Live Through This

COURTNEY: I'm in the middle of having a crisis, a very heavy thing that I'm sure you'll be reading about in the papers shortly. It's the worst time to call. But I'd love to talk to you. Everett is obsessed with you. You're the next star on his list. You know Everett, right?
RD: No.
COURTNEY: Everett's the guy that like runs England.
RD: Oh.
COURTNEY: He makes you famous – Dinosaur Jr, Sonic Youth, Babes, me, etc. Everett runs England and he's wrapped around my thumb. But he loves you totally independent of me. But you know what? Call me later. I'm in the middle of death.
(From the pages of *Rollerderby*, 1993)

COURTNEY: Everett's a great fuck! He's my drinking buddy, and look at all the trouble that I'm in! If it wasn't for him, I wouldn't be sitting here right now with a Gold Card in my bag! Don't fuck with him, or I'll come and kill you! At least he tries to be a rock star, which is more than I can say for any other rock journalist.
(From the pages of *Melody Maker*, 3 April 1993)

COURTNEY: I don't think you should leave this town yet, Jerry [author's real name]. Seattle deserves its reign of terror.
(From the pages of the *Stranger*, 1999)

```
Date: Wed, 16 Sep 1998 22:15
From: Bruce Pavitt
Subject: Re: dear sir
Leg,
   Yes, I have been following your column period-
ically, when I'm in the city. Your inflammatory style
makes for high drama and creates real dialogue. In
```

other words it forces people to think, which is what all good criticism should do.

The Hole vs K Hanna pieces were great. I was proud of how you finally stepped down from your role as Courtney's press agent. As a matter of fact, I don't think I've read any criticism of Courtney anywhere aside from your article, such is the power she wields over the media . . .

I can only guess that your statement about being on the Sub Pop payroll is false. Why DID you move here anyway?

A theme I haven't seen discussed yet . . . righteous moms (Lauren Hill, Liz Phair . . . uh, Courtney). The hottest records out right now are by mothers. When was the last time that happened?

Peace, Bruce

[Everett True also records as The Legend! (hence Leg)]

Live Through This

American Rock Music in the
Nineties

Everett True

DEDICATED TO MATTHEW WHITE (1970–1997)

Remember me, I know that one day you will leave
But I hope
there'll always be something there to remind you
That I still love you
I will always love you

('Ever And Always', Snowbirds, 1990)

This edition first published in 2001 by
Virgin Publishing Ltd
Thames Wharf Studios
Rainville Road
London
W6 9HA

A catalogue record for this book is available from the British
Library.

ISBN 0 7535 0558 4

Typeset by TW Typesetting, Plymouth, Devon
Printed and bound in Great Britain by CPD Wales

Contents

Acknowledgements

I don't put much store in lists like these. They usually either thank people whose job it was to help you, or God: 'I'd like to thank everyone at Sub Pop records for being so friendly towards me over the years, and coincidentally helping me help them make millions of dollars'; 'I'd like to thank the all-bountiful Lord Above for giving us the gift of life'; 'I'd like to thank Nirvana's management for sorting me out on the door at Roseland's, even though they had no choice in the matter if they wanted to keep their artist happy'; 'I'd like to thank my mum and dad for having me.' And what about all those wonderful press agents? They have such good hearts. I'd better thank them as well. Oh, and my editors too. Don't want to upset anyone, certainly not anyone who might help shift copies of this book. Mustn't sound too flippant or cynical. It doesn't help anything, showing awareness of the process. Keep quiet, play the game by its rules.

You soon realise who your friends are, writing a book. Some disappear out of your life for good, despite having taken advantage of you for years, and never return your phone calls. Others refuse to answer emails, or they write one-line replies. Most of them evaporate into the ether. I'm sure they'll return if this book sells a certain amount of copies.

I remember one chum, a couple of months after Kurt and Kristen's deaths, putting the phone down on me mid-call. 'Oh, fuck off back to your famous friends,' she cried, the last words she spoke to me for some time. What, my famous *dead* friends?

I don't want to sound too cynical or jaded, but *'Live through this with me/And I swear that I will die for you'*? Oh yes. As if.

Ah, acknowledgement lists. One of my pet hates. I'll tell you another: history books. Now I'm close to writing the final words for this and sending it away to the publisher, I find myself resenting the whole process even more. It's like closing a chapter on my life, one that I never want closed. History = dead = dull = finished. That's not what music is about. Music is vibrant, living, not to be pored over in dusty corridors and dark hallways. You dance to music, you don't read about it. People only write books when they have no life. Remember that, and chant it before your morning ablutions like a mantra.

You have to move on, though. Life is an ongoing process. The story doesn't finish when you put down this book. Nothing does. This is not a history book. It's just a book about a bunch of stuff that happened.

I am a hypocrite, though.

I would now like to thank the following people who helped me by reading and suggesting changes on the final drafts of this book. Rich Jensen, for being Rich Jensen and inalienably linked to a sensibility that few of us understand. Andrew Mueller, for his hilarious interjections into my copy ('the man sitting on the ledge over there is your lawyer'). Alistair Fitchett, for his intimidating academic overview. David Nichols in Melbourne, for showing such faith in me over the years and being a great copy-editor. Hank Trotter is a fine fellow, opinionated and a creator of ace compilations. Tobi Vail's love of music shone through all our correspondence. Angus Batey was a solid source of support. Chris Letcher is a cantankerous bastard. I'd also like to show my appreciation to Bruce Pavitt for giving me permission to use his quote on the opening page, and Courtney for keeping her distance. Jon Slade helped with the discography. Debbi Shane sent me a harrowing email about the night Courtney and I first met that made me cry. Ian Gittins offered support at a crucial time. Jack Endino, Eric Erlandson and David Bennun helped clarify certain situations.

Each deserves a book far more than I do. Some of them have even written one. A few sent me comments that I nicked and claimed as my own, particularly Chris in the Real Grunge chapter, and *Feminist Baseball* scribe Jeff Smith.

A special shout-out goes to Charlie and Anton and Wyndham and Jenny Boddy and Christof and Beth and Abbo and all the other record industry people who helped make my journeys so fun. I know I'm contradicting myself, but these people are ace too.

Charlotte (my fiancée) has supplied unflagging support and love, despite hating most of the bands and personalities involved. This is devotion far and beyond the call. She also enjoys my singing, so the poor female is clearly deluded.

My main men, ex-*Melody Maker* photographers Steve Gullick and Stephen Sweet, have been as awesome as ever. I send apologies to

Steve's wife Louise for stealing so much of her husband's time during the past few months. Stephen had the right idea: emigrating to Australia with Emma and Otis when I was halfway through writing the book. They are now staying in our old room in Melbourne, the bastards. Oh, and I guess I should give my old mentors Allan Jones and Steve Sutherland a mention, too. Cheers!

All right. That's more than enough dedications already. There were others who gave freely of their time and friendship, and I'm grateful and all that, but shit. This introduction is dull enough as it is. Consider yourself given gold stars, people.

See why I hate these lists?

My favourite question is: 'What motivates you?' Motivation changes, it's not constant.

When I was thirteen, I had to catch the 351 to school from Chelmsford to Brentwood, a 45-minute bus ride. On the bus was a schoolmate named Martin Langridge. He came from the local estate and used to leave his bike at our house, so we'd frequently catch the same bus together and share experiences. One day, I overheard him telling a group of our peers about something that had happened to us. They were held spellbound by his tale. I listened in, thinking, That's not what happened . . . except it was. He, though, made it sound exciting when, in reality, it was prosaic. Or was it? If I'd told my friends about the same incident, they wouldn't have been interested. *It wasn't that exciting.*

God, I was jealous of Martin Langridge.

Years later, I was holding court in the Stamford Arms to a bevy of *Melody Maker* journalists, recounting a recent story of my travels in America. Suddenly, David Stubbs, the well-spoken staff writer responsible for *MM*'s satire pages, turned on me.

'What do you do with your anecdotes, Everett?' he asked, frustrated. 'Take them home and polish them in front of a mirror until they're glistening, and then release them to your adoring public?'

What a compliment, especially from Stubbs, one of the funniest men I've met. No, of course, I didn't, but . . . up yours Langridge! I've finally made it.

Jerry Thackray
1 April 2001

Some of the words in this book have appeared in *Melody Maker*, *VOX*, the *Stranger*, *Hit It Or Quit It!*, *Spin*, the *Age*, *tangents.co.uk*, and quite probably a few other places.

Introduction

Courtney Love
JC Dobbs, Philadelphia
(Extract from *Melody Maker*, 13 August 1994)

Life gets you like that sometimes.[1,2]

I'm with Luscious Jackson, feeling real fine. Maybe this job isn't so bad, after all. The band's just had their first decent meal in weeks, courtesy of *Melody Maker*: they're on a rare day off from Lollapalooza's travelling freak show. We're cruising the main strip, checking out a sighting of Kim and Kelley Deal made six hours previously. We wander into the local rock club – coincidentally the last small club I ever saw Nirvana play – and, suddenly, life hits a major hiccup. Courtney Love is inside, readying herself to play onstage.[3]

(*In my heat-racked sleep, I hear Courtney walking up the stairs – loud, real loud – screaming my name, getting closer and closer.[4] Someone is pounding on my hotel door. I wake in a cold sweat, expecting to find a dead body outside my room. Someone offers me a Rohypnol and I freak.[5] This is not a dream.*)

So, Courtney is about to play a live show and she looks good: real good. But she also looks wasted: real wasted. Over at the back, Kim Deal is holding court, falling over, clutching a carton of cigarettes under her arm. She sees me and smiles conspiratorially. To one side, some members of stoner hip hop act the Goats hang. To another, Tibetan monks are shooting pinball. Luscious Jackson look a fraction bewildered. A cool feminist poet buys Courtney a drink. Billy Corgan is also in the vicinity. Courtney tries to get him and me to make up: 'But Everett, you'd *like* him. You're both scapegoats, you're both my closest friends. And he's so much like Kurt.'

She forces us to touch hands. We both run. Literally.

(*And, in my sweat-drenched sleep, I'm floundering. Famous rock stars queue up to make out with me and I'm helpless to resist[6]. Kim Deal*

1

screams at me for half an hour, is real, real mean to me: and tears flow down my face like blood. Someone calls my name and it's Thurston and Kim[7], holding court with their newborn baby outside CBGB's like visiting royalty. Someone offers me another shot of champagne and I freak. This has got to be a dream. Hasn't it? Please?)

So, Billy is on stage now and he looks pretty darn near wasted, too. He's giving some long rambling speech about his dark side, his misogynist side, and I suspect that in his own fumbling way he's attempting irony and it's mostly aimed in my direction. Do I sound self-important? I'm so fuckin' sorry. It's the way I get treated, OK? Billy's telling the scummy audience about the time some girl/fan came up to his hotel room and asked him to sign her breasts and he refused, he threw her half-naked out of the place. And then he laughs self-consciously and asks us to make way for Courtney Love, widow to the stars.

I blanch, and see if I can't get some industry scumbag to order me a double whisky. No dice. No one knows who I am. When did I start to suffer from such terrifyingly real visions? And why?

(And in my darkest nightmare, people who really should know better are asking me whether I think Kurt would still be alive if he hadn't met Courtney. What, you mean if I hadn't introduced them that night back in LA? Fuck you. Just fuck you. But these are only nightmares, right? Nothing to do with reality.)

And then Courtney is getting on stage, and she's giving a long preamble about ... OK, about Billy Corgan and me, actually, and how we should make up and be friends: and also asking how many of the audience are Pisces like Kurt was and how she'll fuck them all afterwards. We all laugh and clap and smile 'cos you can't help but admire Courtney – her strength, her humour, even through the darkest period of her life. Dont'cha all love a survivor? Ain't they so cute?

(And in my nightmares, I see a totally wasted Courtney Love strap on a guitar in front of a crowd of uninterested people and I find myself unable to reach her, unable to help her. Why is she up there? Why is she putting herself through this? Does she want people to crucify her? Love her? Idolise her? Respect her? Maybe she just wants to prove to herself even someone who can make the front cover of US Magazine can still be real, still have soul. It doesn't seem like her life can be very real right now. Except for the pain. Maybe the only place she has left to be real is on the stage, but she doesn't even have a band left to lend her music the dignity and support it deserves.)

So, Courtney begins her three-song set with 'Doll Parts' and it sounds like the first time she ever played that song to me – down a Cricklewood phone-line at four a.m., her alone in the kitchen at a party. Shambling, amateurish, absolutely painful to listen to, inward-turned, oblivious to what the outside world might care or think. '*I am/Doll parts/Doll face/Doll heart*' . . . it's as fine an example of bitter self–mockery as I have ever wanted to come close to. I can't bring myself to watch her. I hide underneath plumes of cigarette smoke, silent tears creasing my face. People clap and cheer, dutifully. Wow! It's just like being in some crazy movie!

(*And, in my darkest nightmare, it's May and I'm travelling with Hole bassist Kristen Pfaff through Europe, talking about what makes life vital and music worthwhile, laughing even through all the pain and I have a premonition that I'll never see her again. It's a nightmare. I ignore it. I'm still clearly freaked out by that guy Cobain's death.*)

Courtney introduces her next song, 'Pennyroyal Tea', the one she co–wrote with Kurt, with a long preamble about how former *Melody Maker* Reviews Editor Jim Arundel once called it the worst song Nirvana ever played and simultaneously Hole's finest moment. The insult is implicit. But actually, Courtney, this is kinda true – mainly because your version was so much more vicious than Kurt's. He treated the song almost as throwaway; you completely tore it apart. Hole never were Nirvana. Period. Ever. And why the fuck would people – especially you, Courtney – want to compare the two bands? Tonight, 'Pennyroyal Tea' sounds truly appalling – painful to listen to on any number of levels, not least for what it represents and the vast emptiness which is left in Courtney's life, which she will never fill, even if she were allowed to. It seems to last an eternity, what with all the false chords and false starts and Courtney's almost sobbing whisper of a scream dragging through painful evocations. Why is it that her throaty, powerful roar of a voice still sounds so chilling?

(*And, through my pain, I see myself punching walls in Minneapolis, talking death with cool indie rock stars from Louisville, getting wasted on New York sidewalks, tears streaming down my face on planes going nowhere, listening to songs which can never hope to mirror the way I feel inside. A refrain from a Hole song keeps spiralling crazily inside my head,* 'Live through this with me/And I swear that I will die for you'. *I swear that I don't even know what those words mean any more.*)

I have a tape recorder in my bag. Halfway through all this, it occurs to me I should switch it on. But why bother? This is not real. This is just some crazy fucked-up dream. And I can't begin to capture on tape what isn't there.

Courtney starts to leave, but decides one more will suffice, the single 'Miss World'. A friend from one of the bands playing later tonight stands by, to lend support and add vocals where previously Kristen would have done. Her friend has her work cut out, that's for sure. Courtney is almost incoherent by now, staring at the ceiling, not even caring which chords or which notes she hits. *'I am the girl, can't look you in the eye,'* she sings, *'I am the girl, so sick I cannot try.'* For fuck's sake, Courtney. Please.

(*And, in my dreams, I'm quoting lines from Blondie's 'Atomic'*[8] *to my best friend Courtney*[9] *and telling her how her hair looks beautiful tonight. You looked fuckin' great tonight, Courtney. Really.*)[10]

Notes

(1) The review is true, all true. Except, of course, the third paragraph, which was a mixture of fact and a true nightmare. I wrote it in that dream sequence style because I figured that nobody would believe me otherwise. It was written on a beautifully sunny day in a Kinko's – last haven for the travelling journalist – in Louisville, Kentucky, pretty much first draft. I remember photographer Stephen Sweet coming by halfway through, and me showing him the article. Worried by the intensity of what I'd written, I asked his advice. He seemed taken aback, but moved – he told me to keep it exactly as written, except that perhaps I should change the 'tears flow down my face like blood from an aborted foetus down a mother's leg' line. So I did. (Hey Stephen! Good advice! Cheers!)

(2) The photo *Melody Maker* used to run alongside this review was, ironically, taken from the first live Hole show I ever saw – LA, '91. It was used in my absence. By this stage, *Melody Maker* were becoming worried about my state of mind. After reading this piece, writer Andrew Mueller asked our editor, Allan Jones, if he wanted him to fly out and rescue me from the frontline.

(3) I had no idea that Courtney was even on the East Coast when I wandered into the club that night. The last I'd heard from her was when she'd informed me on the phone from Seattle the previous night that she was 'going to fuck me' next time she saw me.

(4) The Courtney dream. Oh yes. A few years later, I woke in a cold sweat on my living room floor to find that my girlfriend had mutated into Courtney and, worse, Courtney was the Living Personification Of Evil. It took about fifteen minutes of wakefulness for the illusion to disperse.

(5) The Rohypnol reference. Courtney offered me one to settle my nerves when flying – I used to be a real bad flyer – and I didn't realise what it was until much later. Rohypnol is, of course, the powerful baby sedative that was part of the champagne cocktail

Kurt deliberately overdosed on in Europe, on his first suicide attempt.

(6) The 'famous rock stars queue up' line. True, although it was two famous rock stars, a lot of alcohol and an industry person performing a striptease for me at five in the morning. I don't quite know why I had become so desirable that night. Something to do with timing, probably.

(7) The Thurston and Kim line is a reference to the then reigning King and Queen of New York counter-culture – Sonic Youth's Thurston Moore and Kim Gordon.

(8) The final line's reference to Blondie's 'Atomic' is there for two reasons. First: Courtney's hair. When I first met her, drunk and tripping in LA, all I could remember the next day was the neon shining through her blonde hair, like the halo Debbie Harry had behind her on *Top Of The Pops* while she was wearing that blue dress, or a drunk man's Madonna. It's a fine trick, to stand so the light hits your hair like that. Second: 'Atomic' is the pinnacle of pop perfection.

(9) Best friend? At that point in time, possibly. Most of my other friends had disowned me.

(10) A week or so later, Courtney flew me over to her house in Seattle where she was auditioning new bass-players to replace Kristen. The review appeared during that interval: she referred to it as 'the nicest Valentine's note I have ever received'. Damn straight. The concert itself was appalling.

Nirvana

Origins

'Other people buy houses. We buy record collections'

SEATTLE PHOTOGRAPHER CHARLES PETERSON

Understand this: I've always despised rock music. For me, it's the language of the braggarts, the fools – those boys at public school who liked to go around sneering at others for no reason except it gave their own pathetic lives some purpose. It's the music of the playground bullies, the fake revolutionaries, the kids whose idea of rebellion is sneaking out at lunchtime to have a quick fag behind the bike shed, the conformists. It's music for people who admire James Dean's vacant, clueless rebel stance and leather jacket, desiring style over content. It's music for the thugs, the beer-boys, the ones who were good at gym and on the sports field, the ones who weren't but always dreamed of being macho somehow. It's music for the proles, the hopeless, hapless masses who like to pretend they're different and daring for a couple of years before growing up to be precisely the same, precisely as conservative as the generation before them and the generation before that.

For me, rock music is about rules, peer pressure, conformity, misogyny, sexism, ageism, hatred of outsiders, mob rule, anti-style-as-fascism. It's dictated to and ruled by people like Aerosmith and Oasis, Slipknot and Jim Morrison, eternally re-treading the path of those who came before. It's about looking backwards, never to the future. It's retrogressive, searching out the lowest common denominator. Rock music leads to exploitation, degradation, humiliation, segregation of any freethinking, revolutionary outsiders. Always.

Understand this: not only do I not believe in utopian ideals (the concept of paradise seems to cancel out that most basic of human instincts – the need to struggle), I don't even believe in rock music . . . if that doesn't sound too stupid. In terms of vibrancy or potency or potential for change or anything, rock was supplanted at the start of the nineties by rave, dance, electronica and their kin. One of the best ways to judge an artistic medium's effectiveness at altering or helping shape popular opinion is to observe the establishment's reaction to it. In the UK, the government has been trying to bring dance music under its control for over a decade now. Contrast this with pop and rock music, where members of the ruling elite hobnob with the rock hierarchy, prime time TV programmes are devoted to musical knowledge, and rock awards ceremonies take on absurd levels of popularity. Rock has the proud boast that it bridges generations: it should not be so proud of that claim, not at all. The vital music, or art, has always been that which creates sociological divides.

Rock music was founded on a lie: white men usurping the black man's heritage, pretty boy Elvis setting all the teenage kids a-squealing with just a wiggle of his white boy hips. It was also exclusively male, created for and by men with a compulsive need to strut their masculinity once they were no longer in the army. God help you if you were female, wanting in: rock's attitudes towards what it perceives as 'the opposite sex' are still mainly stuck in the decade it sprang from: the fifties. Rock revels in its lack of options – unless you think stars like Perry Farrell and Sarah McLachlan with their merciless selling of US 'counter-culture' events such as Lollapalooza and the Lilith Fair during the nineties were providing alternatives. Sure, they were. It's always alternative to be compartmentalised.

Rock'n'roll was a redundant patriarchal language that ceased to be relevant long before I made the trip out to Seattle at the start of 1989, long before I danced upon a table top in *Melody Maker*'s reviews room upon hearing Nirvana's debut single for the first time. I'd grown up with men, knew of men and their ways, found them to be boring and dull. I couldn't understand the need for an art form that reinforced the stereotypes.

Understand this: I've long felt that the only way forward for rock was to give the whole rotting carcass over to women, to do with as they willed. There again, I never understood why women would want to take part in a medium that has been so thoroughly set out in male terms throughout its history.

If I knew anything of Seattle and the Northwest's musical heritage before that fateful plane trip – we landed in such deep snow on my first journey to America that it wasn't possible to see the ground until moment of contact – it was only the following. It was birthplace to Jimi Hendrix and raw-boned sixties garage band the Sonics. Excellent underground comic book company Fanta-graphics had relocated there towards the end of the eighties. Also, a housemate had played me Green River's debut album on Sub Pop picked up on a trip to the States the previous summer. All of us had been rather taken with Green River, and future Mudhoney singer Mark Arm's deranged screaming, if not with the histrionic guitar solos.

There was something else I knew about the Northwest, though, something important. At some point during the mid-eighties I came into contact with this genius singer who danced in an unrestrained and sexy way, Calvin Johnson. Back then, Calvin was in Olympia's minimal rock band Beat Happening. Beat Happening had three members, were supple and seriously salacious. Their songs were formally bare, but mesmerising nonetheless. Lyrics spoke of hot chocolate and special walks in the park, often with an unsettling twist behind the superficial nursery rhyme feel, far removed from the rock mainstream. Lyrics spoke up for those who didn't feel the need to shout to make themselves heard, who appreciated the dark reality behind the façade America usually likes to present of itself.

I met Calvin when his band came across to London to play a few shows. He was expertly manipulating a yo-yo and sweet-talking my girlfriend when we shook hands. Later I was to support Beat Happening on a few intense dates in the south of England at village halls and Brixton pubs. (I played guitar, badly. Eschewing the idea of rehearsing songs as dishonest, I rarely performed with a band.) We seemed to share a similar worldview, one where females are the equal of males; at least. Investigating further, I found Calvin to be responsible for a series of inspirational releases via his K label.

I mention Calvin and my feelings towards rock music now because in all the words I've avoided reading about Nirvana since Kurt Cobain's death, I rarely see any mention of the grunge band's feminine side. Yet to me, this was the most interesting aspect of their rise to fame. Sure, Kurt had a great voice. Sure, Krist Novoselic had the most endearingly goofy way of throwing his bass up into the air and sometimes catching it again. Who cares? The line 'Smells Like Teen Spirit' was taken from a slogan spray-painted on a wall in Olympia by Bikini Kill singer Kathleen Hanna. Ever see a photo of Kurt? Often, he's wearing a Daniel Johnston T-shirt and sporting a tiny K records tattoo. Kurt dated Bikini Kill drummer Tobi Vail in Olympia before he met Courtney. Without a doubt, many of the contradictions that the singer was to feel later about his elevated position came from that period of his life.

When I say Nirvana had a feminine aspect to their music, I don't intend to be patronising (i.e. I'm not trying to substitute the word 'sensitive' with 'female'). All I mean is that Kurt and Krist had a way of looking at the world that sometimes had more in common with accepted female viewpoints than male ones.

Parallels have been drawn between Lennon and Cobain. One of the clearest is the influence that Yoko Ono had on the previously macho, sometimes misogynist Beatle. Kurt too had a masculine side that was all the more intriguing when matched to his Olympian training, and his in-built sensitivity. Most literature refers to Nirvana as a 'Seattle band'. Yet you can't reach their depressed logging hometown of Aberdeen without passing through Olympia, both metaphorically and literally. Nirvana retained the idealism of the influential 'punk rock librarians' and grrrls of Olympia throughout their career.

Who cares if Nirvana could rock and wrote catchy refrains? Anyone can rock and write catchy refrains. Fuck. Give me five minutes and the fingerings to three chords, and I'll write you a song to set the world ablaze. There's nothing smart or clever about having the ability to plug your amplifier into the wall and flick the switch to ON. The chords in 'Smells Like Teen Spirit', that famous guitar riff that helped launch a thousand MTV executives' bank-balances, are basically Boston's 'More Than A Feeling' updated. Chad Channing's drumming on Nirvana's 1989 debut album *Bleach* was directly influenced by the full-on approach of Melvins' super-lative Dale Crover. Melvins were the band Kurt once roadied for. Great, but *male*.

The reinforcement of rock stereotypes wasn't Nirvana's forte, even if it did help shift the units. Nirvana had far more to offer the public than that. Nirvana played punk rock as preached by UK bands like the Raincoats and Slits and the Pastels, not the hardcore (wrongly mistaken for punk) of Henry Rollins and the Exploited. At their finest, at Kurt's finest, Nirvana's music directly recalled the hurt, overly sensitive soul of punk outcasts like Half-Japanese's Jad Fair and Austin idiot savant poet/singer Daniel Johnston. This wasn't rock in the classic sense, far from it. Nirvana's soulful force came from the female side of Kurt's nature – nourished and fed by Olympian people like Calvin Johnson and Bikini Kill and yes, even Courtney Love. Kurt might have loved the heavy metal riffs that helped free him from a life of small-town drudgery in Aberdeen, but he was also aware there was something wrong with the people creating those riffs. Hence the constant reference to sickness throughout Nirvana's career. The mentions of cancer, infirmity and hospitalisation in Kurt's lyrics served as wider metaphors for the corporate rock industry he despised.

This is how it was for me, first arriving in Seattle: attracted by the sound of rock but repelled by its attendant baggage. I felt an instant attraction towards all the longhaired obnoxious laidback rockers like Mudhoney and Tad, despite my training. I might have had my feminist ideals, but when I first heard 'Love Buzz' that chilly November evening in 1988 at *Melody Maker*, I was attracted by the record's power – not because I saw it as part of some wider movement. I played it back to back seventeen times with the U-Men's 'Solid Action' and the split Sonic Youth/Mudhoney twelve-inch as *Maker* staffers walked by the window, laughing at my dance antics. Sure, I liked to rock . . . and having hated rock'n'roll for so long, all this unrepentantly full-on rock – this Seattle grunge, as Mark Arm jokingly referred to it when I first met him on the corner of 1st and Virginia – seemed fresh and unexpected to me.

Let me make this one point clear: before Seattle, I'd never been exposed to ROCK music, always avoided its clothing and deceits. Punk in 1977 had seen to that. It's unlikely I would have been half as enthusiastic about the town and its music if I, like most of my American counterparts, had grown up on a diet of Led Zeppelin and hardcore. But I hadn't, and neither had most of my British contemporaries. Reared on a constantly changing musical culture, where the music press rightly determined that bands grow old very quickly, we were always on the look out for the thrill of the new. The Seattle rock bands, in 1989, both in spirit and in sound, were most definitely new to this naïve English boy.

I'd be lying if I said that I realised Nirvana's potential as soon as I met the band, or even straight afterwards. I was only doing my duty, hanging out with them, drinking and such. What I liked about Nirvana initially was the mischievous glint in Kurt's eyes as we ripped up another seat cover, trashed another amp.

I recall the broad brush-strokes of my first meeting with Nirvana, if not the fine details. It was a sunny winter's day in Seattle along the lake-front about two blocks down from their label Sub Pop's penthouse apartment on 1st Avenue, and five minutes' walk along from Pike Place Fish Market. A little patch of green much favoured by tramps and passing hawkers on bicycles served as the venue for Nirvana's first major press interview. (I remember it well because, on the day of Kurt's memorial service in 1994, the preacher instructed us to all go seek out the place where Nirvana were most special to us, and remember them that way. I thought he was full of bullshit, but walked down there anyway . . . mainly because I felt that almost all the other speakers that day were even more full of bullshit.)

Jonathan Poneman, the affable and extremely enthusiastic co-founder of Sub Pop took me down the steep hillside to meet the four chaps who comprised Nirvana; Kurdt Kobain (as he spelled his name back then), Chris Novoselic (also the original spelling), drummer Chad Channing and extra guitarist Jason Everman. Poneman, a master of hyperbole, was already pumping me full of half-truths and promises about Nirvana's potential.

'This is the real thing,' he told me in a quote I later took word-for-word as my own – which then to my undying shame got repeated the world over. 'No rock star contrivance, no intellectual perspective, no master plan for world domination. You're talking about four guys in their early twenties from rural Washington who want to rock. You're talking about four guys who, if they weren't doing this, would be working in a supermarket or lumber yard, or fixing cars.' Jonathan always did have a great way with words. I'd swear he's missed his true vocation if he wasn't like a thousand times richer than me. You might also note a slightly patronising tone: Jon was firmly middle-class American. 'Kurdt Kobain is a great tunesmith,' he continued, 'although still a relatively young songwriter. He wields a riff with passion. He's your archetypal small guy: wiry, defiantly working class and fiery. His provincial and witty lyrics bring to mind an American Mark E Smith. Nirvana deal a lot with Calvin Johnson type themes, innocence and the repression of innocence. Nirvana songs treat the banal and pedestrian with a unique slant.'

The band themselves were lively, excited to meet an actual music critic from England, eager to lie and distort the truth like their label-mates Mudhoney, not for any sinister purposes, but because it was fun to behave thus. Chris, the lanky friendly bassist, informed me straight-faced that he'd been a competitive tree-climber in his hometown of Aberdeen and had worked as a commercial fisherman in Alaska for three years. Kurdt admitted to a love for the Pixies, told me how the band had been branded as Satan-worshippers back home and then got into a momentary argument with a passing salesman, flaunting tapes.

'How much are those?' he asked.

One dollar, came the reply.

'Shit,' says Kurdt. 'One dollar for a Van Morrison cassette? There are pawn shops around here that will give you twenty bucks for them.'

The guy disappears, after trying to sell us some hash.

'We set that one up, actually,' Chris claims. 'To give you a taste of weird Americana. He's the fifth member of Nirvana.'

11

Jonathan stops by to see how the interview is going and to gee us up into creating more ridiculous quotes. A cat walks by on a leash. I have a five-minute coughing fit and nearly asphyxiate.

It wasn't the most auspicious of starts to my relationship with Nirvana. Although the band did partly reveal their musical taste: 'Aerosmith, Tuxedomoon, NWA, Herman's Hermits, Leadbelly, hard rock, punk rock, power pop, hip hop, Sub Pop . . .' When the interview finally appeared in *Melody Maker* several months later, Everman, later to join Soundgarden briefly as bassist, had left the band. So, in time-honoured music press fashion, I doctored the conversation to make it appear that I'd only been speaking to three people. It hardly mattered. I couldn't tell one speaker from another anyway.

Their all-ages live show a couple of days later at the University of Washington wasn't any great shakes, either. Going on first on a bill that contained Tacoma garage heroes Girl Trouble, early grunge types Skin Yard and the Fluid, and freeloading Englishman The Legend!, the quartet were trounced on almost every front. This was Everman's first show with Nirvana – he lasted long enough to get a credit on *Bleach*, even though he didn't actually play guitar on the album – and he didn't gel. Treading the same fine line between metal and raw power as late sixties/early seventies bands such as Black Sabbath and Blue Cheer, Nirvana veered too much towards the former. Indeed, I remember thinking that Poneman and his business partner Bruce Pavitt's claims that Cobain's outfit were on course for world domination were clearly the deluded wanderings of fevered minds.

In truth, Nirvana barely registered upon me. There was plenty else happening at that time, during my first two weeks in America – a trip to my holy Mecca of Olympia, for one – to divert my attention away from this group of youngsters who somehow seemed separate from everyone else. Sure, I'd made 'Love Buzz' single of the week but I knew plenty of bands that had flamed just as briefly and then flickered out. Bands are like trams. There'll always be another one along in a minute.

Understand this: I used to go to concerts to dance. There was no other reason. If I liked a band, I'd be flailing wildly, often by myself, at the front. If I didn't, then I wouldn't watch them and I'd hide in a corner. It was as simple as that. Attending concerts wasn't a social event for me – I had few friends – and it certainly wasn't an excuse to get drunk and behave obnoxiously. That came later. I wanted bands whose energy I could feed off, and to whom I could give some energy back.

That's why I loved Nick Cave's Birthday Party in the early eighties: the man made an effort. We'd scream our approval when he'd fall back into the crowd, arms akimbo, trusting us to bear him up. We'd punch, kick, scratch to get hold of the microphone and yell a few words down it while Nick's back was turned. 'Express yourself,' the man would scream, possessed, to his adoring faithful, and a few of us did. If you listen closely to the start of the Lydia Lunch/Birthday Party live twelve-inch you'll hear a deep bass voice singing *'Danger zone in the heart of the city/Danger zone in the heart of the town.'* My first recorded performance, thank you very much.

Likewise, Sonic Youth: I remember seeing a 1985 show of theirs in Woolwich, South London, where the sound engineer decided he needed to leave early and started dismantling the PA system around the New York band. It didn't faze them one bit. Shorn of microphones, the band continued to play one of the most exhilarating, frightening wall-of-guitars instrumentals I've ever heard. Likewise, Half-Japanese singer Jad Fair who looks the epitome of a geek with his big glasses, ordinary clothes and battered guitar that he sometimes forgets to plug in. Faced with abuse as he often was, he'd jump into the crowd and face off his oppressor, who would invariably bottle it.

That's why I liked bands like the Slits, too. Conventional rock wisdom ran in the face of these girls' unrequited glee at being allowed on stage and given a chance to scream and show off and wear their knickers on the outside of their clothes, and still create a wonderful, bass-led dub sound ripe for dancing to.

So it was with Nirvana in 1989 and 1990. After the initial shock of seeing them pretend to be a heavy metal band had worn off and they'd lost Jason, they suddenly turned out to be super fine. Hey, the heavy metal tag is fair enough. Would Nirvana have been signed to Sub Pop in 1989 without the hard rock connections? I doubt it. I don't know what fucked-up shit the kids in small-town America have to suffer and lose before they can express their feelings, but I suspect that back in Nirvana's day it included mandatory exposure to Aerosmith and KISS. Yeah, kudos on the rocking front, Tyler. Several thousand minus points for your lack of respect towards humanity, and particularly women, though. Remember: punk rock didn't break till the year 1991 in America when *Nevermind* finally charted. Before then, and before the Internet, Edge City kids had no access to the cool shit which us big city kids from small countries took for granted.

Indeed, Nirvana turned out not just to be super fine, but rather special. That much was apparent from the first time I saw Kurt trying to destroy his amp with the aid of a much-abused guitar and fists. In this, Nirvana reminded me of the glory days of 1985 when John Robb's Membranes would clear college stages of all obstacles within a few seconds. I remember well the look on the faces of London's famed Marquee bouncers when they saw us beating the crap out of their stage with ten foot metal bars, and realised they were powerless to stop us.

Nirvana, particularly schoolyard buddies Kurt and Chris, felt frustration. I could relate to that. After all, what had my frantic teenage dancing been if not a manifestation of my sexual frustration. Nirvana felt frustration with shit club engineers and frustration with the life that had dealt them such a crap hand and frustration with everyone around who didn't immediately cotton on to their genius. Plus, it was almost impossible to express sensitivity within their chosen medium of punk rock/hardcore. This frustration at their surroundings was why Nirvana's early songs – from the nerve-shredding Shocking Blue cover 'Love Buzz' to Skin Yard guitarist Jack Endino's inspired garage production on 'Aero Zeppelin' – sound so brutal and alive. Nirvana had so much angst to get out of their scrawny systems.

That's also why Kurt started leaping backwards into the drum kit, forwards into the crowd, like Nick Cave and Iggy Pop before him. And that's why I loved Nirvana so much initially. They made a goddamn effort – by leaping around and gurning and groaning and screaming so much on stage, it was so obvious that they were merely doing what any half-awake fan would have done in their stead. Get up on stage and have a good time! Put your heart and soul and body into it, because you know what? Outside of tonight, nothing exists. Nothing. What, you want to go back to that crap job as a railway engineer, as a printer, as a nobody? Make some noise! Not along pre-ordained lines, but in your own time and in your own space and inspired by your own emotions.

Years later, Courtney Love explained to me during a *VOX* interview that 'punk rock is a Marxist rite of passage, one that has nothing to do with women'. Unfortunately, by the time bands like Black Flag and the Meat Puppets began to exert a stranglehold on US counter-culture in the mid-eighties, this was true. Initially, punk in NYC and the UK had sought out fresh ways of communication, a way to channel conflicting emotions, and a way in for women previously excluded by rock's patriarchal set of rules. It soon solidified into a uniform, another, even stricter, set of male-centred rules from which you could not veer if you wanted to belong.

Understand this: I haven't knowingly listened to Nirvana since Kurt's death, aside from one brief attempt to understand the

Unplugged release, a record that seemed far too personal to be allowed public access – but hey, wasn't that part of Nirvana's appeal and contradiction? I've just heard 'Aneurysm' (from *Incesticide*) for the first time in at least six years. You must know it. It's the one where Kurt screams *'Leave me out of it'* over and over again. Tears are prickling behind my eyelids, filling the lenses of my spectacles. Understand this: this is what music means to me.

Is it what it means to you?

The following is taken from the pages of *Melody Maker*, 18 July 1992:

'I was always more of a feminine person when I was young,' states Kurt, taking a sip of strawberry tea. 'Then when my hormones started swinging around and I started getting facial hair, I had to let off my male steam somewhere. So I started smoking pot and listening to Black Sabbath and Black Flag. It took the Pixies to put me back on the right track and off the whole macho punk rock trip.'

The trouble with punk is that it thought it was cool to put down women. I could never relate to that. Here was this movement that was supposed to be right-on but excluded over half the people I knew.

'Definitely,' Kurt agrees. 'That was something I realised later because I didn't experience punk in the seventies. There was this live record *Night Of The Living Dead Boys* where Stiv Bators was spewing off about how some girl was sucking his cock while he was on stage. That was the accepted thing.'

Watching *Headbanger's Ball* on MTV, nothing seems to have changed. Music, especially metal, still reinforces all the scummiest aspects of being a male.

'It might be getting a little better because of bands like Soundgarden,' says Kurt. 'They have a good, healthy attitude and maybe others will follow. Even Pearl Jam, who were obviously cock-rock poseurs down on the Strip last year, are preferable.'

The singer pauses, struck by a thought.

'You know, there's an LA band called Love Buzz, and their first album is called *Grunge*. I want to get that album real bad,' he laughs.

Does feminism have any bearing on your life? Courtney has already gone on record as stating that she views herself as a feminist. What does a statement like that mean to you?

'It means women controlling their own lives and me not standing in their way by being a male,' Kurt responds. 'It's not so much of an ideal as a sense. It doesn't seem like there's a recognisable feminist movement like there was during the seventies, more of a collective awareness. It's in the way you live your life.'

What would you say the main difference between having a masculine and a feminine outlook is?

'Being aware of not offending women and of not supporting sexist acts,' the singer suggests, carefully choosing his words. 'But not so you become so paranoid that you can't feel comfortable in a woman's presence. Sexist jokes are harmless as long as you're aware of them. But I also know a lot of people who put on this pretend macho redneck act twenty-four hours a day – they use the redneck lingo and spew out sexist quotes – and then claim they're simply trying to remind you of how rednecks behave. I've noticed that if someone does that for too long they turn into a redneck.

'I kind of respect people who go out of their way to act like an asshole when they're really intelligent, though,' Kurt continues. 'It's a nihilistic statement, like they're saying there's no point in trying to be human any more because things have gotten so out of hand. It's a very punk rock attitude, but I also think it'd be boring to be Johnny Rotten after all these years. I'm not talking about sexism, but that kind of negative attitude when you're no longer able to appreciate passion or beauty.'

The phone rings in Kurt's front room. It's someone from a radio station, wanting to know what type of music the singer listens to. He tells them 'Adult-Oriented Grunge'. It rings again. It's Corey from Chicago alternative label Touch & Go, seeking Kurt's advice over a problem that has arisen with Kurt's management over a projected Nirvana/Jesus Lizard single on his label. Kurt listens attentively and promises he'll resolve the situation with his manager. Despite reports to the contrary, Kurt looks healthier than on previous occasions I've met him. I wouldn't say that he glows with health, but he definitely radiates something – happiness in his new found stability of marriage, perhaps? I suggest to him, when he eventually comes off the phone, that he's much more relaxed today.

'Oh yeah,' he replies. 'But that's because when we last met [in October 1991] I'd been on tour for five months, and I haven't played for a while now. Plus, I was getting pissed off doing those commercial radio interviews with all those DJs with their finely sculptured moustaches, talking in their professional American radio DJ voices and not having any idea who the fuck we were. How much exposure does one band need?'

Granted. At one point, it seemed you couldn't pick up a British music magazine without Nirvana being on the cover – usually with a rehashed or ten-minute interview inside.

'Right,' Kurt agrees. 'I practically adopted the J Mascis Fifth Amendment because I couldn't deal with so many interviews.'

He laughs.

'I don't have narcolepsy.'

Who started that?

'I don't know – wasn't it you? No, I did. It's the only defence mechanism I have.'

Something happened between 1989 and 1990. I don't know what it was. I was too busy enjoying myself to take notes. *Bleach* came out halfway through '89 – an album I listened to about two and a half times before realising that, as ever, with this sort of music records can never compare to the live experience. I concentrated instead on going out.

In the wake of my – and Jonathan Poneman's – rather hyperbolic words in *Melody Maker* in early 1989, Sub Pop came to Britain. Mudhoney supported Sonic Youth on their UK tour. Soundgarden blasted a few heads and collapsed a few stages with their unrequited Led Zeppelin sound. A couple of Lamefest showcases at London's Astoria saw Tad, Nirvana and Mudhoney vying for media attention and to see who could complete the most outrageous stage-dive. First night, Mudhoney bassist Matt Lukin leapt right from centre stage during Nirvana's tumultuous opening set, followed almost immediately by man-mountain Tad. The crowd parted as one, causing the unlucky Lukin to end up on the floor, squished beneath Tad's voluminous mass. It took a good fifteen minutes to scrape the mess up.

It seemed the English music press – which still had some influence back then – was in the mood for some kick-ass American rock after years of ignoring it. Doubtless this change of heart was partly influenced by the rather appalling British shoe-gazing scene that was around at the time. Bands like Ride and the eternally mediocre Chapterhouse were almost the exact opposite of Seattle's maverick, uncool musicians, more concerned with the cut of their hair and shine on their shoes than having a good time.

Nirvana, on the other hand . . .

'Kurdt smashes his guitar by throwing it into the drums at the finale, six-footer Chris lopes around the stage, blind fury on the bass. Nirvana, in their impotency and overwhelming hatred which sometimes verges on misanthropy, create a pop noise equalled only this side of Dinosaur Jr.' (From my review of the Screaming Trees/Tad/Nirvana show at the Pine Street Theatre, Portland, Oregon, February 1990.)

'We're not too worried about being unduly tagged,' Kurt told me around that time. 'It's fine, because we do play a lot of grunge but we consider ourselves a bit more diverse than just full-out raunchy heavy music. We're aiming towards a poppier sound, and we've been into pop music for years. It's just that when we were recording *Bleach* we happened to be writing a lot of heavy songs at the time.'

That was some tour. I rode with Tad, five or six of us crammed into a van built to take one: alongside all the band's equipment. At the all-ages show in Portland, the maitre d' plied everyone with dope; the bar downstairs served tofu and falafel only; beer was strictly limited to over-21s (ID only). (That's not so unusual for the American kids, but an eye-opener to someone reared in a country where alcoholism is almost a way of life. Usually, under-21s aren't even allowed into clubs that serve alcohol – especially in Washington State where the liquor laws are particularly strict. Hence the abundance of 'all-ages' shows in towns like Olympia and presented by hardcore bands like Fugazi where no alcohol is served and anyone can attend.) There was a video crew present to record the three bands and they were rewarded with a show of blistering proportions; metal twisted and distorted and gouged so out of shape its origins were barely recognisable.

I took the stage as The Legend! (my stage name) just before Screaming Trees to a fusillade of broken bottles, sharpened coins and obscene innuendo: civilised people, Yanks. It was the first time I'd ever performed to such hatred, aside from the odd squaddie in Germany, and I loved it, parka tightly buttoned up round my face, winding the audience up further. A tirade of screaming girls hugged the stage, shouting stuff like 'Who the fuck are you?' and 'What the fuck are you?' Trees' singer Mark Lanegan collected $1.71 from the stage floor afterwards. Tad Doyle, standing by the side of the stage, pointed a finger in my direction. 'That guy is pure cabaret,' he announced to the bemused singer of Beat Happening. 'No, he's not,' Calvin replied, before storming off. 'He's punk rock and that's something you'll never be!' It was some night. Dylan Carlson told me a few years later that he'd been inspired to form his deathly drone rock band Earth after seeing me play that night.

Time stretched into infinity between concerts: just an endless procession of highways, byways, houses, factories and the odd traffic jam. You eat a little. You sleep a little. You pray in vain that your van doesn't break down or end up in a crash . . . in Olympia, Calvin Johnson and I hit a patch of black ice at 80 mph, taking a 360-degrees skid across the road. In San Francisco, the Sub Pop tour van ran straight into some guy in the Tenderloin district. You could see him in slow motion, careening and rolling across the windscreen. Our female driver looked about fifteen and had no ID or driver's licence, the van had no insurance and it wasn't her van anyway. Plus, she looked Asian, in a predominantly black part of town. An undercover cop peeled himself off from the crowd, flashed a badge at us and ran off before he could be spotted, saying 'It's OK, I saw the whole thing.'

Nirvana kept themselves amused on the road the usual way – dope, baiting hippies along Haight-Ashbury in San Francisco, playing Witchcraft Coven records loudly out the van windows to piss people off. 'Kiss the goat!' announced the Satanic TV announcer on the record's B-side. If America's maligned West Coast cities heard that phrase once they heard it a thousand times. 'We asked this guy for directions,' Chris recalled about one incident, 'and just when we're about to drive off, Kurt shouts out "Hail Satan" . . .'

Nirvana weren't the only people winding up the locals. Appearing on stage solo in my hooded parka in San Francisco, I taunted the 'assholes' out front to throw objects at me. The power got cut after two songs. Each night, Kurt smashed up a guitar, sometimes two. His actions led Sub Pop, ever on the look out for a good line to feed the press, to announce that Nirvana had been put on an 'equipment allowance'. Like duh. In Portland, it was because he was enjoying himself. In San Jose, it was through sheer apathy. In San Francisco, Chris trashed his bass out of petulance, so Kurt trashed his guitar not to be left out and then trashed the drums for good measure. Meanwhile, Kurt Danielson from Tad was standing by the side of the stage, looking worried. It was his bass that Chris was now using.

'Why do I do it?' asked Kurt. 'Why not? It feels good. Somebody already cut down a nice old tree to make that fucking guitar. Smash it! We only ever do it if the feeling's right. It doesn't matter where we are.'

Of course, if this was all Nirvana had to offer then . . . great. I've never understood why rock bands are so restrained and predictable on stage, why they repeat the same notes and the same chords and the same actions night after night. If that's what you want to do, why not find work on a production line and stay out of my face! Life is grey enough without your kind contributing to the general mediocrity.

The Nirvana shows of this era were great for several reasons. First: the unpredictability factor. However much people criticised Nirvana for merely being the Who twenty years on, no one ever knew quite how a show would end up, whether they'd even manage to finish a show. The trio *cared* about the performance they were giving, even in their darkest days when Kurt would stand stock-still as mayhem reigned around him. If I heard Nirvana fuck around with the start to the 1989 Tupelo single 'Blew' once, I heard them do it a hundred times. If you're seriously telling me there isn't something exhilarating about watching a grown man, or woman, smash things at random, then you probably shouldn't be reading this book . . . or even listening to rock music.

Second: the band's feminine side. It soon became apparent that behind all the bad taste jokes – peeing in Ride's champagne bucket, setting tour van curtains alight – and self-destructive urges, there were some sensitive boys trying to come to terms with life. How else to explain the hurt you can almost taste within Kurt's voice, his inward-turned ferocity? Chris is possibly the dorkiest pop star *ever*. Look at the way he moves on stage and his love for others. Chris isn't rock at all; indeed, he's Mr Anti-Rock. I'm not saying I couldn't hear traces of Nirvana's avowed listening material of the time within their music – the Vaselines, the Fugs, the Rolling Stones, sweet and gentle English band Marine Girls, the Brady Bunch . . . It's just something unusual was happening beneath all the passion and excitement.

Third: the lyrics. 'Sliver' is the story of the trauma a child feels when it's away from its parents for the first time. The song does have a happy ending, though – in the final verse, the child ends up in its mother's arms. Not the standard basis for a full-on rock experience. Or perhaps it is? Your call.

Fourth and most important: Nirvana performed actual living, breathing, disturbing, life-enriching shows. Shows that you knew you'd been to, a part of, witness to. Know what I mean?

Nirvana had actually been playing shows for around two years before the release of *Bleach* in June 1989. (Incidentally, in the Sub Pop promotional literature of the time, the trio are described as 'Olympia's pop stars': not a Seattle band at all, then.) I caught just the one: that Sub Pop showcase at Seattle University in January '89 that so failed to impress. By the time the trio arrived in LA in the spring of 1991 with Killdozer producer Butch Vig to start work on the sessions that would eventually become *Nevermind*, they had toured both the US and Europe extensively, and Dave Grohl had replaced Chad Channing on drums.

Nirvana refused to be drawn as to the reason for Chad's departure in June 1990. 'Religious reasons,' Kurt intoned solemnly when pressed. It was a shame: Chad seemed like fun. After borrowing close friend Mudhoney's Dan Peters for the B-side of 'Sliver', and Melvins' Dale Crover for a brief US tour supporting Sonic Youth in August 1990, the band found themselves with eight US major labels chasing them, and no permanent drummer. That situation changed when Buzz and Dale from the Melvins introduced Nirvana to Grohl, the nineteen-year-old drummer from DC punk/hardcore band Scream, backstage in San Francisco.

It was onstage that Nirvana cemented their reputation as an extraordinary band, especially in the UK – a country that took to them far sooner than America, thanks to Sub Pop's support in the music press. A couple of concerts from the pre-*Nevermind* era stand out.

London Astoria, 3 December 1989 (Lamefest) The first show where Nirvana gave an indication of their true power to their English fans. Playing first, it seemed that the trio had an uphill struggle to impress those of us who'd arrived especially early to catch them. Nirvana had driven all the way from Dover to London in freezing fog, and arrived fifteen minutes before they were due to go on: no sound check, no rest period, nothing. It didn't matter. After 30 minutes, they'd pulverised their way through four guitars and left the stage for dead. I'm not saying Nirvana bettered Mudhoney that night – who were at the peak of their considerable power – but they unsettled and bewildered any number of people with the force of their performance. Or so many of my colleagues insisted on telling me.

Nottingham Trent Polytechnic, 27 October 1990 (with L7 in support) This was the tour that introduced Dave Grohl to Britain. According to an eyewitness account from the balcony (photographer Stephen Sweet), the lights were going up and the crowd trudging off, satiated, home when Kurt rushed back on to the stage to announce, 'We've got a very special guest for you.' The fans all raced back to the front, expecting Tad at the very least, only to hear Kurt complete the sentence with the words, 'Everett True from the *Melody Maker*.' I stumbled up to the microphone and muttered something about how I'd only play a song if Nirvana played one afterwards, attempting to get the kids on my side. Kurt strapped his left-handed guitar over my shoulder – wrongly – and he and Chris settled behind the drum kit, and started bashing away. We lasted about two minutes into my future Sub Pop single 'Do Nuts' until Kurt started to comprehensively trash the drums, upon which I quit my vocal duties and turned around to watch. It wasn't the first time, or the last, I was to join Nirvana on stage.

Afterwards, someone produced a pair of false eyeball joke sunglasses and Chris filmed everyone wearing them. Drunk as I was, and with Nirvana in full support, I managed to convince L7 that I wasn't in fact the London journalist who'd travelled up to interview them. Man, they were mad when they found out the truth a few days later.

Kurt meets Courtney

'I only ever asked Courtney Love out on a date to impress you,' Kurt Cobain once confessed to me.

I never knew whether to believe him. Was he winding me up? For, troubled as Kurt was, he also had a wicked sense of humour. The singer claimed the incident happened the same night that I introduced him to his future wife; at a concert by Austin's favourite retarded sons, Butthole Surfers, in LA, summer of '91. It was possible, certainly. Yet I have almost no memory of the event.

Perhaps this isn't so surprising. Back in the early nineties, I was known for my capacity for drink and its resulting memory loss. Years after that Surfers gig, I was still bumping into strangers who delighted in recounting how they'd helped pour me into a taxi that night, how they'd been personally insulted by me, how they'd heard all about me from other people present that night. Also, as Kurt liked to remind me, when he first encountered us at that show, she and I were rolling around on the floor in the VIP area upstairs at the Hollywood Palladium, totally out of our heads.

'Afterwards, when you and me were back at the apartment,' Kurt continued, 'you kept going on and on about how wonderful this girl Courtney Love was, how you'd only just met her and how you were going to make her into the biggest star in the world and everything. So I decided to act like an arrogant, pissy rock star. I started boasting about how I could get a date with her if I wanted. So I did. I phoned Courtney up right there and then, at four in the morning, and arranged to meet her the following day. I never showed up, though. I only did it to impress you.'

Sure. Maybe it *is* true. Certainly I knew the singer well enough by that point. I'd encountered Nirvana several times over the preceding two years in both the US and UK – although the accidental meeting between Kurt and myself in New York around the time of the rapid ascent of *Nevermind* that led to a more lasting friendship was still some months off. Nowadays, reports of Kurt's life dwell on the negative, disaffected side of his personality. When Kurt killed himself in 1994, dissatisfied with his fame and all messed up by heroin use, it seemed that the sociologists' misconceptions had been confirmed. Here was a band only the alienated could relate to. No, no, no!

Sure, some of the final year was like that; especially that horrendous drawn-out tour of 1993 where no one was saying much of anything to anyone else, and the only person with any sort of sanity left seemed to be extra guitarist, the Germs' Pat Smear. That's not how I remember Nirvana shows, though. Mostly, I recall nights of total passion, scuzzy tours into the middle of nowhere, outrageous pranks and bad jokes. At the time of the Butthole Surfers show, the Seattle-based trio were fast becoming known for their warped, mischievous sense of humour and great live shows.

Back to the main frame.

Maybe Kurt did ask Courtney out that night at the Palladium because he wanted to show off in front of me. Crazier things have happened. Kurt knew me. Courtney knew me. And it's true that he wouldn't have spoken to her if I hadn't been there . . .

Certainly Kurt knew me well enough to recognise the signs of infatuation in his drunken English buddy. Infatuation? Sure. Sure, I was infatuated with Courtney. Even on our first meeting, she had this knack of making you feel you were the most important person in the world while she spoke to you. Kurt realised this. Indeed, he probably couldn't have avoided it. I was drunk. I would have been going on and on about her. So: what better way to show off in front of a friend than to ask his crush out?

Every story has to begin somewhere. Over the following years, both Kurt and Courtney would frequently remind me that I'd introduced them. 'You're the one to blame,' they'd say laughing, aware of how much the critics looked down upon their marriage and saw Courtney as a gold-digger. 'Don't worry, you'll get five per cent of all royalties.'

I remember the concert. It took place during my first visit to LA. How could I forget it? Butthole Surfers, Redd Kross and local all-girl punks L7 – what a great triple bill! I wasn't on the guest list, so I turned up early during the sound check to blag my way in, walking straight past the queue of punks and freaks stretched out across the tarmac, patrolled suspiciously by security with handheld guns. There, I bumped into the manager of Redd Kross, John Silva. Silva also managed Nirvana, Beastie Boys and Sonic Youth.

I told him that I was on a mission. The evening we'd checked into our LA hotel I'd spotted an ad for a Hole show in the local street press eight days away. I didn't know who the band was. I only knew what they sounded like, venom and semen and vitriol and passion all exploding over ferocious Black Sabbath-style riffs. Their two singles 'Retard Girl' and 'Dicknail' had blown my head apart. I was desperate to meet them. I didn't know anything about them, indeed I figured they were from Minneapolis because that city's Babes In Toyland had put them in contact with me. And they were playing so soon! I had to meet them.

So I asked Silva if he knew who Hole were, and how I could get in contact with their singer. Silva was that kind of guy. Knew everybody.

'I can do better than that,' he told me. 'I can introduce you to her right now.'

So it was that I first met Courtney Love.

I can picture her now, walking across the empty dance-floor to meet me: loud, bedraggled, all smudged make-up and tights full of holes, the neon light shining through her dirty yellow-blonde hair. She introduced herself, and within minutes she'd mentioned half-a-dozen famous names that she claimed to be intimately acquainted with: Elvis Costello, filmmaker Alex Cox, cult English pop star Julian Cope. She bought me a whisky and demanded that I buy her one back.

Neither of us had any money, so we raced around the room stealing and begging drinks in equal proportions, becoming increasingly lairy and drunk. Someone introduced us to the curly-haired one from *Bill & Ted's Excellent Adventure*. Someone slipped acid into our drinks. The room spun around our heads as we talked and fought. We got on ferociously well. I was an English music critic, on the look out for the Next Big Thing. She was a struggling musician/actress, desperate to become that Next Big Thing. She loved the attention she was receiving from a 'name' English journalist. I loved the affection she lavished upon me in return. Even if I was annoyed when Courtney questioned my motivation, and started flirting very heavily with me. (What did it matter to me what shape someone's nose was, or had been, when I had the purity of my passion for music to sustain me?) We scammed our way into the velvet-curtained VIP area upstairs, slipping underneath the ropes when security's back was turned. No one was going to stop us. We were untouchable.

Later, Nirvana showed up. The Aberdeen band was in town recording sessions for *Nevermind*, the album that defined an era.

Kurt saw me, and his eyes lit up. It was clear that both Courtney and myself were engaged in some major misconduct. Seeing us there, loud and drunk and behaving obnoxiously, it was natural for him to make his way across to the two most drunken, wasted people in the venue and start rolling round the floor with them.

And that was it. Kurt met Courtney.

I'd like to be able to say that there was instant chemistry, that the light of love started shining through both their eyes as soon as they met, but . . . that's a pile of bullcrap. The only attraction that existed between the future married couple that night in LA was that of the drunk for another drunk. That of two party animals looking for more alcohol, more ways to get high, enjoy themselves and get fucked up. Two minor stars revelling in the feeling of freedom that excess substance abuse brings.

I remember the lights doubling back on themselves, and the way people seemed to be gazing at the three of us tumbling around the floor with a strange look in their eyes, something akin to jealousy. What, were all these beautiful people jealous of me, a drunken English asshole? That couldn't be right.

Courtney departed back to her scummy flat somewhere in Hollywood. Kurt dedicated himself to looking after what was by now his almost comatose English journalist friend and making sure he didn't end up the wrong side of security's muscle. So I was driven back to Nirvana's temporary living quarters, a plastic bag tied on over my face to catch the vomit, one handle per ear, while Chris Novoselic attempted to run over a few wayward Nazi skinheads. At one stage we stopped off in a garage so I could use the bathroom. Incapable of even the most basic of human functions, I staggered rather than walked to the back door, to the sound of the clientele pissing themselves laughing.

'It was so awesome, man,' Kurt later told me. 'Everyone was making fun of you because you were completely insensible. But you got your own back, trust me.'

Why? What did I do? Piss on their rhododendrons?

'No man,' Kurt laughed. 'You walked out of there barefaced, with the complete set of keys to the establishment dangling from your belt hook. They must have been mighty pissed when they realised.'

I awoke the next morning naked underneath a glass-topped table in Nirvana's Oakwood apartment, a thick cloud of dope hanging in the air, the apartment a complete wreck, Chris and *Melody Maker* photographer Phil Nichols engaged in some deep philosophical discussion about drugs (probably). My back was aching from where someone had accidentally hurled a heavy glass ashtray at it. All I could hear in my mind was Kurt Cobain boasting about how he'd asked out some girl we'd met the previous evening. I ignored my fevered imagination, checked the time – fuck, six a.m.! – and wandered out into the street clad only in my underpants to hail a cab back into Hollywood with Mr Nichols.

We had another interview call at eight.

I've told this tale in many forms before, all different and most of them were lies. I've never liked to be pinned down on anything, especially when everyone asks the same tedious questions.

First off, I kept quiet because my good mates and Tiki bar buddies, Chicago's stylin' Urge Overkill, were convinced they'd been present at the great meeting, some time later that year in a Chicago bar. The incident they were referring to was actually when Courtney decided she had to date Kurt come what may, and demanded that the record company trying to sign her band fly her out to the Windy City so she could meet him again. Possibly they were there when the duo consummated their relationship . . . it seems I know a fair few people who might have been present at one of those occasions.

I heard a lot of rumours later about how the couple had first met, including one that doubtless came from somewhere close to Courtney's camp, stating that the pair had known each other for years . . . dating back to when Courtney lived in Portland. Perhaps, but both I, and Courtney's guitarist and former lover Eric Erland-son, doubt it. Still, these rumours did move me to phone Kurt up on one occasion and suggest that we include a section on the Top Twenty Rumours On How Kurt Met Courtney in the book we had tentatively thought of writing together. (I thought I'd leave it until the singer became less famous. Oops.) Unfortunately, Mr Cobain was in a grumpy mood that day and blanked my suggestion.

Later on, I'd deny all knowledge of having known either Kurt or his bride, especially in the months following the singer's suicide. It only led to crap questions like, 'Oh, so what was Kurt really like?' That gambit for conversational chatter has long been replaced with, 'Heard anything from Courtney lately?' Like I'm going to tell you if I have.

Nevermind

By the time I started writing almost full-time about Nirvana, I was living by myself in a one-bedroom flat in Cricklewood, London. There, I wasted many enjoyable hours recording messages for my new answerphone. Mostly, I'd record my favourite bands of the time: Teenage Fanclub, Cranes, Babes In Toyland. Other times, I'd try to create a motif that acknowledged the fact it was an answerphone I was using, not a recording studio. That catchy little jingle from De La Soul – '*Sorry I'm not present/But here's what I'm going to do/Leave your name and number/And I'll get back to you*' – soon went into heavy rotation. It also amused me to sample one of Courtney's frequent (and lengthy) three a.m. phone calls. These were sometimes accompanied by her strumming a few bars on the guitar as she tried to work out one of her new songs. (This, as I've said, is how I first heard the unnerving, autobiographical 'Doll Parts'; Courtney played it to me while she sat alone in the kitchen at a party on the other side of the Atlantic. I advised her not to lose its stark, acoustic feel. Weirdly, she heeded me.)

So imagine my delight one morning in 1991 when I received a tape from Sub Pop and Nirvana's loveable and Herculean British PR Anton Brookes which featured the refrain '*Hello, hello, hello, hello*' over and over again. That song featured on my phone for months before its release, easily enough time for anyone hearing it to become nauseated by its blatantly commercial hook. Not that I featured it for that reason, no.

I just liked the way that during the chorus to 'Smells Like Teen Spirit', Kurt seemed to be picking up the phone to a bad connection.

Events started to move rapidly shortly after that first meeting with Courtney. I have no idea if it was coincidence.

The fact Nirvana had signed a deal with Gold Mountain Management probably contributed more to their rise than any other factor in 1991. It made no difference to me, though. I was aware only of my immediate peers. Perception is nearly all that matters in this life. If you aren't aware of something, it hasn't happened, right? I wasn't aware of Nirvana's rapid ascent into the firmament until long after *Nevermind* had dropped out of the upper reaches of the Billboard Top Forty. To me, they were just another great band, of the sort which we so delighted in covering in *Melody Maker*. Years afterwards people would give me respect as the man who discovered Nirvana . . . but what difference did I make to their career? Someone else would have written about them if I hadn't, and probably with more 'authority'. That's for damn sure.

It certainly helped too that MTV were desperately looking round for a band and musical movement to give their flagging channel the sort of credibility it ill-deserved. Nirvana may well have been punk rock, but they got the sort of major label push and advertising dollar usually reserved for bands ten times their size. Remember those pom-pom girls in the foreground of the school gymnasium in the video to 'Teen Spirit'? Didn't you hate that piece of corporate crap? Kurt also loathed the video and wanted to scrap it – or so he told me during a fit of self-loathing. Fortunately . . . or unfortunately, depending on your stance . . . he never got round to it.

Nirvana played Reading Festival '91 halfway down the bill, going on stage just before Chapterhouse. I have no real memory of that show, despite apparently instructing everyone staying on the floor of my hotel room to get their asses down to the site early on Friday to see them. Chris danced around the stage like a cumbersome anglepoise lamp on acid. Kurt leaped backwards into Grohl's drum kit at the set's tumultuous climax, and was later pictured walking round the site with Eugene Kelly from Captain America (and the Vaselines) in tow, arm proudly bandaged in a sling. The sound was typically obstructive, blustery winds whipping the noise of Nirvana's first UK festival appearance everywhere. I went off in search of solace, and found it in a bottle of Mudhoney's whisky. Later, myself and the 'Honey could be spotted throwing cooking oil around in a vain attempt to catch a fleeing Courtney Love (there with Billy Corgan). We kept that up until an aggressive stagehand tried to rip my head off for throwing oil all over his car.

Still, Nirvana had done enough to impress the rock world at large that they had arrived. This undeniable fact was compounded by the release of THAT album shortly afterwards. When I reviewed *Nevermind* in September 1991 for *Melody Maker*, I stated that the record completed a triumvirate of classic US underground rock albums alongside Hüsker Dü's *Zen Arcade* and Dinosaur Jr's *Dinosaur*. I could just have well as listed Pixies and Sonic Youth, but didn't because I was trying to make a point about trios and their lack of wastage. Courtney criticised me for the review, saying that I was being typically patriarchal by comparing Nirvana to trios that were so male. By doing so, she was showing a deplorable lack of knowledge about another of my reference points, Young Marble Giants. Odd, as she later covered the fragile, minimal, girl-led Welsh trio's 'Credit In The Straight World' on her second album.

'Nirvana have emotion, raw emotion,' I wrote. 'The sort where the singer bares his soul all the way down the line and with the use of but a few simple words and phrases communicates way deeper with the listener than this sort of music is meant to. Take "Drain You" and "Lounge Act" where the words coming from Kurdt Kobain's cracked, hurt voice are almost indecipherable, but dreadfully moving nonetheless. And when he starts screaming, unable to bear whatever demons are coming down on top of him, it's like your worst nightmares about babies crying and buses crashing and skyscrapers falling come true all at once. Never underestimate the power of a good scream. When Nirvana released *Bleach* all those years ago, the more sussed among us figured they had the potential to make an album that would blow every other contender away. My God, have they proved us right.'

Yeah, I know my words proved uncannily prescient, but hell! I was writing exactly the same review of virtually every American rock band I encountered back then.

I love rock'n'roll, me.

All my life I've been looking for a purpose, a sense of belonging, the knowledge that perhaps there are others like me out there after all. All my life I've been looking for a semblance of glamour – '*the nearest thing to desperation I know of*' (The Legend! 1982) – for a sprinkling of stardust to lift me above the mundane. You think that part of me didn't enjoy this strange new power I had in the wake of Nirvana's success? You're crazy. I relished it, revelled in it, rolled around in the dirt with it and got good and mucky. I loved the fact female musicians and groupies and the like were suddenly starting to flirt with me – me! – that notable faces across the underground rock scene wanted to hang out. I was up for it. If people wanted me to get drunk and behave outlandishly, all the better. That part was easy. Hate me or love me ... that didn't matter. At least someone was paying attention.

One event lifted me above the herd who were shortly to follow Nirvana's every move. Shortly after the Reading Festival in September 1991, someone at *Melody Maker* complained that our rival *NME* had been offered the first major Nirvana exclusive for *Nevermind*. This, despite the fact that we and the soon to be defunct *Sounds* had been the major supporters of grunge in the UK. *NME* was the brand leader, even if it wasn't on the ball, and that's all that counts to management types.

'OK,' I stated rashly. 'Get me out to America and I'll do the rest.'

Three hours later, our dashing features editor Ted Mico announced that he'd fixed up a trip for me to interview Kim Deal's post-Pixies band the Breeders in New York. Fine, I thought ... but Nirvana are on the other side of the country! No worries – the night we arrive, the Aberdeen trio are playing at New York's Marquee Club. We go straight over, and sit by the entrance during the sound check until Kurt notices me. The show is blessed with an encore that features just bass and drums and Kurt screaming melodically from somewhere within the audience, he'd fucked his guitars up so badly. It still sounded like there were six guitars playing.

After the show, Kurt asks if I want to come on tour. He also begs for an introduction to Kim Deal, whose debut album *Pod* he loves. I agree to both, with some relief. A few days later, I clamber up on stage at Washington DC's 9.30 Club to scream my a cappella punk/soul songs in front of a sell-out crowd of 800 rabid punks who, to my surprise, all sing them back at me. It's so damn hot, Kurt has to rush off stage twice to take a breather and throw up, before rushing back on to destroy the drums. In Pittsburgh, at JC Dobbs, the show is even crazier and smaller. The queue beforehand stretches all the way round the block. Kurt rams his guitar into the snare drum in anger at the 'punk' rockers who talk through the disquieting rape song 'Polly'.

Remember. This was right when *Nevermind* was starting to explode across America, and Nirvana were booked into a tour of tiny clubs arranged months earlier. Tour manager Monty Lee Wilkes had his work cut out trying to keep the band in check. In Pittsburgh, he was picked up for questioning by the police at two a.m., just after *David Letterman*. The show ended with some harsh words spoken between band and club. Later, someone attempted to set the place alight, piling up cushions, seat covers and carpets in the dressing room downstairs and dowsing them in petrol. 'The Man' figured that perhaps a certain punk rock band knew something of the incident. Not this time, bub. Kurt merely smashed a couple of bottles in the toilet and threw a few things around.

'Maybe I am developing a pissy rock star kind of attitude,' the singer told me two nights later, surrounded by pizza cartons backstage in DC. 'But the exact kind of people who talk really loud during "Polly" and yell for "Negative Creep" throughout the set are the ones who yell "Sell out" after the show because we didn't do an encore, didn't sign any autographs. Yet what could be more rock'n'roll than that?'

'We don't want to be associated with 99 per cent of rock music,' explained Chris. 'The Youth, the 'Honey, the Breeders, the Cross, the Knife, the 'gazi . . . they're the bands we like.' (Sonic Youth, Mudhoney, the Breeders, Upside Down Cross, Shonen Knife, Fugazi.)

Kurt already knew that lines needed to be drawn between Nirvana and their peers. Especially between Nirvana and Pearl Jam, the Seattle 'grunge lite' band formed from the ashes of Green River who were starting to attract attention.

'We're not going to be proud of the fact that there are a bunch of Guns N'Roses fans who are into our music,' he said, in an ominous warning of what was to come. 'We don't feel comfortable progressing, playing larger venues.

'I'm doing this right now because I have to,' he continued, only half-joking. 'Because I'm in fear of having to go to court if I leave the band. If I wasn't doing this I'd be a street musician. That's my goal in life.'

It was easy for him to say that. It's always easier to complain once you're at the top. Not me, though. I would've been lying if I'd said I didn't like all this, the knocks on my hotel door at eight a.m. from security looking for the miscreants who'd trashed a couple of their rooms the previous night. My clothes were covered in vomit, someone was using the back of my head for a pinball machine and the rats in the back alley were so fat and complacent you could use them as footballs. I remembered the decline of the mirrors and general overhaul of a bed, but the television . . .? Sorry, can't help you there. I slipped out shortly after the call, to find tour manager Monty hiding round a hotel corner, waiting patiently for me. Without a word, he motioned me to the exit and I clambered into a van smelling of sick.

Uergh! Who did that?

'You did,' Shelli, Chris's cool wife curtly informed me. 'You asshole.'

Later we went to a barbecue given by Dave Grohl's excellent mom, and Kurt told me of his love for Boston singer, cutesy Mary-Lou Lord. He was also full of admiration for my drinking exploits.

'I don't know how you do it, man,' he laughed. 'I would have been out for days.'

Rock'n'roll, however seedy or disgusting, gave me a sense of glamour. Kurt Cobain understood all about this desire for glamour, it had been his escape from teenage years filled with upheaval. He was also narcissistic in his self-loathing. Many suicidal people are. As he sang on 'On A Plain', *'I love myself, better than you/I know it's wrong but what can I do?'* Oh, but I could relate to that.

Initially, rock music helped to define a new me, far removed from the taunts of schoolmates who looked down upon me because my family didn't have enough money to buy new clothes. When I started making records, records fired with anger and sexual frustration and disaffection, I became someone. I knew finally that I was unique, also that I had a place to turn to when all around rejected me. How could I not love the music that had given me the

Slits, early Ramones, the Jam and Mudhoney? Of course I love rock'n'roll. Even now, especially now, it has the power to move me, to keep my spirits from flagging. Just flick the volume up a notch higher, and play the new CD from Sleater-Kinney or Quasi, search out an old Dexys Midnight Runners album or Stax/Volt single. How can I despise anything that has given my life such validity and direction, that has enabled me to communicate with so many others over the years? It's not rock music's fault that most people are dumb. As a US punk band once said, stupid people shouldn't breed. I love rock music, and they don't come any more rock than Nirvana. Important qualification, though: depending on your definition of rock.

Sure I loved rock. How could anyone doubt it after reading my *Melody Maker* review of 'Smells Like Teen Spirit' in November '91?

'The part I like best for tonight occurs third time through,' I wrote, 'when Kurt [he'd changed the spelling of his name back again by this stage] sings *"I found it hard/Just hard to find/Oh well/ Whatever . . . never mind"*. He nearly gives up, sounding all bruised and little boy hurt, like a favourite toy truck battered and chipped, hidden beneath your brother's bed. He's this close to chucking it all in, but then the inexhaustible chorus breaks through, the bravado guitars rush in and you start wondering if the world's turned mad, that people like Axl and Farrell and the Crüe can dig something this poppy, this puritanical, this passionate. Single of the Year, in case you were wondering how to fill in those Readers' Polls.'

My political awakening came via underground comics and rock. I started listening to pop music late, at the time of punk (1977–8) and so I always, perhaps foolishly, believed that music could change the world. When Nirvana appeared and took the sensibilities of the punk rock underground plus the teachings of Kurt's adopted hometown of Olympia into the mainstream it seemed that finally the dream might be coming true.

Kurt rated the outsiders, those who spoke up for those too timid to shout, artists like Shonen Knife and Young Marble Giants, Jad Fair and Flipper, the sort of people who didn't want to be forever sneered upon for being different but still relished their individuality. This to me is the greatest gift that Nirvana bequeathed; not their own soulful music, but opening up middle America to a music that hadn't been rounded off and polished countless times before being deemed suitable – by who? – for mass consumption. (I say this, but hearing *Nevermind* for the first time in six years or more, I can't help but think the production sucks. It's too rounded off, too polished. If only they'd got someone like Steve Albini in to help them. Great songs, though.) Maybe we all should have waited a few years for the advent of the Internet, and the long awaited fall of the record industry but hell! We had our own battles to fight . . .

On one occasion, Courtney and myself were ribbing Kurt for wearing the same Captain America (Eugene Kelly's rather ordinary post-Vaselines band) T-shirt in all of his interviews. Realising the power the reluctant star had to influence people, I suggested he should change his shirt of choice. Kurt complained that he had nothing to wear in its stead, so I offered him my treasured Daniel Johnston T-shirt that I'd only come by a few weeks previous. He accepted it, under the condition that he would wear it at every available photo shoot afterwards – a promise he kept. A couple of years later, Atlantic Records made perhaps that unlikeliest of post-Nirvana signings: Mr Johnston himself, a tormented schizophrenic who has difficulty remembering anyone he meets, and once pushed a girl out of a first floor window, believing her to be possessed by the devil. He also happens to create some of the most poignant, soulful and rawest blues music in America and so, of course, doesn't sell any records.

In a world where people have nothing to believe in – television, religion, the family unit, all of these have become increasingly meaningless in Western society – rock can provide a rare sense of community. Rock, at its finest, is a club for all of those who don't have the credentials to join anywhere else.

It wasn't all rock'n'roll braggadocio, though.

In Pittsburgh, Kurt walked out of yet another commercial radio interview, fed up with the constant glad-handing his role demanded. This time, he took me with him. We sat outside on a bench with the station's massive skyscraper looming above our heads while Chris and Dave tried their hardest to cover in Kurt's absence, and continued a conversation that had begun days before. We talked about ideals, the bullshit that the record industry deals in every day. We spoke of punk rock, about how people in our cherished town of Olympia were beginning to ostracise Kurt for not being 'pure' enough because he'd signed to a major label.

Previously Kurt had made an inspired rant against rockers like Sammy Hagar and Eddie Van Halen in the van between NYC and Pittsburgh where there was nothing to do but scarf junk food and flip through copies of teen girl magazine *Sassy*. (The red liquorice sticks were our favourites.)

We talked about the past, how Kurt used to practice his guitar in his room for hours on end, shut away from the world. His parents divorced when he was nine, and he went to live with his dad in a trailer park for two years before moving back in with his mother. It took him years to realise that the split wasn't his fault.

'For ages I thought I might be a homosexual,' he told me. 'Because I didn't like the cheerleader type of girl or want to hang out with jock boys.'

His home life was so cloistered it wasn't until about '76 that he realised the Beatles had split. The news shattered him: he'd been looking forward to seeing them in concert for years.

'I wanted to be John Lennon,' Kurt related. 'I was so in love with the Beatles. I would dress up like Lennon and pretend to play guitar, and hold mini-Beatles concerts for my family when they came over.'

In the fourth grade, Kurt had a subscription to *Cream* magazine, which he used to follow the exploits of the Sex Pistols as they trailed across America on that final, fateful tour. He was drawn to the attitudes of the people he read about, even though he'd never heard their music. He would see pictures of Sid Vicious and dream of what his life was like.

'Punk changed my whole attitude to music,' he added. 'From wanting to be a star, I decided what I wanted to do was play rhythm guitar in a band. Every evening all I'd do from the moment I arrived home until bedtime was to sit in my bedroom working on my songwriting techniques and playing guitar.'

It would be years before Kurt even heard a punk record, not until he borrowed a copy of the Clash's *Sandinista!* from the library and was severely disappointed. 'I thought, Christ. If this is what punk is, I don't want to know.'

It wasn't until 1983 when he finally discovered US punk bands like Flipper, Black Flag, Tales Of Terror, MDC and Scratch Acid that he finally found the music to match the attitude.

'I liked anything that was a little bit weird, a little bit different basically,' he recalled. 'I always went for the psychotic, weird, dirgey bands like Butthole Surfers, not for straight hardcore jocks like Minor Threat.'

At the age of seventeen, Kurt ran away from his mother's house and practically lived in the library for the whole of one bitterly cold winter. He'd hang out there, reading books by authors like Salinger and Tolstoy, Laura Ingells Wilder and Laurens Van Der Post, waiting until his friends arrived home from school so he could bum some macaroni cheese off them. By this point, he'd already majored in Custodial Arts. In white trash America, the girls wait on tables and the boys carry the luggage. One job he remembers with fondness was in a large hotel where he was required to clean fireplaces with his bucket and duster. As he was allowed to choose which room he was cleaning, his superiors never knew where he was and he consequently spent most of his time asleep.

'It was a great job,' he reminisced. 'I'd go into a room, lie down on the bed and fall asleep for two hours. I probably slept 80 per cent of my job away. Then one day I got caught and that was that.'

When he was eighteen, he had a job as a lifeguard in charge of 30 children one summer at the YMCA. He taught them how to swim, how to make peanut butter jelly sandwiches and what constituted proper manners. The mind boggles, but Kurt was adamant. 'It was a great job. I used to love working with kids.'

And when he was bored he'd get out of his skull on acid and go around trashing other people's houses. He wouldn't steal anything, just trash them: graffiti the walls and break the furniture, smash the ornaments, anything for a thrill, the buzz. It was around this time that Kurt met Chris . . . but you know all that already from your rock history books, right?

For years, I have been known as 'the man who wheeled Kurt Cobain on stage at Reading'. How sad is that, having your life reduced to one sentence where you play the bit part? Even worse is that I have barely any recollection of the event.

It happened at Reading Festival 1992, right? All day long the rumours had been flying around that Nirvana wouldn't show. Kurt had OD'd on the heroin he was rumoured to be taking. Kurt was with his wife and proud new mother back in the States. Kurt was pissed off with the security arrangements. It didn't look that way to me where I was slumped against a wall, but who really knew? Someone had passed me a bottle of vodka – Mudhoney again, or perhaps one of L7 – and I'd drunk it. Willingly, and with an alacrity that indicated there would be trouble to come.

As you join us, we're hanging around Nirvana's dressing room, listening to the sweet sound of Nick Cave serenading the crowd. Kurt is in one corner, Chris is stretching himself in another and Dave's looking his usual ebullient self by the table with all the half-eaten sweetmeats. (Every dressing room in the world contains a 'food' table featuring the mandatory plate of sweating Swiss cheese and ham, plus several bowls of Smarties and nuts. I've never understood why: because no one, except for starving journalist types, ever eats anything from it.) Managerial types rush in and out the door, making sure I'm well looked after. Confidante to the stars . . . it's a tough job, but someone has to do it.

Someone – Nirvana's wicked new tour manager, Alex MacLeod probably – is pouring me whisky as someone else starts to unfold a wheelchair. Hey, what gives? 'We need someone to push this on,' commands one of the managerial types. Oh, I see. It's a joke! Hardy, ha ha. I like it. Kurt isn't dead, but he's come straight from the hospital and he's going to pretend to rise from the dead. Right? Everyone ignores me.

'I can wheel myself on,' says Kurt, looking for the easiest route out.

'No no no,' I announce. 'I'll push it. And hey, I think I have a blonde wig here that you can wear that'll make you look a little bit more like Courtney too.'

The wig was a present from my sister Alison. At the previous year's Reading I'd been threatened with knives. While talking to Nirvana manager John Silva, a couple of tough-looking types had marched straight over to us and demanded to know if he was Everett True. He reassured them that he wasn't. 'Well, how can we find him then?' the dastardly duo demanded. 'Oh, he's ugly; very, very ugly,' said John, laughing. 'In fact, he's the ugliest person on the site. In fact, I have a feeling I just saw him go into that backstage area over there.' With a gruff thank you, the pair went over to stalk the exit that John had pointed to. Knowing all of this, my sibling posted me the disguise. I danced in it during the rain to Teenage Fanclub on the Saturday. Everyone in the crowd recognised me nonetheless.

Thus we find ourselves hurried along up the side of the stage while out in the distance a mighty crowd clap and cheer. I have little memory of what happens next. There's a drunken wheelchair chase where I push Kurt round in hot pursuit of the L7 girls on the side of the stage, while 60-foot drops wait invitingly and managerial types mutter among themselves about how they're going to 'kill this fucking drunken English asshole journalist afterwards'. Ace Seattle photographer Charles Peterson, the man who defined the look of Seattle grunge in the early years, snaps us while we spin around laughing, framed in the spotlight. Then comes the moment . . .

Picture it. You're on the main stage at Reading Festival with the final act. You can't see a fucking thing. There are just immense spotlights in your eyes, and a hidden crowd roaring approval. I start pushing Kurt to the right-hand microphone stand, and he reaches up from the wheelchair and grabs my neck. 'Cool,' I think in my drunken stupor, 'he wants to wrestle with me on stage like in the old days.' So I start to grab him back.

'You've got the wrong fucking microphone, you idiot,' he hisses. Oops.

We get there without any further incident. Kurt rises slowly out of his chair, I fold it up neatly and stalk off stage again, not looking back but looking rather smug. I stand at the side with my girl for a few songs, and find myself busting for a piss. We aren't allowed backstage again until after the set. Sigh.

So I pushed Kurt Cobain on stage in a wheelchair for what turned out to be his final UK concert. Big deal. He'd have done the same for me.

After the furore from Reading had died down, *Melody Maker* ran a competition to 'win the wig that Kurt Cobain wore at Reading'. (I ran on after the show's end, and grabbed the wig as a keepsake. I thought that perhaps my sister might need it back. I wasn't sure how much wigs cost.) No one wrote in. They didn't believe it. So we trailed the competition even bigger the following week, writing something like 'Listen you morons! This is for real! The first person to write in with the best reason why they couldn't actually get to Reading to see Nirvana wins the wig, and we'll print the winning entry.'

This time, we were deluged with entries. We printed the winning one: it was a pithy, witty, beautifully structured and reasoned piece of writing. We congratulated the winner, commiserated with them for missing Nirvana and informed them that they had by far and away been the finest entry we received.

Trouble was, by this point I'd decided I wanted to keep the wig for myself.

I'm still waiting for offers . . .

In Utero

If Kurt and Nirvana had been allowed to release the original version of *In Utero* as mixed by Chicago producer Steve Albini – he'd reached an agreement with the band that no one was allowed to touch the recording after him – then rock would have been revolutionised. I swear it. Primal screaming was matched only in intensity by Dave Grohl's drumming. Tunes were subverted to Kurt's need to release the anguish he felt at his new unlooked-for role as Spokesman for Generation X. All his hatred, all his drug-fuelled paranoia, all his disgust at a world he perceived, rightly or wrongly, as trying to demonise his wife . . . It all poured out with a bleak fury that was unnerving to listen to. Fuck *MTV Unplugged* being the way forward for Nirvana. This was the real shit, the one where they paid homage to the underground.

I can still remember Courtney's anguished phone call now.

'Jerry!' she cried. (Courtney frequently used my real name.) 'What's your address? I need to send you a copy of Kurt's new album. His record company, his management, everyone, is telling him there aren't any tunes on it. They want him to re-record it. You have to defend him, he's totally depressed about it all.'

A few days later I received the tape: it sounded great. More importantly it sounded like a much more honest representation of Nirvana than anything since 'Sliver'. So there weren't any tunes present? Christ! What about 'Heart Shaped Box' and the traumatic 'Rape Me', with its opening ironic inverted echo of 'Teen Spirit'? (Was that song partially an attack on me? I never did work it out. It was after all a metaphor for the way that Kurt had been treated by the press.) Listen to the plaintive 'Dumb', a tune busting all over with plangent guitar chords. (When I first met Kurt, he told me that he acted according to how people treated him. So if they thought of him as a dumb-ass punk rocker, he was more than willing to be a dumb-ass punk rocker.) Listen to the moving sorry note 'All Apologies' and try denying its effect seven years down the line. '*I wish I was like you,*' sings a jaded Kurt wanting nothing more than an end to all this shit. '*Easily amused. Everything is my fault. I'll take all the blame.*'

God, he tried so desperately to believe in Love.

I sit here and listen to 'Pennyroyal Tea' for the first time in six years and my damn spectacles are again clouding over with tears. Is this the effect that music that is supposed to have no resonance has on me? *Is this what music means to you?*

The brilliantly titled 'Frances Farmer Will Have Her Revenge On Seattle' boasts an opening bass-line that unconsciously echoes the minimal, spooked sound of Young Marble Giants. I wasn't going to deny that overall the album made for heavy listening, but wasn't that the thrill? Nirvana ended up dropping several of the noisier tracks from the finished version, where the management brought in mid-American REM producer Scott Litt in a vain attempt to 'tidy up' a couple of songs for US radio. It's very possible that, the Litt tracks aside, Albini's mixes weren't touched by another engineer. It was when the CD came to be mastered that the sound was cleaned up (mastering and mixing are two very different beasts, each equally as important).

Even the revamped version is an awesome album, on a par with Amphetamine Reptile's hardcore merchants Today Is The Day and Big Black's finest moments. OK, so it isn't the Beatles; but don't you think we have enough new Beatles every other week already?

Kurt wanted to destroy the monster he'd created, that was obvious. At one point, he was talking with me about opening the album with a bass frequency so low it would be able to destroy home entertainment speakers. Now that's subversion. Somewhere along the line – the constant press attention, having to deal with crap like MTV and tabloid journalists, Olympia and the punk rock kids turning their back on him because of his association with Courtney – it had all turned sour. When Kurt formed Nirvana, he and Chris had been as close as brothers. Now when the band toured he and new guitarist, the lovely Pat Smear, travelled in a different van to Chris and Dave. What's the point of that? Why be in a band when you don't even want to speak to your fellow members? Are contractual obligations really that powerful?

I kept the tape safe the only way I knew how. I threw it unmarked into a pile of thousands and tried to forget I even knew the band existed after Kurt died. It remains there to this day, but I have a feeling someone else with soul released the tape to a bootlegger, figuring something this awesome shouldn't stay hidden forever.

The last conversation I ever had with Kurt was on Christmas Day 1993, when he and Courtney rang me up at my house in Brighton, England.

'You're the only person we could think of out of all our friends who'd be in today,' Kurt explained, mindful of an anti-Christmas rant I'd given him and Kim Deal a couple of weeks earlier in Seattle. 'We haven't spoken to anyone all day, except for the postman. How are you? Still miserable? Merry fucking Christmas.'

It was such a shame. Just a year earlier, Nirvana had been so close to disturbing the mainstream and creating a whole new breed of heroes: the Breeders, Sonic Youth, Hole, *et al*. Did that happen? No. Grunge became subsumed by fashion dictates and crap macho bands like Green Day and the Offspring who were all almost the exact opposites of Nirvana in everything but the music. This was, of course, the least important aspect. People's lack of money got turned into a designer clothes statement in an uncanny echo of the early eighties in Britain when *The Face* invented the 'Hard Times' look, the clothes of street bums and moneyless punks becoming off-the-peg delights.

The gestures the band made – Kurt kissing Chris on prime-time TV, the burlesque version of 'Teen Spirit' performed on *Top Of The Pops* which almost certainly denied the single a Number One slot in the UK – might have seemed small in retrospect, but hell. At least they tried.

*   *   *

(The following is taken from the pages of the *Melody Maker*'s 'Sex' issue, 12 December 1992)

ET: Why did you wear a dress in the new video for 'In Bloom'?

KC: I don't know. I like to wear dresses because they're comfortable. If I could wear a sheet, I would. I don't know what to say ... If I said we do it to be subversive then that would be a load of shit because men in bands wearing dresses aren't controversial any more. Basically we wanted to make the video with as little fuss as possible, in as short a time as possible, for a few thousand dollars. There was no hidden agenda. The dresses only came about at the last minute. We wanted to be like the Beatles – no, the Dave Clark Five, I was wearing glasses – we would never make fun of the Beatles. There's nothing more comfortable than a cosy flower pattern.

ET: In your particular context, an MTV hard rock band that sells millions of records, surely it's a subversive act?

KC: It may be subversive as far as a very small amount of people go, who've never seen men in dresses before or who aren't comfortable with the concept, but I don't give a shit about those people anyway. It's not subversive. There's no point in being subversive in rock any more. There's no way you can be, unless you ram a stick of dynamite up your ass. Queen dressed in drag. Male bands do it all the time. It just feels comfortable, sexy and free wearing a dress. It's fun.

ET: How do you feel about the suggestion some of your fans are called 'fags' for liking such a presumably effeminate hard rock band?

KC: I love it. Knowing that gives me as much pleasure as when I used to dress up as a punk at high school and rednecks driving by in trucks would yell 'Devo!' at me. It's good to have a nice, healthy battle going on in high school between the Guns N'Roses jocks and the Nirvana fans. It vibes up the kids who are more intelligent, and at least it brings the whole subject of homosexuality into debate. It's very flattering our fans are thought of as 'fags'. I've heard stories about kids being beaten up for wearing Nirvana T-shirts. It reminds me of when I used to support strange or weird bands who were that little bit more dangerous because they weren't accepted by the mainstream. Devo were a great example – a Top Ten act that were far more off-the-wall than us.

ET: Do you approve of cross-dressing?

KC: Of course. Men shouldn't wear a dress because it's feminist particularly, but because it's comfortable. Sometimes my penis will literally fall asleep or feel like it's dropped right off because it's been constricted by tight Levi's, and I'll have to wear baggy pants or a dress instead.

ET: How about men wearing make up?

KC: Sure. If it's applied in a real gaudy fashion, really thick and makes you look like a TV evangelist's wife. I go through an eyeliner phase about one month every year. Pete Townshend did too, but it didn't last very long. I know all about rock stars who use eyeliner. It never lasts very long. Supposedly it burns into the eyes during shows under the bright lights. Maybe you should tattoo it on. Cross-dressing is cool. I'm sorry I can't come up with any better reasons for why we wore dresses for our video shoot, it's just that I wear them all the time, round the house, wherever. I'd just as soon wear a bathrobe or sheet with a hole in it. It's not particularly because I want to wear a woman's dress.

Six months after this interview took place, several of the Nirvana entourage caught a 'grunge' covers band live in Scandinavia. All songs were performed faithfully – Soundgarden, Pearl Jam, Spin Doctors, etc – until it came to Nirvana. These were sung in a high-pitched squeal, the obvious inference being that Nirvana weren't real 'men' at all. Not like their peers.

I don't recall when it all started to spiral crazily out of control, although that time when a musician died after he'd been drinking all night with me – and I was visited by an Angel Of Death on the exact hour of his death – should have served as a warning. What could I do? I carried on partying, harder than ever. Most of this period was spent in a drunken, happy haze, staggering around the streets of New York and LA, Chicago and Seattle, singing Teenage Fanclub and Guided By Voices songs, unable to figure out exactly where I was. I knew I no longer had any control over my destiny, and that's how I liked it.

In Washington DC I was standing at the side of the stage furtively drinking my whisky, hiding it from the glare of fiery Scots tour manager Alex MacLeod. I wasn't supposed to drink while I was travelling with Nirvana, management orders, for fear of being a bad influence. Frequently though, he would come up to me, check my glass and give me a snifter from a bottle hidden inside his jacket when assured I'd been a good boy. Suddenly I became aware that he was shouting my name. 'Oh fuck,' I thought to myself. 'What have I done wrong now?' I was a bit scared he might have discovered I'd had a hand in Pat Smear's prank of busting his hotel toilet with the aid of a towel earlier. I look up, and see he's rushing towards me.

'Kurt wants you to sing the encore. Get on stage NOW!' he yells above the noise emanating from the PA system. So I rush on, parka pulled up over my head, whereupon Kurt does his usual trick of shoving his guitar-strap over me . . . What did I sing and play? I have no idea. I just kept chanting in some vague approximation of the beat the band was playing behind me. Something to do with doughnuts probably. I was a one-trick pony. This could have been one of the shows where I ended up smashing Kurt's guitar. Who knows? 'If it feels good, do it,' as Kurt himself said a few years earlier. And it feels fucking great to smash a guitar. They're also a lot harder to break than you might think.

At New York's Roseland Ballroom a few nights later, when a whole load of us have gathered on the stage for the encore, including support band Half-Japanese, Jad Fair's young son takes about 30 attempts to break Kurt's guitar. By the time he's finished, the whole ensemble is standing round cheering him on.

It was even weirder in New York at that stadium just by Central Park, where there was just Naomi Campbell and me standing in the VIP area. Huh? The whole time, I kept thinking, I'm going to be up there shortly . . . but that afternoon, I couldn't croak above a whisper in the catering tent, I'd screamed myself so hoarse the previous two nights. The following morning, Nirvana's management and record company offices were inundated with calls from NY press people wanting to know who the mystery 'rock star' on stage with Nirvana had been. Er, The Legend!?

I remember numerous taxi journeys taken across America.

Kurt hopped a lift across town to see genius underrated English Mod band TV Personalities. Arriving at Wetlands, he and his wife espied Steve Malkmus, singer of Pavement, the NYC band who were starting to be talked up in a big way. Not brooking any arguments, they placed themselves either side of Malkmus, remaining deep in conversation all night. Later I saw Kurt walking along the street dishevelled and distracted, on his own, having just argued with Courtney and been thrown out of the cab.

One time, Frances Bean's demon nanny and all-round good sort and professional waster Cali took umbrage with New York's No Smoking rule in taxis and ripped the ashtray straight off the cab door and threw it out of the window. I offered the driver ten dollars, and prayed he wasn't packing a gun. Jesus! I hope I never did anything like that . . . though I suspect I did.

I went to see U2 play in Philadelphia, and Bono got to hear I was there and sent his personal manager across to me with a present: a hatchet. On its handle, he wrote, 'Do your duty! Bono', next to a self-portrait.

I tried my hardest.

One time I turned up in New York to find that Shimmydisc Records had organised two nights of shows especially for me at Brownie's in the East Village. Eleven bands played, including ultra-cool *Sassy* magazine feminist spin-off ensemble Chia Pet. Everywhere I looked, ice cool New York models rubbed shoulders with the elite. There I was drunkenly on my knees in front of Dogbowl, over in the corner playing pinball like no one else existed. What the fuck was going on?

In Oslo 1992, I walk along outside the arena with Kurtney (as the couple became known) as the pair hurl abuse at bootleggers. Courtney tells me of how I remind her of her first husband, Falling James, he a sensitive man who likes to wear tights to bed. Hey, I never did that! Not often, anyway. Back at the hotel, the rest of us – Chris, Dave, Nirvana's road crew including the near-legendary Big John from the Exploited, Teenage Fanclub – stay up until six a.m. performing karaoke favourites.

In Springfield MA, November 1993, we throw a Queen party in Nirvana's tour van: Chris, *MM* photographer Steve Gullick, the Breeders' Kelley Deal, Nirvana biographer Michael Azerrad and me. Gullick ends up winning the prize for best Freddie Mercury impersonation: a bowling ball and a piece of the television screen that we'd been watching the Queen videos on, which Chris ceremoniously presented to him. It was Kurt's video. He usually managed to hide his love for Queen from the press.

LA, September '92: and hunky *MM* photographer Stephen Sweet and me are on an hour-long taxi ride into the Valley, searching for a warehouse where hordes of old film outfits are kept so we can kit Kurt and Courtney out as devil and angel for the 1992 *Maker* Christmas cover. It's an oppressively hot day, and we arrive there only to find all the costumes are vile, musty and old, and that the couple don't want to go through with our idea. We return to the house: Courtney has copper red hair and Kurt suggests painting 'Diet Grrrl' on Frances Bean's stomach when Stephen takes her shot. They refuse to be photographed together, a random decision on the part of their management that probably cost Stephen a new house. Ah, the vagaries of the music business!

Kilburn '91: I attempt to start a food fight with Kurt and Chris, only to be admonished because the band had got thrown out of their own record release party in Seattle a few weeks earlier for doing precisely the same. Scandinavia '92: I'm watching TV with Kurt and Courtney, the only visitor allowed within the Holy Couple's room. Not even the band is speaking to them. Seattle '91: I'm on the phone for hours to Kurtney, off my head through drinking, they in exactly the same state, only through different devices. New York '93: Courtney is telling me how Kurt OD'd only minutes before he was due to go on stage after mates the Jesus Lizard, at Nirvana's big industry showcase. That evening, Big John played his only show with the band as extra guitarist. The kids almost riot when Nirvana throw in a series of quieter songs in the middle.

San Francisco '92: an MTV VJ goes around the Kennel Club's Sub Pop showcase telling everyone what an asshole I am. NYC '93: I'm engaged in a beer-throwing street fight with Gerard Cosloy, future millionaire and owner of Matador Records.

London '92: I watch the brilliant TV Personalities deliberately fuck up their last shot at fame, supporting Nirvana at the Kilburn National, playing all of their achingly honest songs at half-speed. They are so punk rock. Kurt peeks out from behind a curtain to watch. LA '92: Courtney offers to read me Kurt's diaries. In the back room are Kurt's Goya-influenced paintings, strange hybrids of angels and babies and men. At the front of his record collection is a Mavis Staples album, and halfway back, a Legend! single. To enter the apartment, I have to go through a weird lift contraption . . . or was that another house?

Scandinavia '92: and Courtney produces Kurt's lyric book, a scrappy, lined A5 affair, full of crossings-out and amendments, written in blue Biro. 'Here, I thought you might want to take this, Everett,' she cries blithely, seemingly oblivious to Kurt's annoyance. 'What about the lyrics to *that song*, for starters.' Like many successful songwriters, Kurt hated his most famous song with a passion, and would often try to refuse to play it live. I refused Courtney's kind offer. Well, wouldn't you? We watch Eddie Murphy on TV and Kurt remarks how he used to be funny once: 'back before he became famous and complacent, back when he was still struggling to be heard, back when he *had to try*'. There's no need for him to elaborate. We know that he's talking about himself.

Seattle '93: we're singing Bee Gees songs with Kelley Deal again, waiting for Nirvana to finish their MTV interview. The Red Hot Chili Peppers wander by, dressed in drag. I try to convince Kurt that I should pop up wearing an Eddie Vedder face mask during his band's set in response to Pearl Jam pulling out of this MTV showcase hours earlier. He tells me to grow up.

Brighton '92: Courtney is on the phone to me, informing me that she and Kurt want me to go up and accept some big MTV Award on Nirvana's behalf, upon which she and Kurt planned to simultaneously French kiss me. Good plan. How come it didn't happen?

Reading '92: and it's the day after the big Nirvana performance. I'm in hospital with my teenage girlfriend waiting patiently by: alcohol poisoning. Later, I show up in the bar sporting a hospital tag on my wrist, and someone passes me half a pint of vodka. I can't even taste it. I fall over clutching a coloured cocktail and hit the floor, the drink held aloft in my fist, not a drop spilt. I carry on drinking.

London Astoria '91: and Nirvana have set up a food trap for me – cold cuts, pizza, sweating cheese, the usual – on a plate above their dressing room door in response to an article I'd written portraying them as 'rock'n'roll animals'. A British heavy metal magazine writes about the incident and refers to me as 'chubby'.

I can recall a fellow *Melody Maker* journalist screaming at me for the entire duration of a train journey from Brighton to London, 'You're just a fucking music journalist!' No, I wasn't. I was Everett True. I was untouchable.

I hate rock'n'roll.

How can I feel any other way? Look what it did to Nirvana. One moment they're cruising along happily, struggling to make the most commercial album they can to reach as many people as they can. The next, they've achieved their goal and realised that there's no way back, this is their life whether they want it or not.

No one ever tells you about the downside of hedonism: all the nagging headaches and colds and feelings of paranoia that exist for years afterwards. You fly too close to the sun, you're going to get burned.

I Hate Myself and I Want to Die

It all happened too fast.

Somewhere along the line, our dreams came true and we never had a chance to reconcile them with our ideals. Nothing untoward happened for Nirvana that hadn't happened to a thousand other bands, so what was it that felt so bad? Perhaps we were too naïve. We didn't realise that people could take and twist our words and actions into any shapes they desired. Courtney's demonisation was a symptom, not the cause, of all that followed. It's very likely that no one twisted her words in any highfalutin' publication whatsoever, all that was different was the focus applied.

Life is all about context and perception, remember? We were used to existing in our own tiny little insular worlds where everyone knew everyone and everyone behaved in a roughly similar fashion on roughly the same level. In rock, there's nothing unusual or odd about taking drugs, being outspoken or having opinions that fluctuate from day to day. Indeed, it's expected. The world of musicians and the music press is different to the world of the mainstream press. For a start, music critics have no real power. There's far more hypocrisy in the 'real' press than in what to all intents and purposes is still the 'fan' press: celebrities go to extraordinary lengths to make sure their actual characters are never exposed. This was a lesson that Courtney, for one, learned far too late.

Nirvana's 1992 Reading performance was an aberration, chronologically speaking. It was obvious the trio (plus that strange fellow who painted his face and danced on stage. I never did figure out who he was) were enjoying themselves. As a creative unit Nirvana were almost spent.

Look at the songwriting credits to the mighty *In Utero*: see many co-written songs listed there? Chris and Dave – and later, extra guitarist Pat Smear – were still an incredible musical force to be reckoned with. Without them, Kurt would have had real trouble fulfilling his visions. By the end of 1992, though, he seemed intent on reducing their role to that of backing musicians.

Some time between the end of '91 and summer '92, everything changed. Kurt's paranoia and drug-taking became more intense; he became separated from his close friends and in particular Chris when he moved down to LA, fed up with being accosted in Seattle night clubs; Courtney became pregnant. The one focus in Kurt's life became his love for Courtney. Look at the lyrics to *In Utero*; almost every single one deals with his wife and/or her vilification in the press. It's possible, too, that after having been on almost constant tour for over eighteen months, Kurt was never given a chance to return to normality. Indeed, for him, the old normality didn't exist any more. Contrast this with his band mates who both tried their hardest to readjust to their lives. Chris returned to his wife Shelli in Seattle, and began to immerse himself in good causes, trying to make use of his fame. Dave, on the other hand, was always unreasonably well adjusted.

By the time the echoes from *Nevermind* had died down, Nirvana barely meant anything to Kurt any more. Certainly not within the context of being a 'radio friendly unit shifter'. Even worse than that, however, the group found themselves unable to play the small clubs they and their punk heroes cherished. Make no mistake: Kurt hated headlining festivals to a bunch of kids he perceived as only being there because Bryan Adams didn't arrive till Monday. Likewise, the arena rock shows of Nirvana's final US tour. You create music because you feel a primal urge – right? If you want to make money from it, there are far more credible and less soul-destroying ways of doing so than to prostitute your soul.

I stayed in contact with Kurt and Courtney over this period. Indeed, I was probably one of the few who spoke to both sides of the marriage. (Yes, it was sudden, so sudden, in fact, that Courtney realised she hadn't actually ... er ... divorced her previous husband Falling James of the Leaving Trains whom she'd married one night on a drunken whim in Las Vegas. The first I knew of it was when Courtney or someone called me up, and informed me the ceremony had taken place somewhere exotic. It was around then that I also learned Courtney was pregnant.) Yet I had no idea what was going on.

I was too busy enjoying myself.

The following interview takes place in a trailer on the edge of a river in Stockholm. The day is cloudy, with occasional flashes of sunshine. People are drinking Coke and, in Chris's case, red wine. Chris and Dave sit on one couch, Kurt on another. A bowl of chilli-roasted peanuts and some fruit nestles on the table. Someone is smoking. The band seem awkward in each other's presence, slightly wary of each other. When Chris speaks, his eyes are looking anywhere but in Kurt's direction. When Kurt speaks, he does so defensively, as if he feels a need to justify himself in front of Chris. When Dave speaks you can feel he can feel the uneasiness but he's trying to ignore it.

ET: What do you hate most about being famous?
KC: Kids with Bryan Adams and Bruce Springsteen T-shirts coming up to me and asking for autographs. When people in the audience hold up a sign that says 'Even Flow' [Pearl Jam] on one side and 'Negative Creep' [Nirvana] on the other.
ET: What's the best thing about being famous?
KC (ironically): That's a really good question.
CN (joking): We might get some perks here and there. A free drink or two.

ET (sarcastically): Do you get many groupies?

KC: When I was about twelve, I wanted to be a rock'n'roll star. I thought that would be my payback to all the jocks who got girlfriends all the time, but I realised way before I became a rock star that was stupid.

DG: Maybe it's flattering to all those heavy metal bands but we find it kind of disgusting.

ET: What about the free drink?

CN: I came into this tour with a fresh perspective. I would get stressed out and drink a whole lot and react to everything. Now I just go with the flow.

KC (challenging): I've always loved the spontaneity of being frustrated and pissed off . . .

CN: . . . and drunk. Oh yeah! I've had some of my best inspirations intoxicated. It's a different reality. It's like living in a movie or cartoon, where your subconscious takes off. That's where all the good stories come from. But it's such hell on your body.

ET: Has the sudden fame appreciably changed your lifestyle?

KC: Definitely.

CN: It hasn't changed mine. I can still go down to Safeway, buy fruit and vegetables, walk around town. I don't care if people stare at me.

KC: You don't? At all?

CN: No. And the more they see of me, especially in Seattle, the more . . .

KC: Oh yeah, eventually they'll get tired of sniggering at you and talking behind your back. Well, I've been confronted by people wanting to beat me up and by people heckling me. People are drunk and obnoxious towards me because they think I'm this pissy rock star bastard who can't come to grips with his fame.

I was in a rock club the other night and one guy comes up, pats me on the back and says, 'You've got a really good thing going, you know? Your band members are cool, you write great songs, you've affected a lot of people but man, you've really got to get your personal shit together!' Then another person comes up and says 'I hope you overcome your drug problems.' All this happens within an hour while I'm trying to watch the Melvins, minding my own business.

There were about five or six kids sitting there, very drunk, screaming 'Rock star! Rock star! Oh look he's going to freak out any minute! He's going to have a tantrum! He's going to start crying!' Then this other guy comes up, puts his arms around me and says 'You know, my girlfriend broke up with me and took my Nirvana album, so you should give me fourteen dollars to buy a new CD, because you can afford that now you're a big rock star.'

CN: But you have to ignore them or it becomes an obsession. I have dreams about being nude in public and I interpret them as worrying about sticking out. Forget it! It can become a preoccupation. I was like that too when I used to see someone famous . . .

KC: Yeah, but did you pitch them shit?

CN: No, I didn't. That incident you just mentioned seems to be pretty isolated, though.

KC (snarling): It's not isolated. It happens to me all the time – every time I go out, every fucking time. It's stupid. And if it bothers me that much I'm going to do something about it. Fuck it, rock doesn't mean that much to me. I still love to be in a band and play music with Chris and Dave but if it means that we have to resort to playing in a practice room and never touring again, then so be it.

Silence. The mood in the room has turned dark.

KC: I have to hear rumours about me all the time. I'm totally sick of it. If I'm going to take drugs that's my own fucking prerogative and if I don't take drugs it's my own fucking prerogative. It's nobody's business, and I don't care if people take drugs and I don't care if people don't take drugs.

It all started with just one article in one of the shittiest, cock rock orientated LA rock magazines where this guy assumed I was on heroin because he noticed I was tired. Since then, the rumours have spread like wildfire. I can't deny that I have taken drugs and I still do every once in a while. But I'm not a fucking heroin addict and I'm not going to . . .

It's impossible to be on tour and to be on heroin. I don't know of any band that could do it unless you're Keith Richards and you're being given blood transfusions every three days, and you have runners going out and scoring drugs for you.

I never realised that mainstream audiences react towards mainstream rock stars in this way because I never paid attention before. I don't mean to complain as much as I do but it's a load of shit. It's really stupid. I've had days where I've considered this a job, and I never thought that would happen. It makes me question the point of it all. I'm only gonna bitch about it for another year and then, if I can't handle it after that, we're going to have to make some drastic changes.

(From *Melody Maker*, 25 July 1992)

The couple of shows I caught on that tour were painful, easily the hardest to witness of Nirvana's short career. In Oslo, Kurt stood immobile as 20,000 kids went berserk, uncaring as to what reactions his band might or might not have been exciting. And the audience, with their ritualised clapping and banners and shoes tossed in the air and bare chests, didn't give a damn about how good or otherwise the band on stage were. Why should they have done? This was *corporate entertainment*, however much the band decried it. To most of those serenely beautiful, sun-kissed Scandinavians, it didn't matter that it was Nirvana up there. It could have been anyone. It was a festival, see. They didn't give a damn about Flipper or Shonen Knife or punk or Courtney Love or any of those things that were so close to Nirvana's heart. Why should they have done? What mattered was *size*.

Festival crowds know what to expect, or so they think. They've had the parameters of how they choose to spend their leisure time mapped out long ago. On this scale, art counts for virtually nothing. Rebellion? How could anyone be rebellious once they'd conquered the American market? By throwing it all away again? Then you're just termed a failure, or worse, a 'one-hit wonder'.

In Oslo, for all that it mattered, Kurt could have been rampaging drunk and breaking equipment, Chris could have been throwing his bass ten feet into the air and Dave moshing hard, like of old. *But they weren't.* (OK, Dave was). Sometimes Kurt flicked his floor switch from reverb to normal, sometimes Kurt would look across to see if Chris was playing the correct bass part, sometimes Kurt would try and make a self-deprecating remark and fail. There was precious little emotion, humour, angst: just a bunch of incredible songs turned to shimmering dust, some brutally and beautifully evocative lyrics which had begun to mean less than shit, now that the whole world had learned its part and reduced them to the everyday, the mundane.

Even in Scandinavia Kurt was still trying, though. Otherwise, why was he in so much pain? Not for the first time that year, I realised why I considered Bono and Axl and Bruce and all those other would-be rock Messiahs to be so crap. The market forces, the record-buyers, really are that powerful. You either succumb or you go insane. Is there a third choice? Nirvana struggled against it – they struggled real hard and they struggled real strong – but it was impossible to make sense of much of the confusion.

In Stockholm, Kurt was livelier, buoyed by the news shouted to him across the stage by his wife that the concert had undersold by 6,000 tickets. 'Hey! We're on our way out,' he gleefully shouted at me, stumbling across stage to change guitars. But then, Stockholm wasn't part of a two-day festival like Oslo. It was a Nirvana show, for fans only. So Kurt changed the set-list seconds before taking the stage, starting with a classic American punk number, 'Money Roll Right In' (irony!), playing an impromptu 'D7' upon request AND 'Molly's Lips'. He even made a few jokes. Dave and Chris looked happier as well. For the encore, a searing, purposeful 'Teen Spirit' and rampant 'Territorial Pissings', the band dragged 50 kids left outside by the back gate on to the stage. Hell, spontaneous bonhomie *could* sometimes work on this level. Even if it did recall something off *The Arsenio Hall Show*.

But the main set was still as bad as I'd seen Nirvana play, in terms of spirit, excitement, inspiration . . . everything Nirvana used to have in spades. Even if I was almost crying during 'Lithium'. It seemed so appropriate, somehow.

Second night in Stockholm, the assembled Nirvana and Fanclub crews were watching an MTV clip of Eddie Vedder going off the rails in Denmark. There was no appreciable glee at a well-publicised rival losing it, just a sad empathy, a feeling of genuine pity that perhaps here was another singer unable to cope with the lies and pressures and trauma of fame. Here was another singer who loathed and despised the distance forced between him and his audience, who couldn't see any way out of the trap, the role forced upon him simply because he'd written lyrics that reach people. Pearl Jam cancelled the remainder of their European tour that day. Bet Kurt was jealous.

Only one other British journalist was allowed to interview the band in July 1992, *NME*'s Keith Cameron, an early champion of the band. He flew out to mainland Europe, only to be confronted with a far more recalcitrant Cobain, unwilling to talk even to someone he considered a friend. 'I wonder what Keith's going to write, Jerry,' Kurt confided to me on the phone shortly afterwards. 'I didn't tell him anything.' Keith wrote the only possible piece he could in the circumstances: one that showed up the rifts and confusion surrounding the band in far greater detail than in my interview. There again, I *got* an interview.

This later led to Cameron being reviled by the band – a band he loved dearly – or perhaps, more accurately, this led to Cameron later being reviled by Kurtney. This revulsion went to the extent of Cobain naming one of his six guns after him.

'One for every person I want to kill before I go out in a final blaze of glory. There's Keith, [*Vanity Fair's*] Lynn Hirschberg . . .' he told me in a stormy mood from his final Seattle home while I argued with him not to be so stupid. Keith was his friend: an obvious fact that Kurt would have realised if only he hadn't been so blinded by paranoia and hate and of course drugs, not to mention the mealy-mouthed whisperings of certain people close to his management team. Or is that what it's like being famous?

You become so enamoured of the sound of your own opinions and so paranoid about the sound of everyone else's that you can only bear to have 'yes' people around you.

I love rock'n'roll.

When you're at your lowest, when everything comes crashing through on top of you, when gloom has overpowered your life and it seems there's no way out . . . hey! Slap on that stereo and turn the volume up a notch even higher. Doesn't matter what it is, virtually anything will do the trick . . . the Buzzcocks' 'Something's Gone Wrong Again', Altered Images' 'Dead Pop Stars', the Records' 'Starry Eyes', Nina Simone's 'Trouble In Mind' – Love's 'Alone Again Or', even. When I was in my twenties, I used to put Hüsker Dü's desperate, guitar-saturated version of the Byrds' 'Eight Miles High' on my Dansette mono portable record player, turn the volume up to full, turn all the lights off and set the dial to 'repeat'. It was either that or Otis Redding's 'I've Been Loving You Too Long'. When I was sent a copy of Nirvana's 'Love Buzz', I played it on that self-same Dansette, carving a groove into the floor with my head for hours on end. There's nothing to be ashamed of in having a passion for music, although for years after Kurt's death I tried to convince myself otherwise.

So Nirvana in concert during 1992, aside from the Reading Festival headline slot, weren't much cop. You think that was an end to it? Of course it wasn't. (Actually, between that England show and when I next caught up with the band in San Francisco with L7 and the Breeders in April '93, Nirvana played only three times.) As Kurt reassured me several times over the next year, he still loved to make music with Chris and Dave. Forget the rumours and speculation and whatever may have been happening in their private lives. All the band needed was to return to the studio. They did so, with Breeders and PJ Harvey producer Steve Albini at the end of '92, in Chicago. The resultant sessions may not have set the world alight like *Nevermind*, but the band never intended them to. All they wanted to create was great music, and they did with *In Utero*, the album that proved to be their epitaph.

Is that such a crime: creating music with no concern for sales?

Rock'n'roll won't save your immortal soul, but fuck me, I can't help thinking that yes, Neil Young and Kurt Cobain really were right: it IS better to burn out than to fade away. Just ask any old football player.

Oddly, almost all my memories of Nirvana in 1993 are happy ones.

Much of this is down to Nirvana's road crew and tour manager, a great collection of people. Also, it helped that the band had a new collection of songs to tour, once they'd overcome their ridiculous fear of bootleggers. (Hey! There's nothing wrong with the odd live recording. It keeps money away from the record industry, and ensures that the fans are happy. It doesn't stop anyone from buying the actual releases, either.) The fact that Geffen couldn't garnish any US radio hits from *In Utero* – anyone else think that's a cop-out from the working title of *I Hate Myself And I Want To Die?* – must have pleased Kurt. Plus, the genius, mischievous and likeable Pat Smear had joined the band . . . and it's almost impossible to stay miserable while Pat's around.

There's no denying the situation wasn't ideal during Nirvana's final US tour. The band travelled in two separate vans and there was an obvious rift between Kurtney and everyone else. The shows were still great, though. Perhaps adding an 'acoustic' section with a cellist helped pace them; also Kurt was happy knowing his fans weren't comfortable with this new direction. Plus, Nirvana had two brilliant bands in support: Kim Deal's Breeders and Jad Fair's underground heroes Half-Japanese, perhaps the strangest band I've ever seen take a major rock stage. The kids, bless them, treated both acts with more respect than usually occurs at that level, certainly at the shows I saw in Bethlehem, Philadelphia and in Springfield, Massachusetts, and on the following four nights. Maybe some of Nirvana's teachings really were filtering through.

Here are the highlights that I recall from Nirvana's shows in 1993. (I didn't take notes. The main condition Kurt placed on me when travelling in his van was that I shouldn't write about Nirvana for *Melody Maker*. 'You're always doing that,' he complained. 'Why can't you just come along as a friend? I don't mind if you want to do a book, but please no interviews.' Of course, I complied with his wishes.)

Cow Palace, San Francisco, 9 April The Bosnian rape victim benefit show. Nirvana's set ended on a version of 'Endless Nameless' with Kurt and Chris expanding energy like a force nine gale raging across an earthquake-stricken Bay Area. Kurt duck-walked across his amplifier before crashing into the drum kit. I remember sitting up top among the pigeons with Kim Deal and Jo Wiggs from support band the Breeders looking down on Kurt while the achingly poignant 'All Apologies' played. He looked so fragile, so vulnerable, one speck of humanity against a whole generation of curiosity-seekers, fans, the cynical, the bored and a whole bunch of cheerleaders – no tattoos – in butt-hugging slacks. By the door, Chris's wife, Shelli, was handing out leaflets, trying to make people stop and think about why they were there. Some hope! The kids were there because MTV had told them to be there. Still, it's always better to attempt than accept: maybe one or two of the audience went away and thought about the Bosnian crisis because their favourite stars had asked them to. It's possible. After all, didn't Clinton ascend to the presidency partly because of MTV's *Rock The Vote* campaign?

Afterwards, I ended up at Kurt and Courtney's house holding a strange conversation with Kurt about old arena rock shows and being beaten up by bouncers in Manchester, England. He told me about the time he saw Sammy Hagar while in seventh grade: 'Everyone was passing round pot and I got really high and lit myself on fire. I had a Bic lighter in my sweatshirt pocket and I was watching Sammy, swinging upside-down from the rafters, mocking everyone else who were holding their lighters above their heads; I looked down and petrol had spilt out everywhere, and my shirt was on fire. It went well with my piss-stained pants.' So I told him how I thought Nirvana's new songs shone 'as blue and battered as anything from the devastating, forthcoming debut album by Madder Rose, as raw and trembling as any Daniel Johnston live tape'. Of course I didn't say it to him exactly like that: more probably we both yawned and stretched our limbs as Courtney sat by the fire, reading up on some feminist literature. (Really!) As soon as I'd finished the 3,000 words I'd promised *Melody Maker* this time round that I was typing out on the couple's typewriter, we went to bed. We were tired.

NYC Roseland Ballroom, 23 July I can recall the queue outside for this New Music Seminar showcase, and the bullshit surrounding it. Chicago's Jesus Lizard turned in a typically anarchic show as support act: singer David Yow stage-dived before a note was even played. Afterwards, it was oddly restrained backstage. I made a joke about Nirvana's new acoustic middle section sounding just like U2 or REM, and someone nearly hit me. Kurt wore a pair of Devo shades and his trademark, red striped 'Dennis The Menace' jersey.

Krist (the bassist reverted to the original spelling of his name around this time) looked spruce and dapper and exhausted in a stiff-collared black shirt and new short haircut. Dave ran around grinning like a Cheshire cat. I babbled on to Kurt about this great new American rock band I'd seen, Guided By Voices and . . . er . . . that was it.

Springfield MA, Civic Centre, 10 November   All I remember was the rather scary ride from the airport to venue, through endless miles of pitch-black wood in an unofficial taxi – and my feeling of relief when the bright glare of arena lights made itself known through the trees. I sauntered up to the door and told the bullish hicks to let me in. I was Everett True! Me, *Maker* smudge Steve Gullick and Kurt watched Half-Japanese from the side, Kurt at one point running into the crowd to ask a fan for a light. Everyone in the vast hockey arena threw their shoes on to the stage, and walked home barefoot afterwards, in some strange Massachusetts ritual.

Washington DC, Bender Arena, American University, 13 November In the couple of days between DC and Springfield, me and Gullick had flown to Minneapolis to interview Yo La Tengo in bitterly cold weather, and I'd flown back. I recall joking with Kurt beforehand that maybe he should get me on stage that night, as the last time I'd performed live with Nirvana was in DC almost two years before. I never expected him to take me seriously . . . Most of these shows, I was watching from by the guitar racks behind guitar tech Ernie: tapping a sensitive toe or three while cellist Lori Goldston fleshed out newer tracks like 'All Apologies', urging the ever-smiling Pat Smear on to greater heights of glory. Old songs such as 'Lithium', 'Aneurysm' or 'Sliver' seemed to be taking on new layers of resonance with every play. Anyone doubting Kurt's femininity should have caught his confused self-castration on 'Heart-Shaped Box' or fiery 'Frances Farmer' on these nights. Afterwards, I clambered on to a bunk in Kurt's tour van alongside Pat, and we watched videos of puppet sex created by insane Midwest band the Frogs most of the way back to New York. It was a long drive, and no one was saying much.

NYC Javitz Centre Coliseum, 14 November   I was suffering badly from nerves, mainly because I knew Kurt was going to call on me to sing again and for some reason I'd sworn off alcohol, probably because I couldn't speak. The sound was dreadful: echoing around the cavernous, circular venue like a disused aircraft hangar. I'd like to mention the Breeders here but I can't recall a single damn note they played. This is odd because the Deal sisters, with their cigarettes dangling from lips, harmonies loose and graceful, were fronting almost my favourite band of the time.

NYC Roseland Ballroom, 15 November   Another industry showcase, enlivened by the presence of so many friends on stage for the final encore. I never did come to terms with the concept this was supposed to be an 'intimate' concert for Nirvana. Surely intimate means you and perhaps Kurt's mum, and no one else? Or maybe one of the old house parties the band played in Olympia when they were starting out.

Seattle Pier 48, 13 December   The MTV 'New Year's Eve' special. This was the last time I ever saw Nirvana play live. Kurt seemed to have sprouted angel's wings on stage, the band played a mercifully short set and the proles' backstage area was full of Seattle musicians I hadn't bumped into for years. I recall that a close friend of Nirvana's stole all the band's wallets from their dressing room to sell for his heroin fix. I sat around and waited for an eternity, sworn off alcohol once more because I had an important *Melody Maker* joint interview/cover story to conduct with Kim Deal and Kurt, while a girl I'd had a crush on for years suddenly indicated she might be interested in me. I never had the chance to find out. I sat around with Eric, Patty and Kristen from Hole, smoked reefer in Cypress Hill's dressing room and did everything except enjoy myself. Nirvana's set was fine, if you could bear all those MTV sorts larging it all over the place. I couldn't.

I didn't attend the recording of *MTV Unplugged* in November. I can't remember why. I was in New York at the time, and I'm sure it would have been easy enough to go. Kurt had offered me his hotel floor to sleep on a couple of days earlier when we arrived in town. I didn't want to, though. Probably, I wanted no part in the corporate crap surrounding Nirvana. Listen to those wankers cheering every note of each song's introduction on the CD, like it's a jazz concert. Look at all those flowers, cameras and carefully framed screen shots on the sleeve. You tell me I was wrong to stay away. What did *MTV Unplugged* have to do with Krist or Dave or even Pat? Nirvana were a band, remember.

No, it's not Kurt Cobain sharing an intimate moment with the world; you have intimate moments in the privacy of your own bathroom. You don't have intimate moments in front of batteries of soul-sucking video cameras and technicians. I'm not denying that when Kurt covers that Vaselines song or the Bowie song with its mighty refrain, it probably touched chords deep within thousands. But how patronising was the whole concept of inviting Nirvana on to a show like that? The Kurt of old would have scorned it for the shallow façade it was. The singer was in too deep to withdraw by this point, though. (Both Kurt and Courtney had complained to me that MTV had suggested to their management company Gold Mountain that it could jeopardise their working relationship with their other bands if Nirvana refused to play ball. Odious American types . . . I guess that's the way that country is run. The bullies win, every time. Whatever.)

Myself and Gullick skipped across town to where old mates Chicago's Urge Overkill were sitting in a diner, still dreaming of being swank rock stars on a par with Neil Diamond . . . or at least Nirvana.

The Funeral

I was in Cincinnati, Ohio, on 8 April 1994 with Steve Gullick when I first heard the rumour that Kurt Cobain had killed himself.

We were in town to interview Beck, then one of Gold Mountain's rising stars with his slacker anthem 'Loser'. I'd got to town the previous night, in time to catch Tacoma WA skate-grunge band Seaweed at a local venue that also served as a Laundromat. Despite two members being down with the 'flu, the ex-Sub Pop act were in fine thrashing form, reminding me of all the energy and massive power hooks that first attracted me to the Seattle sound. Steve had flown in the following morning and we were sitting around waiting for his room to become ready. It was one of those days you sometimes get while travelling: grey, dull and stretching on forever. We were looking forward to hooking up with Guided By Voices in neighbouring city Dayton later that week, though.

Already, we'd been informed that Beck also had the 'flu, and might have to pull out of both that night's show (at the Laundromat, with skewed LA female pop band That Dog in support) and our interview. So we were sitting around in my hotel room, relaxing, watching MTV and CNN, looking at magazines with pictures of Hole in. The Hole album *Live Through This* was about to come out and Steve, being faintly prudish, was shocked at some of the photographs of Courtney. 'I wonder what Kurt thinks of this?' he asked me on more than one occasion. Despite the weather, though, we were happy; bringing each other up to speed on the last few hectic weeks, when the phone suddenly rings. It's about eleven a.m.

Steve picks it up. It's Paul Lester, my features editor from *Melody Maker* – not always the most sensitive of fellows. 'So what's all this about Kurt Cobain being dead then?'

'I don't know what you're talking about,' Steve replies. 'You better speak to Everett.'

I look at Steve. There's obviously something wrong, I can tell by his manner.

'It's Lester,' he says. 'He says there's a rumour going round that Kurt has killed himself.'

I speak to Paul and tell him that neither of us knows anything but that I'd ring around, find out and ring him back as soon as I could. He asks me to hurry, as there's a whole load of *Maker* journalists waiting in the office late in case the story is true. Steve and I look at each other: it's about then that the façade crumbles and . . . don't ask me how . . . but we both know it's true. Kurt has killed himself.

I don't know what made us feel so certain. It wasn't as if either of us had realised up to that point that Kurt was suicidal. Both of us had thought that the Rome incident where the singer had over-dosed on a cocktail of champagne and Rohypnol a couple of weeks earlier had been a genuine accident. I thought this, despite the fact Courtney had called me up shortly afterwards, asking whether I thought that treating Kurt to a 'tough love' session to help him kick his heroin addiction was a good idea. I had no idea what such a session entailed but I figured anything that helped Kurt sort his life out had to be worth trying. Also, Courtney's personal manager Janet Billig from Gold Mountain had phoned me up personally after Rome to reassure me there was nothing mentally wrong with Kurt. (Whatever. I'm sure Janet was trying her hardest to cope with a crap situation as best she could. It wasn't until a few months later that I'd learnt that Kurt had written a suicide note that night.)

The next thirty minutes were spent in a bad haze of uncertainty as I phoned every number I could think of – Gold Mountain, Bad Moon (Nirvana's UK press agents), my contacts at Geffen, the house – to no avail. Eventually I was forced to call Nirvana biographer Michael Azerrad in New York City. I didn't want to. I didn't like the man. I felt he'd been chosen to write the Nirvana book by Kurt's management simply because he was a 'safe pair of hands'.

'Yes, it's true,' he told me. 'We're all just on our way out to Seattle. I'd advise you to do the same.'

(It struck me then as an odd statement. It still does. What earthly good could I do by going to Seattle? Perhaps Michael was making reference to that job description I'd had screamed at me on a Brighton–London train all those years ago and that I'd vehemently denied: 'You're just a fucking music journalist.' Is that all it came down to after years of passion, that I had a job to carry out?)

I told Steve the news.

I threw the remnants of my bottle of Maker's Mark down the sink, figuring that the worst possible thing I could do at that stage was to get trashed. Steve asked me to inform *Melody Maker* that he didn't want any of his photos used in the inevitable tribute that would follow ... I think that when I called back up I must have spoken to my editor, the semi-legendary old punk journalist Allan Jones. He told me that I should just go and do what I needed to do, 'plane tickets, whatever, it doesn't matter, we'll cover the cost, you don't have to write anything if you don't feel like it'. It's a conversation I'll remember with gratitude until my dying day.

I can't accurately remember what followed. It wasn't real. We sat there dazed. I didn't know what to do or where to go. I didn't want to fly to Seattle to confront a future that I knew would come crashing down around me as soon as I arrived. For the last five years of my life I'd managed to leave my past behind and not deal with the bad side. I wanted to be anywhere but in America, in Seattle, in Ohio ... I started thinking of all those times I'd refused to call Kurt or Courtney, thinking that famous people didn't need friends, not when they had so many managers around them. I knew that if Kurt had just managed to hang out with Steve and me, see a band like Guided By Voices a few times, get trashed with Kim Deal, he'd never have been driven to such an extreme ...

Yeah, right.

The phone rang again. It was Eric, Courtney's guitarist and my (and Kurt's) friend, calling from an airport. 'Courtney wants you to come to Seattle.' So it was I found myself walking through the sterile, anaemic aisles of Cincinnati airport with Steve, clutching a bag full of vinyl albums that I'd bought only the day before. We didn't know what to say to each other. I gave Steve the records to take back to England with him.

So it was that I came to be flying into Seattle on the afternoon that Kurt Cobain's body was discovered, tears streaming down my face, the refrain to a Hole song spiralling crazily round inside my head. *'Live through this with me,'* the lady sang. *'And I swear that I will die for you.'*

* * *

Eric had informed me that when I arrived at Seattle, if I called the house they would arrange for a limousine to pick me up from the airport. It was necessary. By the time the car had got to the gates of the Cobain residence in Lake Washington it was crazy outside. Police tape and small scrums of reporters and the curious lined the secluded road. No one was being allowed in unless they'd been expressly invited. I couldn't help feeling I was being allowed access to the rock journalist's ultimate dream. A guest list to die for. Sorry about the black humour, but you *know* we liked it that way.

Inside the house, it was curiously silent. Mark Lanegan, awesome blues singer with Ellensberg's Screaming Trees and close friend of Kurt's, was standing in one corner. He looked alone and I felt alone, both of us separated from everyone else by our natures and the situation. It seemed natural we should hang out together.

There was virtually no one else there until Krist and Dave turned up with a few friends and family and went and stood on the other side of the room. Courtney and Eric's camp turned up a little later . . . or perhaps it was earlier. I remember some record company types briefly having a fit at my presence there – I was a journalist – and thinking, 'You stupid, stupid fuckheads. I'm not the one being paid to pretend I'm a fucking friend.'

At one stage, Krist came over and asked me if I wanted to come to a wake being held for Kurt that evening by a few of his old Seattle friends. I declined because . . . well . . . I was in Courtney's camp that day, and there was no getting round it. My loyalties had been sorted out a while before. Even though I wanted to speak to Krist, I couldn't because of the politics around Nirvana that didn't die away for one second upon Kurt's suicide, only intensified.

Mark and I stuck around the house after most everyone else had departed. There were some terrible arguments going on between Courtney and Eric, and the nanny Cali, but that was nothing unusual. Some of the people there wanted to take drugs to hide the terrible sudden pain, and others equally as vehemently didn't want them re-introduced to the house. We were introduced to Kurt's mom Wendy by Courtney the following way, Courtney using my real name – 'This is Kurt's friend, Mark, and this is my friend, Jerry.' Both of us were shown and read the suicide note.

And that's almost all I'm going to tell of that terribly sad weekend. Mark and I stayed in the whole time at his apartment, somewhere near the start of the Monorail, downtown. We didn't go out except for perhaps one cup of coffee round the corner. We barely spoke. I was mostly concerned with making sure Mark was all right, and I'm sure he was the same back. We turned on the television once: there was talk of Nirvana and the fans' vigil, and we turned it off again straight away. A load of Sub Pop hipsters were holding their annual party which had turned into a wake at the Crocodile Club. Fair enough, but Kurt hadn't exactly got along with his old peers in recent years. We played a few records, walked around the house, tried to pretend to each other that we hadn't been crying. Mostly however we just sat there and waited for Courtney to call, in case she needed us.

When it came to the day of the funeral service, we realised that I had no appropriate clothes to wear. My only pair of jeans had holes in their knees. We knew that Kurt wouldn't have given a fuck but I still didn't want to look disrespectful. So I borrowed a pair of Mark's black drainpipes and turned up to the service with the top three buttons undone.

It was a gloriously sunny day as we left Mark's apartment to go down to the church – the sort of day when Seattle becomes the most beautiful city in the world, bar none, with Mount Rainer and the Olympics in shimmering crisp detail behind the skyscrapers and Space Needle. It had been raining the whole of the previous week, as is the Pacific Northwest's wont.

'I swear that Kurt would never have killed himself if the weather had been this nice last week,' Mark remarked thoughtfully.

Initially, I felt a sense of betrayal at Kurt's suicide. That rapidly disappeared over the following months. People say that suicide is the ultimate act of cowardice but you know what? It's far more cowardly to let your life disappear into nameless years of drinking and drugs, wasting away the days of your life in a bleak TV-satiated depression because you're too scared to make a change. Sure, I blamed his management for placing too many demands on him while he was feeling so fragile. I soon outgrew that, though. They didn't mean to fucking kill him! They were only trying their best to accommodate everyone, do what Courtney and Kurt and Krist and Dave were asking of them.

Kurt's death was such a shame, such a shame. At one point it had really felt we could've changed things, but with his suicide it was finally proved to me, irrevocably, this is what happens when you try to fuck with the system. There it was in plain black and white. The system kills you.

I know others that the system has killed also; people with fragile, unique voices that became overpowered by the boorish chants of the grey masses, friends and acquaintances and others even closer. They too were unable to cope with the demands placed upon them of everyday life. Maybe someone they loved left them, perhaps they never managed to adjust to everyone else's normality. Who knows? It's not difficult to imagine nothing when you sink into such total depression. Anything is preferable to loneliness: especially death. Kurt happened to be the most famous friend who'd killed himself. He was also the hardest to mourn. Who could I call? Who could I speak to about his death? Anyone I knew that might be able to relate was thousands of miles away and had sorrows of their own. I already felt bad enough about the contradictions of my position as part of the voyeuristic rock press ... Had I somehow contributed to Kurt's death? Maybe the only reason we hung out together was because his glory reflected upon me and gave me that illusion of glamour I'd been searching for all my life?

We had talked about changing things with Nirvana. What would we have replaced the old order with, though? We wanted something *better*. What did that mean? We wanted something less macho, more female-led, more sensitive and spontaneous and fun and exciting: Jad Fair and Courtney Love and Kim Deal, Kathleen Hanna, Daniel Johnston and Dan Treacy. We wanted our friends, our peers, our dreams and our heroes in positions of authority; is that such a crime? We wanted a place where bullies and braggarts didn't automatically rule. We wanted a place where women aren't automatically second-class citizens because they – we – are already part of us. A place where commercial radio counted for shit. A place where no fucking managerial types could make hypocritical speeches about maintaining freedom of speech within the press while simultaneously repressing the press' right to same through use of a few well-placed lawsuits and threats.

What did we want? Not much: just Nirvana.

I returned to England after a couple of days.

Some things were said at Kurt's funeral service that made me realise precisely why the singer had finally given up. They had no grounding in reality, no relation to any man I've ever known. Kurt was referred to as an angel that came to earth in human form, as someone who was too good for this life and that was why he was only here for such a short time. Bull-fucking-shit! Kurt was as pissy and moody and belligerent and naughty and funny and dull as the rest of us, it just so happened he was a little too sensitive for the situation he found himself in, too. After the service I left the church and started walking – to anywhere, anywhere but where all these self-righteous prigs revelling in their own fame and importance were sitting.

I forced myself to return, remembered there were people like Lanegan there, and Calvin Johnson, and Jon and Bruce from Sub Pop, and the Breeders . . . people I loved dearly. Yet in all the days that followed, I only ever found one other person who had been equally upset by what had been said: Kristen Pfaff, bassist with Courtney's band and formerly bassist with great Minneapolis hardcore trio Janitor Joe. (I'm certain there were others but I wasn't in communication with many people right then.)

We chatted about Nirvana that summer as Kristen rejoined her old band for a tour across Eastern Europe alongside fellow Amphetamine Reptile act, Hammerhead. There were nine or so of us all crammed into a dirty old van, talking of love and laughter and life and those small, but so significant, details in between. Everything seemed so right again: punk rock like I'd always loved it practised by two bands to whom it was their natural birthright. The venues were tiny, sweating, crammed with enthusiastic faces and blistering power chords. At night, we would all sleep together in a dormitory, enlivened by whatever cheap alcohol we could lay our hands on. It was like being born again: Kristen was so lively and full of optimism about the future and music and life.

'The rhythm that you hear is the pounding of our hearts,' as one poet put it.

A couple of weeks later, she was found dead in a bath in her Seattle apartment by her former lover and Hammerhead singer Paul. Strangely, the evening was the first time I'd spoken to Courtney since leaving Seattle. She thought I'd heard the news somehow when I called. It wasn't that. It was just that I'd had another premonition of death, similar to the time an Angel of Death had visited me while driving down the freeway between Boston and New York after I'd been drinking with the Unsane drummer Charlie Ondras.

The craziness didn't stop there.

I still travelled to America and Australia and Europe, drinking even harder. What else could I do? It wasn't real, was it? I was sure that somewhere along the line I'd receive a phone call from Anton or Janet telling me that it had all been a ghastly Dwarves-style joke. (Sub Pop's scum rock band Dwarves once put out a press release stating that their bass-player had been murdered in a back alley in middle America. Family members phoned up, concerned. The outrage was considerable when it transpired the whole story was made up.) It was absurd to feel that way, especially as Courtney had taken me into the garage where Kurt's body was found where she had lit some candles in homage, but sometimes the massive events are the hardest to come to terms with. So I continued out-drinking bands and PRs and passers-by in vain attempts to regain my feeling for life; so I became even more desperate in my writing, searching for replacement bands.

It wasn't until my passport got stolen from my hotel room in Chicago while I lay comatose on the floor on the other side of the bed, vomit dripping from my mouth, that I finally stopped travelling to America. Instead, I continued beating myself up on the other side of the Atlantic, reverting to the bleak acceptance of being down the pub beyond chucking out time every night of the week, not even bothering to attend shows.

Music had failed me.

The Aftermath

For once, I thought it would be nice if history was written by one of the losers.

Nothing changes. It's still those with the loudest voices who are heard. That hasn't changed since humans were savages. Everywhere you look, it's the people who have cultivated contacts and bullied their way through life who are at the top. The quieter ones, the people who don't like or understand the need for competition, they're always left behind. Perhaps they don't mind. I do. I've seen too much from the other side.

There is precious room for emotion or actual talent in the pop world. For every Polly Harvey I could show you a thousand Limp Bizkits or Smashing Pumpkins or Poisons. For every Kevin Rowland there are a million Mansuns and Kylie Minogues, Sunny Day Real Estates and Silverchairs. Nirvana succeeded not least because Kurt Cobain had a pretty boy face. Anyone else remember those series of photos where he looks uncannily like Axl Rose? It was a face that could be marketed easily alongside his sensitivity and talent for writing a decent hook. Why do teenagers still wear T-shirts saying 'Nirvana' in 2001? It's because Kurt is a tormented idyllic icon, the nineties equivalent of James Dean and Monroe and every other star who died young and beautiful. These people walking around with Cobain's face and life-dates on their chest are into the image, the pose.

Oh, and of course Kurt left a great narcissistic suicide note behind, one that would ensure he'd be remembered for a fair few years yet. That Neil Young line he quoted in his scribbled handwriting – 'It's better to burn out than to fade away' – what a great way to take that final stage bow! He did us proud with that one, and also with the use of a shotgun to literally put a hole through his head. Say what you like about Kurt, but he certainly had a sense of occasion.

Perhaps that's unfair. Maybe those kids identify with the fact Kurt felt alienated and disaffected with a society that has little to give those who don't grab for themselves. Maybe they too feel that life is cruel, favours only those with swaggering voices and an arrogant macho gait. Perhaps they see Kurt as a symbol of the failings of Western society: why not? Someone has to be. I shouldn't place my cynicism upon another generation's dreams. We all have to start somewhere. I scorned the symbols of the previous generation when I was younger, though – the generation before always betrays those who go after – looking around for my own touchstones. I never held much with the idea of heroes either, believing that the only true hero lies within.

It could be much simpler than that, the secret of Nirvana's enduring appeal. Maybe these backwards-looking teenagers love Nirvana for their *music*. I wish it wasn't only the Goths and metal-heads, the Marilyn Manson and Foo Fighters fans, who seem to like Nirvana nowadays, though. It'd be nice if some of their old fans, the punk rock librarians and Half-Japanese kids, joined in on the choruses. After all, Kurt had a great scream and way round an insidious, gut-churning riff, and both Krist and Dave were awesome musicians and a worthy foil for Kurt's visions.

This is a hard judgement call for me to make. After Kurt died, I didn't willingly listen to Nirvana for several years. If one of their songs came on the radio or television I would get up and walk out of the room, not wanting to be reminded of something that had once been so precious to me and meant less than shit now that everything was dead. I'm English. I don't like to show my emotions in public. I liked Nirvana because their music seemed, to me, to revel in the gift of life, in spontaneous combustion. Not because I liked to dress in black and go around cussing my parents, acting in a bored and apathetic fashion. I used to think 'Smells Like Teen Spirit' was probably concerned with the interface between media and the individual, about the irony of believing in a life of consumerism that continually feeds off itself. Beyond that, I just responded to the rasp in the voice and thud of the drums. Didn't everyone? If you want insights, go read some fucking poetry or JG Ballard or the funny pages. Don't come looking to rock music for answers, because it sure won't provide any.

It's only been in the past months while writing these words that I've listened to Nirvana again ... and you know what's great?

(Aside from realising that *Nevermind* has an early nineties production on it better suited to bad LA hair band Mötley Crüe.) Their songs still sound magnificent. They still make me want to flail wildly, both arms working either side of my body, feet splaying out almost at random.

Even today, Nirvana make me want to dance . . . and what more can you ask for from music?

On my most recent trip to the Northwest, I finally got round to visiting Aberdeen WA, birthplace to Nirvana.

It was a beautiful winter's day, with Mount Rainer looming large and proud next to the road that leads down to the airport. My heart always hits my mouth on a day like this when I realise I cannot stay. Three of us had decided to take a car from Olympia to pay tribute: myself, musician and paper-cut artist Nikki McClure, and Rich Jensen. About a year previously, Nikki was asked by the people at Seattle's rock monstrosity the Experience Music Project, to give them a quote on Riot Grrrl for their museum files. She told them a small story about visiting the beach one fine day with her friend, the artist Stella Mars, and how they made preserves together, building up the fire while the tide was out and then finishing as the tide came in. She had no idea whether the EMP had used her interview segment or not, as she hadn't visited the place.

It was Nikki whose house Kurt crashed at one summer in Olympia just after Nirvana started, and it was Nikki and her boyfriend Ian who Nirvana took with them on their first major European tour, so they could dance on stage. Dance, in the Olympian way . . . until Nirvana's management put a stop to it.

Rich, meanwhile, was responsible for a series of 'punk rock a cappella' releases in Olympia during the eighties, among some of K's earliest, and had been called in to Sub Pop in 1991 to help sort out the company's increasingly tangled finances. He also engineered some early Beat Happening songs.

So anyway, we decided we wanted to visit the famous bridge along the banks of the Wishkah River that Kurt was supposed to have slept underneath when he ran away from home. None of us knew whether the story was true, but all of us realised it didn't matter either.

It didn't take long to find the spot: Aberdeen isn't the largest of small depressed logging towns, and the downtown area near where Kurt grew up is even smaller than Olympia's. The river itself looked gorgeous, wide, glinting in the sunlight and serene in the knowledge that nothing man does will ever alter its course . . . short of a nuclear war or new dam system, of course. We made our way carefully down the riverbank, next to the overpass where a few cars trundled desultorily along. We thought we had the right spot, but we weren't too sure. Only I had seen the Nick Broomfield film *Kurt And Courtney* that pictured Kurt's old family house, close to the bridge: the film director's car drove along while music from Kurt's old friend Dylan Carlson's Earth rumbled ominously in the background. Nikki had a vague memory of picking Kurt up from his house, but wasn't sure from where. Once under the bridge, it didn't take a second to realise we'd come to the right spot with all the broken glass in the mud, torn stumps and graffiti on every available arch. It was one of the most beautiful places I've seen.

The site had been transformed by wandering Nirvana fans. The odd declamatory rant against Courtney scrawled in fluorescent spray-paint aside, the whole place radiated with a clear love and sense of loss it was impossible to avoid. Even better, this symbol of Kurt's alienation from life – real or imagined, it doesn't matter – had been turned into an underground shrine by the Nirvana fans who had made the considerable journey out of their way to be in Aberdeen. This wasn't a $10,000 guitar on display in the EMP, or MTV cameras jostling for a better position. This was personal. You suspect the 'old' Kurt would have approved. We certainly did. We wandered around in silence for several minutes, took a few photos and departed to go thrift store shopping.

Later, several of us decided to make a punk rock record in Amy's front room. Kurt's old girlfriend Bikini Kill's Tobi Vail was there, playing bongos. Amy and Al Larson from Some Velvet Sidewalk played guitar so warm and enveloping, you felt your heart would melt. Rich was in charge of the tape recorder once more. We recorded an Olympian version of the 13th Floor Elevators' 'You're Gonna Miss Me' (the first song I ever played live in Seattle, all those years ago at the University of Washington, opening for Skin Yard and Nirvana). Walking up the steps to join us, Nikki slipped on an icy patch and ended up in the emergency ward, five stitches needed in her chin. The following day saw a constant stream of visitors at her house, bringing soup and flowers and pumpkin risotto.

It was good to be home once more.

'You know what I hate about rock?' asks Kurt. 'Cartoons and horns. I hate Phil Collins, all of that white male soul. I hate tie-dyed T-shirts, too. You know there are bootleg tie-dyed T-shirts of Nirvana? I hate that. I wouldn't wear a tie-dyed T-shirt unless it was dyed with the urine of Phil Collins and soaked in the blood of Jerry Garcia.'

Courtney overhears this last comment from the bedroom.

'Oh God Kurt. How long have you been thinking about that one!' she castigates him, annoyed.

'Well fuck!' he whines. 'No one ever prints it.'

'It's Fifth Grade!' Courtney yells. 'It's so boy!'

'Well, ex-ker-use me!' Kurt shouts back, sarcastically.

(From the pages of *Melody Maker*, 18 July 1992)

Riot Grunge

Revolution Girl Style Now!
(Bikini Kill, Huggy Bear, Olympia)

COURTNEY LOVE: Kurt was pure and he was also insanely ambitious. He wanted what he got, but because of his training, because of Olympia, he decided he didn't want it. One has only to look at old Nirvana when Jason Everman was in the band, to see him posturing like Soundgarden but beating with a pop heart. Nirvana were exposed to what the Olympians did, and none of that is talent-based, and that's where those people bother me the most, Everett. It's not about talent. It's about purity. It's about having a manifesto and it's bullshit.

EVERETT TRUE: Hold on a moment . . .

CL: No. I believe that Ian McKaye [Fugazi singer] had a sacred, divine vision but that by the time it got to Calvin Johnson it was elitist and uninclusive – and it wasn't because they ostracised me, there are plenty of scenes I love that I was ostracised by – and cutie-pie. Listen. I had Marine Girls and Kleenex played for me about the same time Kurt was getting that shit played for him, maybe even before. For him, it was a save because Olympia provided him with some pop, as did Teenage Fanclub and the Vaselines and the Pastels and all those cute personalities I didn't care about. He was as aware as I was of fame. He just couldn't handle it.

ET: Who's that singer who shows off when she sings: Mariah Carey or Whitney Houston?

CL: They both do, with the notes.

ET: Practising their scales.

CL: Mariah. Mariah.

ET: Listen. Mariah Carey has so missed the point. It doesn't matter whether you can do your scales properly, and it doesn't matter how many damn notes you can hit spot on. The purest form of music to have originated in America is gospel. And that has nothing to do with talent, and everything to do with passion, purity.

CL: You and me are absolutely in agreement on that, and you know what I've been getting into a lot is non-Motown soul like Otis Clay. I love the Smokey Robinson stuff, too.

ET: The point about gospel and old school soul wasn't that you hit the note but that you *tried* to hit the note.

CL: Yeah, but that doesn't apply to Olympia and its elitism and its lack of spirituality.

ET: What you refer to as elitism is a couple of people sitting down and working out that what's important in pop music is how personal it is. Pop music is either a personal or communal experience. I'm not denying the two can cross over, but if you want to be purist about it then it's about the personal experience, and that, that is Olympia.

(Taken from the pages of *The Stranger*, 25 February 1999)

Who moved you to thoughts of hatred this year?
'Men I see in the street. I don't know their names.'

JON, HUGGY BEAR

Here's what I hate about '77 punk, and the Sex Pistols in particular: commentators stuck in time, stunting the development of those they're supposed to be informing by their constant referral back to that one moment when everything was still vivid *for them*.

Critics speak of how the Sex Pistols were a one-off, something special beyond everything that came after. 'It was incredible the impact they had, considering how short a time they were around,' reads the standard line. No. What's incredible is how much space has been devoted to one moment that was great, sure, but also would never have taken on such shades of importance if the media wasn't composed of such dullards.

Life is about perception. People are often defined by the moment they are first exposed to the outside world and never move on, least of all in their own minds. Fifteen years ago, it was the sixties' kids, all going on about the Paris riots and how incredible, never to be repeated, the hippies and *Sgt Pepper* were. (Nineteen eighty-five was the exact date critical opinion turned. You could see the new hipsters turning to one another and saying, '*Sgt Pepper*? I don't think so.') Now, it's the turn of Alan McGee and Oasis biographer Paolo Hewitt *et al* to relive their youth while stifling everyone else's.

I never understood the antipathy Riot Grrrl engendered among my colleagues. All the movement was trying to do was kick over the statues – or at the very least, the road cones – and invest music with some excitement again. Weren't Olympia's Bikini Kill basically cherished dayglo punks, X-Ray Spex updated via the kick-ass rock'n'roll of Joan *'put another dime in the juke-box, baby'* Jett and given a fresh, feminist agenda? Nothing to fear there. The second track on Huggy Bear's debut single pays tribute to Sonic Youth's 'Catholic Block': nothing unusual about that. Everyone loves Sonic Youth. So it's OK to be a noise insurrectionist if you're American, over 30 and have 'paid your dues' but not otherwise? Does image really count for that much? The fact these two great bands, the Bear and the Kill, dressed down in retro, almost playground, fashion seemed to confuse everyone.

As Professor X says in every issue of *The X-Men*, 'Humans will always fear and try to destroy that which they do not understand.' When Riot Grrrl burst onto an alternative music scene smug with self-righteousness because it had Nirvana – a band that it had fought the punk wars for, and won – it was reviled. Yet listen to the music and read the doctrines of Bikini Kill, Blood Sausage, Skinned Teen, Bratmobile and the shoe-burning Nation Of Ulysses. How do these bands vary from recent media darlings like Sleater-Kinney, At The Drive-In and Nation off-shoot the Make Up? All create passionate rock music, stripped back, little waste: much righteous fury, similar imagery. Does it really take the record industry and mainstream media ten years to catch up on one simple idea?

Also: how did the definition 'independent' crystallise and become sterilised into one form of music, one that basically meant white boys playing guitars that jangled? You can blame the perpetually frightened breed of A&R men eternally stumbling over one another to sign Last Year's Sound . . . and the media, of course. Critics pride themselves on their impartiality: absolute bullshit! Every 'objective' decision made is based round a purely subjective core judgement, usually informed by others, that there are 'right' and 'wrong' ways to play guitar, or paint a picture, or to read a book. There is no such thing as good art, only good and bad participators. You don't ever have to be ashamed of liking crap like the Verve and the Doors. If something touches you, it touches you. It doesn't matter how facile or ordinary or manufactured it is. Hold on, I think I'm starting to argue myself out of a job . . .

That phrase from Huggy Bear's classic single 'Her Jazz' – *'This is happening without your permission'* – I swear that's what rankled their enemies the most. '*Face it,*' screamed Niki with a searing fervour. '*You're old and out of touch.*' No one likes being told that, certainly not to their face. It confused critics no end: before Huggy

Bear and Riot Grrrl they had been above suspicion, cerebral almost. You could almost sense their brows furrowing: how could anyone like something they hadn't been given a chance to dissect first? Riot Grrrl formed immediate divisions, refused to indulge critics and passive consumers in their usual time-wasting ploy of trying to figure out what is 'good' and what is 'bad'. Why not follow your heart instead? The Riot Grrrls just got on with having a glorious good time, while simultaneously reinventing perceptions and notions of sexual stereotypes . . . and honey, if you weren't with them, then you were against them and yes, that *did* make you old and out of touch. As gender-confusing punk Jayne County once sang, '*If you don't want to fuck me baby, fuck off!*'

Blood Sausage were one Riot Grrrl band who didn't care for the media's close-up examination: a self-confessed 'ugly' boy who read soulful beat poetry over whichever noise patterns happened to be passing at the time.

'I'm the total antithesis of a rock star,' its singer Dale Shaw told me in '93. 'I'm short, fat and ugly, and I haven't any discernible talent. I can't write songs and I certainly can't sing. I'm in a band where nobody can play their instruments, yet here I am being interviewed by *Melody Maker*. I feel like that's some sort of victory: anti-boy rock victory.'

Dale was self-deprecating in his despair, as befitted such a major Daniel Johnston fan. The inner sleeve of his debut EP 'Touching You In Ways That Don't Feel Comfortable' detailed the beatings, kickings and poundings he took when younger. His songs, likewise. One memorable comic strip he drew detailed how he would pick girls' pubic hair out of bath plug holes, in some sort of pathetic fantasy.

'There's a political edge to all our songs,' he said, 'but they don't actually mean anything. Like "Fuck You And Your Underground" and "What Law Am I Breaking Now?" are good slogans, but if you stop and think about it – which no one ever does, thank God – then they're total empty phrases.'

Skinned Teen were even more extreme: four privileged school-girls who flaunted their (lack of) sexuality and youth in an almost a cappella, unrestrained way rarely seen since those original teen Riot Grrrls, the Slits.

'*So what contraception is an angel going to use?*' – Huggy Bear ('Pro No From Now')

I appreciate that *Live Through This* is a history book. That's unavoidable. All I'm saying is that the Sex Pistols weren't a one-off. Sure, Lydon and Co had their own individuality and irritation value that suited their times. But in terms of being a catalytic energising force, they were hardly unique.

'Our fanzines are cut-up to reflect the way we are. Just jab it all down and let people go back to it. Let it repeat on them. Let it be bad crisps.'
CHRIS, HUGGY BEAR

I lived through punk. I also relived the sixties thanks to the underground comics and magazines I so avidly devoured and collected in my time of awakening into the adult world in the late seventies. Both eras were great, and special to me. The music of our nascent selves is magical: that's why we are continually buffeted with the sounds of the late seventies in the media in the first couple of years of the 21st century, whether relevant or not. It's what those in control used to listen to when they cared about music. Anyone surprised at the early eighties soundtrack to 1999's *Never Been Kissed*, the Drew Barrymore 'teen' movie? Don't be. Media people aren't any smarter than you. Something being in print or on film doesn't automatically validate it, whatever friends think. The conversation you have while waiting for a bus holds equal importance to the one you're watching on TV. Never lose sight of that basic fact.

In 1983, the early Creation Records scene based round Oasis 'discoverer' Alan McGee's club the Living Room held numerous thrills for me, not least because I was being given the opportunity to get up on stage and rant at people every night. The Pastels, TV Personalities, Nightingales, Membranes, The Legend! I make no apologies for my elitism. I'm not denying the emotional pull of communal experiences but never understood why anyone would want to listen to music that isn't special to them and them alone.

Stephen Pastel's voice, as awkward and in thrall to Jonathan Richman as it once was, has a trembling poignancy that reaches down to me through the years. Even almost two decades after they first formed, the Pastels are still trying to discover fresh ways of expressing themselves, fresh means of communication, years after most bands have settled into a relentless rut of rehashing the same half an idea over and over. Why? Not because they have any agendas to fill, that's for sure. No, the Pastels will never turn into commercial concerns like Suede or Oasis or Coldplay simply because they don't like being bored. They know that to remain still is to die.

'We feel outside of the outsiders,' Stephen explained in '93. 'We don't deny bands like Manic Street Preachers the right to have their own rebellion but it seems a very conventional rock'n'roll rebellion. We don't behave like that. We're very uptight about ourselves. We're meticulous in every detail and that brings us into conflict in certain areas of music. Most record labels would rather deal with a band of junkies than us.'

I can remember seeing Dan Treacy's TV Personalities one torrid night in '82 or '83. The shy singer was lost to the outside world, his guitar detuned so brutally it was painful to hear. Even now I can't help but be reminded of Kurt, ten years later.

Some of the bands from the Living Room, not the wannabe macho sorts in leather trousers, spawned what we shall call cutie for want of a better word. I've always hated that description with a vengeance, feeling it to be horribly patronising. Rock = cool. Cutie = nerds. And your point is, precisely? We dressed that way – simple bright clothes, anoraks, badges, ankle socks for the girls – because we liked to feel good about ourselves and look smart. Give me an outsider any day. The Pastels, the Wedding Present, Talulah Gosh, Bogshed. Perhaps I liked cutie for the sense of belonging it engendered among like-minded peers and myself, none of us cool enough to be considered 'rock'.

Flash back to rock critic Lester Bangs in the seventies, and the point he once made that people only ever create something of worth when they are at their least cool. He never felt he belonged among the 'cool' rock dudes. Strange then that since he died he has been venerated as the epitome of rock. Now check the quote from Dave Grohl on the back cover of this very book: Everett True is the un-coolest man in rock. He intended it as an insult, but what a compliment! Yet I too defined rock for a generation, and will continue to do so, long after my mediocre, scared peers are forgotten. Embrace your individuality. The coolest people have always been those who know they don't need to prove it.

'When she talks, I hear the revolution/In her hips, there's revolution/ When she walks, the revolution's coming/In her kiss I taste the revolution'

'REBEL GIRL' (BIKINI KILL, 1992)

Across the Atlantic, you could draw parallels between Calvin Johnson and K records' home-recorded tape culture and their rejection of the more boorish aspects of rock, and Scots bands like the Pastels. It was your basic mods vs rockers divide, the snobs versus the populists. Olympia is, to all intents and purposes, the ultimate Mod town, as elitist and extraordinary as it is. It's ironic then that Seattle's Sub Pop Records started as a music and tape fanzine compiled by Bruce Pavitt with help from Calvin. I say ironic, because Sub Pop's populist ideology often seemed at odds with the preciousness of Olympia. Although you could conversely argue that because Sub Pop promoted a scene that was composed of amateurs turned professional, and because they were cultivating a star system, they were the elitists. Whereas Olympia was actually the more populist of the two towns because it believed in the amateur over the professional and in decentralised culture.

Right from the start, K was heavily politicised, mainly because of Calvin's unique way of running his business, no compromise. This was later cemented by the addition of bands such as Canada's female-led duo Mecca Normal with their angry minimalism, and Al Larson's much undervalued Some Velvet Sidewalk.

Future Bikini Kill drummer Tobi Vail was part of Calvin's loose collective, the Go Team. When I first visited Olympia in 1989, I recorded a couple of tracks with the pair in her parents' house. They later turned up among a series of seven-inch records that also included contributions from Kurt Cobain and Australia's sensitive Cannanes. The drummer didn't forget our meeting: an early Bikini Kill song 'Hamster Baby' (it rhymes with 'masturbate me') includes the line *'Oh Everett True/where are you/Who is gonna put in the tape deck/Who is gonna carry the bass amp/Who is gonna buy us a van.'*

I like it. It's on a par with the (Scots pop disco post-Riot Grrrls) Bis song that compares me with Drew Barrymore while she was still cool: *'She is herself/Like Everett True.'*

Sorry, got distracted. Back to the main frame.

Flash forward (and back) a few years. Are you seriously trying to tell me Nirvana and their grunge peers weren't as exciting for their/our generation as punk rock was for yours? Get back in the wardrobe, granddad – and get yourself a new set of clothes while you're there! Hot on grunge's heels came Riot Grrrl, the female answer to its sometimes overbearing maleness. It was cutie, but politicised.

All these movements energised and moved my feet to dance like it was the first time. Sure, the whole Seattle and Riot Grrrl 'explosions' were transient. Hold on, wasn't punk? Understand this. Most bands only ever have one idea: the rest of their careers are spent in diminishing spirals, as they try to find countless ways of recycling that original spark. It's fortunate indeed for record companies that most people don't want to be challenged when they listen to music, but reassured.

Bikini Kill only had one idea – Inspire! Inspire! Empower all females, at least the ones we like! – but the quartet carried it out with such venom, humour and fervour on every record they made, it didn't matter. Indeed, I'm all for arguing that their 1996 swan song *Reject All American*, with its searing tribute to a friend who died of AIDS on 'R.I.P.', is their finest record. Better even than their incendiary singles, the Joan Jett-produced 'Rebel Girl' and 'I Like Fucking'/'I Hate Danger'. High praise, indeed.

Much as I love the Northwest's current bearers of the flame, Sleater-Kinney, none of their albums will ever mean as much to me as *Reject All American*, as betrayed, wanton and cynical as Bikini Kill could sound. Singer Kathleen Hanna's voice was pure punk, absolutely incredible. Perhaps it's my age.

Live, Bikini Kill could be equal parts intimidation and inspiration. Male dancers were instructed to keep to the sides and the back, leading to charges of (inverse, presumably) sexism. Why, because the Kill wanted to even up the odds facing females at shows for once? This was a girl-centric band, make no mistake. Female fans were encouraged to take the microphone and detail when they'd felt abused and/or used by men. The music itself was storming, driven by the heavy repetition of Tobi's drumming and Kathi Wilcox's bare bass. The token male, Billy (he kept changing his second name) filled in on purposeful, abrasive guitar; but the main focus was always Kathleen Hanna, cajoling and tormenting, teasing and pleading, always fully in control and demanding respect in return.

'That girl thinks she's the queen of the neighbourhood/I've got news for you/SHE IS'

'REBEL GIRL'

Bikini Kill shows, at least the ones they played on their incendiary 1993 UK tour with Huggy Bear, were a far less passive consumer experience than most concerts. My role on that tour became confused because of my high profile as a music journalist (the corporate enemy) and refusal to tone down my writing. I refused to speak to the musicians, even though I shared a house with a couple, and had made music with others . . . I didn't want them to feel compromised. I remember one friend telling me how she'd had to argue a gang of 15-year-old females out of setting light to me. Other times, whole pages in Grrrlzines would be given over to diatribes against me because I was perceived as being the personification of (male) rock.

Huggy Bear had so many brittle, wanton, ridiculous ideas that it was scary to contemplate what the future could have held if only they could have reconciled their differences of opinion between wanting female empowerment for all and staying 'pure', untainted in their safe underground scene. So how does Riot Grrrl link in with Nirvana? The answer is simple. In 1991, it was Kurt's 21-year-old girlfriend, Tobi Vail, who provided the link between the singer's cherished naïve pop, grunge and the punk feminists. It was Tobi who played Shonen Knife and the Shaggs and the Raincoats to Kurt. It was Tobi who took all of Calvin's (cutie) Shop Assistants and Talulah Gosh records and wouldn't give them back for a year. The link between Nirvana and K records was cemented long before Kurt tattooed the label's symbol on his arm.

Look at the evidence. Warped joyful Japanese pop trio Shonen Knife were responsible for the first cassette to appear on K *according to Kurt*. (That isn't actually the case. That honour belonged to the Raincoats-esque Supreme Cool Beings, but it's crucial that Kurt believed it to be true.) The singer also described the great childlike seventies group the Shaggs as being the archetypal K band. There are two tracks on Bikini Kill's final studio album that sound like sixties girl group/Ramones fans, the Shop Assistants (a pivotal cutie band). The Pastels have included members of the Vaselines and Teenage Fanclub, bands championed by Nirvana. Get the connection yet?

Kurt Cobain had a feminine side: and it was people like Tobi and Huggy Bear and other, lesser-known Olympian types like Nikki McClure and Stella Mars and singer/writer Lois Maffeo that helped to nurture it.

I never invested Riot Grrrls with sexuality. I don't know why, especially as it was one of their most potent weapons. (Early press about Bikini Kill always harped on about the fact Kathleen was a stripper, something she shared in common with Courtney.) I knew I was doing the women involved a disservice by thinking of them so cerebrally, but perhaps it was the only way I could cope with my own inherent sexism . . . *or so I thought back then*. More probably, I never used to think of females (or males) in those terms. It wasn't that I wasn't aware of sexuality, more that I was hyper-aware of my own maleness – mainly through my training, reading feminist underground comics in the seventies, and listening to cool punk and cutie records. I tried to disassociate myself from my gender. A female friend once remarked that I was the only male who didn't automatically check women out when they walked into a room. It was true. I had to train myself to look at women to become like other heterosexual males – and alcohol helped. I didn't want to remain on the outside forever.

'If you're part of a good band you're supposed to be "good" musicians. Only then are people interested in the ideas behind the music.'

JO, HUGGY BEAR

Huggy Bear were one of the first bands I encountered who embraced the contradictions surrounding their existence. Being contradictory is one of the great joys of life: you should always be ready to discard a lifetime's beliefs for a second or two of FUN. As if that isn't enough reason to love them, Huggy Bear also reminded me of Dexys Midnight Runners' Year Zero soul vision and Nancy Sinatra and Lee Hazelwood's sexually-charged *Nancy And Lee* 1967 album, for both their anti-press manifestos and ferocious male/female vocal interplay. There is rarely higher praise than that. (Year Zero is a punk term. When the Sex Pistols and the Clash first burst onto the UK music scene, they claimed that no band before them had any relevance to the present day. For the punks, this was where history began – in the same way that Christians dated the modern calendar from the birth of Jesus Christ. The punks' Year Zero was 1976. Kevin Rowland's Dexys pulled off a similar trick with their debut album, ridiculing every current musical style within twenty seconds of the opening track.)

Contrast Huggy Bear with their American counterparts, Bratmobile: a great band sure, but basically a straightforward garage band with cheerleader-style nursery rhyme lyrics about grievances with boys and stuff. Odd then that the latter were the most successful band to come from this period. It was because the awesome, subversive mainstream teen girls' magazine *Sassy* used to champion Molly, Erin and Alison's band, particularly in their Cute Band Alert section.

Don't make the mistake of thinking I reckon Riot Grrrl – or even Nirvana – as the time of the last great punk revolution, though.

First, that would run contrary to all my beliefs. The actual idea of 'revolution' comes down to your own personal perception. During the nineties, what was happening in the dance music world in the UK – Underworld, Prodigy, DJ Shadow, Dave Clarke – was at least as exciting and (musically) revolutionary as anything I've mentioned here. I feel 1991 was a Year Zero for many in both the dance and rap worlds, as was every single year that followed. Indeed, if Nirvana hadn't come along when they did, with all the attendant promise of hedonism and free backstage passes and alcohol, it's possible I would have made a switch to championing dance music. It was invigorating enough and also, crucially, made my feet want to move around in odd angles.

Likewise hip hop, with the inspirational, scary sounds of the Wu Tang Clan and their peers sending out shock waves that will be felt for many years to come.

Secondly, most of Huggy Bear's American counterparts like Bikini Kill, Bratmobile and Unwound were too traditionally *rock* to shake things up. Who's to say Bikini Kill wouldn't have turned into Hole (musically, not ideologically), given the same amount of corporate money? The gap between Courtney Love and Kathleen Hanna back then was more confused than many wanted. That's not to detract from Bikini Kill's music, which was always a million times more thrilling than their corporate rivals'.

I'm being extreme here, but I need to make a point. Remember that, early on, Courtney was supportive of her rivals. Perhaps it was because she saw it as a good opportunity to gain some of that all-elusive 'credibility'. I don't know. Perhaps it was the Nirvana connection: Bikini Kill supported Kurt and Krist's band on a few occasions in the States. Perhaps it was because she felt genuine empathy with what Riot Grrrls had to offer. I don't know. There was a famous all-girl London show in April '93 that Hole played with Huggy Bear in support at the old Bay 63. This sorted out the problem of male dancers using their weight to jostle for better position at the expense of Bikini Kill's female fans. Everyone took this to mean that Riot Grrrls hated men. How does being pro-women imply that you're anti-men? That makes no sense. After the show, Courtney called me to complain at how weird it felt to play an England concert without my presence. I was like, why not catch a taxi down to Brighton to visit me, then? Joking. So she did. I still have the receipt for £130 somewhere around here. We sat and talked of . . . damned if I can remember.

Still, the point remains. Bikini Kill were hardcore not punk. That is, their music was formulated along a rigid series of rules and ideologies that didn't brook dissent. It was only later that Kathleen came into her own with the brilliant improvisational low-cost dub-pop of Julie Ruin. Confusion always arises at this point: is Olympia hardcore or punk? It's hardcore, through and through. That's where its sympathies lie. Beat Happening may have been a confrontational – and thus punk – band, but those who followed were already preaching to the converted. Olympia provides a blueprint to live by. Hardcore, too, is about providing an alternative to society's norms, a counter-culture. Punk is far more contradictory: it's where the underground meets the mainstream – the Sex Pistols on British TV, Nirvana on *Saturday Night Live*.

Early Nirvana producer Jack Endino disagrees with this interpretation of events, however. '*Nevermind* was no more of a punk album than Boston's first album,' he states, 'and *Bleach* [the one he produced] was no more of a punk album than Deep Purple's *Fireball*. Their lyrics, pre-*In Utero*, are no more punk than Don McLean's "American Pie". They were a classic rock band. I never heard any punk in them whatsoever. I think this is a convenient myth. If their music had actually been punk then it would NOT have broken. The only punk record they made, sorta, was *In Utero*, which was punk in the same way John Lennon's "Cold Turkey" was punk. Their live show was no more punk than the Who's – which was sorta punk, admittedly. Did punk break in America with *Who's Next* in 1971 then? It did not. Punk "broke", sadly, with the Offspring and Green Day.'

Thank you Jack.

Third, and most importantly, the reason I don't consider Riot Grrrl to be the time of the last great musical revolution, is because Riot Grrrl never was/isn't a musical movement. It was/is a shifting, changing form for female empowerment, a cultural force, one that continually mutates into fresh forms and ideas. There again, I'm a music critic. So check industrial noise terrorists Atari Teenage Riot, London's garage-fed Comet Gain and even the Spice Girls' puerile appropriation of the 'Girl Power' slogan for three remarkably different ways Riot Grrrl has mutated within music.

Intermission

(The Pastels, Beat Happening, Half-Japanese)

Understand this. The Pastels and Beat Happening are behind almost every word I write here in this book.

There is a general lack of individuality in rock music.

This could well be a signifier of the pre-apocalypse, post-everything age we're living in. Everyone is too afraid or too numb or too something to express their true feelings. Or maybe this uniformity indicates that we really do all have the same thoughts, and all this stuff about two human beings being as similar as two snowflakes is rubbish. How else do you explain that at any given point, there will be X number of groups trying to be Beck, Y number imitating Radiohead, and Z being a slavish follower of Oasis who themselves are merely slavish followers of what went before? As, indeed, are both Radiohead and Beck. I'm not saying that originality *per se* is desirable in rock. It isn't. Originality doesn't even exist, as no one exists in a vacuum. It dismays me, though, that those who should be numbered among our most valued creators are forever in thrall to dullard fashion.

Far rather the sound of someone unable to even formulate chords on an acoustic guitar and singing one-word refrains than yet another singer expertly recreating the sound of Aretha Franklin polishing her scales in the bathtub. The difference between soul music in the sixties and soul music now is transparent: once, it was a medium to express emotion within. Now, it's an excuse to show off how well you learnt your maths tables in school.

Likewise, rock.

'I'm certainly not ashamed of my voice,' says Stephen Pastel. 'Admittedly I don't always sing perfectly in tune, but if you go back to great R&B or great soul singers, you'll find they're the same. Although tuning helps to convey a melody, it's not the most important part of having a voice. Ideas are the most important thing.'

The Pastels make me happy for many reasons, but only one important one – they speak directly to me. Whenever Stephen sings in his cracked, mournful voice over a couple of distorted chords he's reaching deep within himself for something pure, something unique. Right from the coy rhyming on the Scots band's debut 1982 single 'Songs For Children' through to their late eighties 'fruity' phase inspired by comedian Frankie Howerd and playwright Joe Orton to 1997's sophisticated, dance-tinted *Illumination*, the Pastels have never lost sight of the humanity at their core.

Some Pastels songs resonate with a glorious despair, some have melodies to send your heart soaring and some stutter slightly like they're aware of the fragility of human happiness. There's hope, joy, tales of solitary sadness and a truly heartrending break-up song ('Nothing To Be Done') among the Pastels' catalogue. Check out their excellent 1993 *Truckload Of Trouble* compilation for proof. The Pastels become more poignant the further they travel.

This Scots collective – Stephen and core members Aggi and Katrina, plus any number of collaborators, ranging from the Vaselines' Eugene Kelly to the Shop Assistants' David Keegan to Teenage Fanclub's Gerry and Norman – are without doubt one of the purest bands around. Yes, it's a badge of pride, but this purity doesn't equate with stasis. The Pastels may well have influenced the cutie movement and the separatist attitude of groups such as the Jesus And Mary Chain, Huggy Bear and Primal Scream, but there's also a whole generation of independent-minded nineties bands who look to them for inspiration.

There are the two labels Stephen has helped run: 53rd And 3rd (with David Keegan from the Shop Assistants) in the late eighties, responsible for a couple of Beat Happening UK releases, and the

21st Century Domino-distributed Geographic imprint, mostly championing music from Scotland. Listen out for the album from gentle Japanese art collective Maher Shalal Hash Baz: they sound like soulful Boston poet Jonathan Richman might have done, if he'd grown up as Tom Waits with an anti-imperial affliction.

I said 'fruity' earlier on. I meant it. Check their album titles from that period – *Up For A Bit With The Pastels, Suck On The Pastels.* People accused Stephen in his leather trousers and duffle coat of being camp for so long he finally decided to roll with it. It didn't detract from the quality of his music, and gave them a very endearingly British, self-deprecating sheen.

In the same way music in Olympia is unthinkable without Beat Happening singer Calvin Johnson's presence – although, some women there may well take issue with this statement – so it is in Glasgow with Stephen. Just under a decade ago, the Pastels set up their 'Friends of The Pastels' organisation in an attempt to network between those distanced by geographic location and lifestyle. For just five pounds, anyone could be Stephen's friend. Musicians from bands like Belle & Sebastian and Mogwai attended the resultant Pastelism gatherings organised in Glasgow, where artists such as Melody Dog, Jad Fair and Calvin Johnson would perform. Scotland has always prided itself on its independence, particularly from the London-centric media: nowhere is there a better example of this pride than among the bands inspired by the Pastels to search out and create alternatives of their own.

In real life, Stephen has alternated between being a librarian and working in a bookshop selling records. Music is too important to him to be relied upon as a source of income. Aggi paints and illustrates for magazines and on Pastels CD sleeves. Her generous wash of colours, scratchy lettering and warm lines mirror the band's music: slightly confusing but so reassuring.

Maybe everyone in corporate rock, and most independent music, sounds the same now because everything has become an excuse for a discourse. With the spread of global communication, the media has become all consuming and artists, in the old fashioned sense of the word, are obsolete. The Pastels and like-minded souls like Jad Fair, Kevin Shields and Domino Records' Laurence Bell are artists. There's no denying it. Yet the Pastels are not obsolete, no way. They're too special.

Often, their songs will communicate a wonderful sense of ennui and desire through the use of a few scattered drumbeats and carelessly whispered vocals. Musically, we're talking Mr Richman and the Velvets' underrated drummer Mo Tucker (who produced the saddest Jad Fair song ever recorded, 1991's devastating Half-Japanese B-side 'Always'). There's also an element of darkness and loneliness hidden away beneath all the Pastels' sugar-bright colours and schoolyard inflections. Latter-day member Katrina Mitchell has a way of singing tunes like 1995's 'Worlds Of Possibility' perfectly in tune but with an off-pitch note thrown in just to let you know that she knows there are always at least two alternate, equally rewarding, melodies close to hand.

In one of my first fanzines, back in 1983, I wrote that 'the day I stop liking the Pastels is the day I stop liking music'. Oddly, this almost held true.

In 1998, the Scots band released an album of other group's mixes of songs from the previous year's excellent *Illumination*, *Illuminati*. This sounded like post-rock noodling nonsense to my ears, despite the presence of illustrious names like My Bloody Valentine, the Make Up and ace Franco-pop retro futurists Stereolab. I didn't like it because I felt that shorn of the fragile, resonant voices and the odd twist of guitar it lacked heart and sacrificed soul on the altar of fashion. It felt like the Pastels were trying too hard to make a point: that after all these years Stephen was annoyed at not having received his rightful dues, and was determined to claim them. This is something that runs contrary to the Pastels' creed. They have always existed separate to This Year's Flavour.

It was all the odder then that I *had* almost given up listening to music by that point. I much preferred to hold court over a pint of whisky in one of Seattle's bars than to sit back and immerse myself in melancholy . . .

Hold up. That is so untrue, I can't believe I just wrote that previous line. What did artists like the Foundations, the Roots, Irving Berlin and Cadallaca do, if not save my life from unbearable loneliness all over again in 1998? Whatever. The Pastels will return and they will remain the Pastels.

I first heard Beat Happening while I was living in Willesden Green, freelancing as a screen-printer and occasional *NME* critic. One day, around eleven a.m., there was a ring at the door. Some skinny Australian kid was standing there. He was in London for 24 hours, stopping over on his way back to Australia from Olympia and had been given three addresses to look up. So he decided on mine. Heathrow to Willesden is a fair journey. It was a good job I was home. So I invited him in, gave him a cup of tea. On departing, he gave me a yellow-sleeved record: the first Beat Happening album. I figured I might as well listen to it, so I did . . . and was overwhelmed by the female voice on the first song on the record, 'Foggy Eyes'. I couldn't get past it.

At the time, I was writing my fanzine *The Legend!* and the only record company who would give me free stuff was Rough Trade – which was lucky, because this was back in the days of the Cartel, so they distributed almost every decent UK label. I thought that maybe I could reciprocate the favour and play them this record I loved so much. Thought that maybe they'd love it too. They did. Later, they released it. This was also the first time I met the Cannanes' David Nichols, the skinny Australian kid. Fifteen years later, we would both live in Melbourne and record music together.

It was Heather's voice that originally drew me to Beat Happening. I've always preferred female singers. That and the bare graphics: the cat on the spaceship! I was a big fan of Tracey Thorn's Marine Girls and their offshoot Grab Grab The Haddock, too: bands 'Foggy Eyes' reminded me of. I responded to the minimal instrumentation. I've always hated extraneous noise, especially unnecessary drumming. I used to sing on stage either a cappella or with the most minimal of backings myself, and was made to feel somewhat of a freak for doing so. It was nice to hear this girl doing the same in some city I'd never heard of before. When I got past the opening track, Calvin's deep-throated singing and the album's production reminded me of early Cramps stripped back to the bone. I loved the directness of the music, the sense of fun, the fact that with a few sparse notes and carefully chosen words, this trio had managed to create a whole aura and mystique about themselves. Beat Happening played with a rigid minimalism that was both highly formed and formal.

So I wrote about them in my fanzine. Pages. What else could I do? All I ever wanted to communicate by writing about music was the love I felt for certain records.

In the context of the British music scene of the time, *Beat Happening* sounded refreshing, exciting to me. Anything I love on first hearing always sounds refreshing to me. It made me feel less alone, made me feel that perhaps there were other people who had the same core values as me. I'm not sure if I heard it the same time as I heard Talulah Gosh, but if I did I wouldn't have connected the two bands, despite the fact they are both often lumped in together nowadays under the tag 'cutie'. They seemed on opposite sides of the world, both musically and literally. The Oxford band were almost deliberately naïve (one early song was called 'The Day I Lost My Pastels Badge'). There was nothing naïve in Calvin's ability to manipulate audiences and tear all opposition down, like a pacifist bully. Calvin delighted in inverting conventional imagery and symbols within his lyrics: his band were truly subversive in the way they superficially sounded so innocent and were actually anything but. Perhaps, though, a certain joy in music for its own sake connected the two bands – and, of course, the Pastels.

I saw Beat Happening live on a number of occasions in England. Calvin Johnson is one of the three most powerful performers I've had the privilege to see. He reminds me of Johnny Rotten. He has the same manic, intense stare in his eyes. The same way of intimidating an audience, the way he'd move so close to them. (That is why he would later be knocked cold by an ashtray hurled by a dumb hardcore kid during a Fugazi support slot.) Beat Happening *killed*. On stage, they communicated with ferocity unmatched by even the most hardcore of hardcore bands, made all the more chilling because of the silences. Calvin had an informed spontaneity behind his music, too. Once in 1990, we played a show as Calvin & The Legend! in Olympia, performing a handful of songs we'd written earlier that day, in support to ex-Shockabilly guitarist and electric rake-player Eugene Chadbourne. We sounded electrifying. Outside, the snow covered everything in a comforting blanket of purest white: and we walked back to Calvin's house through deserted streets, triumphant.

I loved Beat Happening so much when they played in England. It made me so mad they weren't the most massive band in the world. My favourite show was when I supported them and the McTells in a tiny village hall in Hertfordshire. I felt that life didn't get any better than to see three such intelligent, passionate, witty and soulful people on stage.

I still feel that way.

Beat Happening are the most important American band of the last two decades.

It's impossible to know where to start: maybe with K records, the label Calvin set up in opposition to corporate rock, and which has since inspired so many others. From the mid-eighties onwards, K released tape compilations and served as a distribution base for bands across America, eventually spawning what Calvin termed the International Pop Underground. It was via K that I first heard of Galaxie 500, Bikini Kill, Pavement and Chapel Hill's indie cheerleaders Superchunk. Most of these bands had their own labels: it was through K and likeminded labels like Drag City, Merge and Tsunami's Simple Machines that the scene developed a coherency and all-vital support network.

In the summer of '91, Calvin and business partner Candice Pederson helped stage the first International Pop Underground Festival. The event featured over 50 bands including Fugazi, Mecca Normal, Bikini Kill, Some Velvet Sidewalk, Beat Happening and L7. In one of my frequent contrary moods, I refused to attend. I've never liked the idea of going any place people expect me to be. The festival certainly helped catalyse the emergent Riot Grrrl movement which took real inspiration from the 'Girl Day', where in the morning, afternoon and night, only female artists played.

'I've never been to any of those things like Lollapalooza,' Calvin told me a few years later. 'Sounds like a big concert. Fine, if you're into that kind of thing. I'm not. I've only ever been to one. George Michael. That was good. He's got a flair for showmanship that's often lacking. There are a few who share that panache. That's why I like Nation Of Ulysses. They know how to put on a show.'

Beat Happening were an incredible group, full stop. Early albums such as 1983's *Beat Happening* and its follow-up *Jamboree* are the quintessence of heartfelt pop, youth rebellion and full-on independence. Their music was a mix of warmth, hostility and gladness straight out of the adult-rated version of *Huckleberry Finn*. Poignant and direct, the trio mixed metaphor with fuzz-tone. '*Breakfast in cemetery/Boy tasting wild cherry/Touch girl apple blossom/Just a boy playing possum/Welcome back to Indian Summer,*' Calvin sang on 'Indian Summer'. Fellow maverick spirits, Greg Sage (from seminal Portland band the Wipers), Screaming Trees and Steve Fisk helped with production, recording songs that captured the essence of Olympia's seasons – summer, fall, winter.

'I like my rock'n'roll noisy and wild, with a good tune you can whistle now and then,' explained Calvin. 'The third double bill we ever played was with Galaxie 500 and the Go Team [Calvin's other band, with Tobi Vail, pre-Bikini Kill]. We played this real weird party on a ballet stage that started at midnight, but there was no stopping Galaxie 500. We didn't go on till four, the show was over at five, so Galaxie 500 go, "Hey, let's head down to the Staten Island ferry, do an acoustic set and watch the sunrise." '

Beat Happening sometimes recalled the wired country sound of early Meat Puppets in their unsettling fervour. The three members would switch instruments around on stage: vocals, drums and guitar. There was no bass.

'Why should we let technology stand in our way?' asked Calvin when I interviewed him for the *NME* in 1986. 'Less is more in our book.'

Calvin has always been disingenuous in interviews, aware that he has the image of Calvin Johnson to perpetuate. Yet this simple statement holds so much truth. The reason there is so much clutter in rock music, in art, in the world, is that most people have nothing to say and try to hide the fact under layers of extraneous noise. Calvin can perform solo with no microphone and a series of clichés and still sound more vital than a million Rolling Stones records (with which he shares a disquieting sexuality).

As the music progressed, Beat Happening started to write increasingly dark exposés of the traumas behind childish dreams. 1989's incredible *Black Candy* has a surreal suburban beauty to match its starkness and lurking menace, matched by very few – Lou Reed, perhaps. More songs of sex, furtiveness and decay and romping naked through the snow sung in deep sonorous tones of glee. Incredibly, its follow-up, 1991's *Dreamy* is even better. Musicians like Sonic Youth, Hole and post-Vaselines band Captain America among many others agreed, all covering Beat Happening songs. There's a famous quote about the Velvet Underground, about how every person who originally bought their first album went on to form a band . . . this could probably be said for Beat Happening, too.

'I like shows where everybody's dancing,' Calvin suggested in '95. 'No particular favourite step. The dances I like don't have names. They're the ones someone thought up just before they do them.'

Sadly, Beat Happening no longer existed by this point. They had gone into limbo following their fifth album, the Sup Pop co-distributed *You Turn Me On* produced by Young Marble Giants' Stuart Moxham, who was also responsible for the second Marine Girls album. Third member, intellectual radical Bret later went on to form the very fine, minimalist D+ and start his own tape label in Bremerton, Anacortes. Calvin, meanwhile, con-solidated his position as one of his generation's prime movers by building the Dub Narcotic studio above the K offices in Olympia, and fronting a raucous, minimalist dub band of the same name in the tradition of Adrian Sherwood's On-U Sound and Lee 'Scratch' Perry.

Even finer, though, are the Halo Benders, the part time group formed with Built To Spill's Doug Martsch and producer Steve Fisk, after Calvin would jump on stage at the end of Built To Spill shows. They've released three albums of shimmering, ecstatic, subversive pop. I'd recommend KLP46, *Don't Tell Me Now* above all else, with its astonishing incendiary centrepiece 'Bomb Shelter Part 2'. Martsch's searing vocals are a perfect counterpoint to Calvin's deeply felt words of pacifist resistance.

* * *

I will always favour naïve pop.

Take early Ramones. The way they keep their songs so simple means the possibilities and the harmonies in my head and the sentiments and the emotions to be drawn are endless. Joey conveys more with lines like *'Hey, little girl/I wanna be your boyfriend'* or *'I don't wanna walk around with you/So why d'ya want to walk around with me?'* than most 'songwriters' manage in a lifetime of complex couplets and corny imagery. It's what you leave out that matters. The listener should always be left with something to add.

If you're looking for a band that come closer to capturing the secret heart of Nirvana's music than any other, then you need to travel to listen to NYC's Half-Japanese. 'With my headphones on, Jad and I share our little secret walking through shopping malls and airports,' Kurt once wrote in a note to me.

The singer later clarified: 'I like to listen to Jad Fair and Half-Japanese in shopping malls, in the heart of American culture. I just think that if people could hear this music right now they'd melt. They wouldn't know what to do. They'd start bouncing off the walls and hyperventilating. So I used to turn their music up really loud on my headphones and pretend it was blasting through the speakers on the malls.'

I love Jad for his warmth, his spectacles, the way he cuts away all the bullshit and strips music back to its core essentials – humanity, a cracking good story and melody line. I love him for his boundless enthusiasm and shy genius . . . Maybe it's wrong to call Jad naïve because he certainly knows what he's doing, but he has a childlike purity that to me is at the core of virtually any great music you might want to name. (Purity? Actually, children can be among the most evil bastards on God's earth. It's society, via TV and the films, that wrongly perpetuates the myth of children being pure. Maybe that's why Beat Happening are so great: they capture the true impurity of being a child.) Half-Japanese make my feet want to *move*, and there's barely a higher compliment than that.

Jad never tunes a guitar, believing such an action to be the antithesis of what rock'n'roll is about: spontaneity. He very rarely buys guitars: the ones other musicians throw away are perfectly fine. The guitar he played during a 1991 UK tour with the Pastels he picked up in a Glasgow junk shop for £28 the day after he arrived. He sings out-of-key, sometimes gratingly, always express-ively. In his hooded parka and thick-rimmed spectacles he looks like an eccentric favourite uncle.

If Jad feels he's becoming too remote from the audience, stuck up there on stage, he'll jump down and go walkabout with just an unplugged guitar for company. He'll start mugging it up on Jimmie Rogers' 'I Had A Dream Last Night', raising the rafters with a rousing rendition of 'The Sunny Side Of The Street', or sing a soft Daniel Johnston lament. Doubtless, his determined use of untuned guitars and off-pitch singing could be termed avant garde, if you were so inclined. I'm just turned on by the depth of his emotions.

'To me, it is more rock'n'roll to have my guitar untuned,' Jad explained. 'Because I feel that anything that takes time is anti-rock'n'roll. If you say "It's time to rock" but then you have to sit down and tune your guitar for five minutes, well, that's missing the whole point. This way, if I'm ready, my guitar is ready. No matter how many strings it has, even if all the strings are broken and I can only slap my hand on the fretboard, I can go on. As long as my right hand is moving, forget the left one. That's just for show anyway.'

I've seen Jad play concerts with a rolled-up newspaper and upturned wastebasket for rhythm, with just his voice for colour. I've listened to Jad improvise songs on the spot, songs that are heartrending in their simple, direct pleasure and emotion. I've also seen Jad play stadiums in precisely the same fashion – with a band behind him, sure, but with the spirit intact – in front of crowds of over 15,000 in support to Nirvana on their final tour. Now that was a sight. It must have disheartened Kurt to realise his audience didn't spontaneously implode upon contact with the source: but maybe one or two out of the thousands later bought a Half-Japanese record. That would have been nice.

For merchandise, Jad once bought a bunch of plastic Action Men, painted spectacles on them, made up some labels and resold them as 'Jad Fair dolls'. When he stayed at my Cricklewood flat, he left behind an intricate smiley paper cut on my living room floor as his way of saying 'thank you'. That paper cut, alongside several others, is now framed and has pride of place on the walls of my Brighton house alongside some Daniel Johnston felt tip drawings.

There's a famous quote in Jeff Feuerzeig's documentary *Half-Japanese: The Band That Would Be King* about Half-Japanese being better than the Beatles. Can that be true?

Of course it is. For starters, Jad has written more songs – and far more original songs, too – than the Liverpool lads who, much as their melodies might have touched a popular nerve, could never claim originality. His songs are of an equally high standard, he sings about monsters and love, he keeps the torch of rock'n'roll burning every time he picks up a guitar or rolled-up newspaper. He's special. Can you honestly claim the same for the Beatles? That

band are only special when folk like Daniel Johnston or myself –
or even Jad – reinvest their songs with fresh meaning.

Jad is special, just in the way he picks up a pair of scissors.

Rubbing the Impossible to Burst
(Huggy Bear, Bikini Kill, Olympia)

*'Every patriarchal idea implies linear narrative. We have non-linear
narrative. We're like one of those microscopic germs that spread out from
underneath the slide. Our axis points are forever changing.'*

CHRIS, HUGGY BEAR

The first time I saw Huggy Bear play live was at the Tufnell Park
Dome in May 1992. I hung back, didn't want to be caught watching
their inspirational punk-fired feminist noise. I remember thinking
to myself: 'I can't like them. I can't. If I like them, there will be so
much trouble.' I couldn't help myself, though. There was something irresistibly sexy in their fervour, in the clattering drums and
abrasive guitar chords, in the way Niki and Chris screamed at each
other, sometimes dropping into the kindest of harmonies.

Some of those on stage that I found so attractive were my flatmates
and I knew that no good would come of me liking them, because if I
liked them I would have to write about them and if I wrote about them,
well . . . So I kept back despite the chills ricocheting off my backbone,
those chills I had grown to know so well. Instead, it was my colleague
Sally Margaret Joy, the best writer the music press ever screwed over,
who started enthusing, enamoured of their energy and words.

My feet betrayed me (as they often did). It didn't seem fair Huggy
Bear could be creating such energy without the few onlookers
giving any back, so I moved nearer, nearer to the Dome's stage,
bobbing and weaving and ducking imaginary barbs. It would prove
to be good practice for what was to follow later.

Flash forward a few months. It's summer, Brighton. We've been
to the beachfront Zap Club, and now everyone is back at my house
for a party. There's flatmate Jo: she throws up when she hears a
Kendra Smith record. There's flatmate Jon: he walks round the
block in his socks. Singer Chris stands on the stoop and looks at the
stars above the hill for hours. Dale Shaw, later to form the brilliant
improvisational Riot Boy band Blood Sausage, phones his mum and
laughs like a drain when he discovers all the Cadbury's Chocolate
Animals are shaped like squirrels. I'm hiding upstairs with my new
girlfriend. Afterwards, she complains that all she can remember of
that night is constant giggling, and the patter of tiny feet.

That's the Huggy Bear experience.

I wander outside the next morning and a present from Eygpt – a large toy camel – is nestling among the weeds at the end of my garden, next to an empty Cadbury's biscuits box. Huggy Bear all race up to London to see Pavement play the Virgin Megastore, except for Jo who's ill in bed, and then go on to London University where Tanya Donelly's post-Throwing Muses band, Belly, are in support. I walk round the venue covered in lipstick, after Tanya insists on kissing my face several times because I'd . . . well, I'd asked her to. The last time we'd met, she'd slapped me.

Flash-forward to where I'm in Chicago, sheltering from the neon and rain. Cynthia Plastercaster – the delightful lady who was one of the sixties' most famous groupies, most notably because of her fondness for immortalising rock stars' private parts in plaster – is showing me around her collection. There's John Langford from the Mekons, so massive he could make Superman feel insecure. There's Neil Innes from the Rutles and the Bonzo Dog Band, all shrivelled and tiny. 'He couldn't get it up, the poor man,' Cynthia explains, 'so I ended up using him as a door knocker.' The collection's most famous 'member', Jimi Hendrix, is away under lock and key, subject of a court case. The sixties' guitarist was so big he reputedly broke the mould three times. Cynthia offers to preserve my penis for posterity, a signal honour as she'd never considered rock journalists worthy before. I accept, but somehow we never get round to it.

What does this have to do with Huggy Bear? Confusion! Sex! Reduction of the male form to its component parts! I told Cynthia she should start marketing her collection. Imagine pleasuring oneself with a dildo moulded in the form of Jimi Hendrix's pride and joy! Although I guess working out who owns the copyright could be a problem. Bear with me, please.

Fast forward again.

It's early 1993, height of the Riot Grrrl insurrection. I walk into the offices of *Melody Maker* where I'm assistant editor and am screamed at from all sides. 'It's not the new punk,' I can remember one detractor railing at my editor Allan Jones, a man who'd interviewed the Sex Pistols.

No, it was far more relevant, far more exciting than that. It was NOW!

'People don't know how to listen to different kinds of music. If you hear music that is chaotic, fragmented, whatever, it's like "How do you judge that?"'

JO, HUGGY BEAR

Who were Huggy Bear? A brief explosion in time, a distorted mess of vibrato, crackling and noise that we used to call 'music' for want of a fuller word. While all around talked of starting musical revolutions using the same timeworn formats, this English collective were trying to invent a whole new art form, one that bore little resemblance to what had gone before.

Huggy Bear adhered to the Jad Fair belief that there isn't a right or wrong way to tune a guitar, only emotion: and that's about all they adhered to. That is, until they travelled to America and became absorbed into the US rock underground and ended up sounding like a hundred other San Diego hardcore bands. (Someone, some day will have to explain to me how that is a progression. Does conventional proficiency have to equate with dullness? What about the adage it's better to learn the rules before you break them? Huggy Bear did it all back to front, and ended up a shadow of their initial energy.) Right from the word go, when someone placed a Huggy Nation cassette in my bedroom as a Christmas present, they always said they would only exist for three years. Unlike fellow insurrectionists Manic Street Preachers, Huggy Bear were pompous enough to stick with the plan.

The first Huggy Bear tape was extraordinary. On it I could hear tinkling keyboard music, raunchy blues, beat poetry, a cappella nursery rhymes, a slightly misguided attempt at some jazz funk, and songs about transvestites, pirates, dry humping and missing female estate agents. It's no wonder the male-dominated rock press were confused when they finally encountered them. Huggy Bear sounded industrial in a scary precursor of late nineties Riot Grrrls, Atari Teenage Riot, gothic (like my then favourites, Portsmouth's brittle Cranes) and cutie. Of course Huggy Bear were influenced by cutie. All the group had been reared on the sweet harmonies of Pastels fans Talulah Gosh (later to become Heavenly) and the Shop Assistants.

Even then, it was apparent that Huggy Bear were about as far removed from the rock mainstream as it was possible to get – with their home-recorded cassettes and cut'n'paste technique and messages scrawled on parts of their body – while still playing 'music'.

Huggy Bear formed and gestated around two crucial factors. First: fellow prime movers, Olympia's Bikini Kill. This connection came about after I returned from a trip to Olympia in the summer of 1992, and gave a copy of the Kill's *Revolution Girl Style Now* cassette and fanzine to Huggy members Jon and Jo. I'd brought several copies back with me, obtained from Calvin Johnson's K distribution service, excited by what I'd heard. I knew I'd find others who'd be inspired by it the same way. I don't remember either of the pair being too impressed by the music, but the fledgling fanzine network being set up by Bikini Kill's Tobi Vail and like-minded souls like Donna (*Chainsaw*), Erin (the seventies TV star fixated *Teenage Gang Debs*), Bratmobile's Molly and Alison (*Girl Germs*) did interest them.

Second: the Rough Trade concerts. Come the summer of 1992, and Huggy Bear would usually congregate around the Rough Trade shop in Covent Garden, especially on a Saturday when impromptu concerts by bands like Hole, Pavement and Sebadoh would be staged. (The shows helped spawn a fearsome roster on shop manager Gary Walker's Wiiija label, Tindersticks and Cornershop included. All these bands started around the time of Riot Grrrl and were a major part of what was happening.) The afternoons were ramshackle, mischievous and it was supremely inspiring to have such passionate music played right in your face. There was an incredible concert at the Underworld performed by Nation Of Ulysses where the band preached sugar-spun teen revolution – '*Wear your hickey as a badge of pride*' – and burnt their shoes before launching into some blistering rock.

Once, Suede's label phoned Huggy Bear up, seeking a demo tape. 'Not until you drop Suede,' Jo told them. When Sub Pop called looking to do a one-off single, Jo gave the unwary label boss Bruce Pavitt an earful about how much she despised 90 per cent of his roster, not to mention the 'joke' redneck attitude it was then fashionable to sport in US indie circles. Huggy Bear didn't want much: revolution, a little parity in the male-female stakes. Oh, and one more thing – you're not empowering yourself if you're waiting for other people to do it for you.

The point about Huggy Bear is that there never was any point. Like vampires and rain, their image never fades over the years because they never existed. The point is to enjoy life and plot the revolution along with the glittering lips and balloons. The point is that it's always chaos and confusion that produce the most exhilarating thoughts, sounds and ideas. The point is that if you stick to a (male-led) linear narrative, you cut off most of that which surrounds you. Flies have multiple, panoramic vistas of the world. We have one narrow way of seeing life. Who lives the longest? *Exactly!* Punk preached us all these alternatives and then gave us three chords. The Slits were always way more interesting than the Clash.

Don't worry, it's not an examination. All you can fail is yourself.

'I can play bloody thousands of chords, thanks. I made them all up myself.'

JO, HUGGY BEAR

Flash back to *The Word*, 1993.

There's the asinine Terry Christian muttering something about how if these garbage-y bands don't want to come on 'his' programme, they don't have to. So how else do they gain access to the popular consciousness, Terry? Through *Antiques Roadshow*? No one watches *The Word* for you, you prat. You're the cipher.

Usually, the bands needed to be much more established than Huggy Bear to be booked on the show. In an uncanny echo of the infamous *Bill Grundy Show* incident in 1976, however, where the Sex Pistols filled in for Queen's last-minute cancellation and created a tabloid feeding-frenzy with a couple of cuss words, Pulp had pulled out a few days before. Also, *The Word* thrived on what was laughably called 'controversy' (usually some female baring her breasts, or a student downing a bucketload of live worms), so Huggy must have seemed prime fodder with all the attention they were receiving in the music press. For about six months in *Melody Maker*, there was barely a letters page that wasn't composed entirely of rants about the Riot Grrrl 'movement', both for and against.

Huggy Bear on *The Word*: revolution girl style now performed with red hair and space age sunglasses. Girls running rampant, veins bursting, punk rock and Henry Rollins looking upset that his time-slot has been eaten into.

The trouble started after a typically stupid, sexist *Word* segment involving a pair of walking silicon factories called 'the Barbie Twins'. The show was recorded live, so when the cameras cut back to Christian interviewing Rollins, some of Huggy Nation decided enough was enough, and they started to heckle the hapless one. This resulted in a massed game of hide'n'seek among the band's mostly female supporters as they tried to evade a rather surly security force. Oddly, this footage wasn't shown. It could have enhanced *The Word*'s reputation as a hotbed of controversy no end.

The actual performance of the then-current Huggy Bear single 'Her Jazz' was one of the most exhilarating moments of live music television ever, as fans from bands as diverse as original anarchist punks Crass, Pavement and Pulp could attest. It was a moment to remember, cherish and be inspired by on a par with Dexys on *Top Of The Pops*, the Fugees two decades later . . . and, oh, choose your own. Please.

'Someone was saying that Huggy Bear have got to make it succeed, but the responsibility doesn't rest on us. People have got to get out and do it for themselves. There isn't one right way.'

NIKI, HUGGY BEAR

Resting up in a remote Canadian town in February 1993, I flop down in front of a television screen at five a.m. Cut to the streets of New York. Someone's telling someone else about how Riot Grrrls don't talk to the media. The media are talking about how, as soon as Riot Grrrls are talked about in the media, they will be effectively dead. My head spins, and takes several leaps sideways to accusations of 'elitism'. What does this have to do with music anyway? Hold on. Where have you been?

On the *Melody Maker* letters page I am simultaneously compared to 'man-hating' Andrea Dworkin and a sexist middle-aged pig. At the height of all the madness, *NME* offer Bikini Kill five pages and the cover to set out their manifesto if they will speak to them. The Olympian band turns them down flat. A rival journalist sends a letter to Huggy Bear, asking them if they would care to speak to her, now that I've 'fucked them over'. It ends up on my kitchen table. I confront her at a Linus concert at the White Horse: she claims not to know what I'm talking about, although she does have the decency to blush when she discovers Huggy are my housemates.

I find myself in a gutter outside the University of London, talking street poetry with the drain and arguing with the backs of buses. A passing new *Maker* writer, excited to meet me, is pointed in my direction. I'm insensible. 'So this is the great Everett True . . .' Earlier, I'd climbed on board the stage, inebriated, while Teenage Fanclub were playing, in search of my New York friend, producer Don Fleming and his band Gumball. No one stops me, so I set off in pursuit of backstage. I see Don. Don offers me the bottle of whisky he's drinking. It's a third full. I drink it. He looks at me. 'Oh sorry,' I say.

The next day at the Rough Trade shop – rendezvous with Huggy – the singer expresses his surprise that I'm still alive. He claims that I finished two bottles of whisky the previous night. These rock types, they like to exaggerate . . . right?

Three popular misconceptions about pop music:
(1) What matters is the 'song'. Without the 'song', pop music has no context.
(2) We're all on the same side.
(3) People who aren't on the same side as 'us' probably don't like music anyway.

Later that day in Halifax, Nova Scotia where I am attending the Canadian East Coast Music Awards, someone will describe A&R people as the 'true heroes of the music industry'. A friend is dissed by the head of Time-Warner (Canada) because she objects to being called an A&R 'guy'. His excuse is that 'I'm from the old school.' Aren't most of you?

Sub Pop Grunge

Origins
(Tad, Earth, Seattle)

'The "loser" is the existential hero of the nineties. You have nothing to lose because you're already under the minimum wage. You pay too much in taxes, you can never get your head above the ground and you live in a shitty apartment. You work overtime all week and that's still not enough. You own a credit card, but you're always in debt.'

KURT DANIELSON (BASSIST, TAD)

This is where it all started.

People ask me what the attraction of Seattle was. The energy, the insane amount of energy rising up through the boards of that town's clubs, the musicians with their long greasy hair and unflagging sick humour, the thrill of loud music. Bodies tumbling on top of bodies, faces smiling and grinning and lapping up the pain, musicians such as Mudhoney's Mark Arm and the mighty Tad Doyle, and any number of interchangeable grunge bands all merging into one sweat-soaked, glorious whole. The parties where I'd be barricaded into bathrooms by junkie models looking to get laid, and later race through streets in cars high on delirium and alcohol and the thrill of the chill night air. The skyscrapers, towering into the night like a symphony of neon and rich promise, ringed by an almost mythical circle of mountains sometimes not seen for years, such could be the density of cloud and rain. The cheap Mexican beer and endless supply of coffee and trips to the liquor store. The top floor of the Terminal Sales Building where Sub Pop had its offices, world domination promised ridiculously in literature and on the phone, glorious views of the Puget Sound and the city through every window. The warehouse, wandering through a collector's delight of coloured vinyl and coloured vinyl, knowing you could take anything you want and wanting everything you took.

What was there to be excited about? Oh, so much, so much . . .

The numerous late night transatlantic phone calls, enthusing about this or that, not checking facts – never checking facts – only on the look out for more outrageous lies, more tales of glory. The live shows, filled with noise and surprise and the hum of amplifiers always feeding back, the bass always too loud, the whole crowd a hive of wanton activity. Overnight drives spent chatting to friendly dominatrixes, strip bars that doubled as discos with the mirror ball turning and Tad's band thudding, scuzzy joints that threw you straight on to the street when your drinking slowed down too much. Train rides that lasted for days and ended with me taking Sub Pop's bosses for all they owned at poker. Soundgarden boasted of lighting farts: Mudhoney talked of ancient scriptures; the Walkabouts swung with genteel and good grace; Nirvana acted all young and mischievous. What was the attraction of Seattle? It was the lilt in Mark Arm's smile, that knowing smirk as he took another swing at the microphone stand. It was the insane numbers of friendly faces all looking to make sure your good time was your only time; dorky girls who dragged you to ridiculous places and made up songs when the sleep deprivation became too much; conversations that lasted for years.

February 1989 was my first time in America. I took one look at the Seattle skyline as it rose into view over the highway from the airport, like a corporate Emerald City, and fell in love. I remember thinking to myself, 'Don't be absurd. You'll probably feel this way about every city in America you ever see.' I saw many, and never did.

Arriving at Bruce's place, myself and top photographer Andrew Catlin found ourselves expected to share a mattress for a week on the label boss' floor. Our companions were a borrowed record store rack filled with rare – even then – Sub Pop singles and a couple of massive beanbags. Above our heads loomed the twin radio towers of Capitol Hill. I stayed. Sleeping on floors was nothing unusual for me, and I relished the idea of staying with the guy who ran the whole operation. Andy freaked out and checked into a hotel the next morning. The situation led him not to take quite as much care over his pictures as he might have done otherwise. In particular, he didn't bother taking too many shots of one band we interviewed: Nirvana.

I can still picture Bruce and me wandering along Pike – or was it Pine? – across the Interstate 5 bridge in the freezing winter air, on our way past the big department store downtown. He was explaining how 95 per cent of all body heat is lost through the head.

'Excuse me Legend!' he said to me (most everyone on my first trip to Seattle called me Legend, my stage name, probably because Calvin Johnson did), 'but do you mind if I borrow your hood?' So I unzipped the detachable hood from my parka, and he pulled it over his shaved head. We must have made an odd couple, walking around. Me all strained and bubbling with excitement. Him, wearing a weird hood to match his epic beard, filling in my noise with the odd hesitant silence.

The Pavitts and I hooked up with Calvin and Olympian friends for an all-night dance party, no alcohol involved. We danced to the cool sounds of sixties soul and mod, all of us comfortable in our unique dance steps, never growing old. I'd never experienced such rare fun. It felt like it was the norm for Seattle, these fun and frantic and innocent celebrations of music.

I loved the little roundabouts in the centre of each meticulously laid out street around the Capitol Hill area, flowers and trees growing on every one. We'd rise early each day to walk down to Bruce's place of work, on the eleventh floor of the Terminal Sales Building on 1st and Virginia, stopping off for a coffee along the way. There we met ace radio PR Erica Hunter, whose task it was to amuse the eager Limey; sales people Daniel House and Mark Pickerel (drummer with Screaming Trees); musicians like Mudhoney, Chris from Swallow, Nirvana and Tad. People like Bruce's business partner Jonathan Poneman, a man who always reminded me of a big loveable shaggy dog, and spiky photographer Charles Peterson. It wasn't until about four visits in that I got to recognise anywhere in Seattle aside from the tiny strip along 1st outside Sub Pop: all the necessary bars were downtown, either in Belltown or near the Showbox, the opposite way.

Charles remembers that anyone turning up at the office during the two weeks of my visit would be press-ganged into looking after me.

'I turned up there one day,' he says, 'and they asked me if I could look after this English journalist they'd just flown over to do a story. That's how we met. I took you to the Pike Place Market, and my abiding initial impression of you was in the Starbucks along the waterfront, knocking back two large mochas, another one in your hands for later, chewing on some chocolate coffee beans.'

I caught a Greyhound coach over to Olympia, where I spent a happy couple of nights kipping down on Calvin Johnson's hard concrete floor at the Martin, the apartment building where most of that town's musicians stayed. My main image of Olympia back then was of making angels in the snow, and having insane one-sided snowball fights with Al from Some Velvet Sidewalk and Tobi Vail. Mr Catlin, my photographer, also had an up moment when he met slacker cartoonist Peter Bagge and ended up buying several of his drawings.

Back in Seattle, Kelly from all-girl piss-artists Dickless and myself accompanied Jonathan down to a radio show at KCMU and ran the friendly DJ ragged with our double-entendres and impromptu versions of the Ramones' 'Rockaway Beach' and the Beatles' 'I'm Down'. Down at the Pike Place Market, I got my hair cut short. Maybe it seemed an odd gesture as everyone else's hair was way out of control, but I was asserting my individuality.

I was English, goddamn it!

Seattle in '89 had little to distinguish it from the outside world: rain, good coffee, Boeing, a fish market and a beautiful skyline, at the centre of which was the Space Needle built for the 1962 World Fair. It was a remote big city with a small-town attitude, stuck away in the top Northwest corner of the States. It's sheltered by the Olympics and the Pacific Ocean on one side, the Puget Sound (an inland sea) on another, Canada on a third, and is cut off from the rest of America by the Cascades, and 2,000 miles of badlands, cornfields and the Rocky Mountains.

Like any metropolis it had its hangers-on and a handful of cool places: Capitol Hill, 1st Avenue's red light district, home of the OK Hotel and the Vogue where Bruce Pavitt would spin muscle car rock against hip hop DJ sets. 'I moved from Chicago to study in Olympia towards the end of the seventies,' he recalls. 'There I wrote a column on US independent rock for a magazine called *OP* [now *Option*]. In 1980, I started a fanzine called *Subterranean Pop*, dedicated to the same music. It lasted for a couple of years and I followed it with some tape compilations. In '83 I moved to Seattle and started a monthly column in [local music paper] *The Rocket* and a biweekly radio programme, both called Sub Pop.'

Soon afterwards, Bruce joined forces with local promoter and booking agent Jonathan Poneman.

'I'm originally from Toledo, Ohio,' explains Jonathan. 'I moved here to study and got a job at KCMU, the University of Washington radio station. I had a show dedicated specifically to the local scene. For them, I also organised gigs with Washington bands. Thanks to it, I met truly exciting bands like Soundgarden who had a tremendous impact on me. They allowed me to forget my failed musician's glory dreams and get active with Bruce's record business.'

The first vinyl release on Sub Pop was 1986's *Sub Pop 100*, a compilation of US indie music, similar to the tapes. It actually featured only one Northwest band. It wasn't until the following summer, when Sub Pop released the Green River EP, 'Dry As A Bone', that Bruce and John became excited about the potential of local bands.

The factor that differentiated Seattle from a dozen other American cities was its insular self-belief. Seattle groups listened to the same records: Iggy Pop, homeboys sixties garage band the Sonics, and also Portland's Wipers, Led Zeppelin, Black Sabbath, Australia's Scientists and seminal slow-core psychedelic punk rock missing links Flipper. Few of these artists had much time for punk's brevity or holier-than-thou elitism. Late eighties Washington garage bands like the U-Men, Screaming Trees and Green River wanted more from their music than three-minute rants.

'Mostly, these musicians had been in jokey hardcore punk bands in the early eighties,' explains former Sub Pop general manager Rich Jensen. 'After a few years they reacted against the lazy pseudo-rebellious posing of their peers – too many mohawks and too many leather jackets covered with shallow political slogans, no guitar solos allowed – and started riffing out, growing their hair and acting like pre-punk gods of rock.'

Unlike metal, which by the late eighties had degenerated into a bad LA 'hair' parody of itself coupled with dullard sexism, this music had an impassioned urgency. Seattle musicians had learned well the lessons of US punk pioneers like Black Flag, Minutemen and San Francisco's female-led the Avengers. Already, the Northwest had a sound of its own: 'Hard music played to a slow tempo,' as Kurt Cobain described it in '89. This was a sound that took equally from hard rock, punk rock and psychedelic rock, and was infused with a freshness that made it sound unique. A word was needed to describe what was happening: self-deprecating, steeped in garage lore and disposable. You didn't need to look far to find something that matched the dirty, abrasive guitar sound of Mudhoney: grunge.

Looking to discover who invented the word? Infamous early rock critic Lester Bangs described the Groundhogs as 'good run-of-the-racks heavy grunge' in the April 1972 issue of *Rolling Stone*. Even as early on as 'Dry As A Bone', Sub Pop were promoting their label's sound as 'gritty vocals, roaring Marshall amps, ultra-loose GRUNGE that destroyed the morals of a generation'. (The 'Loser' tag that later settled round the grunge generation's neck, and was immortalised by Beck's 1994 single 'Loser', originally came from an early Sub Pop T-shirt.)

'Grunge happened because Seattle had a perfect confluence of good bands, good indie-marketing efforts, camaraderie and people making good recordings and taking good photos,' believes local producer Jack Endino, 'all working for very little money. Plus there was Dawn Anderson's 'zine *Backlash*, which was the only exclusively local music coverage during 1987–90. *The Rocket* caught on somewhat later. It was the right time, too. Eighties commercial rock had become so pathetic and formulaic.'

Endino helped defined the sound of Seattle, alongside Screaming Trees/Beat Happening producer Steve Fisk. In 1989 alone, he produced Tad's *God's Balls*, Mudhoney's *Mudhoney*, Afghan Whigs' *Up In It* and Nirvana's *Bleach* at his Reciprocal Studios. He is still a prolific and opinionated champion of local music through his constant bulletins on the Internet and, of course, his recordings.

(Incidentally, Jack insists that *Bleach* was recorded for $606 and some loose change as legend has it, even though others have since claimed it was more. 'I can show you the receipts if you like,' he told a disbelieving Poneman on a 1998 Seattle 'grunge' panel that also featured Soundgarden/Alice In Chains manager Susan Silver and myself. 'Yes, I kept them.')

In late '88, Bruce and John realised they were nearly out of funds. In what would later become a typical show of bravado, they decided to fly out an English journalist to cover the Seattle 'scene' to stir up industry interest.

I wasn't the original choice of their enthusiastic and dog-loving British PR Anton Brookes. He had wanted my fellow incendiary *MM* writers, the Stud Brothers, as their musical tastes (rock) seemed more in tune with the Seattle vibe, but there were two of them . . . and there's only one Everett True. Score! So he sent me over a bunch of records, the U-Men, Mudhoney and Nirvana foremost among them, and I was absolutely blown away by their energy. Sure, I wanted to dance! The call came at a good time. I'd started writing for *Melody Maker* a few months before, and was fed up of 'the Godfather of Cutie' tag I'd gained through championing bands like the Pastels, Shop Assistants and Beat Happening at my previous paper, *NME*. Unknown to Anton, I'd already been turned on to Green River. My friend and I hadn't totally understood all the Steve Harris triplets that the Seattle band played, but we could relate on a primal level to future Mudhoney singer Mark Arm's howl.

Here were bands that achieved what I had hitherto thought impossible: they made metal sound cool. It's worth remembering that during the mid-eighties, pop music was anti-guitar. You couldn't pick up the *NME* or *Rolling Stone* without reading someone like Toyah or Gary Numan telling you that guitars were old and dead and phallic symbols of repression. Early Sub Pop's guitar-driven rock was a human reaction to the drum machines. John and Bruce's stroke of marketing genius was to push rock'n'roll as rebellion – an ancient credo – while allowing people to listen to big dumb rock and retain their hipster credibility. Up until grunge, there had always been a line drawn between popular and under-ground music, with Journey on one side and the Dead Kennedys on the other. People got beaten up for being punk rock, especially in the US.

Sub Pop blurred that line once and for all.

'There never was anything unique about the so-called "Seattle Sound",' Peter Bagge, the cartoonist behind *Hate*'s Buddy Bradley, the slacker precursor of Bart Simpson, explains. 'It was just your typical white-boy noise: heavy metal with a punk attitude. Identical music was coming out of a lot of places, particularly Chicago, at the same time. It wasn't even a *new* sound. In fact it sounded very retro seventies to me, only louder. Pavitt and Poneman did a great job of packaging the local music scene and making it seem more unique than it really was, providing lazy English journalists with a ready-made hook to write about.'

Anyone walking into Sub Pop's offices in the early nineties would have been immediately confronted with the message 'YOU OWE DWARVES $' spray-painted in angry large white letters on the linoleum reception floor. The words looked apposite next to the confusion of computers, piled-up shipping boxes and fax sheets pinned up on walls already filled with framed Charles Peterson photographs. In one tiny office, Bruce would be sweet-talking a surly independent record-store owner. In another, Jonathan would be spinning a British journalist a fine yarn about the latest Love Battery release. Around the office, sundry local musicians doubling as warehouse packers and marketing agents and wisecracking receptionists would be behaving similarly. For a long time, all promotional copies of CDs were kept in the toilet. (The graffiti from Sub Pop's original bathroom was preserved for posterity by the Canadian Internet start-up company who inherited the premises in 2000, as a foot-wide strip of wall decoration.)

I swear, Sub Pop's early reputation was based around its receptionists. When grunge became an international fashion by-word, one former glory gal Megan Jasper invented a whole lexicon of grunge off the top of her head for *New York Times*. 'Swingin' on the flippety-flop' (hanging out), 'harsh realm' (bad luck) and 'k-ching!' (one more Seattle band signs a major contract) were three of my favourites. As was 'bound-and-hagged' (you can't go out on a weekend evening, because your stick-in-the-mud partner doesn't like your party friends).

Dwarves' graffiti was a fitting tribute to the constant brinkmanship that the company had played since its inception. Nirvana may have eventually delivered the label and the city into the big-time, but there were many close calls before the Geffen money started rolling in. Label T-shirts of the time read 'What part of "We have no money" don't you understand?' in response to bands claiming that the label never gave them any sales figures, and owed them tons of cash.

Many argue that it was Mark Arm's Iggy Pop-inspired stage antics and Steve Turner's brittle, almost mod, guitar runs that put Mudhoney at the centre of the grunge scene, not Nirvana. It was certainly Mudhoney who kept Sub Pop afloat through 1991. In May, *Every Good Boy Deserves Fudge* shipped 50,000 records on word of mouth alone when the label could barely afford to buy them a magazine ad, several months before the Nirvana royalties started to roll in. Indeed, it's rumoured that Sub Pop only received *them* because when the Aberdeen trio came to record *Bleach*, a drunken Krist Novoselic insisted that Bruce gave the band a proper, written contract. Without it, DGC/Geffen could have had the band for nothing.

It was easy to sympathise with bands like the fiery country-rock act the Walkabouts and Mudhoney who suffered because of the label's early mismanagement. It was harder to feel anything for Dwarves, however, a band most notorious for the cover to their 1990 album *Blood Guts And Pussy*. It showed two naked women and one male dwarf, a dead rabbit covering his vital organ. All three were drenched in fake blood and guts. The thirteen songs therein clocked in at just over fourteen festering minutes of splattercore. There were no redeeming qualities there, either. '*Fuck safe sex,*' 'singer' Blag Jesus ranted on 'SFVD', '*I mean I'd rather not get AIDS but I stopped fucking with a rubber years ago.*' At one stage, Sub Pop fell too deeply into an 'ironic' parody of redneck attitudes: nowhere is this better exemplified than the Dwarves.

Earth were another group who were never going to make too many friends, with their heavy drone sound and their guitarist's fondness for hard drugs and guns. Named after an early incarnation of Black Sabbath, their founder guitarist Dylan Carlson gained notoriety as the man who purchased the shotgun that Kurt Cobain used to kill himself. Kurt contributed to their debut Melvins-inspired 1990 EP 'Extra-Capsular Extraction', as did ex-Melvins bassist Joe Preston and Dickless singer Kelly Canary. Unable to obtain copyright permission for any Nirvana songs, filmmaker Nick Broomfield used Earth tracks as the soundtrack for his footage of Aberdeen in his 1998 'documentary' *Kurt And Courtney*, and the music is ideally suited. It's dark, depressing and relentless.

When Dylan finally made it over to the UK for a live performance he played one of the most minimal shows ever. In preparation, he set up his guitar against an amplifier, and when it was his turn to play, walked on stage and switched the amp on. He then walked off again. After 45 minutes of feedback, he walked back on stage again, and switched the amp off. Check out Earth's third album, 1995's *Phase 3 Thrones And Dominions* for one of Sub Pop's most undervalued releases.

Sorry, this too has little to do with the story I'm telling. Back to the main frame.

'That period from May to September '91, when the distributor was obliged to pay for the records they shipped in May, was particularly dicey,' recalls Jensen. 'The bookkeeper, my boss, just kind of quit coming in to the office and got real hard to reach on the phone. Eventually I took over and worked a couple of months without pay. There was a particular afternoon in early August where a potential investor finally came through on a six thousand dollar loan he'd been promising for weeks. The next day the phones were due to be shut off, the van was to be repossessed and the county tax authorities intended to barricade the premises. I think it was 7 August. Anyway, I got the check from him about four forty-five, shook his hand pleasantly, saw him out the door with a smile and then sprinted several blocks to the bank before it closed at five p.m.'

I want to paint a scene for you. We're at the Showbox on 1st Avenue, 1990. The venue is heaving with people. Everywhere is the smell of human perspiration and the hum of over-loaded amplifiers.

On stage, Mudhoney are just finishing their final encore. Mark is lying heedless to the world, in a sea of bodies, on top, beside and underneath him. Around are the scenes of pandemonium: scattered amplifiers, stage-divers nursing bruised tendons, a bouncer at his wits' end at his inability to retain control over the constant stream of people on and off stage. Steve Turner's guitar is howling like the siren of the sexually possessed. Dan Peters has thumped his way into oblivion. Matt Lukin, meanwhile, has been drinking vodka for fourteen hours straight, and he isn't going to stop now.

'Anyone want more?' he yells to tired cheers.

Loud harsh music pumps out from the speakers. A 50 year old in diapers wanders up to me and asks to be chastised. Toilet walls are covered in piss-stains and graffiti from local musicians boasting of their sexual prowess, plus diatribes against Sub Pop's inner sanctum. Enthusiasm oozes from every adrenaline-charged pore. Mark goes over to where Charles Peterson, the man who defined Seattle's look with his hyper-focused highlights stolen from the music's blurry sea of chaos, is standing vaguely shell-shocked. He checks to see if he's all right, then laughs and rushes backstage to throw up from the heat. Ed from fellow Seattle band, the anarchic Thrown-Ups, tries to balance a few beers on his head, not very adroitly. The beer goes everywhere, splattering a couple of Californian wannabe hipsters. In one corner, Sub Pop's human press dynamo Jenny Boddy chats with Seattle's Queen of Blarney Megan Jasper about the latest outrage perpetuated by Mudhoney manager Bob Whittaker. Man mountain Tad Doyle is surrounded by a phalanx of admirers a quarter his size, cracking open a fresh Mexican bottled beer every five minutes.

Similar scenes happened almost nightly at shows by bands like Fastbacks, the Walkabouts, Tad and a hundred lesser hopefuls. Heads thrust in bass bins, obligatory flannel shirts soaked with beer and perspiration, coloured strobes flashed in a dizzying symphony of light. I became enamoured of Ms Boddy and would stop at nothing to shower her with my drunken affections: on my knees at the Crocodile, engaged in a triple tongue kiss with Nirvana tour manager Alex MacLeod and Mr Whittaker.

Courtney Love later included a song partly inspired by Jenny on her *Live Through This* album, 'Jennifer's Body', a revenge fantasy tale that came about after she became apparently convinced, wrongly, the two of us were in some kind of relationship.

It was in Pike Place Market that I experienced my first taste of margaritas and American-style Mexican food, the latter in the company of heavyweight local celebrity Tad Doyle. A butcher by trade – 'there's nothing bad about it, it's kinda pleasurable, the feel of keen metal cutting into raw flesh' – Tad was determined that my first impressions of America would be lasting ones. He wore a flannel shirt, and talked shit with a gruff, insouciant charm. His sweaty presence and guttural roars belied a sharp, malignant intelligence. I wondered if all Seattle musicians were budding college professors, or whether that was just part of the hype John and Bruce were feeding me. On stage, Tad's band was barely believable. They were *heavy*, with a rhythmic density and repetitive force that recalled the industrial metal of Chicago's Ministry, early Swans and brutal hardcore punks Killdozer.

'We just like to write songs about things we find out of the ordinary, twisted; something dark and wrong underneath the placid and seemingly calm surface of everyday life,' explained guitarist Gary Thorstensen.

Early on, there was a triumvirate of Sub Pop bands, Mudhoney, Tad and Nirvana. Many felt that Tad would be the ones to succeed, but they turned out to be too extreme for popular consumption. It's always a bad sign if more than two British music critics like your band, and Tad got lapped up in London. Tad and his musicians personified the image of Seattle, grizzled Northwest lumberjacks playing slow, recycled seventies metal licks. Albums like the Steve Albini-produced *Salt Lick* with its awesome single 'Wood Goblins', and 1991's *8-Way Santa*, burned with relentless fervour. *8-Way Santa* ran into problems rapidly. Its artwork was retracted after the women whose breasts were pictured being fondled on its front cover threatened to sue. (The original photo had been found in a yard sale.) Tad were the last of the original Sub Pop acts to be signed to a major label and the first to be dropped, when Warner Brothers objected to promotional posters for 1994's *Inhaler* album which featured Bill Clinton smoking a joint and a tagline saying, 'This is heavy shit.'

The scene soon degenerated. Grunge started to die the moment it became exposed to the outside world, as all scenes do. As soon as the hangers-on and major label A&R men in town started to outnumber the creative people, the artists, musicians and fanzine editors.

Indeed, some of the folk who turned up in town after the initial (pre-*Nevermind*) explosion began to wonder whether Seattle people weren't living out their rock fantasies a little too literally: particularly when it came to the town's infamous drug of choice, heroin.

'On my first week at the Off Ramp club,' ex-Sub Pop employee and boss of Seattle tape label *homerecordedculture* Michael John recalls, 'I show up at work early and my boss Jan takes me upstairs to an apartment of an ex-employee, a junkie who stole some money and skipped out. Jan tells me, "Keep what you want and throw the rest away, you might want to wear gloves, I think he shoots up." The room was bright yellow, a pigsty littered with garbage, decorated with porn under a fluorescent light. I went into the kitchen and hanging on the wall was a picture of Christ on the cross; sticking into his neck was an actual needle with blood still in the chamber and dripping off the wall. I just stood there. It was raining outside and below me in the showroom, a shitty band was doing a shitty version of the Mudhoney anthem "Touch Me I'm Sick". I was locked in a cliché.'

Sub Pop began to sign a whole slew of mediocre second and third generation grunge bands – groups who'd mostly only formed in an attempt to cash in on the major label feeding frenzy that was starting to take place. Bands with names like Hazel, Truly, the Supersuckers, Green Magnet School, Sprinkler, Big Chief, Canadians Chixdiggit and Hardship Post.

Of them, a few stood out. Olympia/Tacoma's bratty Seaweed were only ever an average skate/thrash band with excess energy, but I was fond of them not least because the first time I ever encountered shaven-headed singer Aaron he was bouncing up and down on Calvin Johnson's knee like a hyperactive puppy. Aaron shared a Seattle apartment with fellow Olympian Rich Jensen later. He and I would take hitched truck rides into the middle of nowhere and blag chocolate cakes at Denny's Restaurant by telling them it was our birthday, or turn up at hipster parties stone cold sober and scrawl messages on the walls. The band gave interviews about masturbation and surviving on five dollars a day, got signed to Hollywood Records in a reputed million dollar deal, and were last heard of living in California as bleached surfer Gods.

Another second generation grunge band, Portland's Pond, were the cause of my getting in a New York taxi crash: both drivers leapt out and began arguing in different, non-English languages while I tried to explain I really did need to get to this club because . . . Pond were sweet, naïve and initially managed to infuse their suspiciously Pearl Jam-leaning rock with a dreamy, psychedelic quality. These three young men, originally from Alaska, sounded as if they'd grown up mostly in bed. Their songs were about dreams and lack of same, about the summer and golden sun-kissed autumn, about trees, sleds, whether or not to get up, whether or not to use charcoal crayons. One great Sub Pop showcase I saw at San Francisco's Kennel Club in 1992 featured them, Seaweed, the mighty Afghan Whigs – then at the peak of their sixties soul-redefining phase – and lesser lights Love Battery. No one watched Pond except Jonathan and me, and I danced and tried not to feel too jittery from an overdose of coffee.

The pure sixties pop thrills of Seattle's hedonistic Fastbacks – singer Kim Warnick was another Sub Pop receptionist – filled many an otherwise dull night. The Fastbacks' original drummer, Duff, ended up in Guns N'Roses: a fair indication of the band's 'hair' roots. Then there was the cleric of cool, the vicar of vice, the deacon of despair, the very Reverend Horton Heat with his three-piece rockabilly band breaking and saving sinners everywhere he went.

'I've been saving souls for nigh on six years now,' the good man told me over a pitcher of water and a shot or two of rum in a Washington DC diner in 1992. 'All over the land young girls will come up on stage asking for the laying on of hands . . . in Dallas, Austin, Houston . . . up to Memphis, Arkansas, Kansas, the Midwest . . . on to Chicago, Ohio, California . . . We're never off the road. Home is just another city we pass in the night.

'I know I shouldn't do it,' he pleads, 'but I've got my own demons to deal with. Some day I know I'm just gonna walk right with the Lord.'

Kurt Cobain's suicide was the final straw for most. There had been other deaths – Stephanie Sergeant from L7-style female punk band 7 Year Bitch, Andrew Wood from Mother Love Bone, Mia Zapata of the Gits – but none with as much impact.

Suspicious of outsiders by nature, the city's musicians and late-come scenesters retreated into a taciturn near-silence. (Seattle, despite all its Microsoft millions, has retained its parochial small-town attitude through to the present day.) Soundgarden and Alice In Chains split a few years later. The first was partly caused by a deep-rooted hatred of the record industry, the latter by the band's continued dalliance with heroin, the drug long associated with Seattle's Capitol Hill area. Even at the time of writing, seven years after Cobain's suicide, it is still almost taboo to speak of Nirvana, or indeed grunge, in public in the Northwest.

Having your lifestyle laid open to ridicule on the fashion catwalks of Paris and in films like *Reality Bites* and *Singles* will do that to a generation.

I'll Take Care of You
(Screaming Trees, Come)

'Stuck in the pits of Cape Coral/Really gave me the blues/Being stuck in one place too long/Makes me itchy to move/There's got to be a better place/So let's get on the move'

'LET'S GO LET'S GO AWAY', THE WIPERS, 1979

Most of America is far different to the image you may have gained from television of glamorous big cities like Chicago and New York.

It's nothing but mile upon mile of the sanitised, white bread, leafy suburbia of the mid-West. It's the home of *The Simpsons*, Beavis and Butt-head, the kids who populate *Clerks, American Beauty* and the Coen brothers' films. It's composed of towns where it's illegal for non-marital partners to have sex, where anal penetration has long been outlawed, whose idea of 'care in the community' is to shove all the black and Hispanic folk away in some rundown corner so 'respectable' citizens don't have to see them. These towns don't have councils as such, or police forces, but private security systems loaded down with guns guarding important community outposts like the local shopping mall. Towns like Des Moines, Iowa, boast about their 'covered walkways' so designed that the few pedestrians still around don't have to leave the security of air-conditioning behind and experience the outside world.

Checking in to a Marriott/Super 8 motel in Rockford, Illinois, we ask the smiling girl behind the desk where we can get a drink. She looks at us puzzled before replying, 'Well, there are a couple of strip bars on State you might want to check out.'

This is the landscape I associate with Screaming Trees' wind-swept rock music, the flatlands, sprawling Edge Cities that have sprung up, unplanned, along the side of whichever freeway happens to be closest. Screaming Trees create neurotic, classic American rock in the tradition of The Band, 13th Floor Elevators and Canned Heat. Whenever I hear *Dust*, their incredible 1996 album, I'm reminded of hours spent driving through the centre, tanked up on Jack Daniels and cheap enthusiasm, singing lustily along to songs like 'Halo Of Ashes' and the affecting love song 'Look At You' with ace *MM* photographer Steve Gullick. That and the rain-swept streets of Seattle – but *Dust* is too epic an album to be confined to one city alone.

Singer Mark Lanegan's psychedelic blues group don't hail from the States' sanitised and scary centre, however. The jail-hardened singer and his guitarists, the two voluminous Connor brothers, grew up in the tiny provincial town of Ellensberg, Washington, alongside brilliant ideas man, recording artist and producer Steve Fisk. There, in Rodeo Town USA – Ellensberg boasts singing cowboy Roy Rogers' Apple Valley housing development – they all attended the same high school. The Connors' dad was the school principal, thereby assuring the brothers of the hatred of all the locals. Lanegan was a transplant, with a dad in Alaska and relatives in Seattle. Inspired by Black Flag, Iggy Pop and the Gun Club, the three schoolmates formed a band to try to get out. Fisk got the band several LA concerts via his connections with seminal LA hardcore/

experimental label SST. Fellow Ellensberg native Calvin Johnson booked the Trees into a couple of out-of-town shows; Sub Pop's Jonathan Poneman set up some Seattle dates. This is important; more than any musician I know, Lanegan has a fierce streak of loyalty running through him. Courtney Love once called Mark 'the most honourable man I know', and I guess she should know. I digress again.

After recording a tape and album with Fisk, Screaming Trees released several records during the eighties. There was a brilliant, warped collaboration on K/53rd And 3rd with Calvin's Beat Happening, and two albums for SST, home of Sonic Youth, Black Flag and Fisk's own group Pell Mell. When the Trees released *Uncle Anaesthesia* on Epic in 1990, they became the first of their generation of Northwest bands to be picked up by a major, before Soundgarden and Alice In Chains.

Screaming Trees' music – certainly the music they made on *Dust* and its predecessor, 1992's bleak and blistering *Sweet Oblivion*, the band's seventh album – resonates with a sense of isolation more usually found in places like Buttfuck, Idaho. There, the only release for misfits like the Trees is rock music, jail or sports. Lanegan's career as a budding sports star disappeared after he broke a leg falling off a harvesting machine drunk one night. He also has neck injuries sustained from playing football. He had little choice but to become a rock star, beyond hitting the ever-present bottle.

'Rockford is a lot like where I grew up,' the singer told me in July 1996. 'But . . . I never had a thing like this.' Lanegan was referring to the travelling Lollapalooza music show, featuring Metallica and Soundgarden and a cast of thousands, that his band were part of, and on whose stage he had just divested himself of all his sweat-sodden clothes: cowboy hat, massive belt, wallet and all. 'I didn't even have a fuckin' record store. I had to take a Greyhound bus a hundred and twenty miles just to buy punk rock records. Where I grew up, there wasn't even a fuckin' place to buy an electric guitar. And if you made songs on your own, you were ridiculed and made fun of.

'You think we had something like this?' he asks rhetorically. 'Fuck no. Now there is. We're playing 50 miles away from my hometown on this tour. These kids are lucky. They're fucking lucky. They're lucky to have my fucking boots and they're lucky to have my pants. They're lucky to see the Ramones, they're lucky to see [hard-edged Australian band] You Am I, they're lucky to see Metallica for that matter. But maybe if there had been something like this, we wouldn't have started our own band. Maybe we'd have been too busy waiting for Lollapalooza to pass through.'

I knew the mid-West reminded me of the Trees for a reason. It's that sense of grief, the knowledge that life has dealt you a raw hand, the anger you get when stuck in an ad man's wet dream of suburbia. Lanegan's astonishing honeyed, silken baritone growl has been compared to Australia's Nick Cave: fine, but way off the mark. Cave has always been a performer and raconteur, y'see. His tales are of other people: murderers, whores, God and the low-life who populate the novels of the Colombian Nobel Prize winner, Gabriel Garcia Marquez. Lanegan, like the bluesmen of old, has *lived* the tale. A loner by nature, he goes wherever the muse beckons.

One night we're supposed to meet him on the Lollapalooza tour, we wait all evening in our god-forsaken motel for him to make the 35 miles from Freeport Holiday Inn. We scorch the microwave popcorn, bust the toilet and argue over who's our scariest co-habitant, but Mark doesn't show.

'I got caught in a lightning storm,' he growls. 'We ran out of money for the taxi halfway to your hotel, met a couple of strippers, got soaked, had to sleep out in the pouring rain, and finally got home this morning wearing the same clothes as you saw just now. At one point while I was walking through the worst part of town, this car-load of brothers come by with a big-ass water machine gun and squirted me right across the face. They totally nailed me! I started laughing so fucking hard, I had to hold my stomach for two blocks.'

Two days later, the singer comes over to congratulate me on downing a whole bottle of Jagermeister and dancing on stage with Girls Against Boys and Rancid the previous show. 'That was real classic Lanegan behaviour,' he laughs. 'Man, I was concerned for you. I was hosing you down where you lay passed out in the sand and dirt because it must have been ninety-eight in the shade, and we thought you were gonna die. Joey Ramone stopped by and remarked, "Hey man, don't rock the floor." Never mind how I feel, how are you?'

I ask Lanegan if he's bitter that Screaming Trees got passed over during the Seattle gold rush.

'I see it this way,' the singer replies. 'In this business, there are sprinters and there are marathon runners. I'm going to be around while these fuckin' *pissants* have spent their last fuckin' royalty cheque and are living back home with fuckin' grandma. I'll still be out on the road playing tiny fuckin' clubs to fifty people when I'm fuckin' sixty-five years old. And that's fine.'

The Trees recorded an album for release in the spring of '94 but it was scrapped after the death of Lanegan's friend, Kurt Cobain. Only one song made it from those sessions on to *Dust* in 1996, the haunted, darkly affecting 'Dying Days': Kurt had written a song specially for Mark, but he didn't record it. (It wasn't unusual for the warring band to go four years in between albums, incidentally: although the Trees split in 2000, they never made another record after *Dust*.)

'I long ago stopped wishing for the pie in the sky, American dream, beautiful wife, beautiful house on the water, fuckin' nice car,' Lanegan says. 'I've never thought that way. I grew up in a time when we thought we'd never live to see eighteen because there would be a nuclear war and everyone would die. When I first quit drugs and drinking when I was twenty-one and the girl I was really in love with had left me because of it, it was like the first time I really looked at myself – "Man, you're still here and you're twenty-one! You didn't even think you'd make it to eighteen!" Music is the only thing that fuckin' saved me.'

The other band Screaming Trees remind me of are Boston's Come.

Like Screaming Trees, Come touch upon a deep wellspring of American music. In their sound you can hear traces of the backwater Delta blues, the lonesome howl of Robert Johnson, the anguished wail of Bessie Smith, maybe the ruthless poignancy of Patti Smith.

'I grew up listening to the blues,' singer Thalia Zedek told me. 'I was attracted to the depth of feeling. My friends would listen to Fleetwood Mac and Linda Ronstadt, but I always hated that shit. Linda Ronstadt said nothing to me about my life, nor did Stevie Nicks, nor Bread, nor America, nor any of those bands. The blues sounded truer. I never listened much to modern music until I was sixteen when I heard 'Gloria' by Patti Smith on the radio. I was going, "Man, who is this?" I'd never heard a female singer like her before.'

Come communicate such raw, basic emotion it sometimes feels that it'd be easier for all concerned not to tune in . . . if only they weren't so damn beautiful. Life is one long, pointless struggle and only the thoughtless can ever be happy. It's better to give up before you start, then at least the fuckers can't get you. Come's debut single 'Car' on Sub Pop is so suffocating, so chilling, you hope it isn't Thalia inside the song, singing so tonelessly of a life that has already finished. You hope to God it isn't, but can't help feeling otherwise. Of course, she denied the charge.

'My songs aren't autobiographical,' she told me. 'Although that single is about stuff I went through. When I wrote it, I felt that I was in a bad place . . . for want of a better word. I was dragging people around me down into it.'

Unlike Screaming Trees and their more recent Northwest Edge City counterparts, Modest Mouse, however, it's obvious that Come's desperate music could only have originated from the city. This is the sound of individuals struggling to make sense of rain-splattered, lonely streets where everyone slams car doors loudly and takes a gun to the floorboards at the slightest disturbance. Lives that have no way out and nowhere to turn to, either. Whereas the music of Screaming Trees echoes with the cavernous empty spaces of the flatlands, Come seem locked within an ever-decreasing claustrophobic spiral of junk, alcohol and overdue rent demands. This seems true, even on more optimistic latter-day albums like the 1998 Domino release *Gently Down The Stream*.

There are echoes of Thalia's previous groups within the layered, slow burning grooves of Come: Live Skull (New York contemporaries of early Sonic Youth, influence on Pixies, Babes In Toyland etc), Dangerous Birds (the early eighties all-female band who *didn't* want to be the Go-Go's) and the gothic Uzi. You can also hear traces of guitarist Chris Brokaw's other band Codeine on Come's 1992 debut album *Eleven: Eleven*. Codeine, who are actually as white and un-funky as American bands get, released a couple of fragile, trembling albums on Sub Pop – *Frigid Stars*, 1992's aptly-titled *Barely Real* – and inadvertently spawned a genre, slowcore.

Slowcore is a sound best left to the sexless and anal. (No disrespect intended.) Someone worked out that music sounds great stripped right back and left to linger softly in the air. True, but without tunes and the requisite psychedelic loveliness of Flaming Lips, say, or Mercury Rev, it also becomes boring very rapidly. Something of which you could never accuse Come or early Codeine. Like the first few Hole singles, like Babes In Toyland, like those traumatic post-Beatles songs that John Lennon formulated out of primal scream therapy, you *know* Thalia is giving all of herself. The art becomes the life.

It's in the voice, mainly. The way it seems dragged down by layers of hopelessness, the way it reaches up to the heavens only to spiral down again into darkness, the way it cries '*I don't remember being born*' on 1992's 'Fast Piss Blues' and scares the life out of you. It's the rasp within the voice, its nakedness, the way it echoes those youthful moments when life span crazily on its head and you were running wild and free, only for some shit-head to glass your mate in the face.

It kills me the way Thalia sings a line like '*Just relax/Just relax/Just relax*' (from 'Submerge') with such urgency, knowing that's the one thing you'll never be able to do. The guitar and drums swell up behind her voice and then die away again, beaten, only to swell up even more magnificently.

* * *

So why have I placed Screaming Trees in the Sub Pop chapter when (a) they have nothing to do with grunge, and (b) aside from the double single 'Time Speaks The Golden Tongue', they didn't even have a release on the label?

The answer is simple. To date, Lanegan has released four solo albums on Sub Pop. Four albums infused with a grace and grandeur and intensity all the more poignant for its manliness. Four albums that have little to do with grunge or indeed rock music, but are the blues laid bare and eternal. This may seem at odds with Sub Pop's sound. Far from it, though.

When I first voyaged over to the city to pump the label up full with half-formulated hyperbole and promises of grandeur, I was excited by the diversity of its roster. On its touchstone *Sub Pop 200* compilation, for every mediocre pop-punk act like the Fluid – great live band, though – there were Tacoma's garage kings Girl Trouble, the country-sparkled Terry Lee Hale and vastly underrated Walkabouts, and Steve Fisk contributing his usual melodic, keyboard-led madness. For every Cat Butt and (shudder) Blood Circus, there was a Beat Happening, a poptastic Fastbacks, a track from the doomed beat poet Steven J Bernstein.

This diversity spread as the label grew tired of the grunge tag that threatened to hold back all but the dullest. Sure, it's had its hard rock, skate-punk and grindcore: the Supersuckers, youthful Calvin Johnson/Henry Rollins acolytes Seaweed, and Tad. To counter them, though, were bands like local emocore heroes Sunny Day Really Lame and Fisk's dance-led Pigeonhed who scored a minor hit off the back of a Lo-Fidelity Allstars remix. There were Japan's female trash merchants Supersnazz, and the British-looking Velocity Girl and Eric's Trip. The 1992 CD *Afternoon Delight!* even boasted that it was a collection of 'Love Songs from Sub Pop', and with such trembling splendours as the sixties-fed Unrest, Nirvana heroes Vaselines, Mudhoney hero Billy Childish (from Thee Headcoats) and lo-fi champs Sebadoh present, it was hard to deny the charge.

By the mid-to-late nineties, the Sub Pop roster had changed out of recognition. It included music as disparate as alt. country (Pernice Brothers, Mike Ireland), warped electro-pop (Six Finger Satellite), dream-pop (Galaxie 500's Damon & Naomi), K-style cutie pop (England's St Etienne), and traditional Stooges-influenced indie fare (Jesus And Mary Chain). In fact, from a decade before, only Lanegan and the evergreen Mudhoney remained.

In the first few years of the 21st century, the Northwest music scene is in good shape. Much of this is down to the determination of those who stuck around long after the media spotlight shifted elsewhere. People like Up Records' supremo and former Sub Pop receptionist Chris Takino (Quasi, Built To Spill, Modest Mouse) who sadly died at the start of 2001. People like the controversial figure of Jonathan Poneman, even if his label did perform an about-face in 1998–9 and reverted to the sound that made the city famous. Banking on people's taste for nostalgia, Sub Pop released a whole slough of neo-seventies neo-hard rock records: Sweden's Hellacopters, Zen Guerilla, Black Market Babies, the Makers . . . plus a compilation from Mudhoney, and two albums from self-styled local 'bad boys', the Stooges-loving Murder City Devils.

'The scene here is as healthy right now as it's been in years,' producer Jack Endino told me in 2000. 'Reality set in after about a hundred innocent bands got their "big break" during 1991–5, and then were dropped as soon as grunge became unfashionable – and because a lot of them blew. Seattle bands are back to doing it because they want to. Those who wanted a career have wised up and are working at Microsoft, Real Networks, Amazon etc. That leaves just the diehards playing in bands . . .'

'Another pleasing result,' the grunge icon continued, 'is that everyone no longer sounds the same.'

Also, Seattle's neighbour, rival and often unacknowledged influence, Olympia, is finally receiving its rightful kudos. Both Calvin Johnson's lifestyle-defining K records (Dub Narcotic, Crabs, Microphones) and Slim Moon's fiery Kill Rock Stars (Bikini Kill, Sleater-Kinney, Elliott Smith, Lois Maffeo) are fine examples of how self-belief will see you through. Both labels have had links with Nirvana (Kurt Cobain shared an apartment with Slim Moon), and prefer not to admit them. Both have learnt from Sub Pop's dance with fame, and realised that that way forward is not for them. Far better to retain your credibility and audience's trust by sticking to your ideals than to court disaster by bringing in the money boys.

'It feels like we've gone back to the early eighties where all the radio and video channels [were] clogged with pricey softcore porn and dancing spokesmodels,' said Rich Jensen recently. 'It means the inspired kids will go on dreaming up a culture for themselves in their basements and at their house parties with no expectation of being recognised or offered a career in the smiley straight world.'

'Thing is,' he explains, mindful of the recent past. 'If you keep at it, figuring out how to keep going with minimal support, making pen pals over the Internet and sleeping on each other's floors, after five or ten years you end up with a society with your own rules and a new little economy the grown-ups won't understand. Eventually, though, they'll figure it out and start to offer you places at their table. Some of you will go for it, make a little scratch and for a couple years maybe there will be fewer dancing spokesmodels smiling on the television . . .'

So why do we select few rate Lanegan so highly? Do yourself a favour and buy a copy of 1999's *I'll Take Care Of You* and lose yourself within its nuances, and the way it sings of life framed by the ever-present desire to move on but held back by the constant urge to get high. The beauty of this collection of old blues covers – and a Gun Club tribute, for Lanegan's dead friend, singer Jeffrey Lee Pierce – lies in its simplicity. Instrumentation, from ex-Soundgarden bassist Ben Shepherd and Dinosaur Jr's Mike Johnson, among other Northwest notables, is kept to a bare minimum, no song is allowed to linger on past a few desolate minutes. The tales Lanegan chooses to re-tell concern betrayal and restlessness: heartbroken pleas for like-minded souls to save themselves, because no one else will, that's for sure. The hymnal 'On Jesus' Program', for example, is stark and blindingly soulful. This is a man so confident, so assured in his own masculinity and sound that it resonates all across his music. Now that Kurt is dead, Lanegan has the Northwest's finest voice without question.

Check his softened version of 'Where Did You Sleep Last Night?' on 1989's *The Winding Sheet* . . . does the song sound familiar? It should. It's the self-same Leadbelly lament that Nirvana later covered on the ill-advised *MTV Unplugged*: no coincidence either. Krist Novoselic and Kurt Cobain played bass and malevolent guitar on Mark's version. I still think it's possible that *MTV Unplugged* was Kurt's way of paying belated tribute to his friend Mark's troubled muse.

These Northwest bands grew up venerating the same outsider music, the same lonely singers, and would frequent the same remainder bins where they would search out the least cool metal bands. That's why Nirvana's heroes Melvins and late eighties Seattle bands like the U-Men and Green River, and Screaming Trees, and Nirvana themselves all share a bond in common – why they used to swap members without missing a beat. Seattle and the Northwest is an isolated area. Who else is going to lend support?

When I interviewed Screaming Trees in 1996, they had an extra guitarist, name of Josh Homme, along for the ride. Later, he formed the magnificent Queens Of The Stone Age with a passing member of Dwarves and a few Kyuss sorts. QOSA produced 2000's finest rock album, *Rated R*, by remembering the three basic rules of rock music: Keep your metal heavy, economic and repetitive;

know when to start; know when to stop. Lanegan contributed a vocal on the Queens' psychedelic 'In The Fade' that made you yearn for him to start fronting a new rock band immediately. Other contributions came from members of Soundgarden, brilliant hard rockin' bands Fu Manchu and Monster Magnet, and the very legendary Rob Halford of Judas Priest. With a pedigree like that, *Rated R* could hardly miss, and it didn't.

Like Screaming Trees, the Queens are infused with the dusty tang of the desert. They match that dry, arid feel to the time when Black Sabbath still sang about fairies in boots, the Stooges ruled the earth and critics understood the veracity of the phrase 'three chords good, four chords bad'. Back when rock was still rock, men were still men and small purple flowering weeds at the bottom of my garden were still small purple flowering weeds at the bottom of my garden.

Metal was a good, a decent, a proper thing back in the late sixties – and again in the late eighties when the Northwest grabbed hold of the genre. In 2000, someone finally realised that again.

Memories of Mudhoney
(Mudhoney)

'Here comes sickness walking down my street/Shaking her hips like she's some kind of treat/All the neighbourhood dogs licking at her feet/Here comes sickness/Here comes sickness/Here comes sickness walking down my street'

'HERE COMES SICKNESS', MUDHONEY, 1988

Newcastle Riverside, Spring 1989 This tour was Mudhoney's first attempt to introduce grunge to an unsuspecting Britain. It was mayhem; pure rock'n'roll stripped back to the bone. Sweat, stamina, steam, sinews, stage-diving, sex, spontaneity, swan-diving, singles and serendipity. There couldn't have been a student union in the country at the time that didn't explode into a riot of moshing at the sound of the opening chords of Mudhoney's debut UK single 'Touch Me I'm Sick'. This was Hendrix played badly with the amps turned up full; twenty years of rock history reinvested with emotion and soul by four no-nonsense working class Seattle lads. How do I like my music? Simple, direct, soulful and rockin'! This band could've been designed specifically for me, with their fondness for destruction. At their laconic best, Mudhoney were untouchable.

I was supposed to introduce the band in Newcastle, then stage-dive straight into the crowd. Dressed in my best suit, I managed the first part OK – with plenty of swear words during the introduction for that extra rock credibility, which I dutifully reported back to *Melody Maker* – and then attempted the second. The crowd threw me straight back on to the stage, where guitarist Steve Turner was already tearing through the super-charged 'Here Comes Sickness'. So I rushed backstage, only to find my way barred by Kim Gordon of Sonic Youth, whom Mudhoney were supporting that evening. 'Uh-uh. You're supposed to be stage-diving,' she informed me. So I rushed back on and off the stage, only to be thrown back on five more times, the crowd was so densely packed. Eventually I clambered off the side of the stage, shamefaced. The humiliation didn't stop me from moshing like a wild beast, though.

'Fuck the kids!' as Mark used to joke. 'Except the kids who buy our records . . . Then they're fucking themselves!'

Seattle, February 1989 I first met Mark Arm, Steve Turner, Matt Lukin and Dan Peters in the Virginia Inn opposite the Sub Pop Terminal Sales Building on 1st Ave. In retrospect, Mudhoney gave me a very warped idea of what American rock bands were like, that they all possessed a brilliantly developed, evil sense of humour and endless stores of enthusiasm. The 'Honey spent the majority of their *Melody Maker* cover story making stuff up, and I loved it.

'The streets over here are paved with grunge,' singer Arm joked with me, in a remark he almost certainly grew to regret. 'We all used to work at Muzak,' he claimed. 'All the people from Sub Pop: me, Tad, Bruce and John [the two Sub Pop bigwigs], Grant from the Walkabouts, Chris from Swallow. We spent our whole time boxing up tapes and sending them to restaurants to corrupt people's minds. All that elevator music was our fault. The whole Sub Pop corporate image is a burn on that.'

We drank Corona beer and shots of tequila, and discussed the Stooges, Seattle's Bundle Of Hiss and Steve's locker in Junior High. Live, Mudhoney were like nothing I'd ever seen: heavy metal matched to basic pop, loose and unpredictable. Matt would spin out entire *minutes* holding his bass above his head. Meanwhile Mark would be bawling to the audience, fixing them in that mischievous full-on glare of his, and Steve was tripping over his guitar case.

'We're probably the clumsiest band in town,' Steve explained. 'We fall down a lot.'

'My sense of balance has deteriorated,' clarified Mark. 'When you get to your mid-twenties, it becomes really hard to stay on your feet. We want to compete with the younger kids who are jumping around and *landing*.'

I'd never hung out with rockers under the age of 30 before. Lemmy from Motörhead, yes, young rockers, no. And Jesus did Mudhoney rock!

Amsterdam, 1995 This was the first time I bumped into the grunge trailblazers after Cobain's death and all its attendant bitterness. For the first and only time, Arm seemed openly hostile towards me, perhaps seeing me as being in Courtney's camp. (Mark, alongside plenty of others, initially blamed Ms Love for her husband's death.) Snide comments were thrown my way, mostly along the lines of being a sycophantic, fame-chasing groupie, one who'd ignore his friends in the pursuit of a good story. They didn't say this exactly, of course. I could just feel the vibes in the air. Nonetheless, we were happy to see one another, even in such strained circumstances. Amsterdam is a good city.

Still, Mudhoney did get one incredible song out of their temporary hatred towards Courtney, the blistering punk single 'Into Your Shtik'. The only record I could possibly compare this blinding, vitriolic, full-on 'fuck you' to would be Thee Headcoats' two-chord thrash 'We Hate The NME'. Hear both now! Mark Arm left no one in any doubt whatsoever as to whom he held responsible for Kurt Cobain's death. *'Why don't you blow your brains out too?'* he demanded, screaming over a guitar line that scorched paint where it fell. It's rumoured that the single was also directed at Winona Ryder, Dave Pirner (Soul Asylum) and other industry insiders, agents and DJs. I made it Single Of The Week in *MM*, probably because of, rather than despite, the line which mentioned the *'scum-sucking leeches who shovel your shit'*. I had an uncanny feeling the criticism of Courtney's hangers-on was justified.

This diatribe must have had particular resonance for Courtney. Not only were Mudhoney a major influence on her husband's band, through both their attitude and music, but the lady had once confided to me that the original blueprint of Hole was based on the 'Honey. Indeed, she did say that the name Hole came from Mark Arm, although I can't exactly recall the connection now (something to do with drugs, I think).

Seattle, WA, 1998 Fulfilling a dream I'd had since first picking up an American superhero comic at the age of thirteen, I was finally living in the States, albeit temporarily. I'd returned to the city that I almost destroyed with my love: I'd written about it and the whole world's attention had then turned its way. So I celebrated the event by calling a debate on the state of music between rockers both old and new for my new employers, the iconoclastic street paper the

Stranger. Steve Turner and Tad turned up, each with their sense of humour and cynicism wickedly intact.

'There are some parts of Seattle I'm scared to walk,' said twenty-stone Tad. 'The first year I moved here I was mugged on Olive . . . course, it would've helped if I could've ran. "Stand and deliver, Doyle!"'

Turner, by now, was releasing records on his Super Electro label, championing garage-style, raw-boned bands that sounded remarkably similar to his own. He seemed to have lost the chip on his shoulder that both he and Mark had temporarily gained during Nirvana, Soundgarden and Pearl Jam's ascendancy to fame. Here was a man happy with himself once more. It was so great to see him like that again. I missed every show Mudhoney played during my tenure in Seattle, though. Perhaps I was scared they might expect me to stage-dive once more.

Bremerton, WA, 1991 (Endfest)   I wrote a one-line review of the Verve from this festival, pointing out what a national embarrassment they were. Years later, their former manager held a glass aloft near my face in a London club in a manner that made me a little nervous, but not as nervous as the possibility of him changing his mood and kissing me instead. I eventually discovered the problem. 'You once wrote that the Verve should be bottled off stage and they were!' he raved. No, I replied sedately. That doesn't sound like me, no imagination. I may have said they should be thrown down the stairs and have their fingers broken one by one so they could never inflict their horrible sound on my ears again, but I would never have written anything like that. I was winding him up. I'd never written that either. Oddly, the explanation didn't placate him.

. . . Now I come to think about it, I saw the Verve at Lollapalooza in 1994. It was the Charlatans I laid into at Bremerton. Ah well. All these fine, sun-baked American festivals and crap English rock bands tend to merge into one.

Mudhoney were sweeter than a very sweet thing indeed that afternoon. Never has a band been named so aptly: equal lashings of muddy sound and honeyed harmonies. Even now, it's almost impossible to hear their first album *Superfuzz Bigmuff* or any of the fine, two-fingered salutes to the commercial market on their debut major label excursion, *My Brother The Cow*, without my chest racing up and meeting my mouth halfway. These kids could ROCK!

London Astoria, 1991   We're backstage after a show, and I'm drunk as usual. Waking up in one of those rare moments of clarity you get when totally frazzled, I'm suddenly aware that Mark Arm has walked into the room, and is joking about something to his band-mates. What's that he's saying to Steve? 'The Legend! has scored.' Hold up, that's me!

I look around in a haze, and find Courtney Love on one knee and a voluptuous PR on another fighting over me. Well, they're fighting about something, certainly. I'm not dreaming this. I *think*. I don't understand how I'm in this situation. Does glamour surround me at every turn? At least two members of Mudhoney take photos as evidence.

One of my fondest memories from those crazy, fucked-up years involves Mudhoney's manager Bob Whittaker. He was driving me back to my hotel after a late-night party along a sidewalk in his huge limousine. A terrified major label record company executive was sitting cowering in the back. At one point, there was a hedge coming up on one side, a lamppost on the other, and I knew there was no way we could make it through intact. So I leant across the front seat . . . and started to strangle Bob and to punch and hit him.

It was the only possible reaction, given the circumstances.

Brighton, England, 2000 If you're looking for one band that sum up the spirit of those early Sub Pop years, then look no further. The more I think about Mudhoney over the years, the more I love them. The 'Honey started almost by accident, never expecting to make any money . . . unlike certain other Northwest musicians. The only thing the four members have ever cared about is the music.

Chaps!

'Fame and fortune [were] never a motivating factor,' Mark told me in 2000. 'Looking back, I've kind of decided that I've been doing vaguely the same thing since 1980. It's been like this rock'n'roll, punk rock thing. It's always trashy, loose and usually loud in one form or another. I don't know why, but it's what I'm drawn to. It's rare that any of the bands I've admired and respected were popular on any level, the exceptions being Alice Cooper, Black Sabbath, Jimi Hendrix and Creedence Clearwater. So I knew from the get-go that we'd never be rich.'

What has been your proudest achievement?

'Getting away with it,' he replied instantly. 'The whole thing has been somewhere between a miracle and a gift. To tell you the truth, when I started playing, inspired by punk rock and hardcore and stuff, it was inconceivable that I could quit my day job and start being a musician. I never imagined in a million years that anything

I was doing musically could be remotely involved with a popular trend. If I'd known that at the time, I probably would have started doing something else.'

Seattle, WA, 2001 Mudhoney have just finished a storming set at the old Off Ramp, one that could have happened any year of the past decade; three attempts on 'Touch Me I'm Sick', Charles Peterson thrashing his head next to me, beer poured over sweat-addled bodies and all.

I'm in the corner nursing a quiet glass of Coke, no ice. In the centre of a packed floor of drinkers, Bob Whittaker is holding court. He's falling over, leering, holding his mobile phone the wrong way up to his ear and issuing orders, propped up by sympathetic security men. 'I'm being under served!' he roars accurately before adding mendaciously, 'I'm on fire!' Seeing our coterie of *Stranger* drinkers he makes his way over and lurches at us, falling splat upon the table. Cue mayhem and much hilarity.

Suddenly, a drunken lucidity overcomes Bob – he's been REM's tour manager for years now, you know – and he spots me. 'Hello Jerry,' he remarks, coming over and shaking my hand politely, 'didn't know you were in town.' The next moment, he's back into his act full swing, yelling at the top of his voice. He stumbles towards the *Stranger* table again, and proceeds to give everyone a full frontal, trousers and pants down. The room explodes in laughter, and a passing Irish band – Therapy?, in town to record with Jack Endino – start chanting, 'There's only one Sammy Hagar,' in reference to Bob's unruly mop of curly blond hair.

A wannabe hipster sitting near to Fastbacks singer Kim Warnick and myself begins to whine. 'How come whenever I behave like that, no one laughs?' We look at the moron, sadly. Some people never get it.

Fell on Black Days
(Soundgarden)

'Bart Simpson has more to do with grunge than we do.'
BEN SHEPHERD, *MELODY MAKER*, 25 MAY 1996

It's 1996. There's an oppressive cloud hanging over the Northwest. People talk in hushed voices, looking downwards onto streets filled with grime and torn paper. I'm seated in Linda's, the Sub Pop hang-out ever since about '92, but a bar I'd managed to ignore up till then, preferring instead my old hang-outs of the Comet, and

Eileen's up on Broadway with the bright lights and pint glasses full of chilled vodka, no ice. Around me are seated the Seattle old guard: producer Steve 'Pigeonhed' Fisk, Sub Pop founder Bruce Pavitt, slightly deaf photographer Charles Peterson, Soundgarden guitarist Kim Thayil. A couple of the newer breed of Sub Pop musicians sit nearby, awed by our august presence. We're another generation. Kurt is dead, and the taste of hype that was so sweet when it was just me and a couple of my companions creating it has long turned sour in our mouths. It's my first visit to the city in eighteen months. As ever, the weather is brilliant and sunny, throwing the leafy, spacious streets into sharp relief, mocking all the dark lyrics and moodiness that have become the city's musical stock-in-trade.

Bruce chooses his moment well. Once we're all assembled, he tells us that he actually bothered to turn up to work that morning, only to tender his resignation. He doesn't feel the company bears much resemblance to the one that grew out of his Sub Pop column in the *Rocket* during the eighties. He wants to buy a warehouse, host dance parties, get away from this stinking beast that no one calls grunge even as a joke nowadays. Except, that is, for all the bands that followed from the outside like Candlebox, Alice In Chains and Silverchair. He wants to build a house on an island: follow the teachings of LSD guru Timothy Leary, maybe start a book imprint.

We drink to that, and old times.

Later, I'm sitting in a millionaire's club with Kim and Soundgarden singer Chris Cornell. We're looking at a pamphlet detailing the addresses of Seattle's more famous musicians, plus the sites of infamous drug busts and deaths, with matching photos. It's a Seattle version of Hollywood's Map Of The Stars. The pair tell me about a long-running cable TV programme called *Kurt Cobain Was Murdered*, the gist of which is . . . ah, you guessed it. The room is massive, opulent, adorned with busts and gold leaf like its founders believed in the veracity of Ancient Rome's splendours. You could fit a football pitch between the occasional resident. I check my jeans, and notice that they no longer have holes. We sprawl in armchairs not designed for scum like me. Somewhere far above my head is the ceiling.

I feel dwarfed, insignificant like Charlie Brown or his nineties cartoon counterparts *Calvin and Hobbes* staring at the night sky. Why am I here? What is my purpose? Are rock musicians really so paranoid that the only place they feel secure hanging out is a place designed for arms dealers and corporate stealers? I don't understand what we're doing talking in such sterile surroundings. Chris speaks in a near whisper. I can barely hear him as he attempts to explain why the band's new album *Down on The Upside* is so dark.

Your new album seems a little bit . . .

'Too sober?' the singer suggests.

I was going to say diverse, chaotic.

'Yeah, that's sort of true,' he agrees sombrely.

'It's like a dust devil or something, with different objects floating,' says the band's main songwriter, bassist Ben Shepherd, later. 'It's not as dark as before. In Japan when we last met, I was ready to jump out one of those windows. I was on a downward spiral. I thought it was all falling apart. There's a weird delirium I get if I have a lack of sleep going on where everything becomes too surreal and too fragile.'

Do you agree with the people who describe Soundgarden as depressing?

'Everything is sometimes,' Shepherd says. 'I thought *Super-unknown* was pretty optimistic, inspirational. It might have spoken of dark things or a dark feeling but there was always something in it, even lyrically, that suggested, "Hey you've hit the bottom, now there's only up." It offered people a chance to get dark without having to be there. Having said that, I've never written a song that'd make you laugh.'

I'd say. My main memory of meeting Soundgarden in Japan '94 was being out late, drinking triple-strength Long Island Iced Teas at the Underground club. I shattered Ben's concept of Western culture by informing him that it was Jane Fonda, not Raquel Welch, who starred in *Barbarella* – one of several, mostly Kung Fu films starring Bruce Lee that were showing on screens behind us. We had a long drunken discussion on how we both see people as shapes, blurred impressions, rather than actual figures. It was snowing gently as we walked back from the club, incapable. Ben threw a glass. It shattered on the street. 'Respect the country,' a female voice admonished us.

'Tokyo is like the part of the beach where all the garbage washes up,' the bassist later told me during a bleak diatribe against the music business. 'I used to feel way more into this whole business. Now I play the songs and get the fuck out of there. There's always something slowing the process down, some dumb kid whacking some other kid in the head. It never stops.'

MM journalist Mat Smith once recounted a story wherein Soundgarden threw a hissy fit because their van driver refused to drive them to the doors of a club where they were playing, 200 yards away. They sat there, arms folded, until the coach finally moved. Frowngarden, as they were known in the office, for their moody lyrics and pompous self-regard.

Years later in 1999, I bear witness to a Kim Thayil paranoia fit. He and Matt the Tube from the Jim Rose Circus are chugging beers at five a.m. in my Capitol Hill flat that I share with ex-Nirvana and Hole soundman Craig Montgomery and sister Carrie, ex-girlfriend of both Mark Arm and Mark Lanegan. Suddenly, Kim notices that the red light on top of Craig's phone is flashing.

'Are you recording this, man?' he roars, oblivious to the fact his band split up some months before.

I get mad. I think he's accusing me of being a scummy tabloid-style journalist, so I turn on him. 'Oh, so because I'm a music critic I must be like the lowest of my breed. Well get the fuck out of my house, you drivelling session musician!'

Matt, meanwhile, is trying to separate the pair of us.

We might have loved their music, and the individuals when they weren't being too insecure, but Christ, could Soundgarden be obstreperous.

Early on, Soundgarden threw in some humour to offset the pomp. Their debut SST album, 1989's patchily astounding *Ultramega OK*, contained a cover of John Lennon's finest ever moment, 'One Minute Of Silence'.

'We had a minute to fill on the record,' explained original bassist Hiro Yamamoto in Holland.

'The real deciding factor was that we knew there wouldn't be any publishing problems, because you can't copyright silence,' added Chris.

Then there was the psychedelic, spooked-out instrumental '665–667', the two neighbours of the beast, which fitted neatly either side of the epic 'Beyond The Wheel'. Not entirely seriously, Chris explained Kim came up with the idea while he was levitating above a shopping mall, that if 666 is the number of the beast then the numbers either side must be all-encompassing. 'He thought that once it was played, the Pentagon would actually levitate.' The band's live show at the time included a version of the Beatles' 'Everybody's Got Something To Hide Except For Me And My Monkey' – a song later covered just as effectively by brilliant Welsh hard rock band 60ft Dolls.

At Soundgarden's first UK show, I helped their PR Charlie Inskip (of Real Time Travel Agency, as it became known after my cheekiness in constantly requesting trips from them out to America to see my friends) lift out table after broken table that the stage had been resting on. Earlier, the security men had walked out of the London college venue, claiming conditions were untenable: they also objected to our edict that no kid should be roughed up for stage-diving. The pay-off came when Cornell launched into one of his ear-splitting screams fuelled by one of the loudest sound systems ever, and the crowd clambered as one up on to the stage to be thrown off by a handful of friends. Cue mass confusion. Anyone walking into the hall late was almost physically forced back out through the door by the waves of noise billowing from Kim's guitar. Sub Pop's early image was encapsulated within the beards and shoulder-length hair of Kim and Chris being tossed around furiously in time with the giant squalls of sound: male, but blisteringly fine nonetheless.

During our first interview, Cornell and a youthful Thayil tried to light their farts in their Dutch hotel room. The drinking was intense. Drummer Matt Cameron has vivid recollections of seeing me puking up blood in his sink in our shared room. In the same interview, Chris claimed he modelled his high-pitched wail on his mum screaming at him when the police came round. Oddly, in an annual poll of Best Bands to play at Holland's famed Vera Groningen venue that year, The Legend! came several places higher than Soundgarden after my impromptu support slot. Perhaps it was the disruption caused during the Seattle band's set when T-shirt man (and future Pearl Jam tour manager) Eric brought me down with a rugby tackle after I'd sung with Chris on an ad-libbed version of 'Some Enchanted Evening'.

Who knows?

Years later, I'm on stage in a shopping mall in Osaka. Chris Cornell has just announced me as special guest mid-set to the confusion and polite delight of 500 hard rocking Japanese Soundgarden fans. The following night, the band's tour manager has to physically lift me out of my seat after the band's set, I'm so gone.

'I'm used to doing this with rock stars,' he announces to the world at large, shaking his head. 'But rock journalists . . .?'

Here's what I like about rock. Anything that isn't flash, that does the job.

That's not true. I revel in flash. I love bands that dress up, who look the part. Give me the surrealist, Futuristic robots of Kraftwerk over a million 'new' American punk/frat bands or Blur, who can't even be bothered to change out of their street clothes to climb on stage. Give me the sleazy, easy cocktail dress of jazz chanteuses

Billie Holiday and Carmel rather than any band who believe that looking smart is paying to advertise someone's label on your shirt. I'm resolutely camp in my fashion tastes. My ideas of glamour were shaped by sixties British TV game shows, most obviously *The Generation Game* as hosted by Bruce Forsyth. I love the Spice Girls, Barbie Dolls and any traditional female diva. That's what so attracted me to Courtney Love initially. Really.

Still, it remains true . . . when it comes to rock groups I've always been a little alienated by smoke bombs, by stiletto heels, by eyeliner. I've never quite understood it, thought that the early seventies androgyny of boorish stars like Bowie and Bolan was simply another excuse for male rock critics scared of the potential of women to celebrate more men. Image was never much of a substitute for content for me. That's why I've always hated and despised the long line of Rolling Stones imitations, from Aerosmith, Guns N'Roses, Black Crowes, Poison, the Verve onwards. If it has to rock – and yes, it *has* to rock – then let it be basic, heavy, strong and unashamed. I've always thought that space, silence between the grooves, is one of the most vital aspects of any band's sound.

I grew up on Motörhead, UFO, AC/DC. How could I think otherwise?

Balance that against rock's tendency to be out-and-out macho. No wonder I avoided the genre for so long. I know we all like to indulge in a few playground fantasies now and then. It's just that mine never revolved around the typical boy thing of chicks, dicks and cars. So I was a freak. But I knew that I couldn't be alone.

'We are a male band, and there's no way round it,' Kim told me in Japan. 'We're also incredibly fair and intelligent. We're not criminals. We're not abusive. We don't exploit women or people we come into contact with. Maleness is no more an obnoxious quality than being effeminate. We're not pick-up driving, beer guzzling, "Hey, look at the pussy on her!" guys. Our maleness comes from our creativity, our aggression and our intelligence. When I was younger, I had a real problem with maleness. Between the ages of 18 and 25 I thought that was the thing that sucked most. I felt that in itself it was wrong, and I was very protective towards women I came into contact with.

'But it's very macho to say that, to behave in such a condescending fashion,' Thayil added, sighing. 'It's one thing to respect someone, it's another to be someone's dad and say, "Women should be treated like this! Homosexuals should be treated like this! And dumb pig men shouldn't do this!" It's probably true, but you can't treat people like children. That's also a very male, heterosexual thing to do. Maleness is something we, as Soundgarden, wrestled with for a long time.'

I'm certain that Soundgarden and their Sub Pop brethren weren't the first cool metal bands. It sometimes seemed that way, though. Would Bruce Pavitt, a champion of unknown bands through both his newspaper column and tape label, have released Soundgarden's 1986 'Screaming Life' EP if the band had been jerks? I doubt it. (OK, I know Jonathan signed them. I'm making a point.) It was almost mandatory for Seattle bands to have cool attitudes because of their joint metal and punk influences.

Soundgarden always were more Ozzy than Dio, early Plant than Palmer, right from the start. *Louder Than Love* betrayed their love for early seventies riff-o-mania long before it became fashionable again, while 1991's *Badmotorfinger* was merely a continuation of their overriding regard for Black Sabbath guitarist Tony Iommi's fretwork. People said they sounded like Led Zeppelin: I'm sure that was true. Certainly Cornell's high-pitched vocals and sex god bare chest seemed familiar even to me, a rock virgin. I've long maintained, however, that the past has no bearing whatsoever on what is happening right up there on stage in front of you . . . as Soundgarden proved countless times.

The last time I saw Soundgarden, they were in Spain or somewhere, 1997 or some time, fending off advances made towards them by a drunk English journalist clutching beakers filled with gin in each hand, there to interview Metallica. I remember little of their support slot, except they refused to allow me on the arena stage beforehand to introduce it. I do recall, however, that songs like 'Black Hole Sun', 'Fell On Black Days' and 'Blow Up The Outside World' resonated with a dark, gothic splendour like nothing could exist outside their cavernous sound and Chris's brooding, shrieking wail. They sounded like the end of the world, almost literally. They sounded so final, so total that I could forgive them all the pomp, the bluster, the occasional rock star attitude, the sulks and fits.

Kurt's death wasn't the end of grunge. Examine the sales figures. Those who had jumped on the bandwagon late and called themselves 'grunge' sold far more post-1994 than the entire Sub Pop catalogue put together. The end of grunge came when Soundgarden split at the end of the nineties and Chris Cornell released that rather ill-advised stab into Billy Joel territory with his 1999 solo album – even though the band had existed mostly outside of the Seattle 'scene'.

Now, if only someone could tell Bush and whoever is next off the production line, we could all get some sleep.

Grunge Lite

Pomp and Circumstance
(Smashing Pumpkins)

'Some people are just so full of shit. I want the pill he has. The pill that makes him so fucking important.'

KIM DEAL (BREEDERS) ON BILLY CORGAN, BIG DAY OUT FESTIVAL, AUSTRALIA 1994

Pomposity isn't automatically to be avoided in rock music.

I personally prefer music kept raw, simple, direct. Yet one of my favourite singers – Kevin Rowland of Dexys Midnight Runners – is also, undeniably, one of the most pretentious. He used to ban alcohol from his shows, believing that substance abuse interfered with the purity of his soul vision. He took out full-page adverts in the music press rather than speak to journalists, fearing they would warp his words. He and fellow conspirator Kevin Archer banned their group from speaking to other groups, and designed a blueprint for life that annoyed a fair subsection of the press and music fans alike. Unable to cope with the impossibly high standards placed upon them, the collapse of Rowland's first and second bands left him in high dudgeon. None of that mattered, though. Why? Kevin had *soul*. His music was shot through with both intense paranoia and a basic humanity that touched every quavered note he sang and every mirror-bright brass refrain. When he based his third album *Don't Stand Me Down* around an extended fifteen-minute argument between himself and a band member – oh, ultimate pretension – he did so because he felt a burning desire to communicate a love that went deeper than words.

OK then. Pomposity without humanity is bad. And, as *MM* critic Jennifer Nine memorably remarked in her review of Smashing Pumpkins' flatulent and festering *Melon Collie And The Infinite Sadness* 1995 opus, there wasn't enough of 'the milk of human kindness present to make a cup of tea'.

It still doesn't mean you can dismiss a band for being pompous and soulless. Look at Queen. No one is in much denial that Freddie Mercury could be a complete dickhead when he chose, and no one bought seventies albums like *A Night At The Opera* for their sensitive insights into human nature either. It was the opposite, in fact. People loved Queen for the bombast, the vast explosions and the overkill. Only a singer as arrogant as Mercury could have sung 'We Will Rock You', 'We Are The Champions' and that ultimate faux-angst fest 'Bohemian Rhapsody'. Magnificent, they were too, if you could forgive Freddie his operatic but essentially grating voice. (I couldn't for decades.) Queen at their height were unstoppable: Lloyd-Webber's musicals given fresh, weird shapes, the Who's grandiose vision for rock music taken to extremes.

The Who, though, were appalling around the time of their 1969 rock opera *Tommy*, as bad as Smashing Pumpkins at their most histrionic. Why?

It's for this reason. If you're not going to mix your pompous tendencies with humanity, if you can't handle putting any emotion into your music, then at least learn to laugh at yourself! Think Queen, and what image comes into your head? Freddie Mercury mincing around in a leather skirt, doing the vacuum cleaning during the video to 'I Want To Break Free', Mercury making lewd, suggestive forays into sexism with 'Fat Bottomed Girls'. (All right, so Queen's humour could be seriously bad.) I'm not saying that a band's every action should be tempered with a knowing wink, a crafty nudge like in that famous *Monty Python* 'suggestive' sketch. Heaven knows, I abhor post-modern artists like Beck and late eighties 'joke' indie/hip hop act Pop Will Eat Itself. The ability to laugh at oneself, though, is a fundamental. It's also an ability that I think Billy Corgan and his Smashing Pumpkins sadly lack.

See much humour in their music, beyond that appalling CD title pun *Melon Collie And The Infinite Sadness*? Exactly. I have a vague feeling I made that joke in a singles column about six months earlier, incidentally.

There's one more thing. Pomposity is almost invariably a male attribute. It would be ridiculous to claim that women can't be prigs – look at Alanis Morissette, for land's sakes – but it seems that females usually temper conceit with a little soul and humour. This is probably because women have been the underclass for so long, and it's the losers who need their humour. The winners have no cause for it. Hence the lack of the ability to laugh at oneself in your average American.

Who cares if an artist is 'honest' either? As Bertolt Brecht once said, 'the guile-less word is folly'. History is about perception: any given situation can be viewed in countless differing ways. Honesty *per se* does not exist. Also, it can often be much more fun when the artist wears a mask or takes on a persona, rampantly lying as if his or her career depends on it. Where would life be without a little confusion and mendacity? Pop music cannot exist in a vacuum; the concept runs contrary to its very nature. As for the whole debate against manufactured bands . . . I have three names to throw at you: the Ronettes, the Spice Girls and the Supremes. Still feel like arguing?

Don't be so superficial.

After I reviewed a Smashing Pumpkins appearance at Reading Festival 1991, Billy Corgan informed a fellow *Maker* critic that he'd written 'Rocket' from the dreadfully overwrought *Siamese Dream* about me. The initial review was fairly innocuous: something about how the Pumps weren't particularly good, or feminine, or soulful, or honest, or any of those things Billy was so laughably claiming for himself. I stated *my* truth boldly, yet without rancour. In response, he told the journalist that he'd been moved to write the song after figuring he would rather take a rocket ship away from this earth, never to see anyone again, than spend five minutes in my company.

I have no idea if he was joking. It's possible, although even his main supporters had to admit that humour wasn't exactly Bill's strong point. See above. Bill was too single-mindedly ambitious and felt his music far too important to waste time on such trivial, lesser emotions.

He was also obsessed with Courtney Love, whom he's dated on and off over several years, and through her, Kurt Cobain. Kurt, needless to say, hated Billy: seeing him as a clown, a charlatan, fraudulent and virtually bereft of talent too. Corgan would frequently stoop to making references to Ms Love in early nineties interviews, in misguided attempts to lend weight to his own sorry muse. For example, when he suddenly discovered that he had a 'feminine' side to his music in the wake of Nirvana's success, he qualified the statement by adding 'that's a very Courtney Love thing to say'. Like Courtney is the final bastion of feminism! All Courtney ever wanted was success on *everyone else's terms*, not her own. Hence the boob jobs and flirtations with Hollywood nobility as she strives to loose herself of her individuality and become *just another starlet*. Sorry, I'm getting ahead of myself.

Mostly, however, Billy seems to me to be a pitiful, self-deluded Cobain wannabe. So deluded, in fact, that even to the present day

he doesn't understand why more critics don't give him respect. Er
... because your music is woefully pretentious, doesn't even have
the basest spark of humanity within it, and could only appeal to an
eleven-year-old with aspirations to be thirteen, perhaps? Sorry. I've
allowed myself to be diverted. Back to the main story.

If Corgan was joking when he made that comment about
'Rocket', he certainly regretted it shortly afterwards when I wrote
an 'answer' live review of a Pumpkins show at Chicago's Metro club
in 1993. The article started by drawing a line in the sand between
what I perceived as soulful music (Nirvana) and the fakers (Soul
Asylum, Porno For Pyros, Smashing Pumpkins). It continued by
making reference to Billy's chest-clutching falsetto and went on to
accuse the band of being a calculated, sordid amalgam of every
saleable moment in rock from the last fifteen years (ELO, Warrant,
Jane's Addiction, Soundgarden). The final paragraph was particularly choice:

> Someone recently made a remark to the effect that God is cruel,
> and it's just not right that all those perfectly poised goths like
> Bauhaus' Peter Murphy and David Sylvian should have no talent
> while fat chumps like Cocteau Twins' Robin Guthrie have the
> magic. It's perfectly fair! Billy Corgan is a media slut, a corporate
> whore in the lowest, most pitifully sycophantic way. He doesn't
> have a trace of originality, of poetry, *of soul* inside of him. He is
> all smugness, all knowing steals and money-grabbing finesse. He
> is an irritation, a minor one, but one which grows with each
> passing sales figure.

The day the article appeared, his press agent called up and
cancelled *Melody Maker*'s forthcoming trip to the States for a cover
feature. On every date on the UK tour that followed, he dressed up
in a clown suit for the encore, in riposte to my calling him a
'clown'.

'I'm a faker, I'm a media whore, I'm a complete phoney!' he
raged from on stage during the entire month of September 1993. 'I
just hope all of you can make up your own minds.'

It was kind of Billy to credit me with that much power over
people, but truth to tell I never possessed a thousandth of what he
was implying.

Several times, he refused to go on stage until his manager had
made sure the venue was cleared of my presence even if I wasn't
there, and at one year's Reading Festival Billy came looking for me
with a bodyguard in tow. Maybe they wanted to make up a

foursome to play Scrabble, but I doubted it. It became a favourite topic of conversation, something to dine out on: 'How's the feud with Billy going?' Once, shortly after Kurt had killed himself, Courtney tried to introduce me to Billy. She made us shake hands as industry scumbags chattered and knocked back doubles of Maker's Mark around us in a tiny Philadelphia bar. His grasp felt clammy to the touch.

It seemed absurd that an artist selling millions of albums could be so insecure and up his own arse that he could be so upset by one critic, but perhaps it was what I represented. Back then, I was the Dude, and didn't Billy know it. His record company had early on tried to fly me out to Chicago to interview the singer/musician. I refused. I was always up for a trip to America, especially to Chicago, where I could hang with my Urge Overkill buddies and discover fresh and exciting tiki bars, but unfortunately someone had played me his songs.

I didn't like them at all. It was obvious even then Smashing Pumpkins were going to be massive.

Other times, I was even more succinct in my insults.

One Smashing Pumpkins single I dismissed with a concise two-word insult, thus reprising a motif that I'd used earlier to surprisingly devastating effect on Paul Weller's comeback solo single. I thought I was being witty. Not everyone agreed. Especially his press agent, who thought I was going out of my way to be offensive. Not so. I just didn't want to waste any precious space explaining why I disliked a band that everyone knew I had no time for, space that could be spent praising the latest single from Some Velvet Sidewalk or Madder Rose or Swell.

Back then, when I hated a band I wanted to destroy them, no messing. Why? Because I *cared* about the music I was writing about. I only ever became a critic because I felt a deep-down love for music and wanted to communicate that passion to others. If I hated a band, it was for what I saw as their cheapening of the quality of life, for adding to the greyness all around me, for inflicting their turgid sound upon my ears. I couldn't escape them: it was my life, remember? Forget all that 'they do what they do very well' bollocks. That has nothing to do with anything. Talk about a trite homily! What? So Mansun and the Wonder Stuff are very good at being mediocre, grey Britpop bands with a passion for copying whatever sound happened to be trendy six months ago? Radiohead are very good at producing pretentious, overwrought, muso ramblings? (Actually, I pity Thom Yorke *et al* more than I despise them. Fancy never being able to better your first single, no matter how many years you linger on.)

Think about that phrase: *They're very good at doing what they do*! Why not say they're 'interesting' and really go the whole critical hog?

So I hit back at the bands polluting my ears the only way I could, through my writing. Sure, I went over the top sometimes, but what would you have me do? I thought critics were supposed to *criticise*. Or perhaps you enjoy reading yet more anaemic advertising copy, more writing that adds to life's mediocrity?

I always thought that if rock music should stand for just one thing, it was the emphasis on the individual. I now know that's not the case. Once the marketing departments and T-shirt bootleggers and production assistants get their hands on music it becomes 'product', indistinguishable from a thousand supermarket items. Music as seen on the TV is a lifestyle accessory, something as throwaway as last year's video of *Big Brother*. Oddly, I don't have a problem with that – shine brightly then disappear, that's fine. It's the way they take away everyone's identities that sticks in my craw. When I write about music, I want bands that are individual, bands to whom I can give something back in return . . . the same way that I could when I'd be dancing down the front at concerts, by myself. I want to increase the energy.

Readers often thought of me as negative. This was ironic considering that 95 per cent of my writing in the eighties and nineties was positive. In retrospect, the praise was often undeserved, but I couldn't stop myself. I felt passionate about music, and also felt that the only service I could provide to my readers was to write in a style that reflected my feelings. How could I expect bands to be artistic and honest and soulful if I didn't behave the same way back?

Since then I've learned that there are worthier targets in life than bands like Smashing Pumpkins or music itself, but none more fun. Of course I didn't watch the Metro show in Chicago that I was attacking in that *MM* live review. I had better things to do with my time, like watch crazed, euphonium-touting country band Bad Livers at the Lounge Ax, for example. We were only at the Metro because we were interviewing the support band – Arcwelder? Tar? It was one of those cool Touch & Go hardcore bands, certainly.

Courtney was dating Mr Corgan during 1991, and, on a couple of our early rendezvous in London, she would depart early to catch up with Billy at his hotel. (A strange leap between two people, I've always thought: myself to Bill. God, that's scary now I think about it.)

I've always been an emotional writer, and knowing that truth can take many different forms, my writing usually only attempts to capture how I feel at the time.

Oh, and in case you're wondering whether time has mellowed my feelings towards Billy and his ridiculous Smashing Pumpkins outfit, have a read of the following:

Smashing Pumpkins
Machina: The Machines Of God
(Virgin)

I do not like Smashing Pumpkins. Smashing Pumpkins probably do not like me, either.

I think they're smug, supercilious, pompous and priggish. Their new album stinks of self-regarding portentousness and naff schoolyard symbolism. Songs like 'The Everlasting Gaze' would've been rejected by even Pearl Jam as being too cock-rock based, and its lyrics are all sub-Marilyn Manson schlock horror. I do not like the way Billy Corgan sings like his ass has been sharpening pencils, his whiny complaining look-at-me style of falsetto flatulence. I do not like his band's music: their faux-techno drum patterns and anonymous, bad metal riffs. I do not like the sleeve to this album. It reminds me of the religious imagery of bad popsters Sixpence None The Richer. I feel that Smashing Pumpkins are a massive pose, a boring petty lie, and one that far too many children enjoy. I do not understand how anyone over the age of five can enjoy this shit. I hate songs with titles like 'The Crying Tree Of Mercury'. I do not even have to hear them to know that . . . but I listened anyway. I hate songs with titles like 'The Crying Tree Of Mercury'.

Smashing Pumpkins probably think I'm disrespectful.

I am not a lapsed Catholic, nor do I have any pretensions to be one. I do not like wallowing in my own guilt and sorrow. I especially do not like multi-millionaires who behave like that. I hate the way all 74 minutes of this album is an anonymous wash of sound, no dynamics, no direction, just fuzzy early eighties bad gothic abrasions. I despise 'I Of The Mourning' and 'Try Try Try' (Corgan's vocals are particularly heinous on the latter). I think all 9.56 minutes of the churning needless 'Glass And The Ghost Children' are 9.56 minutes too much. I've always hated seventies prog rockers and disposable pop stars that believe that because millions of people are dumb enough to buy their turgid self-wallowings their art possesses some worth. Haven't you heard of the Law of the Lowest Common Denominator?

I despise pomposity above almost everything, even when it's hilarious. Smashing Pumpkins aren't hilarious. They're a sick, squalid little joke. And they probably wouldn't like me much if we met either.

(Everett True, *Stranger*, 16 March 2000)

One Against Five
(Pearl Jam)

My feelings towards Pearl Jam have mellowed since Kurt's death.

Initially, I hated the Seattle five-piece. You have to understand why. I grew up with punk, the Beatles (on piano) and soon thereafter sixties soul. I had no empathy whatsoever with the pomp and bluster of mid-American rock. If I thought of seventies bands like Whitesnake and Aerosmith at all, it was with a shudder. I've always found it hard to swallow unrestrained maleness being rammed down my throat.

My adolescent years were spent reading Graham Greene and George Orwell, and maybe the odd superhero comic, not indulging myself in puerile, American-led fantasies of going on stage and strutting my stuff. I had no desire to become one of those men sporting codpieces and string vests, baring my chest at every opportunity and treating women like shit. If I wanted enter-tainment and gigantic light shows, I would far rather watch a musical like *Oliver!* or *The Sound Of Music*. Sure, I was puritanical. I liked the clean-cut, sharp, all-night lines of mod and Northern soul. I had little or no time for music that I'd been trained by punk to distrust, that had clearly degenerated into pitiful self-parody. The Rolling Stones were old men in the *seventies*, for Christ's sake!

I found rock shows intimidating, sure. I have never made a secret of my elitism and paranoia. I didn't want to escape reality via the tongue-wagging felicitations of KISS or Journey. I didn't like the idea of showing off like Roger Daltrey. I liked my music to have style, soul and integrity. All of these factors mainly run contrary to the very spirit of soft rock and heavy metal. It wasn't until I discovered Soundgarden and Mudhoney that I realised that yes, it *was* possible to be cool and rock out. It was then that I started to go backwards in time and appreciate the raw-boned minimalism of

Black Sabbath, the full-on sonic overload of Led Zeppelin. That took a long time coming, though.

Indeed, it's possible that I would never have fallen so heavily for Sub Pop's charms if I hadn't been such a comparative rock virgin. Everything seemed totally fresh and new to me, when in reality it was almost the opposite. Who cares? Mudhoney singer Mark Arm's great charm is that he's always managed to invest the music he loves with an integrity and passion light years away from his chundering peers. Perhaps it's because his band were always more mod than many people realised. When I first met them, guitarist Steve Turner admitted to being influenced by seminal garage man Billy Childish, The Vaselines and bands on 53rd And 3rd, one of my cherished Scots cutie labels. Also, they had a wicked, almost English, sense of humour. No wonder we hit it off.

I'd always dug Lemmy's gravel-gargling roar in Motörhead, though. Even as early as 1983, I could be caught carving a groove into the Hammersmith Odeon's floor with my head, and had to be restrained from doing myself serious damage by a couple of passing fans. Who can resist rock that stripped-back and powerful? I can still remember the sight of Lemmy breaking all four strings on his bass with his opening chord. A roadie lifted the instrument off him, seamlessly fitted another one over his shoulders and he continued playing.

For me, mid-American rock like Pearl Jam is the antithesis of Motörhead. It's far more concerned with parading on stage than rocking out, always spouting 'Look at me! Look at me!' There are too many frills and guitar solos. There's not enough good solid dancing music. It wasn't just coincidence that the outside world – fashion, film, mainstream magazines – only started to treat 'grunge' music as a serious phenomenon once Pearl Jam started making it big in 1992. The true innovators quickly got left behind, as MTV and their kind championed the safest of rock: Pearl Jam, Stone Temple Pilots, plus the morbid and dull Alice In Chains. Seattle may have been the adopted hometown of Nirvana, the Last Great American Rock Band, but even before *Nevermind* came out it was the place to be. Less credible bands such as Mother Love Bone had attained respectable sales figures in 1990, much to the sneering dismay of their more punk-inclined brethren. Mother Love Bone singer Andrew Wood died in 1991 and the band split, bassist Jeff Ament and guitarist Stone Gossard going on to form Pearl Jam.

At last, here was a group the men behind the corporations could understand. They didn't mess around or throw confusing amounts of punk attitude and subversive humour into the equation. Pearl Jam took their music seriously, had 'adult' lyrics and played ball big time. They were the first Seattle band not to object to being labelled grunge. This was clearly ironic. Far from being soulful iconoclasts like Mudhoney or Screaming Trees, Pearl Jam were merely LA hair bands like Poison and Motley Crüe given a fresh set of clothes and a bad hairstyle. Listen to the music. So, of course, their tame, unchallenging, ordinary rock albums went on to sell millions more than the group whose coattails they rode into town on, Nirvana.

When I saw Pearl Jam's first UK show at London's Borderline in December 1991, I had no axe to grind. Sure I didn't like Mother Love Bone, but I was rather fond of Ament and Gossard's previous band, Green River. There again, the River boasted Mark Arm's laconic vocals and fellow future Mudhoney guitarist Steve Turner's innate pop sense. Also, neither Arm nor Turner cared about careers or anything boring like that . . . which is what led to the original Green River split.

'Some of the other members started getting the idea they could be popular,' Arm told me in '89, 'and at the age of 24 started to see music in terms of a career. Steve left at the peak of that, while I was blowing myself away by being in the junior Rush or whatever. So Green River got into the idea of signing to a major, and that's how *Rehab Doll* was recorded. Too many compromises were made. I was listening to far simpler stuff, such as the Stooges. We split on Halloween, 1987. I formed Mudhoney and the others became Mother Love Bone and signed to Polygram. So I guess we both got what we wanted.'

The fact that Ament and Gossard's new singer Eddie Vedder had been recommended to them by the Chili Peppers didn't exactly endear him to me, though. The Chili Peppers represent all I loathe about rock, with their muscles bulging and tattoos sweating and twenty minute 'funky' bass solos before even a song has been played. Still, future Hole/Smashing Pumpkins bassist Melissa Auf der Maur was recommended to Courtney by old mate Billy Corgan and it didn't mean I hated her.

So I had no hidden agenda when I went along to check out the latest new American band in town that night. Indeed, in my guise as 'the Godfather of Grunge', I'd been asked to review the show for *Melody Maker*. What I saw astounded and sickened me. There was none of the good-natured, self-deprecating humour of Pearl Jam's fellow Seattle bands. There was no desire to play the songs, or rock the joint. Instead, we had Jeff Ament wearing his funny hat, vest with his nipples hanging out, a pair of basketball shorts – if ever a fashion should have been strangled at birth – and playing one of those really crap battery-operated basses. Instead, there was Gossard and Mike McCready wanking out on guitar. And there was Eddie Vedder, long hair flailing all over our faces in the cramped surrounds of this tiny West End industry joint, leaping around and baring his chest, and doing everything that was anathema to my mod sensibilities. Ugh! It still makes me shudder to think of it.

What could I do? I knew that if I wrote about this, Pearl Jam would never speak to the *Maker* and it was obvious they would shortly be massive. How couldn't they be, with their butt-kissing attitude, inexcusable arrogance and the traditional rock songs? The timing was perfect. Everyone, but everyone, was looking to Seattle bands to be the saviours of rock.

I passed on writing the review, gave it over to a more solid metal-loving sort. There is an unwritten rule at music papers rarely broken. There's no point in slagging off a band if no one has written about them yet.

Oddly, when I returned home to my Cricklewood flat that evening, I got a call from Nirvana manager John Silva. 'I hear you saw Eddie's band tonight,' he chirps. How the hell he knew that, I never worked out. I guess that was part of his job, to be in the right place at the right time. 'And I hear you hated them.'

Spooky! I hadn't even spoken to anyone after the show.

My friend, photographer Steve Gullick – a man who's seen Pearl Jam more times than is fair or just – has a unique take on what makes them great *to his ears*. 'Smashing Pumpkins were Queen,' he explains. 'I used to like them because I was young. We all make mistakes. Pearl Jam are Whitesnake, though. I don't have a problem with that. I've always liked Whitesnake. Pearl Jam never claimed to be anything more than a straightforward rock band from Seattle who play heavy rock with personal and impassioned lyrics.'

When I remind Steve of Eddie Vedder's ridiculous 'I'm not your Messiah!' speech he came out with in the wake of Kurt's suicide, he retorts with a 'Yes, but he was going mad at that point.' Like Mr Gullick wasn't! There's a memorable shot of him from after a Marquee concert in London 1992, standing next to Eddie Vedder. Eddie is proudly holding a T-shirt aloft that Steve had been wearing. It has footprints *on its back!*

Steve does have some justification for saying this, however. When the band's second album *Vs* was released in 1993, Eddie gave out his personal phone number on the radio, 'in case any fans need to talk to me'. Temporary insanity might also explain why he came out with crap like 'I always thought I'd go first' upon hearing the news of Kurt's death. Oh, poor sensitive, trembling Eddie! The band later cancelled a tour, partly because of the knock-on effect Kurt's suicide had in Seattle. That too was ironic, considering how snide and mean Kurt had been towards Eddie's band while he was alive. He called Pearl Jam a 'bunch of careerists' – one of the worst insults the avowed anti-rocker could throw a musician's way – and said the band was 'simply corporate rock dressed up in grunge clothing'.

Despite reports by revisionist historians since, Kurt never called a truce between Nirvana and Pearl Jam. Possibly he might have done if he'd lived long enough. Everyone who knows Eddie makes a point of saying what a thoroughly decent chap he is. Yet at Nirvana's final Seattle concert in December 1993 – a show that Pearl Jam bottled out of playing, citing 'illness' – Kurt was making jokes about how terrible Pearl Jam were, although most of his bile was directed towards those two Seattle scene stalwarts, Gossard and Ament.

Some of us felt that Eddie's depictions of the confusion of childhood on Pearl Jam's debut album *Ten*, especially the story of emotional abuse told in 'Jeremy', were predictable, if not cynical, attempts to cash in on the prevalent climate. Especially as that album's centrepiece, 'Alive', is, to my ears, a straightforward rehash of the old Lynryd Skynryd staple 'Freebird'.

People ask me why I used to be so down on Pearl Jam. Here's the reason, nice and simple: Kurt Cobain loved rock with a passion, so much that he wanted to destroy it. Like the Sex Pistols before him, he understood that it was the only possible way to invest his cherished music with meaning. Cobain's roots were in punk as much as they were in seventies rock, in the burgeoning Riot Grrrl scene in Olympia, in the naïve rock of Half-Japanese and the Shaggs. Where is the connection with Pearl Jam, a band who stood for everything the punks reviled? Everything Nirvana was trying to do – invest rock with a fresh attitude and outlook – Pearl Jam would undo, even more forcefully. How thin is the line between great music and self-indulgent whining? As thin as the line between Nirvana and Pearl Jam.

At the start of this chapter, I said that my feelings have mellowed towards Pearl Jam in the last five years, and so they have. I couldn't give a crap about them now. I'm too jaded to think that it matters they're corrupting their fans with their inflated sense of self-importance. Those fans deserve all they get. I'm too cynical to think it matters that Pearl Jam are simply going through the same tired moves rock bands have been making ever since Jagger first learnt he could get laid if he pretended he wasn't middle-class and swivelled his hips a little. The fans will learn, and if they don't, what of it?

At least Eddie is a decent chap.

Jeff Ament, Stone Gossard and Eddie Vedder all have cameo roles in *Singles* – Cameron Crowe's 1992 ode to Seattle twenty-somethings – as members of a fictional local band called Citizen Dick. There's one telling scene where the three of them are sitting around in a coffee house discussing a bad review they'd just received in local paper the *Rocket*. (In reality, this scene would probably never have happened. The *Rocket*, and its Bruce Springsteen-loving publisher Charles R Cross, was more noted for ignoring local bands than slating them.) They shrug, and laugh it off. The inference is obvious: Citizen Dick, and Pearl Jam, couldn't give a damn about bad press. It doesn't affect or change anything.

When it came to real life, however, the reaction was very different.

Picture the scene. Pearl Jam are being interviewed for the music fogey's bible Q for a cover story. The mood in the room is affable, if a little fraught, as pizza-loving journalist Mat Snow questions them about recent events. All of a sudden, Eddie spots a copy of the new *Melody Maker* lying on a nearby table among other magazines. Inside, there's a review I've written of his band's recent show at Finsbury Park, supporting Neil Young. He picks it up and begins reading while his band mates chat among themselves. In it, I compare Pearl Jam to rock journeymen . . . er . . . Journey, and claim that Eddie 'sings like Phil Collins with a backache'. I say that his band are 'cock-rock strutters *extraordinaire* who missed their true vocation as extras in the last Heart video'. Among other great phrases that leap out is the alliterative insult, 'pompous, pedantic prats – everything that punk was against'. I go on to add that I think Eddie is a 'sensitive, overblown, preening, gibbering pretence of a poet' and accuse him of suffering from a messiah complex.

In short, I don't like them.

If this was *Singles*, Eddie would just have shrugged the review off. He'd know that it didn't matter, right? Right. This wasn't *Singles*. This was real life, or what passed for it. And anyway, I'm a far better writer than most.

Eddie continues reading through to the end of the review, face as black as thunder, throws the paper down and launches into an expletive-laden tirade against the British music press. He then storms from the room, and refuses to come back in, refuses to do any photos. The cover session is most definitely *off*.

Revenge at last!

I'll Stick Around (sigh)
(Foo Fighters)

When the Foo Fighters played their first UK show at King's College, London, in the spring of 1996, I blanked Dave Grohl to his face, fucked up on confusion and alcohol and resentment. I wrote a strange review of the concert the following week. In it, I took sideswipes at Nirvana's management, friends and fellow musicians, but in such a way that only insiders could have understood my references. I was moved by the energy and passion of Dave's new band on stage – particularly the figure of ex-Nirvana guitarist Pat Smear, still smiling – but couldn't figure out whether this was because they were any good, or if it was because I was emotionally vulnerable. After all, I'd barely been out since Kurt's death, and Dave was far closer to the singer than me. There was a fair amount of bitterness behind my article: like, 'How dare Dave get on with his life!'

Also, the Foo Fighters sounded astonishingly like Nirvana, something that seemed to border on bad taste. Not fair, I know, but that's how I felt. That's how it was. At least Krist when he re-emerged even later had the grace to return with a band called Sweet 75 who were so blatantly not commercial that you couldn't doubt his integrity.

The next time I met Dave was in Texas three months later, where we waited for the bats to come flying out from underneath Austin's main bridge at twilight. I mumbled an apology for the review. He smiled, and told me not to worry. That made me feel worse.

'Go speak to Dave Grohl,' Breeders singer Kim Deal had told me in Brighton a year after Kurt's death. 'He'll make you feel better.' I had. I felt like crying. What is the point in trying to reclaim strands of your past life when they seem so unreal?

'It's like this,' Dave said when we spoke together again, in Barcelona, later on in 1996 for a *Melody Maker* cover story. 'I can't sit on my ass and do nothing. I had almost a year of that [after Kurt died]. I realised that I had to get out and do something now or else sit on my ass forever. I can look back at the past and think of all the good things that happened . . . and I think of the bad things that happened too . . . but there's nothing you can do, there's nothing that you can do to change what happened and that's the bottom line.

'Doing all these interviews it's hard to think about the future sometimes. People will ask me about the future, but only after seventeen questions about the past, and it's sort of like ... well, how do you expect me to get on with the future when you won't let me out? And you *have* to look forward to things. There are still so many things to look forward to. There are. Shit, I fucking think about Kurt every day, every fucking day, every day, every time I get onstage and, you know, it's difficult, but it's the kind of thing which you have to force yourself to deal with, you really have to keep going, because ...'

Otherwise there's no point living. Exactly. Shame then that Dave had to form the Foo Fighters as his escape route. I've always thought of them as a pale imitation of former glories. Music is black and white to me. If it's not brilliant on one of a thousand myriad levels, it shouldn't exist. Initially, the Foos had a resonance and charm because of the context they existed in. Now, long after, the charm has tarnished and they could be anyone.

On one hand, it's brilliant that Dave is still creating music he loves, and is obviously having fun and letting others have fun while he's doing it. On the other, his group are mediocre. If Mr Grohl hadn't drummed with Nirvana, I would have dismissed the Foos out of hand, as being even worse than Gavin Rossdale's grunge revivalists Bush. At least Bush can hold down a tune, and Rossdale has a honeyed rasp that is far more evocative than Dave's hoarse bleatings. But Dave *did* drum with Nirvana. There's no getting around it. Expectations are unrealistically high because of it. So let's get this straight from the start. If I dislike the Foos, it's nothing personal. It's because I really do think they're a dull band.

'I'm not a very emotional person,' Dave states. 'If I'm watching a movie and there's this mushy goodbye dialogue and there's no music, it means nothing to me. But if there's some Steven Spielberg fucking *ET* music, then I'll be in tears. Music is one of the few things that can spark that kind of emotion in me. After Kurt died, I couldn't even listen to a fucking Cornells song, I couldn't listen to any music for fear that the refrain would have some minor chord in it that would make me bawl ...'

I went to see that stupid *Backbeat* movie shortly after Kurt died, and I knew that when Stu Sutcliffe died I wouldn't be able to handle it. I knew.

'Why? Why did you go to see that?' Dave laughs. 'Then it took a little time,' he continues, 'because ... I guess it's different for me, I guess it's different for everyone. Nirvana's music meant something different to each person. Like, with my wife Jennifer, there was a time when we weren't together, and the song "Come As You Are" reminds her of that period, so if that song comes on the radio, she can't listen to it. I prefer not to listen to Nirvana music on the radio. If a song comes on, I'll search for something else. And it seems like there are times when it's four o'clock in the morning, everyone's asleep, and I'll go down and pop in a bootleg and listen to it. It's strange. Emotionally, music can do different things to different people, and it's not that you should force yourself through it . . . You shouldn't walk out of this interview and go home and put on *Nevermind* and drown yourself in sorrow. It's not going to happen, but I just think the whole Nirvana experience was such a good thing, it's a shame to try to forget it.'

I know that you must have had this a million times worse than me, Dave, but I get so fed up of going to concerts and being asked, 'So what was he really like?'

'Fuck,' the singer agrees. 'I get it every day, three times a day you know, and it's almost like I have a rubber stamp answer now. Fuck you if I'm going to tell you exactly.'

Nowadays I just tell people I never met Kurt.

'I wish I could do that,' Dave laughs. 'But . . .'

It was one of the reasons I didn't want to do this interview. It was obvious we'd talk about Nirvana.

'Well, if it wasn't you, then I wouldn't sit here and talk about this kind of thing,' he replies. 'Ultimately, I don't want this to be the big Dave interview, but it's fine because at least the conversation won't be so shallow as to ask, "What do you think about the rumour that *blah blah blah?*" '

He's referring to all the stupid questions people used to throw his way like, 'What do you think about the story that Courtney had Kurt murdered?' What is he supposed to think?

'I don't know,' he continues. 'Maybe I'm so naïve and stupid and childish to think, Duh, life must go on, but if that's what's going to get me by, then shit, I'll take it. There are times when I think, All right, here I go, this is it, today is going to be the big freak-out – but it's kinda gradual, and you have freak-outs once in a while and then you feel lucky in many ways. Sometimes I feel jinxed, sometimes I feel like the rest of my life will be spent in the shadow. I do.'

On the positive side, there was the late seventies Manchester group Joy Division who meant so much to so many. Their singer killed himself too. Obviously, they weren't in the same sales league as Nirvana, but the group that came out of them, New Order, did pretty well for themselves.

'Right,' agrees Dave. 'That's true. So how did you feel when New Order started?'

I really fucking resented them.

We both laugh.

It wasn't fair that so much of the first Foo Fighters UK interview was taken up with the past, but what could I do? Pretend nothing happened? Sometimes, it seemed like Dave was determined to keep the flame of Nirvana burning single-handed in his music. Sometimes, it seemed like none of us would ever escape the shadow of the past: not me, not you, least of all Dave. Especially when there were people like me around who refused to even acknowledge the past, and in refusing to acknowledge it, couldn't let go. It's unfair. Foo Fighters mean plenty to a whole new generation of fans to whom Nirvana were just another band. Grohl's grunge torchbearers touch people in their own way. Reaffirming the very human desire to survive. Taking pleasure in the thrill of being alive. Reacting against all the shit that went down back then. Back then, no one suspected that Dave Grohl would turn into such a front man, even if he did release a rather fine full-length solo tape on Tsunami's Simple Machines tape label. He was only the bloody drummer.

But back then, no one expected a lot of things to happen.

'Sometimes,' Dave says carefully, 'if you think about the good things that happened and take comfort in them, it sort of eases the pain of the bad. Nothing lasts forever. Sometimes I'll talk about Nirvana and remember things openly about Kurt, and it freaks people out. They think it's really strange I'm like that – "I think Dave might be about to lose it. He's talking about Nirvana, what's going on?" It was a big part of our lives, and to start thinking about it and then cut it off is not right, because it's five years of your fucking life that you're cancelling out. You can't do that.'

It wasn't fair. I shouldn't have been discussing the past with Dave, especially not when there was such a joyful abundance of life going on around us in Spain. I should have been discussing . . . what do I discuss with rock stars in interviews?

Beer and prostitutes – our upmarket hotel was a haven for streetwalkers. Normally, you don't even notice this sort of thing. It's standard in the hotels bands stay in, classy and otherwise, to have prostitutes hanging out in the lobby. It was blatant in Madrid, however: especially as there were policemen on the pavement outside touting guns, and making sure the residents weren't hassled too much.

Tour jokes – Dave: 'What was the first thing OJ Simpson said after the trial finished? Please could I have my hat and gloves back now.' The blacker the humour while on the road, the better it is for most musicians.

Food – the evening meal saw bits of asparagus flung by drummer William Goldsmith at Pat, later blamed on the journalist. William and I and photographer Steve Gullick talked long and emotionally into the night, bonded by the warm glow of empathy that alcohol brings. Unfortunate, then, that when I next encountered William it was two years later in his hometown Seattle and his pompous emocore band Sunny Day Really Lame had reformed and I couldn't resist making several jibes in the direction of their musical wankfest. I thought the drummer would take it all in good heart, we were drink buddies after all! He didn't.

Live shows – for the Foos' Spanish Halloween performance, guitar tech Eddie wore a hockey mask and Dave's wife Jennifer donned a fluorescent blue wig. Dave himself was unrecognisable in black wig and beard, while William painted war-stripes on his chest. The crowd was suitably manic and stage-dived like America did five years before; i.e. like they'd seen how they were supposed to behave on MTV Europe.

What do I ask bands about usually? You know . . . life in general.

Oh well, whatever. Never mind.

Listening to it now, 1996's debut album *Foo Fighters* has a real poignancy, even if it does sound like a collection of hastily recorded demos – rightly so, as Dave plays all the instruments on it, aside from one brief contribution from Afghan Whigs' Greg Dulli. Maybe its unfinished quality is part of its charm. How can it not be poignant, though? Much as Dave might have denied it at the time, there are clear references to Kurt in the lyrics: the prophetic 'I'll Stick Around', the frightened 'Alone + Easy Target'. Obviously that was going to give the record an edge that folk less connected with the Last Great American Rock Band couldn't hope to match.

After that album, shorn of its tragic context, the Foo Fighters were just another band. The second album, 1997's *The Colour And The Shape*, the first (and last) to feature Pat Smear among the full band line-up, was a fine hardcore record, if a little standard. No shame there – after all, you can include most rock music under that description – but nothing to take pride in either. After Smear's departure, it's been one long slide back into sub-Nirvana territory, culminating with 1999's *There Is Nothing Left To Lose* with its lack of a solid, metal heart. Does it matter? Dave always wanted to be a pop star. Foo Fighters now play commercial rock in the American tradition. KISS, Cheap Trick, Bush . . . I know the latter have British passports. I'm talking *sound*.

I asked a friend and Nirvana fan recently why he didn't rate Foo Fighters particularly highly. 'I don't like Hüsker Dü,' he explained. 'I don't like pop music either.' Yet Hüsker Dü's eighties albums had a resonance to them that transcended the pop wash that afflicted their singer Bob Mould's solo work. Dave's band has no such charm. They're just another minor diversion for the kids to bounce up and down to before they settle back down to a lifetime of TV, more kids and insurance brokers. There's not even the pretence of rebellion, or being an alternative. Foo Fighters revel in the fact they are a continuation of that long line of formulaic middle-American rock bands. It's almost like Dave thinks there's something wrong in giving too much of himself to the Foo Fighters. You can't blame the man for that. He's seen first-hand what happens to musicians who invest too much of themselves in their music. You can certainly criticise his art, though.

There was something strange about Nirvana that went beyond MTV and couldn't be manufactured. I have the same feeling from Wales' Manic Street Preachers. Maybe it's their lack of irony. Everyone seems so damn ironic now, as if that excuses all failings. Kurt was for real: Dave is playing the Scooby Doo version.

Nothing has changed in Dave's plan. Foo Fighters still play loud, abrasive rock: grunge. The main reason I don't like them now and think they're a tenth-rate version of Dave's former band is that he has lost both his original drummer (William) and the incomparable Pat Smear. Yes, it really can make that much difference changing musicians. I see nothing wrong with the musical form of pop-grunge if performed with enough style and soul. I like Hüsker Dü and Cheap Trick, remember?

As a front man, Dave makes a fine drummer. Sure, he's cute. That doesn't mean he should be ignoring his strengths and contributing to the general aura of grey that surrounds corporate rock music nowadays.

Let's be fair. Dave foresaw the criticism cynics like me would throw his way right from the word go.

'What people don't fucking realise,' Dave told me back in '96, 'is that this type of music has been around for years. Often, journalists don't even see the correlation, that Nirvana's music had snowballed from so many different things. It came from Flipper, it came from the Pixies, it came from a lot of different punk bands, bands that were around ten years before *The Year That*

Punk Broke [Sonic Youth video that referred to the success of *Nevermind*].

'So then they look at what I'm doing and wonder why I'm not Edwyn Collins or someone,' he continues. 'They don't understand that when I was fifteen and had *Zen Arcade* [Hüsker Dü], that's when I decided that I loved this music. For me to do anything else for the sole reason of doing something different would be so contrived. For me to put out a freeform jazz record to be as far away as possible from Nirvana would just be ridiculous.

'I knew that when I was recording the album, people would say, "OK, that song has some distorted guitars and heavy drumming and a strong melody to it, it must be like Nirvana." The instant I realised that, I thought, Fuck it, I don't give a shit! What else am I going to do? It's just what I love to do. The stuff I do at home on my eight-track, whether it's acoustic or just noise, is not the kind of thing I like to walk onstage and do. It's fun to bounce around to this kind of music in front of people.'

I'm sorry Dave. What you're saying may be true, but the fact remains. Foo Fighters are the antithesis of Nirvana on every count except where it matters least – the music.

The Real Grunge

The Primordial Ooze
(Melvins, The Jesus Lizard)

The greatest pop music is throwaway. There to be listened to one moment and discarded the next. I can understand musicians not liking being told this. After all, they are trying to create a living from durability, but critics have for too long indulged them on this point. Many bands have only one idea, and most not even that. The rest of their careers is then spent in a hopeless quest to recapture the initial buzz. Why else do so many musicians turn to excess drink and drugs after a few years in? It's because they have no way of *feeling* otherwise.

I love Melvins because they are loud, basic and primal. That's it. They've had their one idea and they're not budging from it. They want to rock, and they do just that, with no consideration for taste or sales or carving out a place in history. It's the real grunge. Dale Crover hits the drums harder than anyone else around. Singer/guitarist King Buzzo writes a great heavy, dark song in the tradition of early Black Sabbath. Together, this relocated Californian trio have a knack of slowing time down so each bass note seems to last an eternity. Doesn't matter who the bassist is: it could be Olympia's Joe Preston (also of Earth), Aberdeen's Matt Lukin (also of Mudhoney) or Shirley Temple's daughter Lori 'Lorax' Black (who played on 1989's *Ozma* and 1991's *Bullhead*). It could be *Ozma* producer, Englishman Mark Deutrom. More recently it's been ex-Cow Kevin Rutmanis who has supplied the big ugly noise. This slowing down of time is indubitably a good thing, if only because life is too short. Less is more, as hair designers always say, simpering. 'A little more off the top, sir?' Yes please.

Melvins received undue attention because Kurt and Krist of Nirvana were fans, but even without their patronage they would have attained cult status. Bands as focused as King Buzzo's lot always do. Even their fiercest enemies have to admire their singularity of purpose. In their inexorable grind, Melvins provided a sense of community to the two Aberdeen friends who felt outside of their peers, outside of most music. Everyone needs to feel special, and if that means supporting a band few others understand, all the better.

Melvins played a major role in Kurt's career. He roadied for them early on, and they also encouraged him in his musical aspirations, even introducing him and Krist to their future drummer Dave Grohl after Chad left the group. You can trace Melvins' music through to latterday Nirvana improvisational encores such as 'Endless Nameless', where the trio would take a riff and build upon it for as long as it took. (As far as actual *songs* went, Portland's brilliant late seventies punk-pop band the Wipers were far more influential.)

In the eighties, while Lukin was still in the band and Melvins lived in the Northwest, they scared and confused the hardcore punks by playing even slower, heavier chord sequences than Flipper. Not in a guitar store show-off way, more like James Brown or Ted Nugent, where everybody played the same thing: the music was one huge power riff. Dale Crover hit the drums so hard he would wear gardening gloves, underwear and nothing else on stage.

I've called this the Real Grunge chapter. All I mean by that is that the bands included here are here because they were clearly creating this sound, because it was the sound they clearly loved to create. Sorry if that sentence is repetitive – not that being repetitive is any crime when it comes to rock music either. As the Fall's Mark E Smith once sang: *'Remember the three r's. Repetition, repetition and repetition.'*

I knew little of Melvins as people, except that Dale and his partner Debbi Shane used to let me stay on their floor in San Francisco, and made great flavoured popcorn. Both liked comic books. Dale doubled for grunge icon Neil Young as his younger self in the video for 'Harvest Moon' after answering an ad for extras. He got to drive – and crash, because he couldn't actually drive – Neil's Cadillac, kiss the young Mrs Young and go dancing in the moonlight like a wayward character from a Thin Lizzy song. The directors wouldn't allow him to keep the stick-on sideburns, but later we went driving up to Half Moon Bay through a myriad of pumpkin patches that could have been drawn by Charles Schultz, to find the bar where the video was filmed.

Traditions in Western and Eastern music differ greatly. In Eastern culture, the moment is what matters, what you're experiencing at any given point in time. This means that concepts such as 'songs' are meaningless. You carry on while it feels good and you stop when you've had enough. Experimental US noise bands like Savage Republic and early Sonic Youth realised this. Their guitar sound borrowed heavily from the Greek bouzouki, repeated endlessly until the emotion became overwhelming.

This is also what makes side two of Melvins' incredible 1993 major label debut *Houdini* so very cool. It may sound to the unwary like a bunch of inebriated men very slowly and very painfully falling down an endless flight of stairs, but there's far more to it than that. It's soul music, spontaneous and carried through with a minimum of fuss. Sure I like bands that are intelligent, but I don't like bands that make a point of it (REM being a prime example of this trait). Give me the brutal honesty of Melvins any day. I *like* the way jungle has rid itself of even the vocals and retains a similar beat throughout. Motörhead and similar acts like Melvins are great because they know precisely what they want to achieve.

You don't need a degree to appreciate this music, just a love for the hum of an overheated amplifier, a desire to escape the everyday via full-on sonic assault, a need for some loud. It was strange, then, that the same kids who went to Soundgarden and Guns N' Roses concerts never understood Melvins. Perhaps it was that the Northwest band, and likeminded souls like the Butthole Surfers, Cows and Steve Albini's Big Black, had a grunge aesthetic too extreme for the mainstream. Real grunge is about noise and chaos and psychedelia – confusion as sex. I don't want to mess with people's perceptions too much here, but most of the Sub Pop bands didn't actually play grunge, at least not grunge as defined by Lester Bangs and Mudhoney and Everett True. Most of Sub Pop was punk dressed up in rock clothing, except for their most famous band . . . who were, of course, rock dressed up as punk.

Enough already with the textbook definitions.

The reason Melvins and their kin weren't more popular is that they unsettled and upset and, in the main, record listeners don't want that from their music. Life is upsetting enough as it is. It takes a true punk sensibility to reject the mainstream the same way Johnny Rotten did when he wore his 'Pink Floyd sucks' T-shirt, or Kurt did when he posed for a *Rolling Stone* cover with a shirt boasting 'Corporate Magazines Still Suck'.

'Usually the bad reviews say all the same things as the good ones,' explained King Buzzo to me for *Melody Maker* in 1993. 'It's all, "They're slow and they're heavy and they make me puke". We play slow because we're getting old . . . What's that? We've always played slow? That's right. We've always been old.'

Kurt half-produced *Houdini*, taking his task seriously, calling Steve Albini up in Chicago to get information on how to set up the microphones, before he walked out, telling the band to 'write more songs'. Even so, I swear *Houdini* could've taken Metallica on in the metal stakes if Melvins had been so minded. Of course they weren't. There was a great version of KISS's 'Going Blind' among the debris of busted guitar strings and shattered skins. Importantly, Melvins were very Olympian in their approach: no self-indulgent, mystical lyrics or overbearing guitar solos, everything was one gigantic, minimal sprawl of primordial ooze. Perhaps that's part of the legacy of growing up in Aberdeen.

The first time I saw Melvins live was also the first time I caught Hole. It was in LA '91, and they almost overwhelmed my nascent Courtney Experience, except that I had to run screaming from the strip club venue after 30 minutes of Melvins – roughly one song – friends pacifying my ears with the promise of pizza. Melvins were never under any illusion regarding their commercial potential.

'Why did we call the album *Houdini*?' asked Dale. 'Because it's magically going to be in the bargain bins a week after release.' In fact, Melvins sold a decent number of records for their record label Warners, but were more of a 'prestige act' like Lou Reed, Van Morrison and Bob Dylan.

To celebrate the fact the unlikeliest of all rock bands had been signed to a major, simply because Mr Cobain liked them, WEA flew me to Disneyland. It was an appropriate setting for an interview with a band so in love with the comic book imagery of KISS. The hyperactive King Buzzo lived in a house filled with Pee Wee Herman memorabilia and cow skulls, Mexican candles and mummified bats. It was his idea to visit the 'happiest place on earth' and it was he who bounced hardest between rides. I found it hard to believe that someone so childlike could sing songs so nightmarish. The resulting article was an A–Z of Melvins, full of:

C is for Curry – what the *MM* journalist who reviewed the last Melvins show in England went to have instead of watching them play.

R is for Rubbish – what Melvins think all English bands are.

A is for Aberdeen – a small logging town in the Northwest of America.

P is for Promises – Melvins have seen many broken over the years.

Chicago's Jesus Lizard also became caught up in the undertow of Nirvana's success.

It was absurd, absolutely absurd. There was no way this rude, crude rock'n'roll band could ever have sold millions of records. They were perhaps a little more commercially viable than Tad, Melvins or Daniel Johnston but only because the frontman was slimmer. I've seen shows where the singer – I use the word in its loosest sense – David Yow would be stage-diving before even a note had been played. He looked unholy, righteous and possessed by the same elusive demon of rock'n'roll that overcame both Iggy Pop and Nick Cave in their day. His performances belonged to another dimension – one where creatures with sadistic, nihilistic, whip-lashed, growling, gruelling, beer-speckled, irrational, pummelling, surreal, leering, terrifying tendencies were allowed to roam free in front of bands playing primordial blues so fierce they burned brighter than all hell. Tales of his stripping off and sweaty bear hugs and charges of obscenity in uptight states just because he liked to 'whale his winkie' were legion. The Jesus Lizard might not have been too strong on the melodies or helping MTV shift units, but they knew how to *entertain.*

'It's absolutely impossible we could be as big as Nirvana,' Yow said in '93. 'We're not that easy to swallow. I like Nirvana a lot, but they're abrasive pop. Our music is heavy on the abrasive side and not very substantially pop. I can't sing my way out of a wet paper bag.'

This didn't stop Capitol Records from signing them in '95 for *Shot,* a development that led to a rift forming between the band and producer/fan Steve Albini. Before that, the Lizard had been signed to Chicago's proudly independent Touch & Go label, even releasing a split single with Nirvana, 'Oh, The Guilt'/'Puss' most notable for its strange sleeve of an Indian chief on one side, and a poodle in a dress on the other. If anyone had bothered to flip the Nirvana side over, they would have heard a song that extended long talons of guitar to scratch deep beneath the surface. The voice hollered, the drums thundered with a driven force. In the distance, it sounded as if someone was exorcising the last remnants of emotion out of rock's bloated corpse.

Business as usual for the Lizard, then. As 1990's vulgar and violent debut *Head* and the following year's *Goat* proved.

You could argue major label bucks were the Lizard's rightful dues. Long before they signed, the quartet – Yow, suave guitarist Duane 'The Silver Fox' Dennison, incredible bassist David M 'The Little General' Sims and youthful drummer Mac (aka Laughy The Tallest Elf) – had gained a reputation as one of America's most exciting live acts. They also had some heritage. Both Yow and Sims had been in Scratch Acid, the pioneering noise deliverance mid-eighties band from Texas acknowledged by everyone from Nirvana to Sonic Youth.

The Jesus Lizard weren't ever going to be an easy band to sell, even bearing in mind genres such as death metal's penchant for degradation and misery. The Jesus Lizard always were a King Crimson for the insane (and now dead) NYC scum rocker GG Allin set.

'When I hear the Jesus Lizard,' guitarist Duane told me, 'I think of flashing lights, ugly faces, bad smells, bad aftertastes – a trip down bad memory lane. I picture myself back at junior high in front of kids who used to laugh at me in school assembly. And I'm playing the songs in that kind of "I told you so, ha ha ha, look at me, you all have boring jobs, I don't, you're all divorced fucks, I'm not" way. Beautiful fucking images.'

When I first met David Yow he was slumped out on the pavement a block down from Cagney's, a lingerie bar in Chicago's warehouse district, drinking a bottle of beer with his belongings scattered around him. We ended up conducting an interview in the bar, interrupted only by pitchers of beer, scantily clad waitresses, free stale tacos and bourbon. Oh, and the Real Serious American Males all wearing their 'American flag and a two by four' express-ions and a 70-year-old female barfly who insisted on juggling her breasts in our faces.

Ugly American Overkill
(Amphetamine Reptile)

I understand ugly, the need to wallow in the darker, sleazier aspects of life, its use in music as a cleanser and an antidote against the worthy and the artificial, its healing power through catharsis, its sheer brutal splendour and forgiving grind. Much as I appreciate the beauty of Galaxie 500 or Mercury Rev, beauty cannot and should not exist without its bestial counterpart. The reasons I like Boss Hog's debut 1989 AmRep album *Drinkin', Letchin' & Lyin'* are almost exactly the same as why I appreciate labelmates Today Is The Day's *Supernova*, even though the two groups are different in every other respect. Both have an almost searing beauty to their repellent noise.

The first record comes from a bunch of bored rich New York folk (Cristina and her paramour, heir apparent Jon Spencer) wallowing in their own decadence. It revels in its depravity. On the sleeve, Cristina is posed naked except for a pair of thigh-high leather boots that couldn't have hurt sales. While other punk acts wallowed in the overt, the first two Boss Hog records were about the *implied*. Guitars squealed and fed back, Cristina and Jon mumbled and exhorted in a call to a backwater sexiness that had been lost up till then. This was straight tight rock, though, however disjointed the vocals sounded.

Supernova shares a similar disgust for the trappings of normality as *Drinkin', Letchin' & Lyin'*. What is rock music if not a fantasyland for those wishing to rebel against the hypocritical, squeaky-clean façade of corporate America? Recorded by three uptight, almost religiously fanatical hardcore boys from Nashville, Tennessee, *Supernova* has an intensity few bands achieve. You got the impression that, like 2001's rightly praised hardcore band At The Drive-In, Today Is The Day would have willingly abstained from everything that makes life worthwhile if they'd thought it helped their music. *Supernova* lies somewhere between Throbbing Gristle and Melvins, a noise that can take your head apart. Every ounce of passion, every last iota of soul that singer Steve Austin possessed was screamed out through his lungs. Where were the tunes, the songs and *the ideas*? Who cared? We wanted more volume, and pain, and veins busting out from foreheads.

Maybe it was a testosterone thing. Certainly it was no coincidence the two bands were signed to the same label alongside Cows, the incredible God Bullies, Chokebore, Hammerhead and many more. Charismatic label boss Tom Hazelmyer liked to surround himself with musicians who had the same no-nonsense, warped view of life. Most of these people were male because Haze was male. Early on, Amphetamine Reptile gained a reputation it never quite shook off as being the label who never signed a female musician ... Cristina, Nashville Pussy and one-time Hole bassist Kristen Pfaff from Janitor Joe aside, presumably.

The AmRep bands were as close to the real grunge as I encountered in my travels through America. This was the circus of the insane, the overspill from Butthole Surfers' deranged visions of the eighties, where singers would stab themselves in the ass with large crucifixes while singing about salvation and serial killing, where it was as important to be a showman as to rock out. It was also important not to care about conventional truths like *beauty*: one tour was called 'Ugly American Overkill'. Imagine John Goodman from *The Big Lebowski* playing rock with his loser bowling alley pals, and you're halfway there.

One time Kevin from the Cows was setting up his bass in a Washington DC club, and the soundman came running out of his booth, saying 'There's something incredibly wrong, your bass is feeding back and is horribly distorted!' Kevin pointed to the top of his bass amp and said, 'Maybe it's all those distortion pedals that I have it plugged into.' The guy wandered off, shaking his head in disbelief that anyone could want to sound that way.

This was the sound of America's underbelly rumbling, where artists revelled in playing whatever roles society had forced them to take on. The Cows gained notoriety for singer Shannon's live antics. He enjoyed playing trumpet wearing nothing more than a big hat and a bigger smile. Punk rarely came more unhinged than Minneapolis' Cows. They were almost avant-garde in their shuddering, feral blast of noise matched to some surprisingly melodic four/four pop structures.

Shannon was one of the best lyricists from the underworld, writing songs like tiny Charles Bukowski vignettes about the dark side of life. There was a deep, burning intelligence behind those heavy lidded eyes as he painted a Theatre of the Absurd with a surrealist passion. If the Cows scared people it was because Shannon showed us the part of ourselves we hide so we can look in the mirror in the morning. He sang with all the sarcasm in the world, secure in the knowledge of how fleeting our rotten lives are.

I tried to interview the Cows once, in a seedy midtown Minneapolis pool bar, buzzing with chatter and smoke – but instead of answering my questions, they started laughing because I was so drunk.

Haze came over, incensed. He thumped down hard on the table, breaking a few glasses. 'I'll fucking put money on this man,' he said, pointing at me, 'to drink you fuckers under the table any day. You think he's wasted now but in ten hours' time he'll still be like this when you're puking your guts out.'

The band laughed even harder.

'Four hundred and sixty dollars, next month's rent, says he can do it,' stormed Tom.

The Cows were aggrieved at the unfairness of this bet. It was clear that I was a hardened drinker, but equally apparent that Haze wasn't someone you say no to. So they tried to argue themselves out of the situation.

'You've got to understand, he's pointing at someone over there and saying that's us, he says he doesn't drink and he's clearly wasted, and anyway we have no money,' a Cow complains. 'You say he can hold his drink, but fuck. No offence, Tom, I'm sure we believe you and everything, but the Hammerhead guys said he lost consciousness through drinking ten years ago.'

I hurled my tape recorder at them, narrowly missing Shannon and his shaven eyebrows, and stormed off. The interview never happened.

* * *

Hazelmyer was an ex-Marine – 'the only difference between that and other shitty jobs was that you couldn't quit' – who used to keep a street sweeper on the window ledge above his desk in AmRep's Minneapolis offices. (His street sweeper was a six-foot semi-automatic, kept in readiness for the 'day America finally turns on itself'.) This was the man rumoured to have thrown lanky Sonic Youth guitarist Thurston Moore into a garbage dumpster, and who'd posed for the front of a single by his mod-influenced hardcore band Halo Of Flies wielding a baseball bat, after all. One time I hooked up with Haze in New York, he picked up a punter who'd been ogling his wife down the front of a Chokebore concert in CBGB's and brought him down on the ground so hard, I swear I heard bones crack. The next time we met, he introduced me to a cocktail sensitively entitled a 'Dead Nazi', one part Jagermeister, one part Rumplemintz (a strong, almost hallucinogenic German schnapps). It caused a few problems later.

When I first spoke to Tom in London 1989, he was playing stand-in bass for Madison's seminal Killdozer – a band who were a big influence on the early Seattle scene. The brutal, sometimes hilarious trio played rock with all the subtlety of a jackhammer on a throat, and had their albums produced by folk like *In Utero*'s Steve Albini and a pre-*Nevermind* Butch Vig. Another, *For Ladies Only*, was composed entirely of covers. They did for Don McLean's 'American Pie' and Deep Purple's 'Hush' what Exxon did for the environment.

When Haze finally quit the music industry in 1998–9 to concentrate on managing his bar and keeping his toy collection up to speed, he had pulled off that rarest of tricks: a man who'd got rich while keeping his integrity. That's perhaps what happens when you have major labels looking to release music they just don't get: post-Band Of Susans grunge outfit Helmet and the libidinous Nashville Pussy were just two AmRep bands who signed major label deals. Haze stayed true to his independent, hardcore roots. All he ever did was release music he liked – and he saw no reason to apologise for being male, either.

I remember Haze once giving me the lowdown on cheating on your partner.

'It's like this, Everett,' he explained as we bit down on half-pound steaks and the odd burger in a shitty American motel. 'I have three criteria that a woman has to pass before I cheat on my partner. First, she has to be more beautiful than her and that counts out 99 per cent of them. Second, she has to be more intelligent and funny than her and that also counts out 99 per cent. And third, she has to obey both those rules *and* throw herself at me. It hasn't happened yet.'

Tom offered to put me up after he heard the news about Kurt killing himself. I caught the slowest train ever – 27 hours from NYC to Minneapolis seated next to a mid-West beauty queen into the Lemonheads – and we spent a fine week shooting rifles, drinking and eating almost-raw burgers. I only punched the wall once.

After the Portland leg of the aptly named Clusterfuck tour, *MM* photographer Steve Gullick and I are recuperating at the side of the stage. Haze is waltzing with an equally drunken Pete from Guzzard to the strains of Psychedelic Furs and Nirvana, chasing those elusive disco spotlights. The club is almost empty. Various musicians stand around chatting to an odd friend or two, drinking the remains of the rider.

Suddenly, Haze spots us.

His reaction is instinctive.

Heads down, shoulders out, he body-charges us. Steve throws up an arm to protect himself. It's too late. The damage is done. A large 'crack!' is heard, followed by an ominous silence as the photographer surveys the damage caused to his £1,500 camera. It's ruined.

Haze looks up, momentarily dazed. He reaches into his pocket and pulls out a twenty-dollar bill.

'Here. Will this cover it?'

This is What Thurston Moore Called Foxcore
(Babes In Toyland, L7, Lunachicks, Dickless)

'First of all,' begins singer Kat Bjelland, 'what's it like being in an all-female band? Lori, what's it like being a girl?'

'I love Kat and Michelle's tits just as much as I love my own,' laughs the drummer.

'You know,' continues bassist Michelle Leon, 'when we're in New York, us and Dickless and L7 all sit around and go "yeah" together.'

'YEAH!' shout all three simultaneously.

'And we all get our periods at the same time,' adds Kat.

This is where my betrayal comes in.

The band I loved more than anyone in 1990 was Babes In Toyland. Everything I understood to be important about rock was tied up with these three women. Kat Bjelland would stand there on stage, face contorted with fury, spitting out her love–hate lyrics over a battered guitar lick. In her flat heels and chiffon she had an odd girlishness: pseudo kindergarten curls, crudely bleached, tattered baby doll dress, red lipstick and wide eyes. Her legs would be covered in bruises by the end of each show from contact with the guitar, pain dulled by a constant stream of whisky.

There was nothing 'girlie' or childish about her performances, though. Her screams sounded ghastly and cleansing, an exorcism of her past and a recent succession of bastard boyfriends. To her side stood Michelle, able to hit her bass with a demonic force that belied her size. Behind them, Lori Barbero, the brash, loud one, everyone's favourite sister, would be kicking up a major league racket on the drums, and occasionally singing in her operatic, drawn-out voice. At the set's end, she'd jump up and take a photo of the audience, like we'd all been invited to a private party. It was Kat that your attention was always drawn back to, though, her eyes rolled back wide to the sky, stamping her foot and grinding her sticker-covered guitar against her hips. Kat was the *electricity*.

So what do I understand to be important about rock? It's simple.

It has to *rock*. In other words, there needs to be a primal fury and power that goes way beyond the three or four chords being played. Babes In Toyland had that fury, certainly early on. They rocked as hard as anyone in Tad or Killdozer. Babes had a brilliant grasp of dynamics. They used silence and anticipation as effectively as noise.

It has to *challenge*. Mostly only art created by women has any validity. The male experience has been created and recreated so often. The female perspective has barely been explored in rock music. Hard rocking music created by intelligent females is still a rarity, and you can forget the juvenile, PVC-clad charm of Kittie and their breed in 2000. They are so clearly women (*girls*) shaped by men into their own fantasy images of what a strong woman should look like. Babes In Toyland never cared about looking cool, not in a traditional sense. How could they, with Kat standing there, glowering and sweating several layers of hatred? This was almost revolutionary: three women creating a metal/New Wave-based sound who didn't dress in combat boots or leather or lumberjack shirts or PVC, yet who sounded better than virtually every male band.

Somehow, Babes In Toyland were creating a new language, astringent but oddly tuneful within all Kat's roars and lyrics like '*Fry fucking fry/Fuck and fry my blue boyfriend*' ('Pain In My Heart'). Most of Kat's words came out as soul-searing screams or five-second blasts of lucid hatred, but then the *past* had every bearing on the Babes. Kat's mother left her when she was five, so the straight As student quickly learnt to look after herself. There were two Kats growing up: the high-school cheerleader, and the tormented, Kahlua drinking, Sylvia Plath reader.

The Babes were the flipside to Madonna's all-conquering power trip, her ability to mould men as and when she liked into her image. But the Babes approached it from another direction altogether, using darkness and torn emotions and every rotten mean trick in the book. Or rather, Kat did and the others tempered it and made it palatable. There was a balance to Babes In Toyland. Without it, they would have tumbled straight into the giddy chasm that made folk like Lydia Lunch impotent as far as the outside world was concerned. (I use the past tense. After 1992's *Fontanelle*, the Babes lapsed into self-parody, confusing the line between genuine emotion and cartoon imagery. It wasn't until Kat formed Katastrophy Wife with her husband Glen Mattson several years later that she rediscovered her power.)

The band's raw, blistering music recalled the primeval metal attack of early Sonic Youth and their Blast First label-mates, NYC's abrasive all-female UT. I would dance around on no feet to the sound of Kat's voice, as I used to with UT, laughing at all the squares who never did understand soul music.

The Babes' 1990 Sub Pop single 'House' describes a woman's stubbed toes, broken arms and various wounds before concluding *'Oh my God/Is this what it's like/To fall in love?'* Songs from *Spanking Machine*, released the same year, were equally unsettling. 'Swamp Pussy' advised we should all *'cease to exist'*. 'Dust Cake Boy', with its *'Pow! Pow! Pow!'* refrain, echoed the jazz textures of the Birthday Party's 'Big Jesus Trashcan' from several years before. Easy listening this wasn't. Except, of course, the Babes were fun: fucking ace, delirious, down-on-your-knees-and-bloodied fun. The Babes played with punk aestheticism. Raw and furious, Bjelland flirted between self-indulgent and revolutionary with a flick of her caustic tongue. The lyrics straddled an uneasy divide between scathing bitterness and an almost naïve fairytale ('Hansel And Gretel') outlook on life.

I was unable to resist the trio. It wasn't just that they could rock, taught me how to drink (via Kat's love for Jagermeister) and took me on tour with them. It was that they satisfied a need deep within. It was the real grunge.

Dickless' one-off single from 1990, 'I'm A Man', articulates rage and passion for me perfectly. It's impossible to make out a word of what singer Kelly Canary is screaming about over the abrasive wash of white noise. Sure she sounds angry, but maybe she's just happy at being given the chance to exercise her lungs.

The all-female Seattle group never really existed as such. They'd get together and not practise, just drink, rely on their mates from Tad to write a couple of riffs, boast about their dominatrix friends and then fuck the music up good and proper. They had a great name. What more do you need? In interview, the girls were immaculate.

'I'm Kelly from a trailer park somewhere in the Southwest and I'm pretty much white trash, although I'm trying to get over it,' announced Dickless' singer. 'And I'm an alcoholic! I scream, that's about all I do.'

'Do you scream like that in bed, babe?' asked her guitarist Kerry Green.

'I got asked that by the Red Hot Chili Peppers guitarist,' laughed Kelly. 'Sure, tiger. Give me a quarter and I'll show ya.'

In concert, Dickless were nothing short of phenomenal. Rock is about spontaneity, remember? Supporting bands like Mudhoney, the girls would take to the stage like oysters on acid and have people stage-diving into silence. The standard Dickless song lasted under two minutes, lifted the riff from 'Smoke On The Water' and was lucky if it found itself with all the instruments playing simultaneously. Kerry in the clown suit played road-mending guitar. Occasionally, she'd glance over at Jenny (bossa nova bass) and attempt some semblance of rhythmic order, a notion that Kelly would always put a stop to with another licentious screech.

Nothing ever appeared after that single: a perfect career. I don't know why the projected UK tour didn't happen. Years later, Kelly formed the dynamite Teen Angels with marginally more tunes but not as much presence. The riffs were more recognisable, but the scream remained the same.

'How did Dickless come about?' asked Kelly. 'We were born without penises and then we learnt how to swear and use the word "dick", and put it all together.'

'I've just thought of a great thing to say at an AIDS benefit,' interrupts Kerry. 'We'd just like to make it clear we'll open up for any boy band as long as they have a condom. We'll open up for free!'

If you want another example of a perfect career, track down STP's single, 'Hey Bastard', also released in 1990. It's a great visceral blast of female empowerment, one of the finest from the grunge/grrrl era – abrasive guitar, scolding out-of-control vocals and a mean, lean production courtesy of Velvet Monkey Don

Fleming and Sonic Youth's Kim Gordon. Four songs that blister paint where they fall. NYC guitarist Julia Cafritz (formerly with Pussy Galore) later formed Free Kitten with Gordon. 'Hey Bastard' was STP's only record. Who cares? It was a perfectly formed moment in time.

'*Hey bastard!*' the girls screamed. '*Love me for what I am.*'

There were other female bands around almost as fine – Portland's Calamity Jane, Mudwimmin, Frightwig – but none of them claimed a place in my heart like Dickless or STP. They were so *natural*. It was the first time I'd encountered American females in the flesh, and they warped me for life.

It's October 1990.

Kat and myself are at a student flat in Liverpool. Around us, hippies and debutantes stand around stoned, talking to each other on their way out, ignoring us. We're mad. It's five a.m., we've only just got here and the party is finishing. I look at Kat, and see that she's drinking from the only whisky bottle in the place. So I grab it and we run outside, hurling the bottle at the front room window as we leave.

We run so fast and we run so far. We can't go on because we're laughing so hard, and we're on our knees, still trying to put distance between us and our supposed pursuers, but we can't continue because our trousers and tights are all ripped, and our knees are bruised and bloody . . . Eventually, we find a cab and clamber into it, still laughing.

A few months later, a package arrives in the post for me at Cricklewood. It's a copy of the debut Babes In Toyland single, 'Dust Cake Boy' signed by all the band. Kat writes, '*to the sweetest skin yr. knees pal & nippin' thee 'ole naughty bottle with me mate of mine.*'

New York's Lunachicks played a biker Monkees to Dickless' white noise Beatles.

First time I saw them, their singer Theo was drenched from head to toe in fake blood, having just ripped off a wedding dress to reveal a tacky plastic mini-skirt and a pair of glowing eyes doubling as a bra. A carnival queen in stripes, Squid pounded her bass like a professional weightlifter. Dina and Sindi (low-cut blouses, sneers on faces) screeched and belly-danced their way on guitar through the mega 'Cook Fuck + Rock' and 'Cookie Monster'. Musically . . . um, musically, they sounded much as you'd imagine. Rock with plenty of blunders and missed starts and howling solos thrown in. Theo sang in a disconcertingly operatic manner.

Trouble was, this sort of one-dimensional cartoon soon began to pale, however enticing the bright primary colours of the 'Chicks' debut 1990 album *Babysitters On Acid*. Early on, I said that Dickless made Lunachicks sound like Kylie Minogue with a bad hangover . . . a comparison the East Coast quintet didn't take kindly to.

'If you say that again,' yelled drummer Becky, 'we're going to open up your mouth, rest it on the kerb and hold you there while one of us stomps on your head. Then we're going to tie you to the back of my 750 Honda and drive you down Broadway, all the way to the Manhattan bridge and throw you off.'

'And then you'll be sorry,' added Squid.

'Oh, I don't mind people being nasty,' tempered Vegan Theo. 'I just hated being called a bimbo.'

When I saw the 'Chicks ten years later in Melbourne, they were still ploughing the same groove as a walking, talking, brawling, bawling punk cartoon but without as many bum notes. Their sound had progressed to borrowing heavily from the first couple of Runaways albums, while their lyrics could have been taken from a Hanna-Barbera clip, albeit one with a racy, adult theme. More songs about tits, ass, bad ass bitches and car wrecks. Theo had progressed from a plastic skirt to full-on fetish rubber dress, but other than that Lunachicks were almost identical. Talk about thrashing your one idea into oblivion! You just knew when Theo was going to throw in an insult, a cuss word or an eating disorder. It didn't matter what the year was.

I guess consistency is to be admired, but give me a one-off, flaming bright and then gone, any day.

I said earlier this is where my betrayal comes in.

Here's why. Babes In Toyland had an almost unique sound. It wasn't until Courtney came along shortly afterwards and ripped off Kat's image and music for Hole's *Pretty On The Inside*, did I hear it duplicated. So what did I do? Go with the LA girl, the one able to flirt better. It wasn't deliberate. It was just that I partied with Courtney more, and she didn't hit me every other time she saw me. (Well, not after the first few occasions, when she thought that calling me 'sexist' would help further her career.) The music Babes In Toyland created was so close to my core, the way Kat would take a split-second pause before launching into another scream, those powerful rolling drums and bass.

I never came close to capturing the essence of Babes In Toyland during interviews, I was too shy, too embarrassed to talk about music that mattered so much. During our first encounter, I only asked questions in words of one syllable and even referred to their music as a 'cartoonish assault', albeit one as harrowing as *The Shining* or Windsor McCay's nightmarish *Little Nemo In Slumberland* comic strip. Even the title of *Spanking Machine* would, I told them, be taken to refer to the way the band treated their instruments.

'That's cool,' Michelle laughed. 'That's the best one so far. Babes In Toyland: three retarded musicians beating hell out of their equipment, treating it like a toy.'

The second time (for 1991's mini-album *To Mother*) I'd got more of a fix on the music, but the band refused to take too seriously someone who enjoyed his alcohol so much. I suggested to Kat that perhaps some people might find the Babes' music a little, uh, *upsetting*.

'Why?' she asked, perplexed. 'Because I scream? It's not like I say mean things.'

Right. So lines like '*I know the sugar plum fairy/Her name is Mary/She's halfway inside my arm/She halfway does great harm/So she charmed herself into a toilet/And fucked herself/Gold and holy silver beads shot out her eyes/Then the pain comes . . .*' (from 'Catatonic') aren't distressing?

'I suppose,' the singer stalled. 'But one man's upsetting music is another's beautiful lullabies.'

We swapped stories instead, like Lori being fed tequila until she couldn't pronounce the name of the brand any more, and the Babes signing a deal with Warners in America. The tour was typically chaotic: in Leeds I had to crouch at the front of the Duchess Of York's stage, holding Kat's microphone stand upright against the hordes of maniacal stage-divers and body-slammers.

The Liverpool date was even more intense. The ceiling was about seven foot off the ground, and a lack of ventilation meant that perspiration was dripping everywhere: faces, hands, feet, the rafters, walls, the microphones, the floor . . . *everywhere*. Only fifteen people could actually see the band that were playing behind some sort of cage, much to Kat's discomfort. Halfway through the show, Michelle called for a bottle of whisky and by the end it was empty. A girl crawled backstage, vomited and keeled over at my feet, unconscious. Still the kids were stage-diving in that precious six inches of space, and still songs like 'Vomit Heart' and 'Ripe' sounded like the most precious jewels in the world, precious because they were so tarnished and unafraid of their own beauty. The tour manager was kept busy darting around, holding up wooden crash barriers, placing (Lori's) socks over microphones to stop electric shocks, holding up the drum kit, pushing back stage invaders.

'You have to stop thinking in those situations,' explained Michelle afterwards. 'Get a little shot of whisky and do it.'

I tried one more time with Kat later: why do you just write songs about bad situations?

'Because when you're having a good time, you don't have a catharsis with yourself, you just go and have a barbecue or something,' she replied, shifting the sleeping bag on our shared floor that night to a more comfortable position. 'This is good therapy, like going to church or something.'

Ever appreciate L7? You should.

All they ever wanted to do was rock – rock hard, rock strong. Rock like sex never mattered. One of their earliest songs, the Sub Pop single 'Shove', is their greatest and most revealing moment. It's a diatribe on the treatment women get in the moshpit when all they want to do is . . . altogether now . . . SHOVE! That was L7 in a nutshell: equality around a guitar tuner; equality around an overloading amplifier; equality so equal that equality shouldn't even be mentioned in a discussion of their music. (Sorry.) The fans liked L7 because of their no-nonsense punk-influenced grind, somewhere between Richie Blackmore and Tad Doyle, not because they played up on their sex. L7 were hard and heavy, with (as they sang on 'Fast And Frightening') 'so much clit, she don't need balls'.

This is what L7 had to say on the idea of 'foxcore': 'We all have vaginas and instruments – and that's all we have in common.' The band rapidly got tired of sensitive fanboys wanting to make a big deal out of their womanhood and having to justify their music as a gender statement. That's not to say L7 weren't feminists – they were – but they and like-minded musicians such as Babes In Toyland refused to take the more overt approach of the Riot Grrrls, where gender politics crept into interpersonal relationships. Kat Bjelland, for example, was just pissed off that some guy left her or whatever. She didn't view it as a patriarchal thing, more of a 'you fucking asshole' thing. Likewise, L7. The cover of their debut album *Smell The Magic* depicted the head of a man, on his knees, being pulled towards the crotch of a plastic-clad dominatrix.

L7 used the same pummelling four-chord refrain throughout the nineties. Their minor hits, 'Pretend We're Dead' and the rather menacing 'Andres', were indicative of their appeal: primal rock, played smart and given a slight New Wave sheen by whichever major label producer was passing. Given a different climate, one that allowed the Go-Go's and Joan Jett to hit big with similar, almost cartoon-esque songs a few years earlier, L7 could have been massive.

Sub Pop Grunge

▲ Mudhoney's Mark Arm: Reading Festival, England, 1991 (Stephen Sweet)

▲ Chris and Kim of Soundgarden: Arizona, July 1994 (Steve Gullick)

▼ Everett True aka The Legend! – perhaps the worst-selling Sub Pop single ever (cover: Colin Bell)

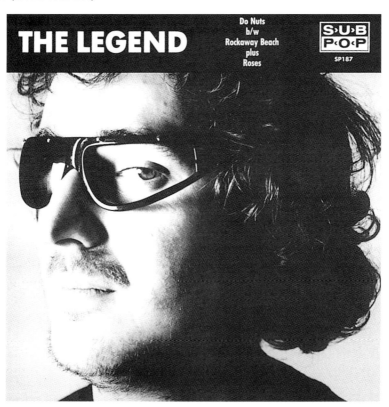

THE LEGEND

Do Nuts
b/w
Rockaway Beach
plus
Roses

S·U·B
P·O·P
SP187

▲ Nirvana
(Dave, Krist, Kurt):
Stockholm,
June 1992
(Steve Gullick)

◄ Kurt Cobain and
Everett True in
matching spectacles
and T-shirts:
Stockholm,
June 1992
(Steve Gullick)

▲ Kurt, November 1993 (Steve Gullick)

▲ Courtney, March 1994 (Stephen Sweet)

◄ Hole (Eric, Courtney, Patty) in the back garden of the Cobain residence: Los Angeles, October 1992 (Stephen Sweet)

Everett, Courtney and   ►
Frances, backstage at
Nirvana's MTV 'New Year's
Eve' show: Seattle,
December 1993
(Steve Gullick)

Riot Grunge

◄ Jad Fair, singer of Half-Japanese and his £28 guitar: Bristol, England, 1991 (Stephen Sweet)

▲ Niki and Chris of Huggy Bear: London, Valentine's Day 1993 (Stephen Sweet)

▲ The Pastels (Stephen, Aggi, Katrina): London, 1997 (Steve Gullick)

Grunge Lite

◀ Eddie Vedder of Pearl Jam: NYC, April 1994 (Steve Gullick)

Art Grunge

Mark Ibold and Steve Malkmus of Pavement: February 1992 (Stephen Sweet) ▼

Beck and Lou Barlow: October 1994 (Stephen Sweet) ▼

The Real Grunge

Babes in Toyland ▶
and Everett True:
Birmingham,
England, 1991
(Stephen Sweet)

▲ The Jesus Lizard: Chicago, 1993 (Stephen Sweet)

Pop Grunge

◄ Urge Overkill celebrating a Bulls victory: Chicago, 1992 (Steve Gullick)

▲ The Breeders: Sheffield, England, Halloween 1993 (Stephen Sweet)

◄ The Lemonheads at singer Evan Dando's old school: Boston, Massachusetts, 1992 (Steve Gullick)

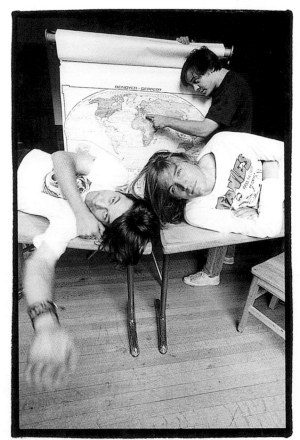

The self-explanatory 'Freak Magnet' (from 1994's rather OK *Hungry For Stink*) rocked like rock should never have moved on from the Motörhead and Girlschool collaboration. As indeed it shouldn't. By the time 1997's *The Beauty Process: Triple Platinum* appeared, it was mostly over. There's only so far punk bands can carry their youthful aggression and energy.

Give me catharsis.

Back in the early nineties, I wrote a series of misinterpreted and slightly clumsy articles explaining 'why women can't rock – the rules don't allow it'. For example, both musical instruments and the entertainment industry's power structure are weighted heavily against female interlopers. I cited examples of how stereotyping helped keep power away from potential insurrectionists like Polly Harvey and Babes In Toyland. I explained how men would always find words to dismiss what they didn't understand or found threatening – the obvious ones like 'man-haters' for women who stood up for their own sex and 'hag' for anyone who wore combat boots. No wonder Riot Grrrls and cutie bands like Heavenly sometimes tried to make themselves look as unthreatening and childlike as possible: subversion can only occur once you're inside the system.

The two great role models for women in the fifties when rock was invented (to suppress black culture) were Doris Day and Marilyn Monroe: the homemaker and the bubbly sex kitten. This still mostly holds true in rock music. Women who don't slot into these pigeonholes are marginalised. Take a quick count of the number of women you see fronting TV programmes, or acting in films, or creating music. Is it a 50-50 split with men? If not, why? Equality is now a given in many workplaces in Britain, but it still hasn't reached that status in the music industry. The day is some way off when we'll have a female Marilyn Manson, or Bruce Springsteen. Clearly the reason for that isn't lack of talent, either.

Oh, and please don't cite the dreadful whining hippie Eastern student Alanis Morissette or any of her kind as positive role models. Does it come as a surprise that she – and not the Breeders or PJ Harvey or Kristin Hersh – sells millions upon millions of records? It shouldn't.

Babes In Toyland could clearly rock and yet never achieved anywhere near the degree of success once predicted. Part of this was down to timing and luck and lack of MTV-acceptable videos, doubtless. Part of it was down to the fact the media only ever has time for one strong female in any given field at any point in time (unlike with male performers) and by the time Babes signed to a major they already had their Courtney 'Kinderwhore' Love, thanks very much. Mostly, it's because what people – even Korn fans and bloody Limp Bizkit and Slipknot fans – are really searching for from rock music is reassurance, not something that disconcerts.

Michelle left the Babes after her boyfriend, Henry Rollins roadie Joe Cole, was shot dead outside Rollins' Venice Beach home by an LA gang member, shortly before Christmas '91. Her replacement was long-time friend Maureen Herman, but it wasn't the same. Maybe the Babes left a little of their soul behind when they let Michelle go; maybe they should have given her more time to recover from the tragedy. Instead, they went back into the recording studio with Sonic Youth's Lee Ranaldo and recorded *Fontanelle*, their cleaned-up major label debut. Less than a year later they split up for several days before reforming to record the stopgap *Painkillers* 'album' and tour with Lollapolooza.

When I caught up with the Babes again in June '93 in Seattle, it was the first time the band had seen each other for several months. Kat was (briefly) married to Stu from Lubricated Goat, and had formed a band (Crunt) with him. It seemed like an appropriate time to ask Babes In Toyland about the movement they'd helped influence, Riot Grrrl.

'Movements?' asked Lori, characteristically refusing to be serious. 'Ugh! I wish I could go to the bathroom! God! I was tour-managing Silverfish for five weeks and I only went once. It was like the tour joke.'

'Kathleen [Hanna, Bikini Kill singer] once gave me a really cool dress,' revealed Kat, after I persisted with my questions. 'All right,' she added, looking at my face. 'I think anyone who stirs up controversy is cool, it's better than sitting around on your ass, doing nothing. I like the way it goes "Grrrrrrr!" That tiger power.'

'We were foxcore, now we're Riot Grrrl,' sighs Lori. 'Is that any better?'

'Quit labelling us!' the singer complains. 'It's taking the importance out of things.'

Uh-oh. Here it comes, the answer that every female rock band since time immemorial gives when questioned about support for their own sex . . .

'Anyway,' she adds. 'Music transcends all genders, or it's meant to.'

Kat and Courtney's sibling-like rivalry started back in the eighties.

The two women were briefly in a band together in LA called Sugar Baby Doll, with future L7 bassist Jennifer Finch. (Sugar Baby

Doll sounded like a youthful gothic monstrosity. Their instrumental 'The Quiet Room' later turned up on 1991's *To Mother* and, oddly, *Fontanelle*.) Both singers were strippers in Portland, Oregon, and had a similar taste not just in dress sense, but in men. Kat included the vicious hate song 'Bruise Violet' for Courtney on *Fontanelle* after Courtney claimed the credit for the 'kinderwhore' look. *'You see the stars through eyes lit up with lies,'* Kat spat. *'You got your stories all twisted up in mine/You fucking bitch/I hope your insides rot/Liar liar liar.'* Courtney responded with 'Violet' on 1994's *Live Through This*. Shortly after this I met Kat again: she was at the Cobain residence to comfort Courtney after Kurt's suicide.

This love–hate relationship continues to the present day.

Pop Grunge

I Just Wanna Get Along
(The Breeders, The Amps)

Kim Deal. All I know is that she made a great drinking buddy.

I lost count of the times she would join me after shows, determined to see who could last the pace till dawn. It was usually a raucous draw. We'd sing Bee Gees covers and songs from *Oliver!* in a corner with her twin sister Kelley, end up knocking back triple Pernods with Alex from Blur in a hotel bar, perhaps partake of her favourite tipple, the lethal Mississippi Mudslide. I would go off home or back to the hotel and recuperate. She'd repeat the feat night after night. At one stage, she and Kelley were said to be drinking half a bottle of whisky each before hitting the stage. Some occasions I don't recall, others I do all too vividly. Once, the first time I met her after Kurt's death, she yelled at me until tears ran down our faces. People stepped over us as we fought in the corridor: what else could they do?

'Do you think Kurt would have killed himself if he hadn't met Courtney?' she asked me again and again, just months after she'd invited me to travel with her band, on the day of Kurt's memorial service. What, if I hadn't introduced them to each other, you mean? Fuck you, Kim.

Kim Deal. All I know is that, for the longest time, she was my definition of rock.

She had impeccable credentials, of course. She came from white trash central, Dayton, Ohio. She'd been in the Pixies, the group who had such an influence on Nirvana's sound. The first two Pixies albums (released in 1987 and 1988) rank alongside *anything* by an American band in the nineties. Rarely has Halloween sounded so catchy, or spooky. I can recall pogoing my way across several tables in the balcony of London's Forum as the Pixies played and friends tried to hush me. How could I be quiet? A massive shadow was on the wall and was bouncing up and down in perfect synchronisation with the music. Kim was undervalued in Pixies, but responsible for one of the Boston band's finest songs, the eerie 'Gigantic'.

The Breeders' first album, the sparse, Steve Albini-produced *Pod* appeared in 1990 while the Pixies were turning into a lame surf rock parody of themselves. Kurt wanted the Breeders as support for the *Nevermind* US tour, but he couldn't get them. They were still a side project. Kim Deal. She was so casual about her genius it was genius. Most artists would've killed to be blessed with the lilt in her voice. A few years later, Portland's Dandy Warhols wrote a song about wanting to be her. Many people pretended to be fucked-up on drugs and alcohol, and not care what others thought. Kim didn't pretend.

Impeccable credentials? I'd say. *Pod* was created by what amounted to an alternative super-group. There was the vivacious Tanya Donelly (Throwing Muses, Belly), deadpan English bassist Josephine Wiggs (Perfect Disaster), Brit Walford aka Shannon Doughton aka Mike Hunt (from Slint, a band who revolutionised the Chicago underground scene with 1990's *Spiderland*) and Carrie Bradley, the violinist from brilliant human Boston band Ed's Redeeming Qualities. *Pod* was one of Kurt's favourite albums. Even now, the sparseness behind its shifting dynamics and warped pop sensibilities delights. It took just 21 days to rehearse and record, as every album should.

Early Breeders lyrics concerned themselves with abortion, weird sex and death. 'Doe' was written about the patronising attitude of men towards women giving them head.

'They pat you on the head,' explained Kim, 'like you're a tiny female deer.'

Everyone looked to Kim for approval. Like she could care. Courtney Love described her as 'the most empowered person I've ever met. She's got this huge sense of entitlement'. After Black Francis abdicated from his position in rock's forefront with a series of bad, whining post-Pixies albums, suddenly everyone wanted to know the Breeders. Especially as they were mostly female, and known for their fondness for partying. *Pod* was about sex, as was the title track on its 1992 follow-up, the orgasmic 'Safari' EP.

'That song,' Tanya Donelly informed me, 'is mean and has a sexual element.'

Which is . . .

'It's about coming,' explained Kim.

The Breeders weren't shy. Our first interview contained a massive argument about what constituted losing one's virginity.

Newest member, puritan Kelley – who'd joined, never having picked up a guitar before – thought it needed to involve penetration. Tanya argued passionately, and drunkenly, that it didn't.

'You can't consider lesbians to be virgins,' she said, 'because they have sex with each other. I consider losing your virginity to be the first time you get into a bed or the back seat of a car or a bench or the park or the bathroom sink . . . There are so many levels to sex. Penetration is just a formality.'

Eighteen months later, we were still talking about virginity. Only now we'd moved onto the circumstances under which the band themselves had lost theirs.

'Kelley didn't have sex during her adolescent years,' jokes Kim.

'Wait a minute,' her twin interrupts. 'Let me hand the mic to Kim. OK, she's right. But I did decide to have sex before my nineteenth birthday . . .'

'I don't want to know this,' says Kim. She starts humming loudly and places her hands over her ears. Her sister asks her if she wants to take her turn first.

'No,' replies the singer. 'It just grosses me out too much.'

'Why?'

'You're still a virgin!'

'God, Kim! You had sex!'

'I was married, that's different.'

'What? You were a virgin and then got married.'

'It's depressing.'

'When I was nineteen,' continues a determined Kelley, 'I decided I had to lose my virginity. So I had sex with this guy and it was awful. I didn't have sex again until I was twenty-five, and that was when I lost my virginity, because my hymen didn't break with this other weirdo guy. So that's it. And we fucked for twenty-five hours continuous. It's way too big a deal, holding this cherished thing. You're supposed to enjoy it when you're young.'

Affable long-term drummer Jim MacPherson's first time was even odder.

'All my sexual experiences from when I was young are blurred,' he laughed. 'I started at such an early age with alcohol and drugs that I can't remember anything. You know that first time? I was taken advantage of by a thirty-eight-year-old woman on a Florida beach. I didn't know what I was doing. How old was I? About fourteen.'

Kim Deal. All I know is that there was something about the way she used to stand there on stage, cigarette hanging from her lips as she bent down to change another string, smoke stinging her eyes.

Isn't that right there the definition of rock, doing something pleasurable, for the quick fix, even though you know it will ultimately hurt you?

What wasn't there to love about Kim Deal? Aside from her fearsome temper, scathing tongue and dismissive attitude towards anyone too slow to keep up. One sure way of irritating the singer was to ask her a question about 'women in rock'. Muttering the words Riot Grrrl in her vicinity was like holding an extremely large red rag to a particularly belligerent bull. This, despite the fact Kim Gordon from Sonic Youth and the Grrrl-influenced Free Kitten co-directed the Breeders' 'Cannonball' video. Kim just wasn't having any gender issues brought into discussions of her music. She saw it as demeaning.

'It doesn't wash,' Kim Deal told the *NME*, 'because when I think about music I think about strings and bass parts and little things that are actually going on during the song. Feminine chord progressions? I don't think so. That's the Beach Boys. Masculine chord progressions? That's L7. Feminine and masculine don't exist in music. It's like a masculine and feminine cigarette: it's all tobacco.'

Every decade has its Chrissie Hynde, its Cerys Matthews. The former Mrs John Murphy wrote the finest pop songs of her generation, never pandered, did things by her rules – could turn out a mean country song, too – and got into bar brawls with Ohio truckers. She never apologised for her drug taking. Even rarer, she was prepared to discuss the pros and cons of heroin use in public, even though both she and her sister had been in trouble over the drug. Indeed, Kim had seen Kelley OD.

'All those bad things that have happened on drugs,' she told me in '95. 'Kelley's arrest and Kurt's death and everybody who's high on drugs . . . Maybe Kurt did it because he was high on heroin and couldn't stop and hated himself for that . . . I still believe in being able to do drugs and being able to learn from them. I haven't changed my mind. I like drugs and I don't care.'

'There is no one in this room right now who could honestly say that drugs have not played an important role in their lives,' she began another of our interviews, her whole band present. 'Drugs are no more dangerous than driving a car. If you decide to put your foot down to the floor and see how fast you can possibly go, and you crash and die, that is not the car's fault, it's the driver's fault. Taking drugs requires judgement.'

Kim was a control freak. How couldn't she have been?

'Kim's greatest asset is her unpredictability,' her bassist Josephine Wiggs told me in '93. 'Coupled with her single-mindedness. I like her ability to constantly surprise me. She won't even consider what's going to happen tomorrow because she's dealing with whatever it is right now.'

Kim dressed like a mechanic and sang like a drowsy angel. Her voice oozed lasciviousness and *smouldered*, while her hedonistic bent rivalled Keith Richards. Breeders songs sounded delirious in their pop magnificence – a perfect mix of sixties girl group harmonies and mid-eighties Middle American rock power. Want proof? Look no further than the Aerosmith cover 'Lord Of The Thighs' on 1993's 'Cannonball' single, the Ohio girl's way of paying tribute to her heritage. It's also the weakest Breeders track ever recorded.

Kim listed 'seeing a passed-out drunk girl being carried away over the heads of the audience at an early Rush concert' as being a formative musical experience. She so wanted to be that girl. Kelley discovered rock'n'roll after seeing classic rock film *The Song Remains The Same* at a drive-in, high on acid. All three American members of *Last Splash*-era Breeders listed Rush as being among their influences. Only Josephine was savvy enough to namecheck brittle English post-punks Gang Of Four.

A dirty fag and her cheeky grin, that's all it took. The Breeders had a coy playfulness to songs like 'Don't Call Home' (from the 'Safari' EP) that masked the often sinister undertones going on behind the warped guitars and restrained beat. Why is that siren wailing in the background? Why is Kim whispering *'You never can call home'*? A sudden chill runs down your spine while you're tingling from pleasure . . . and then another intoxicating guitar line starts up breathless, as you fall all over again.

That's the Breeders effect.

I want to set a scene for you. The year is 1995. The Breeders have disappeared, gone the last time Kelley got busted for drugs. Perhaps Kim didn't like playing stadium Lollapalooza shows, who knows? In their stead we have the Amps: rough, raw, righteous and even more bewildering than the Breeders. One minute blasts of pure energy, five-minute tales of disillusionment. Everything teeters on the brink of collapse. During shows, ex-Breeder Jim MacPherson vomits between songs, and hands out pieces of his drum kit. Kim laughs and sways dangerously. The two new Dayton homeboys flex their tattoos and grin with obvious pleasure. Think back to that lovely moment when you discovered how easy it is to create a melody with three chords and a crate full of beer. That's the Amps.

It's late. We're in Kim Deal's hotel room in Glasgow: I'm sprawled across the bed, she's checking her reflection in the mirror. We're surrounded by tour debris – clothes, guitar strings and beer bottles. Downstairs, people drink *heavily*.

I ask Kim whether she thinks she's attractive and she replies, 'Well, Everett, when people get to our age, if they like someone then they find them attractive, and I know you like me . . .'

Kim gives a brilliant rant about thirtysomething men, unable to get it up unless they're confronted with 'strange'. Strange, according to Kim, is strange pussy: pussy that is different or young or wrapped in a tight mini-skirt; pussy that is fine unless it happens to belong to the person the man's been in a relationship with for several years. Objects are hurled across the room in anger. Voices are raised and lowered conspiratorially. One long stream of invective follows another: junkies and in particular Kelley, 'fools in love' and assholes who use the word sexism gratuitously, celibacy. Tape recorders are switched on and off. Topics become too personal for public consumption. Afterwards, Kim goes down to the lobby and, somehow or other, gets the mother of all bruises on her forearm. It's a cracking interview. An interview to end all interviews.

So, wouldn't you know it? Not for the first time while talking to Kim, the tape fails to come out. When it's finally sorted out, it's next week and we're still talking about sex.

Don't you hate that whole thing where people say they love you just to get you into bed?

'No one's ever said that to me just to get me into bed,' Kim moans, before realising what she's said.

She laughs.

'That makes me sound like a slut! If someone told me they loved me, I would leave, because that's uncool. You don't start getting *gushy-gushy* on the first date like that. That's gross. I would just giggle.'

So how would someone get you into bed?

'Get me drunk.'

She shows me the bruise on her arm.

'I'm too macho,' she sighs. 'I'm too macho.'

Later, an inebriated Kim gets into an argument with an equally inebriated Debbie Smith from Echobelly, and starts smashing the dressing room up, throwing bottles at the wall. Within half a minute, the room is a mess of broken glass and alcohol, Jim cowering behind an amplifier and myself too shocked to have moved. Another 30 seconds and Kim is all smiles again, joking and rasping in her nicotine-stained voice.

* * *

Kim Deal. All I know is that she was (briefly), as *Feminist Baseball* put it, the college rock Ava Gardner. She looked beautiful and big and tough in person, but didn't photograph that well. Did that make the Pixies singer Black Francis her Frank Sinatra? I introduced her to Mr Cobain, you know ... and then reaped the benefits a few years later when I conducted a joint interview with the pair in Seattle, December 1993. The interview had been going great for about twenty minutes – an argument about sexism, an argument about menthol cigarettes – until I noticed the recorder wasn't switched on. Sigh. Fortunately, this was seen to be typical ET behaviour. Kim claimed to have been popular in school, a cheer-leader and captain of the gymnast team. When she was young, she wanted to be gymnast Nadia Comaneci.

'Basically I just wanted to be someone before they were hairy and ugly,' she explained.

The Breeders were so underrated just because Kim wouldn't wear lip gloss in their videos. She was willing to wrestle with journalists, shout loudest and be flippant and genius simultaneous-ly, however. Courtney claimed the singer was the only woman Kurt ever admitted to having a crush on. It wasn't like her band-members were lacking in smarts or charisma, either.

Brighton's Jo Wiggs, for one – her down-to-earth, sardonic English manner was a perfect foil to Kim's flights of fancy. At Lollapalooza '94 she came over to where we were standing, just so she could laugh at our plight at not being able to blag any kind of backstage passes at all. Cheers, Jo!

'It's gold! Gold sparkle is our theme,' she informed us, in case we got thrown out before the Breeders played. 'We have gold sparkle risers and our monitors are covered in gold lamé. We never got as far as all dressing in gold, because we felt we'd disappear against the background.'

You could have dressed in silver or red.

'That's true. That's very true.'

'Josephine doesn't talk a lot which is a big plus in my book,' explained Kim. 'She dyes her hair, dyes her lips, slut, and is very particular about what she wears – the colours, everything.' This was in direct opposition to Kim and Kelley, of course. It was rare that the twins dressed up. 'She's frequently paralysed by her extremely broad overview. She once had a plectrum for seven years. There was nothing special about it, she just didn't need a new one.'

Jo wanted to be leather-clad, high-kicking, immeasurably cool Avenger Diana Rigg when she was young. But, as she explained: 'I always knew the only time you saw her was when she was acting cool, but wouldn't it be great to exist in those half-hour long, superficial situations? It would like being in a rock band without all the waiting.'

Kelley, on the other hand, wanted to be Samantha from *Bewitched*. Good job David Yow from the Jesus Lizard didn't know that. He used to have strange pre-pubescent fantasies about the character.

'Kelley's not particular, she'll wear just about anything,' says her twin. Sure, the two Deals were identical twins. Kim used to carry ID bearing Kelley's photo. 'Right now [in the tour bus] she's smoking as usual, reading as usual – some sort of soft erotica. She's a sweet girl unless she's being a roaring, drunken broad of a bitch! My mom and dad always said she was a bad influence and that I did what she did. She was the one who first smoked cigarettes, skipped school and took drugs. I would have turned out really good, I bet, if it hadn't been for her.'

Jim MacPherson was plain sweet. He reckoned *Pod* had one of the best drum sounds ever and wanted to be GI Joe when young.

'Jim grew up with lots of sisters,' related Kim. 'His parents took him to a psychologist when he was eight years old because he talked like a girl. Jim, poor guy. Had six cups of tea at six this morning. He misses his kid, and his hand hurts. He's very unimpressed by travelling.'

The last time I met Jim was in Melbourne, 2000. He was playing drums alongside a fellow Amp in Robert Pollard's exceedingly drunk Guided By Voices. Backstage, Robert grabbed me round the neck and started yelling to everyone what I'd last said in his presence. 'You were awesome man,' he laughed breathlessly. 'We were standing there with Jim Greer [ex-guitarist and *Spin* journalist] and you started ranting, "I'm famous, you're famous, he's famous, we're all fucking famous – but nobody else here is!" '

So Bob insisted I go up on stage to tell everyone in the audience the story. It made a change from him going on about how I'd discovered his band.

US Pop Catharsis
(Urge Overkill, Girls Against Boys, Afghan Whigs, Madder Rose, Scarce, Rodan)

It's June 1992.

There we are – Urge Overkill's mob and the British press – on the roof of an apartment block overlooking Chicago's impressive skyline, sitting round a table consuming Schlitz beer and slices of watermelon, watching the big basketball game between the Chicago Bulls and the Portland Trailblazers. Above our heads in the overcast sky, a police helicopter circles in case the Bulls win and rioting erupts like it did last year. Across the way, the Puerto Ricans are celebrating independence weekend. A partial solar eclipse is predicted. All hell is gonna break loose if the Bulls get their shit together.

There seems no chance of that happening. The Bulls are 79–64 down, with just one quarter to go. The Yanks' faces are glum. The Brits are triumphant.

'Hey! There's no way the Bulls can steal it now,' I yell. 'If they do, you can shave my head like Michael Jordan.'

The final whistle blows. The Bulls have beaten Portland. Pandemonium breaks out: fireworks explode, guns are fired, a whole crowd heads for the nearest big department store, overturning a car on the way. Nash Kato (guitar/vocals) picks up a giant bollard and uses it to foghorn people passing by on the street below: 'Booooollls! Booooollls!' A red moon appears behind the Sears Tower.

Blackie Onassis (drums) turns to me with an evil grin: 'What were you saying about Michael Jordan, man?'

Oops.

There was far more going on in rock music during the early nineties than just Seattle.

Across America, there was a minor revolution happening, fed by bands on small labels previously ignored by the media. Bands like Chapel Hill's clean-cut Superchunk with their Merge label and churning 'Slack Motherfucker' single that fast became an underground anthem. Bands like DC's Unrest and their colleagues the pop-fed Tsunami and their inspirational Simple Machines tape label. Bands like New York's feral and mean Action Swingers, and Dean Wareham's Galaxie 500 offshoot Luna. Bands like the salacious Girls Against Boys, fearsome Cop Shoot Cop and all their Touch & Go relatives in Chicago. Bands like the ridiculously arrogant Afghan Whigs, the Sub Pop group that got away. These were bands that made music not because they thought they'd become rich or famous but for the thrill of it. All right, maybe they thought they'd attain a tiny degree of fame . . .

Seattle was merely a microcosm of what was happening in America, 1990–91. This microcosm was repeated numerous times across the country. Louisville (Rodan, Slint); Chicago (Tar, Arcwelder, Urge Overkill); Boston (Blake Babies, Buffalo Tom, Lemonheads); Rhode Island (Scarce, Throwing Muses); Portland (Pond,

Calamity Jane, Dead Moon); Minneapolis (Zu Zu's Petals, the Amphetamine Reptile bands); Olympia (K records, Some Velvet Sidewalk, Kicking Giant, kill rock stars records, Yoyo records); Washington DC (Fugazi, Dischord records), and so on.

One fine example was Robert Pollard's gorgeously unpredictable Guided By Voices from Dayton, Ohio. Robert was an ex-schoolteacher who claimed to write up to 100 songs an album. 'I have no way of knowing how many songs I've written,' Pollard told me in 2000. 'It could be ten thousand. I have a whole suitcase full of songs on tape that I carry round with me. It depends on your definition of a song. I have loads of ten-second songs. I'm writing a song as you type.'

When I talked to Robert and his fellow musicians in New York 1993 for their first ever interview, GbV had already released six full-length albums recorded on four-tracks and in friends' basements. That was some meeting. Every time I put down my glass in between sips of beer and whisky and tequila, there was another full one waiting for me. Sure, the group had reason to celebrate. They'd waited ten years to be interviewed by an actual music critic, and they weren't going to let it slip by unmarked.

As you catch up with me again, it's 1993 . . . or maybe 1994. We're driving to Lafayette or perhaps Kansas City. It's hard to know. It's a college town, certainly. You can tell by the drunken population wandering the streets, tanked up on Bud and testosterone looking for something, anything to fill the void. It could be Madison. It's a town in the middle of America, in the middle of nowhere, certainly.

We've been driving for ten hours now – racing through the flatlands, hungover and eyes barely open, horizon stretching out endlessly in front of us in our crappy, crammed, smelly van. Trucks with large stickers reading 'How's my driving? Call 1-800-ADVISE' roar past at 100 miles per hour. Breakfast is biscuits and sausage gravy, Taco Bell bean burritos and coffee. Unless we're sleeping on a fan's floor, in which case American (cardboard) bacon creeps onto the agenda. Tapes of the Pastels and Eddie Bond, the singing sheriff telling the story of Buford Posser, American folk legend and bad ass lawman, keep our eyelids from closing. Our arms rest on windowsills in the hot afternoon sun, no seat belts in sight. We drive past the home of the original McDonalds, through industrial garbage dumps and on to an interview at a Chicago video station where the VJ asks the band's one female member for her cooking tips. Detroit Rock City is even colder.

Rain drips through the roof. Beastie Boys and country singer Iris DeMent cause us to give voice, lustily. We wrestle as we roll down green hills, and laugh. We cruise down a freeway from Kentucky to Missouri in an ice storm past overturned vans on the verge, sleep caressing our eyes. We share scatological puns and Chicago gossip, try to work out what the main ingredient of the Midwest's favourite soft drink Big Red is. There are five, six of us in the van – a dusty torn mattress up back serving as impromptu rest spot for those who didn't manage to sleep last night, too much drink and partying. We chew on some wickedly tart Lemonheads candy sweets. We eat chocolate Easter Bunnies. In Kansas, it's warm beer and pinball flippers, paternal soundmen shouting down the PA to 'quit this joint'. In Lawrence, it's all freezing hallways and icy blue glances, guitars blasting holes through our hearts like piss in the snow.

Towns of leafy suburbia give way to towns of concrete under-passes give way to towns of scary shopping malls. Where are we playing tonight? Want me to do a slot?

I swagger on stage in Kansas City in front of a crowd of a thousand drunken frat-boys, much to the surprise of Come who are also sharing the bill. Somnambulist pop group Madder Rose – or is it those loveable post-rockers Rodan? – have consented to allow me my ten minutes of infamy. And I'm determined not to let the moment slip away.

'Last night,' I begin, swaying precariously in the spotlight, 'I had a quart of whisky . . . [cheers] . . . and a quart of vodka . . . [more cheers, as someone passes me a pitcher of beer] . . . I don't feel so hot tonight. This one's an old Beatles number you might recognise. It's called "I'm Down".'

Few bands lusted after fame as much as Urge Overkill.

When I first interviewed them, the Chicago trio took 40 minutes to decide which sunglasses to use for the photo shoot and treated myself and photographer Steve Gullick to a ride downtown to a few tiki cocktail bars in their electric blue 1973 Cougar XR7. For the actual photos, they posed with cocktail glasses, wearing matching green polo-necks and UO medallions and white trousers that they changed into and out of a dozen times a day. Other bands sweated. The Urge *perspired*.

'What we really aspire to is making a splash in the fashion world,' explained Blackie Onassis. 'Like George Harrison at an airport, 1968, flying in to the premiere of some film he's just produced. We like fashion because it's nonsense, but done with a flair that's missing in the rock world.'

This attitude and regard for sartorial elegance led some critics to dismiss the Urge's glamcore sound as throwaway. A shame, because Urge Overkill played a hard, shiny kitschadelic power pop that assimilated both the bell-bottomed past and 'cool jam' present, most notably on their taut, Cheap Trick-influenced 1993 Geffen album *Saturation*. Like Killdozer and Nirvana, the Urge recorded with Steve Albini and Butch Vig. They made records in tune with the Gestalt of rock'n'roll: peerless pop composer Neil Diamond and deep-voiced sex man Barry White, what rock was and what rock could be.

'We met Dean Martin in Minnesota,' King Roeser (vocals/bass) revealed in 1992. 'He gave us a metaphor about life involving plenty of dry martinis. We've met Jimmy Webb, one of the Cassidys, George Clinton ... "Urge Overkill?" he says. "Like a woodpecker in the hay!" We're like celebrant dabblers, drawn to the powerful forces of the universe.'

It was doubly appropriate that when the Urge finally attained some of the success they'd been grooming themselves for, it was on the back of an old Neil Diamond cover ('Girl, You'll Be A Woman Soon') used in 1995's *Pulp Fiction*. (It was the part of the movie where Mia/Uma Thurman dances alone in her apartment, pulling back her gloved hand across her face.) All those years spent knocking back flaming cocktails and dining out on local takeaway Duk's infamous non-dairy cheese substitute – 'You're not paying for the water, you're paying for the plastic cup' – hadn't gone to waste. Now they could party with Uma and John Travolta.

Urge dreamt of being stars on a par with Liza Minnelli and Barbra Streisand – real stars, in other words. 'Real stars know if they're overweight and can't sing,' Nash explained. 'Real stars don't ever pull an "Elvis" or a "Michael" [Jackson].'

Finally, they had a chance to live out their dreams.

Of course it didn't last. At the end of 1996, following a disastrous tour of America, Roeser left. Little has been heard from the band since. Don't cry for Urge, though. They always knew what stardom and fame entailed.

'Spend all your money!' Nash cried to me in a New York diner in September '93. 'Every last note and coin! You can end up broke on welfare in a homeless shelter and you'll still be a star. No one will know what became of you and you'll live forever. That's why Axl Rose is a star and Billy Joel isn't. These people spent their money when they had it. They did NOT put it by for a rainy day!'

'Fans give you their money,' added Blackie. 'They expect you to have a good time with it.'

Afghan Whigs made songs for the ladies. Cruel, fierce, enflamed, swaggering, licentious songs that managed the neat trick of being explicit while still hinting at so much. *'Ladies, let me tell you about myself,'* sang Greg Dulli on 'Be Sweet' in 1993. *'I got a dick for a brain and my brain is going to sell my ass to you.'* Dulli had a paradoxical belief in, and loathing for, his own masculinity. He'd frequently flagellate himself inside his songs, and then go out and make the same mistakes all over again. Greg revelled in his sex, even while he tortured himself as to how he could be such a bastard. *'My lust, it ties me up in chains,'* he lamented on 1996's 'Blame Etc'. Sometimes, he tried to write songs from a female perspective. Hence the presence of a lead vocal from Scrawl's Marcy Mays on *Gentlemen*. It was his male strut that set him apart from his more self-conscious peers, though.

The hard drinking Cincinnati, Ohio (later Seattle), group claimed to have met in jail. Bassist John Curley was Dulli's old friend, while drummer Steve Earle joined after his motorcycle crashed into the singer's car. The Whigs' debut album, 1988's self-released *Big Top Halloween* sounded derivative of Dinosaur Jr and the Replacements, but then so did everyone else back then. It didn't matter. Much of its follow-up, their Sub Pop debut *Up In It,* had a ferocity and love for pure rock that rivalled even Mudhoney.

Like label-mates Tad and Nirvana, the Whigs were fascinated by society's underbelly: the serial killers and religious bigots. 'The fact someone would want to rape someone else, the fact someone would want to kill in the name of God . . . I'd never do these things,' Dulli told me in 1991, 'but I'm fascinated by these acts.'

Both Dulli and Kurt Cobain came from towns with a 70 per cent white trash population, plenty of trailer parks and a whole load of narrow-mindedness. Like most of Washington, in fact. When I visited Olympia the weekend the Gulf War started, I saw rednecks and hillbillies cruising around in pick-up trucks, waving American flags and yelling pro-war sentiments, looking for hippies or local college students from Evergreen to beat the shit out of. (Washington State's Fort Lewis army base is situated between Tacoma and Olympia.) A pro-war rally in Olympia's tiny main square attracted 200 people and three times as many flags.

Early Afghan Whigs songs were extremely cathartic. Witness the incredible 1990 single 'Retarded', wherein Dulli screamed in his gravel-throated voice, *'Motherfucker lied to you/motherfucker told you no'* over and over. You didn't quite know who or what he was singing about, and you didn't care to find out either.

By the time Dulli had found his own voice – or rather, that of the great old female soul and Motown singers from the sixties – on 'My World Is Empty Without You' and 1992's 'Uptown Avondale', his band had moved far away from charges of revivalism. The idea of a grunge band moving into old school soul territory seems incredible now. Not as incredible as it sounded back then. Know what was great about Afghan Whigs? The way you wouldn't have trusted them even if they'd been your closest friends. The suits. The way Greg sounded like he'd kill for whomever he was singing about. The womanising. The compassion. The bellies. Their *soul*. Those goddamn bastards. Dulli's strained feckless croon owed far more to the tortured legacy of OV Wright than any rank male Ozzy imitators. The guitars would blur and bite like a pack of wildcats let out for the season. The drums leapt back and forth warily, like they knew they'd be fined for one missed beat, one fluffed roll.

The Whigs slipped slightly into parody by the time of 1996's *Black Love*. Dulli had taken his swagger beyond humour, thought it was enough simply to stand there and smoke another cigarette and look cool. Of course, he was probably right . . . If only the Whigs hadn't created such a legacy over their previous four albums, all those brooding, smouldering soul covers, and inflamed live shows.

American rock in the early nineties was varied, continually surprising. Half these bands played support to the other half, the order changing depending on which year it was. Without Nirvana, most of them wouldn't have been signed to a major. Where was the link, though? The fact that myself and *Melody Maker* (and thus *Spin*, *NME* and a thousand lesser lights) championed them? That they all had a legacy in common: bad mid-American seventies rock, as personified by *Frampton Comes Alive*, matched to the spiky aesthetics of New York and British punk?

Maybe the link was Matador Records, the New York 'independent' label that started from a (brilliant) acerbic fanzine written by owner Gerard Cosloy and ended up signing almost every post-Nirvana band in America. Or so it seemed. The slacker generation, that's what they called us, the bastards. Maybe the link was Lollapalooza, the travelling festival that would feature any local band prepared to compromise a handful of barely formulated ideals in exchange for a few dollars. Maybe there was no link, beyond happenstance. Still, perception is all that counts, right? Most of these groups had similar record collections, though, and weren't shy in parading their influences.

Take Girls Against Boys.

Remember Psychedelic Furs and how they managed for a split second to capture the darkness and claustrophobia of city life, the repetitive clickety-clack of trains running non-stop through the centre? Remember how, in Richard Butler's half-drawl, half-whine and the relentless thunder of drums, they offered escape through immersion, a way out by sinking deep within? OK, then.

Now imagine all those coked-out, bright-faced kids roaming free in *Pretty In Pink* confronted by a place like Brooklyn. Imagine if, instead of slumming it around art galleries and openings the rest of his life, Butler had taken to hanging with Fugazi's Ian MacKaye and Steve Albini. Imagine how *awesome* the Furs could have sounded with a little more imagination and guitars that blew cold sparks of fury, with words that resonated crazily through crowded clubs and empty streets. Imagine how *great* they could have been if they'd buttoned down the noise a little, started experimenting with silence. OK, then.

'Kill the bass-player, kill the other bass-player,' comes a Mark E Smith-esque chant above a dark bass line on the menacing 'Kill The Sax Player'. 'Kill the drummer, he can't play. This is way too fucking strange . . .' Girls Against Boys singer Scott McCloud starts choking back laughter in the studio. Time to switch allegiances again, time to get back to St Mark's Place, NYC. I turn, and there's Scott, wicked grin on his face, egging me on to punch the rock star, punch the rock star. I plead with him to leave me alone, but he's too slick and he's too sexy, and the night is too young. I have to obey him. It's out of my hands. Time to find another party.

Now, take a fast car. Please. Drink a bottle of Night Train in a side alley, ride Brooklyn's Queens Expressway at night, find an apartment where you can't hold down a conversation for more than three minutes because of junkies arguing on the stairwell. Start bugging out because you can't cope with all those feelings of anger, frustration and ecstasy swirling through your head. Whoa! Calm down, boy. Take it easy.

'When I hear our music,' says Scott, 'it's like being in a dark club with people talking to each other constantly. The incessant chatter, that's the murkiness I like to hear in music – the constant wash of everyday sound, trains running overhead.'

Like the Whigs, GVsB had a reputation for being a 'ladies' band'. Maybe it was something to do with the coiffeured hair, suits and sex within Scott's incessant drawl and founder member Eli Janney's brushed-aside spectacles.

'I wonder all the way down,' Scott chants on 'Learned It', Eli and Johnny's twin basses complementing Alexis' chaotic drum sound. 'You're nowhere at all/I've got one shot . . .' He gives a sigh, then leaves the band to carry the swagger and chill through. Time to switch. It's Seattle '99 and there are a few of us in a van with GVsB, throwing sneakers

out of windows, knocking back Maker's Mark. 'Say you're the greatest
rock critic in the world,' Scott evilly instructs my writing companion.
'SAY IT!' 'She can't, not when I'm here,' I tell them. 'I'll say it.' 'Yeah,
we all know that you don't mind saying it . . .' repeats Scott maliciously.

My nadir occurred in 1996 when I failed to make a Girls Against
Boys show in Madrid, because I was drinking somewhere in
London and couldn't be bothered catching the plane. There's no
snappy anecdote to round this section off. I wrote the review
anyway, and carried on drinking.

Days blur into nights, nights into days. We race around the centre
of Amsterdam on the backs of bicycles, swinging crazily round
lampposts, shouting until our voices crack and beyond, watching
Scarce bassist Joyce Raskin perfect that crazed dance of hers
onstage – halfway between AC/DC's Angus Young and something
far sexier. It's April 1995, and I'm in Holland with Rhode Island trio
Scarce, there to support Hole. Days blur into nights, nights into
fights and I'm listening back to a tape of me talking to the band, four
a.m. in a fountain, except it's not the band speaking on the tape . . .

'Jerry, Jerry, Jerry, Jerry,' the tape goes. 'Jerry, Jerry, Jerry,
Jerry, Jerry, Jerry, Jerry, Jerry . . . stupid asshole.'

It's Drew Barrymore, saying my real name over and over again
for two minutes. She's in Amsterdam with her date, Hole guitarist
Eric Erlandson, and knocking back shots with the worst of us. Ah,
huh. Time to start the interview again. It's May '95, and we've
moved to England. So we travel through darkness between Nottingham and London, knocking back shots of cider and vodka, tumbling
out to shoot pinball against a kidnapped Eric, sitting up till five a.m.
talking about hatred and old English movies and music that never
takes off. We race around the streets of Kensington, tear the roof
off Frankfurt, smoke dope till the whole world becomes one fuzzy
balloon.

It's June, and we've moved to Germany. Somewhere along an
autobahn, we break down and just *need* eggs over easy. Scarce
singer Chick Graning claims not to like people, but on the night of
our third attempt at an interview, he spends his time nursing me
back to something approaching health. Joyce claims to like
everyone, then tells us about how she hospitalised a schoolmate
using just a tennis racket. I'd mention the drummer too, but they
never lasted longer than a month.

We were together to celebrate the release of 'Glamourizing
Cigarettes', possibly the greatest song written about an ex-girlfriend
of Chick's named Tanya Donelly who was always pictured smoking

a fag because she thought it looked cool . . . ever! (Tanya didn't actually smoke.) The dangerously volatile 'All Sideways' and 'Days Like These' singles were even better. I've always been a sucker for male/female vocal interplay. Scarce had such passion and self-belief, it hurt.

Scarce were so cool: they would grab hold of all the cracks other bands fall through and make something of them. Dead sexy motherfuckers, Scarce sounded like all those parts of REM and Bowie no one is supposed to like. The trio also rocked like Soundgarden with serious distemper. Fugazi once snagged a plectrum Joyce had been using in a show, claiming they'd never seen as much blood on one pick before. Chick was straight out of the Marcel Marceau school of expression. His grimaces, the way he thrust his guitar into the air, his leaps and bounds were inspirational. His silken shirt and jacket didn't just get soaked. Little rivulets of sweat would continue to form on his back an hour after Scarce had finished playing.

'It's the blues man, it's the blues,' Chick explained to me over an espresso in New York once. 'They just grab hold of me. It's fun, you know. I can't imagine getting up on stage and simply standing there. You've got to sweat like a pig.'

Chick was formerly in Nashville's long haired, flannel-shirted Anastasia Screamed, a band I described as having spent their entire career trying to recapture the sound of Bob Mould's scream on Hüsker Dü's version of 'Eight Miles High'. This was an honourable occupation, the search for the inarticulate language of the soul. Chick hated US indie (college) bands with a vengeance.

'What's indie supposed to stand for?' he would ask, sneering. 'Independently wealthy?'

The singer grew up surrounded by bikers and listening to deep Southern country music like David Allen Coe. His mother befriended ghosts: he smoked 30 packs a day just to achieve that killer gravely effect in his voice; and he had the wildest staring eyes. Joyce drew children's books and painted in warm bursts of colour. She studied ballet for eight years. With Scarce, she practised it on stage while thinking about 'sex, happiness, spirituality, love and eternity . . . but mostly sex'.

'We want to be a sexy band,' she told me. 'Not in the way we look, but in the way we sound. Sexy makes you want to shake your hips.'

Shortly after Scarce finished that 1995 European tour, Chick suffered a brain aneurysm, and lapsed into a coma for several weeks. He recovered, but later decided he no longer wanted to be in a band with Joyce.

It was a sad end to such a great band.

* * *

Understand this.

These bands are close to the core of what this book is about. Pop music and spontaneity. I could barely have survived without it – whether it be the sweet, melancholy pop of New York's Madder Rose (the ones with the Buford Posser tapes) or the abrasive, jagged guitars of Louisville's Rodan (the ones with the Easter Bunnies). It's so vital to my life, a way of coping with all those bleak lonely hours where nothing seems to matter, except a lingering drawn-out minor chord or burst of molten guitar fury.

How could I resist Madder Rose? They wrote songs about displacement and loneliness, and suffused them with such hypnotic, dreamy tunes – this at a time when I had no home, when I was almost continually on the road. On a couple of occasions, I called *Melody Maker* to inform them I'd missed the plane back from Chicago to London and the next one wasn't due for a week. 'Have a good time, and don't forget to write,' my editor Allan Jones informed me. Chap! I would celebrate with a few cocktails with Urge Overkill's manager Beth, being sure to take in whatever was happening at Lounge Ax that evening.

Madder Rose captured the feeling of insomnia, a constant malaise of mine, that all-consuming desire to attain sleep whatever it costs. Know that deliciously drowsy feeling you get on a Saturday morning when there is no alarm clock to stop you from drifting back to dreamland? That's what listening to Madder Rose songs like 'Swim' or the beautiful, drawn-out 'While Away' feels like to me. When they agreed to let me travel in their van, I leapt at the chance. Sure, get the critic to ruin your version of Jonathan Richman's 'Sleep In Your Arms Tonight' with his fumbling backing vocals every show. It's fun! Forget friendships, though. Although neither of Madder Rose's two good albums, 1993's debut *Bring It Down* and its successor *Panic On*, captured their live magic, they still contain more moments of post-Velvets grace than anyone this side of the Pastels.

'*I guess you never know/I think of you all day long,*' Mary sang on 'Car Song'. '*So try to get some sleep.*'

If only I could.

If only I could.

It's a Shame about Evan
(The Lemonheads, Buffalo Tom)

Nineteen ninety-three's *Come On Feel The Lemonheads* is a much underrated album, each song an imperfectly sculpted exercise in gentle paranoia and loving despair. There are luminous tunes to swoon over, lyrics that mean everything and nothing in their self-doubt. There's a voice that cracks and ravishes simultaneously, seductive in its silken empathy. There are moments of straightforward adrenaline rush ('Dawn Can't Decide') and unashamed hedonism ('You Can Take It With You'). There's a duet with Belinda Carlisle of the Go-Go's, a compassionate look at LA's 'grip and grin' world ('Paid To Smile') and loads of insidious pop refrains concocted by singer Evan Dando and his Australian songwriting partner Tom Morgan.

In many ways, *Come On Feel* is the ultimate travelling companion for one lost in a world of superficial friends and 'paid to smile' benefactors, forever flying high. Where are we? Who cares? Here comes another radio station middle management disc jockey VJ reporter image consultant type, another distributor to make nice with. That part in *The Wedding Singer*, where Adam Sandler serenades Drew Barrymore on a plane over America. I swear that must have been based on Evan. Only Evan would have had both the arrogance and naïve belief in romance to attempt a trick like that.

During 1993 and early 1994, *Come On Feel* soundtracked my life, a life that was becoming increasingly surreal with each airport I visited and every LA club I found myself drunk outside. Its music caressed and comforted me, caught somewhere in a lightning storm between New York and Boston, thrown off a plane before it even took off from Heathrow at eleven a.m. for being too drunk, comatose in a Hollywood elevator. Every time Evan stumbled over a harmony, or soared off into the stratosphere with backing singer Juliana Hatfield in tow, there were my dreams and helplessness captured for the briefest of interludes.

Here's my take on that classic fucked-up rock star of the nineties, Evan Dando. This business is superficial, insidious. Some people like bubbly grunge singer Dave Grohl and stage school graduates like the Spice Girls are lucky. They fit right in. Either their personality or their training enables them to ride the wave of insincerity that surrounds almost everyone involved on the way up (and down). Evan, despite popular perception, never fitted in with all that, even if he was great at acting the part to people he didn't know – and even to those he did. Well I recall his (and Hole's) manager Janet Billig trying to tell him how much I loved his new album, more than even Nirvana. Like he could give a fuck. It was LA, 1993. Evan was stoned, disinterested and oblivious to real emotion. What did someone's passion for music compare next to the need to score more drugs?

Once Evan wouldn't have behaved like that. Once he was too smart, had too much soul. When I met him in a Stuttgart hotel lobby in 1991, his lazy drawl masked a keen knowledge of pop culture. We chatted about tormented British cult hero and friend TV Personalities singer Dan Treacy and Giant Sand's country-fried Howe Gelb, and swapped Milan Kundera quotes. There was no pomp or cynicism, just another sweet American boy in love with rock.

Evan always wanted fame, though – or so those around him at his major record label thought, mistaking talent for sales. (It's easily done.) So the New England boy started living down to his 'bleached surf bum' image, an airhead to compete with all the other airheads on offer.

'I'm starting to believe in it,' he told me at the end of '92. 'Maybe I'll take "Dippy Dando" on as my new persona. The tabloids say I don't like hotel suites so I'm going to take the bus and pitch a tent in a friend's garden and eat at cafes. The press says I'm planning to live in Australia, because America is no longer a safe place to hitch around.'

We both laughed. But then Evan went and did almost exactly that.

'We're Atlantic's glam grunge band,' he added. 'All I know is that they want me to smile into the camera.' He chuckles. 'Oh yeah man, I'm happy to do it.'

Other rock figures believed he was that way all along. Influential NYC Matador Records boss and ex-fanzine writer Gerard Cosloy attacked his band as being an 'A-ha lookalike', even when they sounded pure grunge. Kurt Cobain ridiculed Evan, something the Boston boy never quite got over. After the Nirvana singer died, he claimed the pair had been great friends. That wasn't how I remembered it.

Maybe you really do have to mess yourself up to sing the blues if you never suffered while growing up. Evan comes from a privileged upbringing similar to that of the amoral characters who populate Brett Easton Ellis' novels. He bunked off school to smoke pot, became obsessed with trendy pop culture murderer Charles Manson and decided he would be a rock star dropout. Evan took his obsession with hedonism too far, though, and spent a year stoned on acid in Australia in the early nineties. When he came back to America he was too fucked to concentrate on his career. During one *NME* interview he spent the entire time scribbling notes to the journalist, having lost his voice smoking crack cocaine. Meanwhile stories filtered through about Evan's sexual encounters with young girls and models.

Lemonheads drummer David Ryan feels the reason Evan turned to hard drugs in 1993 was simple. He was lonely. 'After you've been touring for a year,' he told me, 'you start thinking of your band-members as your only friends. Then when they leave, you're alone. That's what happened in LA. So Evan started hanging out with a crowd who seemed cool because they were junkies, and they became his professional friends. And for the ten minutes you're on it, crack makes you feel that the person you're with is your best friend in the world.'

Oddly, Evan's benign, almost naïve, outlook on life survived most of this, perhaps helped by the drugs that caused him to lose focus. He's always had an incorruptible pop sensibility. Trouble is, the Lemonheads' roots were strictly Massachusetts hardcore. Listen to early records like 1989's *Lick* or its predecessor *Creator* and you'll hear some solid Boston pop/rock: vivacious, but interchangeable with a dozen other Massachusetts bands like Angry Samoans, Volcano Suns or Big Dipper. It wasn't until Evan's co-singer Ben Deily left – a short while before the band's major label debut in 1990, the disappointing *Lovey* – that the Lemonheads began to take a more overt pop/country direction. Evan was the group's original drummer. If they'd stuck with their original sound they might have ended up like Green Day.

The group got signed to Atlantic on the strength of an inspired, feedback-drenched cover of Suzanne Vega's 'Luka', included on *Lick* at the last minute. The band considered it throwaway, but it didn't stop them releasing two more delightfully lightweight cover versions ('Gonna Get Along Without You Now', 'Different Drum') as singles immediately afterwards. It was thus unsurprising that when the Lemonheads' brief moment in the spotlight came a few years later, it was on the back of yet another cover, a flimsy reading of Simon and Garfunkel's ode to teenage lust, 'Mrs Robinson', used in the smash hit slacker lifestyle movie *Wayne's World 2*. Evan always did have a way with other people's words, and thoughts.

As a group, the Lemonheads were an OK live act.

I don't mean to deny the contributions of others, notably the Blake Babies' Juliana Hatfield and John Strohm, and long-time drummer David Ryan; also bassists Jesse Peretz and Nic Dalton. It's just a fact: Evan's voice and songs never fitted in well with their abrasive, collegiate rock sound. I say this, despite the Lemonheads' fabled appearance at Reading Festival circa *Come On Feel*. There, the band laid right back for Evan's mellower songs, and he roughed up perfectly for the more aggressive ones. 'Big Gay Heart' was phenomenal. It left some of us hardened critics feeling distinctly teary-eyed.

The other members could be vital, though. Dalton has an earthy honesty that served him well when, concerned for Evan's health, he gave an interview to the *NME* shortly after Kurt's death, bringing into question the techniques of Evan's, and Kurt's former managers. The scene around his Sydney-based Half A Cow label served as inspiration for several songs on the Lemonheads' fifth album, 1992's *It's A Shame About Ray*; in particular, the debutante song 'Alison's Starting To Happen' and wistful 'My Drug Buddy'.

Juliana was the foil for many of Evan's more romantic interludes in the studio. She played bass on *Ray*: she sang on several songs on *Come On Feel*. The Blake Babies were a fine, spunky take on the Go-Go's bubblegum pop, several years on. For a while Evan and Juliana posed for pictures together, an anaemic, strangely sexless counterpart to Kurt and Courtney. The Boston-based singer had an ambiguous sexuality herself. For a long time, she made a point of saying she was a virgin, even though friends said otherwise. She was also known for making stupid comments like how women weren't designed to play guitar, and they shouldn't scream or shout because it's 'physiologically not female'. (It was the wrong way around. It should have been 'guitars aren't designed for women to play'. But don't start me on that whole 'rock is a male construct, created by and designed for men' theory again, or we'll be here all night.) Despite all that, some of Juliana's solo albums have a disquieting charm.

By himself, Evan could sound incredible. One show in December 1992 at Ronnie Scott's in front of the London media stands out. Evan took the stage with an acoustic guitar, no set list, no plan except to run through some of his favourite songs. His voice sounded effortless yet full of emotion as he glided through covers of Cole Porter's 'Miss Otis Regrets', 'Gloomy Monday' and 'Brass Buttons', plus any number of sweet originals. Someone was meant to record the show for potential release as a live album and forgot to hit play on the machine. (I know because I met the guy responsible on a Glasgow train the following day.) I swear that if the recording had happened, Evan would've been massive. The concert could have been that pivotal.

The singer Evan most recalls is the Flying Burrito Brothers' doomed Gram Parsons and his tormented, mid-seventies country soul. He has the same love for tradition, and same knack of stepping slightly to the shadows when writing about subjects. Evan enjoys writing about special inanimate objects, such as 'Favourite

T' (shirt) or 'Stove' – a song inspired by a routine call from the gas engineer. Evan is even better than Gram, though, because his songs are of my time. They have extra resonance for my generation. It always matters, the context in which you hear pop music.

Perhaps *Come On Feel* confused commentators with its schizophrenia. The first side is a near-constant stream of pure rush-of-blood-to-the-head pop: the nonchalantly resigned 'The Great Big No', the teen romance of 'It's About Time', the dewy-eyed 'Big Gay Heart'. Everything is going swimmingly until Evan Dando reaches the *second* version of the hedonist's handbook 'Style'. The first time he tackles the song, it's fine – an upbeat, self-assured rock song with a snappy chorus of '*I don't wanna get stoned/But I don't wanna not get stoned*', just ripe for wannabe fuck-ups watching MTV. Second time around, however, he sounds all drowsy and resigned, with disgraced LA soul man Rick James singing falsetto in the background.

'Evan changes his story about the meaning of "Style" every time you ask him,' reveals David Ryan. 'Frankly, it's less about drugs than it seems. It's a song about indecision, when you don't want to do anything and then all these LA-style people come in and tell you how great you are – "Style!" Likewise, "My Drug Buddy" is more about friendship and loneliness than the obvious. The drug motif is the shotgun on the wall, the prop for the song.'

After 'Style', *Come On Feel* is punctuated by silences, studio chat and extraneous noise, finishing with a meandering freeform piano solo called 'The Jello Fund'. As a reflection of Evan's confused state of mind at the time, it couldn't be more appropriate. I loved it. It was a reasonably accurate reflection of my state of mind, too.

Come On Feel failed to shift units like Atlantic expected. Then Kurt died and everything turned strange.

Reports of Evan hanging around with his new buddies, such as Manchester's ELO wannabes Oasis and INXS singer Michael Hutchence, started filtering through. There was that famous photo of a rumpled Evan and Courtney in a compromising position on a hotel bed with a 'mystery' third person. If memory serves correct, the chap in question was either Blake Babies drummer/drug buddy Todd Phillips or fellow hedonist, long-term Frances Bean nanny, Cali DeWitt. Evan retreated back to Australia. Odd stories surfaced concerning Evan's state of mind and prodigious drug intake.

A seventh album, the subtle and bewildering *Car Button Cloth* was released in 1996 with help from passing friends, but it too straddled the divide between grunge and pure pop uneasily, too uneasily for most commentators. I loved it, for the way Evan's voice sounded even more tormented and wracked with doubt on the slow-burning ballads 'Losing Your Mind' and 'Break Me'. There were still moments of pop perfection: the upbeat single 'The Outdoor Type' and nonsense 'Hospital', for two. For the Bristol date on a rather subdued UK tour, Evan invited me up on stage to sing the encore while he thundered away on the drums.

Early on in their career, I referred to the Lemonheads as the Fifth Best Live Band in Boston.

I wasn't trying to be nasty. Being a college town (Harvard, most notably), Boston had more than its share of great rock bands at the turn of the nineties: Dinosaur Jr, Galaxie 500, Blake Babies, Pixies, Soul Asylum, Come, Sebadoh, Buffalo Tom. There was something in the night air. I spent many happy hours there avoiding monsoons and dancing on car roofs, travelling the underground. Appropriately enough for the hometown of that great naïve seventies singer Jonathan Richman, all my memories of the city seem to belong to another, more innocent era. (Like my recollections of Olympia.) We went shopping for Folkways records, and found Legend! singles as well. At Newbury Comics, I bought Fantagraphics books by artists like Peter Bagge and the Hernandez Brothers. There was a chase after New York's narcoleptic pop stars Mazzy Star down storm-battered streets

The first time I met Buffalo Tom in 1990, I watched the entire first season of *The Simpsons*. We drank milkshakes for breakfast and hung out with Damon and Naomi from Galaxie 500. Later, everyone came over for an anti-Superbowl party. I slept on bassist Chris Colbourn's floor. A week after I left, his flat burnt down.

Originally, Buffalo Tom sounded similar to their fellow Amherst University student J Mascis' Dinosaur Jr. This wasn't so surprising as J produced the Tom's first two albums, but Bill Janowitz sang with such passion, it never mattered. Like Australia's Go-Betweens, these three unassuming soda-loving Yanks proved it was possible to be male, perceptive and write great riffs. Indeed, singles like the almost unbearably poignant 'Taillights Fade' and 1990's mighty 'Birdbrain' have more in common with the alienated distances of New Zealand's Flying Nun label than any of the grunge bands the trio usually got lumped in with.

There was a terrific rasp in Bill's vocals, a wonderful restraint behind the harmonies and molten guitar heroics. It's almost impossible to describe the appeal of Buffalo Tom without sounding desultory: a good solid rock band, full of decent people and decent chords, capable of moments of extraordinary passion. Of course, they never made it big.

Ill Communication
(Beastie Boys, Beck)

Mike D grabbed me backstage in Philadelphia, Lollapalooza '94.

'Hey, Everett,' he yelled, as we sat on one end of a long wooden catering table, girls giggling to each other a few feet away. 'Usually my main mission is to get on stage and rock the house. Today it's to keep you and Billy Corgan apart.'

Mike was well aware of the long-standing feud that had begun after the slap-headed pop star wrote a song about me on his dreadful *Siamese Dream* album. I knew Mike because I'd met him when he'd got me past security at some hip 42nd Street club in NYC to see his label's band Luscious Jackson (an all-female hip hop quartet who once spent an entire interview with me talking about furry tongues and salt canisters). Now here he was warning me off my main sport, baiting major league rock stars. Who did he think he was . . . aside from being one-third of the event's headliners, of course? In the backyard, I could see Corgan playing basketball with members of rap band A Tribe Called Quest. He wasn't shooting too straight, but looked irritatingly at peace with the world. My companion (and inner demon) Scott from Girls Against Boys was clutching a bottle of whisky and threatening to withdraw its supply from me unless I went over to Billy and created some mischief.

'I'm warning you, Everett . . .' glowered Mike.

Early on, I felt ambivalent towards the Beastie Boys. I appreciated the fact they were brats, the way they caused shock horror headlines in the tabloids. I even thought the idea of giant phallic symbols and dancing girls in cages on stage was neat, mainly because it was all so obviously ironic. It wasn't like they were killing or harming anyone. Nobody got hurt.

It was only later that I grew to despise the hypocrisy of those around the Beasties, and their predictable humour. It was only later I learnt that the vast populace has no sense of irony, especially in America; and that the Beasties utilised frat boy facetiousness, something I undoubtedly would've hated if I'd known what it was. Don't get me wrong, though. I loved the first Beasties album *Licensed To Ill*. 'Fight For Your Right To Party' had a great snotty feel; 'No Sleep Till Brooklyn' is the best song Motörhead never wrote. The Beasties started off as a NYC thrash-core punk band, with a Luscious Jackson on drums. When they switched genres they retained enough of their original sound to be attractive to a rock audience – or, more importantly, to the Aerosmith audience: metal watered down and thus ripe for mass consumption. In many respects, the Beasties were the first grunge crossover band: loud, obnoxious, with abrasive guitars and lyrics. They were smart, too. Smart enough to play it dumb when required, like John Lydon and Kurt Cobain before and after them. Their interview technique was pure Bob Dylan.

Punk wasn't so far away that I'd forgotten the attraction of behaving badly for its own sake, and shocking people. One year, it's the Sex Pistols. The next, it's the Beasties. Is singing about wanting political disruption in your home country ('Anarchy In The UK') really that different from standing up for youth's right to enjoy itself? Some of the fiercest inter-generation battles in the late eighties were fought against the dance-heads and their right to congregate and imbibe substances whenever they chose. Consider the Criminal Injustice Act. What is 'Fight For Your Right' if not a clarion call to dance?

Even then, I was aware that the Beasties' occasional 'violence against women' lyrics and bad-mouth boasting were only there because they were parodying the media's image of them as trailer trash. Also, pre-Niggers With Attitude and the rise of gangsta rap, most hip hop wasn't as misogynistic as its nineties brethren. The rap pisstakes were more to do with conspicuous consumption; VW badges instead of Mercedes logos, White Castle and Budweiser instead of Cristal and Budweiser. The sexism in their lyrics was aping the metal morons from the Beasties' hardcore (punk) background. The Beastie Boys weren't serious.

I know: when does the line between parody, irony and reality become so blurred that it no longer exists? That's impossible to call. I would contend that intelligent people have the hardest time being racist or sexist, though, simply because prejudices usually come about through fear or lack of information. Prejudice is caused by stupidity mainly. (That seems as good a defence of Eminem as any. Also, his music *rocks*. Even if most of his audience falls precisely into the 'dumb trailer trash' demographic the Beasties were mocking.) I liked the 'post-ironic' *Viz* comics, too, which parodied prevalent working class male sexist attitudes in Britain by taking them to logical extremes. It felt liberating to laugh at un-PC humour, knowing we were aware of our frailties while laughing.

It was only later I realised I was a perfect target audience for the Beasties; a white middle class kid with aspirations to being an outsider, who'd never experienced black culture beyond the odd trendy late seventies deep reggae outfit and anything condoned by Abbie Hoffman.

That was in retrospect, though. I was gutted when *NME* asked me to review a Beastie Boys show in 1986 and I couldn't because I was supporting the Shop Assistants in Switzerland at the time. I wanted to be *bad* so badly. I thought it'd be a hoot, a slap across the face to those who thought of me in one way and one way alone. Even then, I knew I wanted to have fun. And the Beasties, for better or for worse, were the living embodiment of fun.

The Beastie Boys' Def Jam label-mates like Public Enemy were a little too close to the truth for comfort. That's why the Beasties held so much appeal for us suburban kids. They gave their fans the veneer of street credibility, without any of the danger. Plus, you knew they were golden-hearted sorts underneath it all, and smart. I first realised that in 1989, when their second album *Paul's Boutique* flopped. (I've always favoured bands that don't sell records. They seem so much more artistic, somehow.) All of a sudden, I found myself loving the Beasties' arrogance even more, the way they thought that overnight they could change from being a loud-mouthed brat-rap act into something of worth! How excellent. Even now I don't know anyone who's actually listened to *Paul's Boutique*, although I know plenty of hipsters who claim to have done. It wasn't the Beasties' fault they almost ruined English culture by inspiring new lad magazines to think they were clever. Perhaps they were. Perhaps it was those that followed who dulled every-thing.

Whatever. There'll always be people around who'll miss the point. And most of them will be journalists.

I didn't realise how truly smart the rap trio were, though, until the early nineties, when they hooked up with all the credible alternative rock sorts – Sonic Youth, the Breeders, Nirvana and, erm, all the other bands managed by their livewire manager John Silva – and began to exploit their credibility. If the Beasties could come back from their second album's 'disappointing' sales, they could come back from anything. (Actually, *Paul's Boutique* sold a cool million in the States alone, but because those sales came on the back of the seven million-selling *Licensed To Ill*, it was perceived as a flop.)

John flew photographer Stephen Sweet and me to San Francisco to witness the Beasties' comeback gig, shortly before the release of their third album, 1992's *Check Your Head*, the one where they realigned their hip hop credentials and got serious. We get to the venue, and there are kids outside on the street touting sub-machine guns. We're told we're not on the list. Fine, we say, and go back to the safety of our porn-laden hotel rooms. We don't need that macho shit.

The Beasties came of age in 1995 with *Ill Communication*.

It was the perfect summer record, the kind of bomb you wanted blasting out of every tenement window and car stereo as the long, hot, interminable months dragged gloriously on. *Ill Communication* was the moment the Beasties gelled, when their years of hangin' with the Rock Underground elite finally crystallised into something of artistic worth. The album was even savvy enough to contain a reference to Riot Grrrl: *'So I'll say it like the group Huggy Bear/There's a boy-grrrl revolution of which you should be aware'* ('The Scoop'). They even got in on the UK Rough Trade Covent Garden scene (with a little help from big brothers MTV) at a show for the skater kids and Donovan's daughter Ione Skye, star of *The Rachel Papers*. The magazine they started around this time, *Grand Royal* was great, too; dense, fannish and packed with information on what were then cult topics like Moog synthesisers and kung fu.

Suddenly, everyone who owned a Soundgarden or Nirvana album also had a Beastie Boys record in their collection, to prove how 'open-minded' they were about music. Perhaps unfairly, the Beastie Boys became known as the rap group for people who don't like rap groups.

Ad Rock started dating Kathleen from Bikini Kill, and it was clear that her sharp-edged feminism rubbed off on the former 'bad boys'. You could also hear the influence of Kim and Thurston from Sonic Youth creeping into the sassy, smart rhymes and sharp bursts of rock guitar. *Ill Communication* was the pivotal moment in the Beasties' career. It came out before they started wearing their NYC street cynicism as a badge of cool, but long enough after their brash impetuous beginnings to realise that boasting about beating up women just isn't that funny. The record was aware without being preachy or overbearing. Mike D knew that if they could get people to forget their misogynist past and reinvent themselves as caring, sharing men with an eye to the political action (Tibet was Adam 'MCA' Yauch's pet cause) they could create a much longer-lasting audience. It oozed cool from every pore. Not put-on hipster fake sunglasses-after-dark cool, but the cool that only comes about when people are operating at the top of their form.

And it's a record the Beasties are almost certainly doomed to copy forever. Unless, of course, their projected *Full Country Album* ever appears and they do a Beck, and reinvent themselves as rootsy, 70-year-old, ornery Ol' Opry folks. I hope not. I'd much rather hear the jaded, business-like retreads of 1999's *Hello, Nasty* than more cosmopolitan white boys pretending to be Southern rednecks.

The Beasties' defining moment came with the video to 'Sabotage'. In it, they played to their strengths (confidence, humour and the funk) and knew when to quit. The *Starsky and Hutch* pastiche was clever because it was restrained and spot-on. The humour was implicit. It wasn't shoved in your face. By the year 2000, the Beastie Boys seemed to be growing ever more desperate, what with their Japanese boiler suits and protective eyewear. Please! I'm not saying I like pure rap Beasties. I don't. The time I liked them was when they could switch effortlessly between different genres without sounding contrived, when they were grunge rap. *Hello, Nasty* felt contrived. With it, the Beasties turned into just three more corporate rock stars up there pretending to be young.

Hello, Nasty let the side down by using tired samples, by being in tune with a mentality that went out of fashion several years back. Maybe we should've seen it coming during the long years of artistic wilderness, filled by crap like the compilation of early hardcore singles *Some Old Bullshit* best left festering in Greenwich Village collectors' shops. Hardcore is not punk and it never has been. The sooner people realise that, the better. Then there was that dull collection of funk instrumentals *The In Sound From Way Out* where the Beasties proved that the more funky you try and get, the less funky you actually are.

As musicians, the Beastie Boys make great politicians. I hope to see Mike D standing for Mayor of NYC before I die. That would be so cool. As long as he doesn't then whip out a saxophone and start jamming along to an old Money Mark record.

Gold Mountain Management's other major act, Beck, is just as smart as the Beasties.

The trouble is, though, that for all his cleverness and ability to reinvent himself every other year as This Generation's Prince, This Generation's Kurt Cobain, This (Gap) Generation's Alternative Icon, Beck has no soul. Once, when he used to wander out into the audience mid-set to sign autographs and dance to the sound of his cult hit 'Loser' played on a Dansette record player, it was both cheeky and amusing. Now, when he manages to convince half the record industry that he really is His Purple Highness with 1999's lifeless, transparently charlatan album *Midnite Vultures*, it just feels like he's snickering, laughing in the faces of his adoring public.

They're not clever enough to engender his respect, and he doesn't care who knows it.

'Look at me,' he seems to be saying, with every insouciant toss of that carefully sculpted hair and Devo sunglasses. 'I know that what I do is worthless pap for the self-consciously hip. But it's OK *because I know it.*'

Beck is the ultimate post-ironic chameleon, a cipher for a generation's fantasies for times long gone by. If it's 2000, it must be time for some more eighties funk. It's obvious that if Beck had a choice, he would be releasing Woody Guthrie-influenced acoustic country albums like his rather affecting 1994 K record *One Foot In The Grave* (produced by Beat Happening's Calvin Johnson). When he cares to, the singer can turn out a fine minimal, girl-choking-on-candy song of lo-fi beauty in the style of Lou Barlow's Folk Implosion. *When he cares to.* He must have been thrilled when Johnny Cash covered one of his songs.

He's bloody irritating, full stop. 1996's Dust Brothers-produced *Odelay* is a great, state-of-the-art pop album even if it does reek of De La Soul's Daisy Age pacifist hip hop seven years on, and also *Paul's Boutique*, with whom it shares producers. Even if it did inspire a whole generation of hopeless chancers to copy his sound wholesale, up to and including 2000's Mercury Music Prize winner, Badly Drawn Boy. No reason to hate Beck, perhaps. There's something insufferably smug about Mr Hansen, though. It's the way he can complain in a *Face* interview that people are obsessed with his haircut and then spend hours talking about nothing else. In Beck's public persona he continues to play the class fool, the slacker generation's very own David Cassidy.

When I caught up with him in 1994 for a joint interview with Sebadoh singer Lou Barlow on the rather spurious premise that both had released singles with the word 'loser' in the title, I was already suspicious. I wasn't sure whether his ability to switch between Sebadoh and Slayer with a flick of the wah-wah pedal was an asset or a liability. The latter, probably. I was already using phrases like 'the blue-eyed boy of corporate rock management' to describe him, and found it strange that he should have been so seemingly 'in' with people I admired, like Calvin and LA skate-punk fanzine *Flipside*, when I barely knew anything about him. I thought of Sebadoh as the spiritual heirs to Nirvana's throne. The record industry clearly thought Beck should be the one. Weirdly, the second time I was scheduled to interview Beck was in Cincinnati on the same day Kurt was discovered dead. Beck contracted pneumonia. I didn't stick around.

That was just one in a series of coincidences that made it seem like he wasn't the boy for me. Once, he blew me out for an appearance on *Top of The Pops* where he performed 'Loser' with a bunch of old men. 'It is sort of an obnoxious song,' he admitted, 'if you take it out of its context and put it on a big radio station.' Didn't stop him from recording a whole series of similar-sounding songs like 'Devil's Haircut' and 'Sissyneck' though, did it? Then Beck started freaking out, perhaps fazed by all the US press attention (two US music magazine covers in one week – not even Nirvana managed that while Kurt was alive) and refused to talk to anyone. Then when we finally did meet up, two days after the interview, my hotel room in Chicago was turned over and everything stolen, including the Beck/Lou tape.

Fortunately, the tape featuring these two slacker icons was found a few days later. Clearly, the thieves couldn't . . . uh . . . be bothered to take it.

Beck knows how to mix art with commerce and so has persuaded millions of people into thinking the end result is worthwhile, while simultaneously deriding his fans. He's a Thunderbird puppet for the Gap generation with his roots in hardcore and lo-fi, not to be taken seriously and most definitely not soul, despite all the funky rhythms. 'MTV Makes Me Want To Smoke Crack', he sang on his debut single, and Beck should know by now, having almost single-handedly propped up the dying corporate beast with a series of releases that make Prince look like he's still got his old pizzazz.

Still, he's written a few nice tunes.

Art Grunge

Smash Your Head on the Punk Rock
(Dinosaur Jr, Sebadoh, B.A.L.L.)

I interviewed J Mascis on top of a mountain in Vermont as his band Dinosaur Jr got kitted out for a hard morning's skiing. Close by, people stomped ponderously over to the edge and disappeared with swan-like grace down the slopes. The temperature at base was 28°F; at summit 25°F. The *MM* photographer got frostbite in two fingers while snow bunnies chatted excitedly.

Later I spent a fruitless couple of hours playing chess against Teenage Fanclub producer and temporary Dinosaur member Don Fleming. I beat him through use of a nifty knight sacrifice, levelling the series to 1–1. Meanwhile Mascis and his fellow musicians answered every one of my 80 questions with an 'uh-huh', 'oh man that's way too heavy' or 'oh man, I can't think of anything to say', followed by protracted silence.

The scene was straight out of a tour brochure: a blanket of white outside, warm fire and solid pine furnishings in, ski equipment stacked up in one corner, TV blaring away in another. We briefly discussed favourite colours. We briefly touched on the difference between metaphors and similes. I briefly banged my head against a hard wooden table. There was no malice, just honest bemusement that I should want to talk about music. Once the skiing season finished, that incarnation of Dinosaur Jr split up, leaving *Melody Maker* with a rather expensive restaurant bill to pay.

When I caught up with J ten years later to celebrate the release of his second solo album, 2000's *More Light*, he was equally laconic.

Do you think Dinosaur had an influence on grunge?

'Um, maybe to some people,' J replies. He's fine if you question him about scuba diving or skiing, not so great on his chosen profession. 'Don't all bands just rip off other bands they like? I've heard a few things that sound like Dino rip-offs, but not that often. Other people say they hear it.'

Were the early nineties the time of the Last Great Explosion in Rock?

'What, for businessmen?' the singer drawls. 'I don't see that. I see Nirvana as separate to everything else. They were good and actually got big. It was bizarre because that doesn't happen very often. The other bands got caught up in the undertow. Nirvana were definitely more commercial-sounding. It seemed like they should make it over other bands. You couldn't see Scratch Acid being on the radio.'

What do you think the relevance of your music is in the year 2000?

'Relevance?' asks J, surprised. 'To who? I don't know.'

I knew East Coast 'pop grunge' producer Don Fleming for several reasons.

One was that he and his conspirator-in-arms Jay Spiegel aka the Rummager (drums) were insanely good company. One occasion I turned up in New York to find the pair recording a track for an REM tribute. 'Come on over,' Don instructed. 'It will be fun.' I got to the studio to find their band, the rock beasts Gumball, watching old KISS videos and stumped as to how to record the vocals on their New Wave take on Stipe and Co's 'Stumble'. 'Hey, why don't we get The Legend! to sing them,' the Rummager suggested. So I did, after a cursory listen to the tune we were meant to be covering. I nicked the melody from *The Magic Roundabout* and gave a rant about 'monkeys on the shoulder' straight from the Reverend Horton Heat school of sermonising. It took two takes, and it was still the best damn track on the resulting *Surprise Your Pig* compilation.

Every time I met Don and the Rummager, they seemed to be in a new band, shortly about to split.

In 1989, I conducted an interview with the pair in the *Melody Maker* offices while they held up a black plastic bin-liner with the name of their third member on. 'Where's Kramer? He's in the bag!' The band was B.A.L.L. Renowned dope smoker, bassist and Galaxie 500 producer Kramer had left three dates into their UK tour with Das Damen.

Das Damen were considered heirs apparent to both Dinosaur Jr and Soundgarden's throne back in 1989, and had an equally warped sense of humour and love for Beatles harmonies and Sabbath licks. The New York combo also starred on The Legend!'s Sub Pop single 'Do Nuts'. I showed up at New York's Fun City studios to record the a cappella A-side by myself, no guitar, nothing. Engineer Wharton Tiers looked surprised and peered round outside to find out where the rest of the band was. 'No, that's it,' I told him. 'Just plug a microphone in, and we'll ROCK!' When they showed up later with their guitar, Das Damen took one listen to work out their parts.

B.A.L.L. were an insanely great rock band with a keen sense of humour and revisionist rock history. The sleeve to *Bird*, their second album, featured a parody of the Beatles' banned 'butcher cover'. *Trouble Doll*, the 'disappointing third album' (their words) was based on the concept that every title should contain the word 'trouble', even the final one, song number thirty. 'Trouble Finale' was actually a satirical, high-pitched reading of Neil Young's 'Hey, Hey, My, My'.

Kramer ran B.A.L.L.'s NYC Shimmydisc label, encouraged maverick spirits like Jad Fair, Daniel Johnston and the peerless concept musician Dogbowl and his King Missile . . . hold on. Let's get this right. Kramer played bass in Shockabilly, who were warped psychotic blues played at 100 mph, was also in the Butthole Surfers, made an album with Jad Fair and . . . hold on. Let's get this straight. Bongwater were Kramer's main band, a delirious psychedelic sex machine formed with TV actress Ann Magnusson. Their fourth album *The Power Of Pussy* has an undeniable sadness, as well as a rampant carnality, obscenity and pornographic quality. I met Ann once, at Camden Underworld. She composed a nine-verse, intricately layered song on the spot, entreating me not to leave her behind. We then got in a major barney with a bartender over the amount of whisky he'd poured into Ann's glass. Kramer and Ann later fell out acrimoniously, so much so that the resulting court case led to Shimmydisc going bankrupt. Before that happened, Kramer recorded a triple concept album based on George Harrison's *All Things Must Pass*.

That's enough about Kramer already.

After B.A.L.L. split, Don and the Rummager briefly reformed the Velvet Monkeys with J Mascis, Sonic Youth's Thurston Moore and STP/Pussy Galore guitarist Julie Cafritz to record the Blaxploitation spoof *Rake*. That project didn't last long because, as Don explained, 'When you have to write eight guitar leads for each song, it gets kind of limiting.'

The *dynamics* duo also joined Half-Japanese long enough to record about ten albums (a couple of months, then). Gumball followed, giving Don a chance to indulge his obsession with pop culture and noise, from the Monkees to the Damned to Faust. He was confusing pop boundaries (bubblegum, symphonic, punk, seventies rock) long before Fountains Of Wayne and Weezer made it fashionable. Perhaps his work with Sonic Youth, Alice Cooper,

Seattle's Posies and on Hole's debut album helped ferment the musical brew.

When I caught up with the nascent Gumball, Don got me stoned and took me to a Greenwich Village chess shop where we did battle to the sound of three Greek guys screaming 'Master Dick!' and betting openly on the players sitting at the table next to us. The only rules of the place were 'no gambling, no eating, no iced tea'. Within five minutes we'd broken every rule between us. My concentration shattered, Don thrashed me to go 2–1 up. We drank beer, smoked more dope, watched bad Beatles videos and hung out with Kramer's parrot. Straight afterwards, the pair left Half-Japanese.

That's enough about Don Fleming already.

Except, the last time I encountered the producer we invented a whole new musical genre, Nemocore, based on the non-rhythmic, oblique cadences of experimental band Amon Duul 2. I played the theremin the way my living room table dances. The movement's central precept was based around a psychotic hatred of drummers and, indeed, melody. It was rumoured that audience members had been thrown out of gigs just for clapping. Nemos told cruel anti-stickmen jokes to one another ending with the punch line '. . . Shoot the fucking drummer.' ('Why did the Nemo cross the road? To . . .' 'How many Nemos does it to take to change a light bulb? Two, one to change it and one to . . .')

I wrote up a series of reviews, and Don went on the Internet to sell tapes of our band Turbulance (the misspelling was deliberate). Taking the whole affair one step further than strictly necessary, Beach Boys fanatic Don was last seen playing around the East Village in a real life Nemocore band, Foot, with fellow overgrown schoolboy Thurston Moore.

If you're telling me that you don't understand the beauty and poignancy and place in history of Dinosaur Jr's second album, 1987's *You're Living All Over Me*, then perhaps you shouldn't be listening to music. J never recaptured its full-on slacker charm, probably because founder member Lou Barlow (bass, ukulele, tapes, vocals) left between the release of 1988's *Bug* and major label debut, 1991's *Green Mind*. The balance within the band never existed again. To all intents and purposes, Dinosaur became a solo project after Lou's departure – especially as J, like Evan Dando, was originally a drummer.

Dinosaur's first three albums have a raw passion to match the pyrotechnic guitar splendour. At early shows, the UK press venerated Dinosaur for their loudness. Walking into a Dino gig you could almost physically feel the waves of volume emanating from the stage. Late eighties, I would be on my knees at the front of the Fulham Greyhound, next to future Wiiija 'Huggy Bear' Records boss Gary Walker, mock genuflecting as J flicked a switch and breezed through another windswept guitar solo.

Dinosaur who? Their first album *Dinosaur* appeared in 1985 in a US post-punk underground climate that favoured short, acerbic bursts of noise over *anything*. Just when everyone reviled the seventies as being a decade of dinosaur (ha!) bands, here were J and Lou and drummer Murph to reinvent a musical genre. Suddenly, it was hip to like Lynryd Skyrnryd and the Allman Brothers again: something Seattle bands like Mudhoney doubtless appreciated a few years later. Oh, and Neil Young . . . but he never did go out of fashion.

Dinosaur who? Their feedback-drenched version of the Cure's 'Just Like Heaven' rates alongside Hüsker Dü's take on the Byrds' 'Eight Miles High' and This Mortal Coil's 'Me And My Sister'. As does their cathartic, sugar-sweetened retake on Bowie's 'Quicksand', the lyrics rewritten to talk about the near-fatal car crash that also went on to inspire the brilliant one-off Dino single 'The Wagon'. 1993's *Where You Been* should have catapulted the band into super-stardom, but maybe J went overboard with the searing guitar solos, spilling out every which way. It didn't stop *Spin* magazine from printing a photo of the shy, almost diffident New England boy under a caption saying 'J Mascis Is God'.

Dinosaur who? Ah, just the band who inspired Teenage Fanclub, Nirvana, Buffalo Tom, Lemonheads and . . . thousands. Ask any indie guitar band. The Fannies' 'Everything Flows', in particular, is as fine a Dinosaur tribute as they come, written long before the loveable Scots quartet turned into an excellent modern-day version of the Byrds. The description that Kurt applied to grunge early on, 'hard music played to a slow tempo', could have been designed for Dinosaur.

'Freak Scene' is the single that invented the slacker generation. J plays guitar on it like he skis. Effortlessly, yet fully in control. The song slows down, catches on fire, whispers sweet harmony to itself and then starts blowing a tornado. *'So fucked I can't believe it/If there's a way I wish you'd see it,'* J sings with heavy resignation, a sentiment Nirvana could only echo with their *'I found it hard/So hard to find/Oh well whatever, never mind'* line from 'Smells Like Teen Spirit'. *'Don't let me fuck up will you?'* J pleads, helpless in his slumber. *'Because when I need a friend, it's still you.'*

It's one of the greatest singles ever.

* * *

I got my revenge on J for the ski incident later.

One night, '92 or something, I was watching Dinosaur Jr play a typically epic set in Boston, headlining over My Bloody Valentine and slo-core kings Codeine. It was a great evening, one of those shows where the Valentines held a chord for 35 minutes, but my teeth were hurting. During the nineties, I used to keep a bottle of Jagermeister by the bed in case of toothache. A few gulps of that, you drop off to sleep, no worries.

'No matter man,' their tour manager tells me. 'J's dad is a dentist, I'm getting my teeth fixed up with him tomorrow. Drive with us overnight to Amherst for their big hometown show, and he'll see to you first.'

J also mentioned that we could do a Dino interview, something the music press were always on the lookout for back then. So the three of us drove back to Amherst, listening to some obscure mid-American rock shit like The Band or Quicksilver Messenger Service on the tour bus.

J's dad fixed me up real good, filled my tooth with some US drug called Novocaine or something. It felt odd, though, like I was flying through a big fuzzy wad of cotton cloud. Next thing I know, I've freaked out and left town, and I'm on a Greyhound bus in the middle of Massachusetts, not having told anyone I was going – or indeed done any interview.

Next time J sees me, he backs away slowly. 'Stay away from me, man,' he growls. 'You're weird.'

Here's what makes me different to you.

I always knew the Smiths were charlatans, frauds. There was no way Morrissey really felt the way he sang, otherwise he wouldn't have been up there on stage throwing gladioli over us. It was cabaret, the lizard's tongue. I didn't understand how my friends fell for it every time. Here he was, with his messages of melancholy and despair and loneliness, all polished to perfection, all suffused under the glow of a commercial radio station-orientated production. Where was the honesty? How could he reduce his (presumably heartfelt) words to simple repetition? Is this romance, that someone repeats the same statements to others, time after time after time again? I didn't understand where individuality came into it. I *like* the feel and hiss of a tape recorder sullenly turning in the background. Everyday life isn't cleaned up. Why then is the music that is supposed to mirror it?

I loved Nirvana because, on stage, it was impossible to predict the mood. There was nothing mundane about Kurt's performances.

The guitars would flicker and burst and die, the voice would sound different every time. Perhaps hearing John Lennon's first solo album, the primal scream therapy outing, affected me more than I realised. The ex-Beatles' melodies were great, certainly, but what I really liked was the spontaneity, the way it sounded like it was the first time he'd even thought about tackling the songs this way. Perhaps the reason I liked anarchist, true punk collective Crass wasn't for the sentiments or anthemic choruses, but for the starkness of the recording: *the humanity at the core.*

I understand music. I live and breathe it. I love a pop sheen, an over-polished Pet Shop Boys or Destiny's Child or Beach Boys harmony. I also don't need to be patronised. If music is special, if it's supposed to be communicating emotion then I don't need it dressed up. The whole genre of lo-fi has become just that over the years: a genre. Groups searching for a certain sound that they heard other groups obtain years before. Fuck that. Deliberately sloppily recorded albums aren't what I'm talking about here. That's just as cabaret as the sickliest Britney Spears or Debbie Gibson single. The beauty of Lou Barlow's collection of solo recordings, Sentridoh's *The Original Losing Losers*, isn't that the songs are brief, or that the tape sometimes crackles and wobbles, or that his guitar is occasionally out of tune. The beauty of Lou is that he records as he sees fit, and moves on when his mood changes. The beauty lies in his wavering voice, his direct words that he never labours over or dwells on, the awesome tunes he stumbles over because he isn't looking for permanence.

It could be even simpler than that. His voice reminds me of my own when I used to record myself at the piano back in the seventies. On those early recordings he is clearly as unable to cope with life as I was. Maybe others relate to pop chameleons and the frauds because that's what they're like. Good for them.

Kurt once stated that he felt special listening to Half-Japanese because it was a secret that he shared between just him and Jad. That's why I love Lou Barlow's songs. They make me feel special, unique. What more could you ask from music?

Sebadoh Incident One: In 1994, Courtney Love and I reviewed the singles for Melody Maker, *the same day Kurt tried to kill himself in Rome. Among them was Lou Barlow's solo Sub Pop seven-inch, the stark 'I'm Not Mocking You', 'He's the kind of guy you'd fuck and the next day would be hanging from a tree in your backyard,' stated Courtney. 'Lou Barlow and Steve Malkmus [Pavement singer] . . . which one is hotter? Which one would you marry and which one would you fuck on the side?'*

Good question, C.

Sebadoh started 'for real' after J split Dinosaur in 1989 and then reformed the band a couple of days later without telling Lou. It was his loss. Sebadoh's sound is more instantly recognisable than Lou's solo stuff. Over several albums of varying consistency, the trio have come to represent a certain strand of American underground music. This is ironic. I'm sure that was never the intention. Yet on records like 1994's biting *Bakesale*, 1996's patchy *Harmacy* and 1991's sprawling *Sebadoh III*, Sebadoh have become standard-bearers for a generation. Sebadoh sing directly to the geeks, the kids who got left behind while their jock mates went off and slammed to Rollins and their smart friends were out romancing and dancing. It's odd. I would claim that Sebadoh – Lou and bassist Jason Lowenstein and a couple of drummers – are very sexy, the way they lay themselves bare, their unshakeable belief in love and humanity. Yet look at the media definition of the word 'sexy'. Sebadoh don't exactly fall under it.

Lou's other band is even stranger. The Folk Implosion – Lou and fellow Bostonian John Davis – started off by creating homemade cassettes, similar in sound to Sentridoh. Yet, after the filmmaker Larry Clark was inspired enough to include their 'Natural One' on the soundtrack to cult movie *Kids* (alongside a Daniel Johnston track or two), the duo found themselves with a Top Forty hit and major label contract. In recent years, they've sounded different again. Over a sparse electronic beat and threadbare guitar, Lou croons gently to himself on their most recent album, 1999's *One Part Lullaby*, quietly invoking the barely audible calm and coldness of his new hometown, the City Of Angels.

Sebadoh Incident Two: 'Remember when Kathleen [Billus, wife] made you introduce me to Kurdt Kobain?' writes Lou Barlow via e-mail. 'I don't remember much of that. In fact I don't think anything really HAPPENED. I remember drinking the Breeders' whisky and not even getting buzzed. It was a hockey rink. You said something about Pat Smear flushing something down some toilet somewhere and then, either that day or some other time, you came to Kathleen's birthday party, remember? I think that there was whisky involved then, too.'

The two events happened separately. The Nirvana introduction occurred on the Seattle group's final tour. Both Kurt and Lou wanted to meet, felt empathy for each other's music. Indeed, nothing happened. Both parties were too shy to speak. At the birthday party, Lou's wife produced a jam jar and proceeded to fill it right to the brim with Maker's Mark for me.

Sebadoh's 1999 album, *The Sebadoh*, invokes the original spirit of Nirvana (the *spirit*, not the sound: there's a crucial difference), especially when Jason screams out one of his plentiful noise cleansers. I never understood Jason's songs before, thought they were only included to prove that old truism every band trots out when blessed with a strong front-person, 'Sebadoh is a band.' Now I understand. Oh man, I do. The album's *pièce de résistance*, though, is Lou's self-doubting 'Love Is Stronger' where he keeps reiterating *'Love is stronger than the truth'* like a mantra he could believe in if only he repeated it enough. *'Pleasure takes its toll/People lose control every day/Hypocrites like us/Deserve a little trust along the way.'* In 'Love Is Stronger', Mr Barlow has written the equal of his own incredible break-up song from 1993, 'Soul And Fire'. No idle compliment.

In places, *The Sebadoh* sounds like punk rock, like it's just been invented and not defiled by countless generations of Alan McGees and Offsprings claiming that they MUST be punk because ... er, they once heard a UK Subs record. It has spirit, beauty and a determination to keep things moving. 'Flame' lifts a simple self-sample and repeats it wordlessly over and over until your heart melts. *'See how we've grown,'* Lou wails. No idle boast. To make the album, Sebadoh uprooted themselves out of their comfort and security to move to new cities across America, and lost a drummer. Thank God Sebadoh know creativity comes through adversity. *'Thought I'd get my shit together,'* Lou sings wistfully on 'Thrive'. *'Now I know I never can.'*

Sebadoh Incident Three: When I first saw the 'Doh play, in their hometown of Boston, '92, they stopped me dead in my tracks and caused me to shed tears. With a few chords and words, they made me question the purpose of live music. My existence felt like a sham, a charade, a bogus rigmarole of drink and chat and the odd knowing wink. After seeing them, I was unable to watch Pavement, back then my favourite band ever. Perhaps in Lou's presence there on stage, I saw something of my old self, reflected back at me. All those years of homemade cassettes and crappy recordings, and songs sent via the post to friends. Maybe it was just that Sebadoh were real, *not an MTV-manufactured concoction. Swapping instruments around between songs only further endeared them to me.*

'They're survival songs,' Lou told Olympian singer and journalist Lois Maffeo in 1998. 'They're about trying to survive whatever love is. I think that's really an important thing because it is a real thing not to survive it. You've got to be careful not to let it ruin your perception of yourself and your self worth. People slide into schizophrenia and all kinds of good stuff. It just alters your brain chemistry.'

* * *

What happened to Dinosaur Jr anyway?

'I decided to bag it, man,' replies J off-hand. 'No reason.'

No reason?

'No reason.'

Blue Thunder

(Mercury Rev, Galaxie 500, Flaming Lips)

The finest story I have involving Mercury Rev happened in Portsmouth, England in 1995.

Long before that, though, we'd noticed the upstate New York band's fondness for sport. Sport as in game – or should that be prey? There had to be sport when Mercury Rev were together, whether it be watching a drunk critic gamble their PDs away in a Melbourne casino (PDs are *per diems*, pocket money: the currency that bands get paid in while on tour) or watching the same drunk critic rip the piss out of unwary bands in New York bars. Refused their sport, Mercury Rev would turn on themselves, leading to fights. Singer Jonathan Donahue tried to gouge out guitarist Grasshopper's eye with a spoon on a transatlantic flight. Original front man David Baker would go walkabout into the audience during live shows. The rumour was that the rest couldn't bear being on the same stage as him. Trouble was sport, that's for sure.

'Of course we'll always have the infamous Portsmouth incident involving you and yer photo friend, the police and the stolen liquor from the hotel bar,' writes Jonathan via e-mail. 'You whining and scratching at my hotel door . . . only to barge in . . . only to be kicked out . . . only to grip the door frame like grim death as we dragged you out by only yer ankles.'

That's not how it happened. We raided the bar, got drunk and made up a story for the benefit of my photographer Stephen Sweet about how I'd been arrested. So Stephen went stomping off down the station. The next morning, the management stopped him on the way out, small matter of several missing bottles of champagne.

'I was livid,' Stephen informed me. 'I told them in no uncertain terms what I thought of them calling the cops in to arrest one of their guests for such a trivial offence, and they looked confused. Especially after they called the police and they denied all knowledge. The hardest thing was to stop the bottles from clinking together in the Sainsbury's bag I was holding at the time . . .'

See, Jonathan! I wasn't the fool that night. It's you bands, trying to look cool. It's like the time I interviewed your old New York labelmates Cop Shoot Cop in an apartment on the corner of 14th and A. During the course of the interview, we got a death threat shoved under the door: 'I'm going to take my fucking GUN and fucking blow your heads OFF if you don't KEEP QUIET.' The band left shortly afterwards, belying their reputation as a tough, hardcore industrial outfit. I stayed. In the morning, the apartment owners (and label bosses) were due to switch buildings. They gathered me up and deposited me in the back room of their new flat. It turned out that they'd bent a few too many rules to get their new place, as the Secretary of the Residents' Association informed them 30 minutes after arrival. She insisted on being shown around, and opened the door to the room where I was laying naked on a mattress, swigging from a bottle of Jack. I offered her some, sociably.

Five minutes later, we were back in the old place.

When I interviewed Mercury Rev, Mr Baker tried to smash my tape recorder. 'I hate awkward questions,' he said. 'You fucking liar,' he continued, as I accused him of being insensitive. 'You talking to me here? Someone once said to me, "How come you totally give a shit about every single person in the room while you play?"' David left the group soon afterwards. Who knows where he is now? Probably holding conversations with scared rabbits in upstate New York as to who is the most paranoid being in the field.

I drunkenly tried to chat up flautist Susie Thorpe. Jonathan revealed his misanthropic side and told me how much he loved guns.

'Don't want to miss the big day, man,' he said, shortly. 'Do I practice? Sure, got to. Revenge is the motivating factor. It's driving me to make music and wipe away all the gravel, all the slow people in my way. Things are simple really.'

Jonathan played lead guitar with Flaming Lips around the time of Mercury Rev's debut album, 1991's *Yerself Is Steam*. The two ensembles often shared members. Mercury Rev pianist/bassist Dave Fridmann produced several Lips' albums, including 1999's rightly venerated *The Soft Bulletin*. *Steam* and the following single 'Carwash Hair' contain some fine moments of crazed, multi-faceted beauty. I compared Mercury Rev to the rain falling off a Thunderbird T's side. Indeed, I went stranger than that. I said that listening to their second album 1993's *Boces*, was like falling down the rabbit hole in *Alice In Wonderland*, and every time you try to hold onto something, another shape, another texture, another colour will attack and transform you.

'Guitars meld, and fuse into one gigantic, multi-headed beast,' I wrote. 'Flutes whisper in and out like the wind on the Interstate 5. Drums echo cavernously and spring off on multiple paths of exploration. Yet there's a core that holds it all together and gives it some semblance of form. Listening to Mercury Rev is like slipping down a shopping mall of freaks and hairdressers, only to be confronted by wilderness.'

Mind you, I was typing those words in the beautiful San Francisco sunshine.

'That was the same nite you drank the entire band's alcohol rider before we got off-stage,' continued Jonathan in his mail, referring to Portsmouth '95. 'It was probably the same nite you told me for the twenty-second time how in love you and Courtney Love were, or some strange variation on this theme as only you in yer un-right mind could develop – along epic tragic lines of course. It was very Salingeresque as I recall.'

Shut up! I never said that! You see what I mean about Mercury Rev's fondness for sport. Even when writing from across the Atlantic, Jonathan can't resist an opportunity to wind me up. Maybe that's the juvenile side of his character. His group have an almost childish belief in the healing power of music. Nineteen ninety-eight's *Deserter's Songs* sounds like a fifties Disney soundtrack shredded down through three generations of rock's wayward outsiders, songwriters, drifters all. It sounds like how Neil Young might have – if he wasn't so goddamn Republican. It haunts and swells and staggers in its breadth of imagination.

I once saw Mercury Rev play an entire Phoenix Festival show tuning up. It sounded like the whisper of angels choking back laughter on the breeze.

'Other than this story,' Jonathan finishes up his e-mail, 'there's only eleven other stories involving you an' yer arch-ego-enemy David Baker. You two would have made great comic book super-hero fodder.'

I guess so. Like the time photographer Steve Gullick drove up to Springfield MA with David to see Nirvana play. Afterwards, Kurt told me to 'never let that man near me again'. This was odd, because Kurt was usually tolerant of my companions and David was very likeable. He could be intense and paranoid, though. We fought as much as we hugged. I've always thought of him as Soundgarden guitarist Kim Thayil's psychic double.

'Mercury Rev is like a satellite that is getting signals beamed in, but is always sending them back scrambled and jumbled up,' guitarist Grasshopper told me in '93. 'Some of the time we're gonna suck, sometimes we're gonna be cool. We just try things. But at least we try, you know?'

*   *   *

Someone, some day, is going to have to explain the music business to me.

Around the start of the nineties, Rough Trade US went bankrupt – meaning that all the company's assets, including master tapes and record contracts, were up for sale. In 1991, Damon Krukowski, drummer with Galaxie 500, purchased his own band's master tapes with the only bid at an auction in New York. How can this be right? That people's beauty and art can be bought and sold so randomly? It's especially upsetting because Galaxie 500 had such a special radiance.

I first met the Boston trio at a party in 1989. I was in awe of their debut album *Today*. Its passion and sombre beauty was reminiscent of Joy Division and the Velvet Underground, two groups that had influenced my teenage years too much. After Joy Division singer Ian Curtis killed himself in 1980, I had to get rid of all of their records because I became too obsessed with his tragic story, his terribly dark lyrics and Peter Hook's bass sound. I wouldn't listen to them again for another seventeen years.

I wasn't sure I wanted to meet Galaxie. They were geniuses and I was a punk kid. I didn't know if I wanted to cross the line between fan (possibly their only English fan at that time) and acquaintance. Someone insisted.

I went into the next room, and there were the three of them sitting round the table drinking beer. I couldn't believe how *normal* they looked. Or that they seemed more in awe of me than I was of them.

That was the last time I ever felt quite that way about a band.

Looking back on Galaxie 500 now, it's not surprising I fell for their charms. Their cover versions – Young Marble Giants, Jonathan Richman, Joy Division, Beatles, Rutles, Yoko Ono – were so in tune with my own musical tastes. They loved Beat Happening and thought that drummer Mo Tucker's primitivism was at the heart of the Velvet Underground. How few of us agreed with that! Everything about Galaxie 500 was so restrained and unhurried. Naomi Yang's chthonic heartbeat of a bass sounded almost sepulchral, the drums were a whisper of percussion on the windowpane.

At the heart of *Today* is Galaxie 500's tumultuous reading of Richman's chilling Modern Lovers song 'Don't Let Our Youth Go To Waste'. The original is a plaintive a cappella chant. On Galaxie 500's version, Dean Wareham's guitars roar like the fury of the ocean unabated, while his quavering, eerie tenor echoed Richman's words of hope and despair. Producer Kramer, meanwhile, kept adding more reverb until it felt the whole world was ringing in your ears.

Kramer produced all Galaxie's three albums. He also played occasional guitar and sound effects live, and supplied the dope and jokes. He was the invisible fourth member. Not only did he run Shimmydisc and play in B.A.L.L. and Bongwater, he also owned Noise New York, the studio where Galaxie recorded. Costs were kept to a minimum because Kramer was a believer in recording everything on first take. The first Galaxie 500 album cost $750 to record. Whereas the third Hole album was rumoured to have cost anywhere up to £1.25 million to record, My Bloody Valentine's final studio album nearly bankrupted their record company but Nirvana's *Bleach* cost $606 and 'some loose change'. Spontaneity is at the heart of all great rock music.

Galaxie 500 should possibly be placed under 'naïve grunge' alongside Jad Fair and Half-Japanese: but the almost psychedelic guitars, the self-consciously arty videos that frequently utilised blurred scenes of death, and Naomi's earrings, assure them of their place in 'art grunge'. Also, Galaxie 500's music – icy, powder-blue: a stark, almost terrible beauty behind the humanity – is a perfect counterpart to the reassuring, warm red contours of Mercury Rev and Flaming Lips. Their songs celebrated youth, albeit those decaying, deliciously decadent hours of youth spent wondering whether death wouldn't be sweeter after all.

Certain songs are evocative of certain scenarios. Even now I can't listen to 'Fourth Of July' without seeing the Empire State Building all lit up at night. Snow is falling in the East Village, alcohol courses through my veins and Dean is creating mischief in Joe's Bar on 7th with a few industry friends. 'Tugboat' reminds me of Olympia, of Calvin Johnson's story about how Galaxie 500 defined rock'n'roll for him. 'Sorry' recalls Damon and Naomi's Boston apartment, paintings and books all around, the three of us recording music on a four-track to back spoken word renditions of Mazzy Star reviews.

I think of glaciers, diamonds and fuzzy pain. I think of an acid trip I once took listening to Sonic Youth's *Daydream Nation* where the nerve centres on our bodies lit up like Christmas lights on Sunderland bridge. Time slowed down, reversed, so the digital clock was counting backwards and each guitar note oscillated into infinity and even the click track sounded unbearably poignant. That's how Galaxie 500 sound to me, without the drugs.

I used to heckle down the front of Galaxie 500's UK shows around the time of 1989's incredible *On Fire* with shouts of 'play quieter, softer'. It was the direct opposite of the war cry I'd shout five years earlier at bands like the Membranes and Dog-Faced Hermans: 'faster, louder'.

Beauty is such a strange concept. During our one interview, Naomi felt it was 'something that's not afraid to be intuitive'. Dean thought it came down to 'nice legs, bare white walls, bent guitar strings'.

'I was reading a history of bent guitar strings the other day,' Damon interrupted. 'Apparently, in the original blues guitar scale, people went out in the fields and recorded notes that no longer exist. This guy reckons that's where the bent note comes from, through reaching for notes that don't officially exist.'

You might have guessed Galaxie 500 wrote songs about nature, emotions, alienation, hope and torment. You'd be wrong. The band were named after an American Ford car.

' "Blue Thunder" is about my car which is blue,' revealed Dean. 'It's got a gigantic engine, but good mileage.'

'Before he told me that,' laughed Naomi, 'I thought it was about storms crashing against lightning-flecked mountains, cities afire on a summer's day. That sort of thing. I was very disillusioned when I found out. Still, we actually wrote the music with that in mind.'

'And "Snowstorm" is about static on the TV,' added Damon.

'We're a typical American rock band really,' explained Naomi. 'More songs about TV, fast cars and alienation.'

After Galaxie 500 abruptly split, much to Damon and Naomi's shock, the two factions formed bands not too dissimilar from the original, although lacking crucial components. Dean moved to New York. I have any number of anecdotes from those times . . . walking into the Windmill Obstacle on Central Park's miniature golf course at nine a.m., cross-dressing at drag queen parades, cramming into tiny vans to see his band Luna play at Maxwell's, Hoboken. Luna's initial recordings were made with the help of various members of Mercury Rev, and they later turned into a creditable reflection of former glories, particularly on 1995's *Penthouse*. Dean still doesn't have that magical drummer, though, one that breathes and lives in the spaces between the beat like Damon did in Galaxie 500. Drummers are often seen as the least important part of a rock band, but a bad – or worse, a *competent* – drummer can ruin a band's sound like no one else. Why bother to include a rhythm track if all it's going to do is fill in space?

I despair of rock bands sometimes.

Damon and Naomi, with the help of Kramer, continue to plough the same furrow they first ploughed fresh out of college. Their albums have their moments, but they are lacking a charismatic leader – Dean Wareham, say.

* * *

It's hard to explain Flaming Lips to a casual observer.

There are some obvious facts.

To achieve the symphonic splendour of 1999's *The Soft Bulletin*, the Oklahoma band recorded up to 200 tracks separately: gongs, oboes, choirs, upright pianos and any number of percussive instruments. Imagine *Fantasia* mixed in with all the spacier parts of Neil Young's early seventies work, throw in unquenchable melodies and a voice that defines melancholy. This is fantasy pop. The supporting concerts were deliberately upsetting. On video screens behind the trio, a civilian was repeatedly executed, while seconds later girls in one-piece swimsuits jiggled their toned buttocks in our faces, and worlds exploded. Singer Wayne Coyne bashed a giant golden gong and his own bearded face, until fake blood trickled everywhere. The music was played loud past the point of distortion.

Its predecessor, 1997's *Zaireeka*, could only be listened to in its entirety by utilising four CD players, and sequencing carefully. Not one listener heard a similar version to another. The concerts featured 150 friends and industry observers all holding boom boxes, playing various Flaming Lips music.

Nineteen ninety's inspirational *In A Priest Driven Ambulance* features Jonathan Donahue, and a version of 'It's A Wonderful World' that brings tears of joy to my eyes. Jon also plays on its follow-up and major label debut *Hit To Death In The Future Head*, which is notable for its 29.16 minute-long final track – the entire album played in reverse, but a little faster. At this point, their UK label had such little faith in the band, the press office refused to pay my train fare to travel from New York to Philadelphia to interview the band. No matter. After Jonathan's departure, and the resulting sublime *Transmissions From The Satellite Heart*, the band scored the unlikeliest of US Top Forty hits with 'She Don't Use Jelly'. The resulting media parade saw the band featured on *Beverly Hills 90210* where the character Steve Sanders remarked, 'I've never been a big fan of alternative music, but these guys rocked the house!'

For *Clouds Taste Metallic*, *Melody Maker* travelled to Chicago to interview the band, where our plane was hit by lightning during take off and I forgot to switch the tape player on (again). The album failed to chart, despite the presence of the painfully wistful 'Bad Days' on the *Batman Forever* soundtrack, and the drop-dead gorgeous singalong 'Guy Who Got A Headache And Accidentally Saves The World'.

When I saw Flaming Lips play Lollapalooza in 1994 my head exploded. The drummer fed me Jim Beam in between drum rolls.

A bubble technician sat up in the clouds, and afterwards we sat around and eulogised ELO. Next time I saw them, they'd elevated me to role of 'snow mechanic': one of the greatest honours I've ever been awarded. The following words are taken directly from my *Melody Maker* report of their shows in Chicago, '94:

The lights. Fairy lights spinning round on bicycle wheels and in streams; eyes that flash evil red from badges; the odd lighter held aloft in sanctification. The snow. Great cascades of paper snow, billowing out over the drums and the whisky and the photographers and the electric piano. Bravo, oh wizened snow mechanic! The crutches. Crutches being waved wildly above the heads of the audience at the Double Door. The Flaming Lips can make the lame walk! The unborn baby. Pulsating inside its mother's belly at the Metro. Kicking madly at every extraneous roll on the cymbals. The language. How many different languages can you say 'the Flaming Lips are the best fucking rock band in the world' in?

Les Flaming Lips sont le meilleur groupe du monde. Los Flaming Lips son el mêjor grupo en el mundo. Il Flaming Lips é il meglio gruppo nel entro mondon.

The sleep deprivation, man. The sleep deprivation.

The midnight Tower Records showcase is acoustic, drummer Steven making the odd roll (*of course* with 'Jelly'), but mostly behaving all mellow and stupid on piano and guitar. The odd wail of extraordinary distortion is elicited from Michael's bass amp; the crowd have to teach Wayne the words to one of his old songs; *Clouds Taste Metallic* is treated with jollity and soul; but otherwise this is . . . weird actually. Some kids sit and swoon, others stand and swoon. Afterwards we lick guitar straps, puddle ducks and step over comatose bodies. Whatever.

The drugs, man. Where?

The Metro show is darker, much darker. There's sweat, semen, smashed-up skinheads and strangeness, sangria, and no new songs. Often, it sounds like the world is ending. Sometimes it sounds like one extended plaintive cry submerged under layers of darkly psychedelic guitar. No one jumps into any garbage trucks, but they *could* have done. I never take notes, but if I had they'd have read '*rapsodija u ponon, mali bag, I KNOW A WOMAN GOES TO SHOWS, il ne faut pas souhaiter la mort des gens, DON'T RUB IT DON'T RUB IT*'. Something like that. Something to indicate how I started speaking in tongues after their closing, sorrowing interpretation of 'It's A Wonderful World', anyway.

The drink, man. Oh cheers, Steven.

The Double Door is . . . let's put it like this. Nervy. Numbing. Nauseous. Nice. *Neon*. The last time I took drugs, the world lit up in fairy lights then split in two (and two and two) and carried on splitting. *Carries* on. Most bands have the germ of an idea and grab onto it greedily, scared to let go. The Flaming Lips have a whole bloody virus – and it carries on splitting, fuelled by the most glorious, coruscating guitar harmonics and effects pedals. Fuelled by that and Wayne's cute quiver of a voice; imagination; verve; fever; firmaments; follicles: and everything magical that ever caught fire.

The States, man. Altered States.

When I interviewed the Lips drummer Steven, he started freaking out just like Mercury Rev's David Baker when confronted by my tape recorder.

'Are we still friends?' he asked, shaking.

Sure.

'So what do you want to know?' he continued, scared. 'I get drunk and try to play my drums and have a good time. And that's it. People play music and whether you like them or not, they have their own trip. We try to make people walk away thinking, "That was worth the time."'

Your favourite colour?

'Blue. I don't know why. Blue. What kind of question is that? Blue. It's just there. Blue. OK?'

So tell me something about your band . . .

'It's rock music,' Steven said, worried. 'That's hard to do, Everett. I don't know why you'd ask me to do that. It's rock music, man. There's nothing wrong with it.'

Daydream Nation
(Sonic Youth, Pavement)

So we drive down to Binghamton, through all the gorgeous oranges and browns and hazels and auburn and brilliant yellows and ochre and lively reds of Broome County in full autumnal bloom. We arrive at the campus of Sonic Youth guitarist Lee Ranaldo's old school just as our gas runs out. Another hour passes, and we find the building we need. We're late, and our breath freezes in spurts of near ice as we attempt to gain access to the packed campus gymnasium doubling as tonight's venue. Sheriffs tote ten-gallon hats and guns, and kids wear flannel like it's the state costume of New York.

We reach the venue. There are kids in security T-shirts holding mobile phones, looking like raw army recruits with their first rifle. Bassist Kim Gordon is inside, sporting a 'Girls invented punk rock, not England' shirt that was thrown on stage a few nights earlier in Toronto.

Sonic Youth are a flurry of flames, cartwheels and sardonic anger. '100%' is illuminating in its rushes of noise and all-powerful choral release; 'Silver Rocket' a vivid outburst of screaming guitars and drum thunder. The young audience love it. Thurston introduces Kim's searing feminist diatribe 'Swimsuit Issue' with the words, 'I'd like to send this next song out to Axl Rose and all those dicks, hyuk, hyuk . . . they're probably very nice people.' The single 'Youth Against Fascism' is storming, a metal sucker of a railing punch. There's plenty of cool ruined glamour on offer too, if that's what you're after.

Tonight is the first time I've been sober and watched Sonic Youth since 1983, almost ten years previously. They're great. Back then, they were a terrorist noisenik quartet with attitude and I was a geek. Since then Thurston Moore has both discovered and created art-rock, grunge, 'foxcore' and flannel shirts. According to him, that is. Sonic Youth are now an ace corporate rock squall of beauty and noise. And me? I'm still a geek.

So I rush back to chat, but the band's disappeared with my photographer. I sulk and play *Addams Family* pinball until they reappear.

Where should one begin with Sonic Youth? Their music and attitude influenced an entire generation, and of course Seattle. What follows then is An Idiot's Guide To Sonic Youth.

Sonic Youth formed when visual artist and bassist Kim Gordon moved to NYC from LA at the end of the seventies. There she met up with future husband, guitarist Thurston Moore, and they started playing music together: harsh, challenging, abrasive music influenced by free jazz, art, punk rock and cheap beer. Future SY guitarist Lee Ranaldo and Thurston had already collaborated together, as part of New York composer Glenn Branca's experimental guitar orchestra. Early band names included Male Bonding, Red Milk and the Arcadians.

'I always say we're excused from any analysis as far as other bands are concerned,' laughs Thurston. This quote, and all the following, are taken from the upstate New York interview I conducted with the band in 1992. It took three false starts before we managed to determine what level we could relate on. The previous year, Thurston had gone on record as saying he wanted to rip my head off for perceived 'sexist' comments about Courtney. (He later rescinded.) I'd avoided speaking to the Youth before because . . . well, I've never liked doing the expected.

'You can lump us in with Mudhoney and Nirvana, but we started before all those bands,' he continues. 'Who are our peers? Swans? We're totally seen as parental by people like Kurt and Courtney. When they got married, they sent us a postcard, like, "We're here mom and dad!" It's very endearing but kind of faulty seeing as how Courtney is five years older than I am.'

Ooh, bitch! I don't think that's true, either. That would make Courtney . . . erm, *old*. How do the band feel about their 'God-parents of slacker rock' tag?

'It's gross,' Kim shudders.

'Slackers are people like us, only they don't do anything,' explains Thurston. 'Rather than *No Future* it's *No Present*. I find slacker endearing, if annoying. We don't subscribe to it. Our influence is on the music.'

'It's more like us and other bands through the eighties have built up a vocabulary of sound that is drawn upon by bands like Pavement,' thinks Kim. 'It's almost like folk music. All this dissonance contrasted with melody has become a new musical language.'

Sonic Youth's first drummer was Richard Edson, who later acted in a couple of Jim Jarmusch films. His replacement, Bob Bert, went on to play in New York's groovy hate fuck noise eighties band Pussy Galore, and write a great fanzine *BB Gun*. Pussy Galore spawned several bands – Jon Spencer's Blues Explosion, Boss Hog, Royal Trux, Action Swingers, STP, Free Kitten among them.

Thurston has collaborated with everyone from jazz pianist Cecil Taylor to hardcore Scots band Prick Decay and free guitar-player Derek Bailey. Yes, you could say he's promiscuous. His solo album *Psychic Hearts* sounds like the Male Riot Grrrl. It's grrreat!

Lee released a solo record in the eighties. It was on clear vinyl with an etching on the flipside, while each track was contained within its own locked groove. Yes, it was unplayable. Some of Lee's Sonic Youth songs are actually the best ones – 'Eric's Trip', 'Genetic' – despite conventional critical opinion.

Kim is a fashion designer with her own label (X-Girl), a video director (she directed the Breeders' 'Cannonball'), a celebrity mum, and record producer. She produced STP, Hole (*Pretty On The Inside*) and was a major influence on Riot Grrrl. Her anti-commercial music band, Free Kitten – who she formed with Pussy Galore/STP's Julie Cafritz – later went on to embody many aspects of the Grrrls.

Drummer Steve Shelley runs his own record label, Smells Like. In 1999, he started reissuing old albums from ace sleazy sixties producer Lee 'These Boots Are Made For Walking' Hazelwood. Hazelwood, of course, is a major influence on both Calvin Johnson and Stephen Pastel. Smells Like have also released Catpower, Two Dollar Guitar and Blonde Redhead records.

Looking for a record to start your Sonic Youth collection with? Try the double album *Daydream Nation*. Just its first song alone, 'Teenage Riot', inspired a whole generation of disaffected youth – Pavement, Nirvana, Huggy Bear, Blur – to pick up their guitars and start experimenting with molten noise. On the labels to *Daydream Nation*, there are four symbols, each pertaining to a member of Sonic Youth, in tribute to Led Zeppelin. The female symbol represents Kim. The infinity symbol is Mr Locked Groove himself, Lee Ranaldo. The omega symbol is Thurston. And then there's a little devil with a halo, sunglasses, drumsticks and bat wings . . . Steve Shelley.

Sonic Youth recorded the 'Death Valley '69' EP with fellow NYC noise-head Lydia Lunch. It was written about the Charles Manson killings, and is still possibly the most thrilling death ride via guitars available on vinyl. New York photographer and filmmaker Richard Kern (*New York Girls*) shot the accompanying video full of gore, band-members the victims of a Manson killing, blood pouring out of them, organs exposed.

In 1988, Sonic Youth released a split twelve-inch with Mudhoney, each band covering the other's song, 'Hallowe'en' and 'Touch Me I'm Sick'. Thus Sonic Youth ushered in the grunge era while simultaneously proving their impeccable garage credentials.

The video for 'Addicted To Love', the Robert Palmer cover released by Sonic Youth under the name Ciccone Youth, was shot at Macy's Store in New York City for something like twelve dollars. It features Kim Gordon miming in front of a standard Macy's video trailer. The *South Bank Show* once screened a special featuring 30 minutes each on Sonic Youth and John Zorn, with interviews from Glenn Branca, Lydia Lunch, Matador boss Gerard Cosloy and Lenny Kaye, during which the video was mentioned a lot.

Sonic Youth live shows are memorable for Thurston's individual guitar technique: sawing the fretboard across the edge of the stage, hitting the strings with drumsticks, wedging screwdrivers underneath the strings. I have no idea what definition of punk rock you care to use while reading *Live Through This*, but Sonic Youth and Beat Happening are as close to the core as it gets.

* * *

We're sitting around post-concert in Binghamton, having a few vodkas. There's Kim and Thurston, photographer Stephen Sweet, me, a few members of Japanese band the Boredoms, a sound engineer or two . . . The usual array of sweating meats and cheese, plus bowls filled with M&Ms sit on the side tables: for food, we order Chinese takeouts and pizza. We're not talking about much: idiot music journalists, MTV, the usual, why the US underground is so fascinated by punk. The Sonic Youth documentary, *1991 – The Year That Punk Broke,* which was filmed around various European festivals with Nirvana, even mentions the word in its title.

I ask the married couple if they think Nirvana are punk rock.

'In the context of the whole macho redneck mentality that is a lot of America, yes,' replies Kim. 'Kurt and Krist grew up in a small town. They are subversive so that although their music has some elements of heavy metal, it possesses a real radicalism. They make rock stars that grew up in the same white trash fundamentalist environment nervous. They're subversive because they represent so much power and vulnerability at the same time.'

'They're subversive in their whole "we don't want to be famous" thing,' Thurston laughs.

In the UK, that is seen as whining, as an inability to cope with success.

'I see a lot of that too,' agrees Kim. 'From the beginning, Kurt was like, "Oh yeah, I wanna sell a million records. I don't see anything wrong with that". When you're faced with the reality of it, though, it's totally different. That's called psychosis when you can't accept what you want. You think that you'll have the power to do whatever creative things you desire and maybe you do, if you're Guns N'Roses and all you want to do is tour.'

'Punk is an elitist kind of aesthetic, a dividing line,' Thurston explains. So speaks the man who used to follow Sid Vicious round the streets of New York. 'It's a way of separating yourself from all the attitudes you want to extinguish, like the whole macho thing, the whole idea of competitiveness, the way big business dictates youth culture. That's punk rock.'

'Punk rock right now is also Riot Grrrl,' adds Kim.

But Riot Grrrl US is a mostly middle-class discourse.

'Original punk rock in England was too,' the bassist shoots back. 'Class never had anything to do with whether something was punk rock or not. A lot of kids came from the suburbs, where they didn't have an identity or a culture of their own.

'In America, there's always been an urban versus suburban faction,' she adds. 'And suburbia is represented as white. That's why punk has connotations in the US. Riot Grrrls aren't espousing any quality, but everything they say and do is very punk. When Bikini Kill take off their shirts and it says "slut", or when they sing songs about how they were abused as children, they're being confrontational. Bikini Kill are a politically correct band who are doing all these contradictory things, which is almost anarchy. And anarchy is a natural place for most women, because this society is pretty much run by men and men's morals.'

Do you think men can be revolutionary in rock music any more?

'If they wear pyjamas,' jokes Thurston.

I seriously think men can't be punks.

'I'd almost agree with you,' says Kim. 'There's nothing for them to be confrontational about. The only way they can be punk is by imitating girls who are punkers.'

Lee shouts from across the room something to the effect of 'that's bollocks'. We ignore him.

'They can be brats,' Kim adds. 'They've only got their nostalgia. Fugazi are hardcore, not punk. That's something else entirely.'

Thurston disagrees.

'Fugazi are punk,' he claims. 'I have an interview on tape with [singer] Ian MacKaye in 1981 where he said, "When I wake in the morning and I look in the mirror, I see a punk. I don't use the word hardcore." '

'What year was that?' Kim asks her husband. 'Nineteen eighty-one? OK. What year it is now? Nineteen ninety-two. Hardcore was about kids educating other kids. It was anti-corporate, but it wasn't confrontational. It was about creating a culture.'

'I don't agree with you,' Steve Shelley chips in. 'Hardcore was totally confrontational. In the Midwest it was always a fight to get a show or make anything happen. It was about getting beaten up by the jocks because they thought we were fags.'

'But it was all by men,' Kim argues.

'You should ask Richard Hell about punk rock,' Thurston tells me, referring to one of NYC's original '76 punk rockers. 'The secret is locked inside Richard Hell's brain.'

Here's what makes me different from you: I understand the power of music.

I recognised Pavement's talent when they were a loose fragmentation of varying musical styles. The sleeve to their debut 'Slay Tracks 1933–69' single was cryptic and uninformative, the music even more confusing. A college graduate joined forces with a Stranglers fan and an acid casualty and recorded five songs on a whim, the day before they went on vacation. Scrapings of noise, mixed in with flashes of pop brilliance. The record unsettled Mark Ibold from NYC's Dust Devils, later to become Pavement's bassist.

'I thought it sounded very weird and dangerous,' Mark told me during our first interview, round the corner from Matador's offices in New York. Label boss Gerard Cosloy had given me a tape of Pavement and told me I should talk to them because they were great. So I interviewed them on spec. It was only years later, when Malkmus told me that I'd reviewed his first three singles, contrasting them with rudimentary electronica and unfathomable dry rot, that I realised I'd already heard Pavement.

'I took the record home,' Mark continued, 'opened it up and took a peek inside. The label was called Treblepicker and it was from Stockton, California. I didn't even know people made music out there.'

It wasn't until I heard 'Summer Babe' that I realised Pavement's true potential. Not only did the single boast a melody that would have made any sixties girl group want to burn their stilettos in jealousy, it also rocked with such delight and strangeness, you couldn't help but tumble headfirst into the giddy mêlée of sound. No wonder Pavement later hooked up with Huggy Bear and Winona Ryder and that whole crew. Malkmus and gang's ability to straddle divides while rejecting inertia was mind-boggling.

'The songs on *Slanted And Enchanted* are about personal girl–boy relationships,' Malkmus revealed before correcting himself. 'Sorry, man–woman relationships, that sounds tougher. These are emotional angst songs. Some are improvised stories. Others are truisms and aphorisms. They're flip, but emotional too. We're not into being empty or surface cynicism. We're not as pretentious as someone like Bryan Adams or maybe Hole, where Courtney Love is always giving her urban nightmare to you. Our music is both visceral and just cool images.'

This was in early 1992, before Courtney attained worldwide notoriety.

I don't need to be told what is great or good or glorious. I am capable of making my own mind up. I recognised Pavement's talent long before they turned into the credible alternative to REO Speedwagon, drive time music. Back in the mid-nineties when people were concerned with the notion of 'cool', I was arguing with Malkmus on icy New York streets about irony and self-consciousness, the end of rock music. Pavement were initially compared to the abrasive guitars and sarcasm of the Fall, but that was like comparing mountain streams to icebergs. Looking back, it's strange that a band so traditional could be hailed as new. Like every great rock band since the Sex Pistols and Nirvana, Pavement looked to destroy rock while reinvesting the form with hope and meaning. They wrote great *pop* songs, songs that drew heavily from America and the UK's mid-seventies period (Cheap Trick, Steely Dan, Badfinger) yet retained enough of a twist and overflowing love for music to keep them away from the traps of their forebears.

You could draw parallels between Malkmus' smart, sassy music and that arch chameleon David Bowie, but Steve never struck me as cynical. Disturbed, maybe, but cynical, no. Pavement's 1992 debut album, the still-glistening *Slanted And Enchanted*, rocked with an urbane freshness reminiscent of Jonathan Richman's Modern Lovers. Pavement regularly discarded songs that most musicians should kill for.

If this section of the book was like an early Pavement song, there would be precious few tangible points of reference. Everything would be a fog of confusion. There would be plenty of strange and intriguing interruptions, a handful of tangents and quotes that might or might not reveal something, and a little humour. If this section was like Pavement, it would be self-effacing yet quietly confident. It would *rock*. There would be plenty of mystery, much seriousness and not a little intelligence. The words would flow not for the sake of meaning, but for the sake of sound. Tunes would be at a premium, noise levels too. It would roll and sway and rumble along merrily under its own steam. But writing about Pavement is like skiing with marshmallows.

If you had five words with which to describe yourselves, what would they be?

'Wow, words,' Steve exclaims pleased, and then pauses. '*Slanted And Enchanted*. Actual fantasy count. That's only three.'

'Coming To Your Town Soon,' offers Mark.

'How would you describe yourself in five words?' Steve asks me.

One of them would be chameleon, and another would be cipher.

'That sounds like a Pavement lyric,' he laughs. 'We're into the secret ichnography stuff. We like spies, the idea of Switzerland. What happened to the British bobsled team?'

Some critics despise Malkmus because he's a rich kid who's always in the toilet when it's his turn to buy a round. Not me. I think he's a force for The Good, a smart charlatan with diamond fingers that loves to create and amplify. Over the nineties, Pavement inspired so many bad bands – New York's Sammy, Blur on a down day, Grandaddy and the Eels are just four that spring to mind. All their pretenders failed to capture the essence of Pavement, not least their spontaneity. Achieving a particular sound isn't an end in itself, nor is the ability to poke cruel fun at those less able-bodied members of the rock community (e.g. Smashing Pumpkins). The cheekbones don't matter, nor does the ability to imitate at will. Like Kurt, like Lou, like Evan Dando when he wasn't trying to impress some crap supermodel, Malkmus has a casual brilliance to his music. This is natural. This is fun. Sometimes it seems like Malkmus will fall into the Beck trap, laughing at an audience clearly not smart enough to catch his every nuance, but every time his *soul* and beating pop heart sees him through.

When I last met Malkmus in his new hometown of Portland in 1998, he offered to write about free jazz for the *Stranger* for me, and we swapped drunken taunts. Like that other great purveyor of Art Grunge, Mercury Rev singer Jonathan Donahue, it has always amused Steve how many people hate me. Like the Rev, Pavement are very New York. You know that if Steve spotted someone wearing blue shoes in a cafè, and then got to know the person real well later on, he'd forever say to them:

'Hey blue shoes. How's it going?'

Much as I rate *Slanted And Enchanted,* Pavement's more rounded-off 1994 album *Crooked Rain, Crooked Rain* is the one that occupies a special place in my heart. For a start, there's the plaintive soft rock classic 'Fillmore Jive' with its lines about '*rockers with [the] long curly locks*' and '*the street full of punks*'. Those lyrics remind me of standing outside CBGB's in the summertime, with all the dead industry hangers-on and soulless rockers. The people who thought Beavis and Butt-head were revolutionary. People stuck in a time warp they will never escape. It almost seemed to be heralding the end of rock, the way it finished, suspended in midair on the line '*When they pull out the plugs and they snort up the drugs*'. It was like Pavement knew rock had nothing unique to offer, so they might as well fuck around and confuse shit.

'It could be interpreted about how rock people in the nineties behave exactly like the rock people in the seventies,' Steve shrugged. 'There are analogies to bigger bands like Pearl Jam. It's back to that old "alternative to what?" thing. There is no alternative music.'

I was speaking to Steve in January 1994, on the coldest day New York had seen in a century. My hands were chapped, my chest was heaving and I felt like I'd been hanging upside-down in a meat freezer. This time, it wasn't because of the cheap late night alcohol down Max Fish.

I appreciated the fact Steve was always willing to draw lines. Remember those brilliant *'Out on the road with the Smashing Pumpkins/Nature kids, they don't have no function/I don't understand what they mean and I could really give a fuck'* lyrics and splurge of piano on 'Range Life'? Like Peter Bagge in his slacker comic *Hate*, Malkmus parodied his peers, sometimes cruelly, but with such wit and style that no one minded. Except, of course, the most pompous.

'I really do not like myself much and feel guilty for even expressing myself,' said Stephen to me, quoting. 'That's the classic line everyone comes out with. I feel like that and I'm sure the Kurt Cobains of this world also do. What are you supposed to say? *I Hate Myself And I Want To Die* is a great title for a Nirvana album. It's a shame he didn't use it. What can you do? Love yourself and start to live.'

Do you sleep at nights?

'Yeah. Takes some drinking, though. I never lie awake wondering what's going to happen the next day because I know what's going to happen the next day. It will be similar to the day before.'

Crooked Rain, Crooked Rain was great in the way that Bowie used to be great when he wasn't just a pile of pompous shite in a greying suit, cool in the way Bryan Ferry was cool when he wasn't pretending to be a simple, soulless lizard in carpet slippers. It had poise the way Tony Bennett imitating Fred Astaire has poise. It breathed despair and lust the way New York breathes despair and lust. It oozed with a slow-burning groove and faux-cool white boy indie sophistication. It was cleansing, the way that having a deliciously wicked sense of humour is always cleansing. And it took pot shots, at peers, pressure, punks, prats and the pointlessness of its own existence.

'I don't think rock music as a language is totally dead,' Malkmus told me in '94. 'The death of it is there, but within your own reference field there's room to grow. Our music is anti-PC to an extent because, as "Elevate Me Later" says, *"there are forty different shades of black"*. Why are people complaining about the words we use? We've lost poetry, some of the good things about life, because people are too uptight. Everything you say will always hurt someone else – take it lightly, it's not indicting you. These minor rivalries are what makes life interesting. The way it's going now, we're all just going to have one song by the year 2000.' . . . and it will be written by Spacemen 3.

'That's fine by me. I like that band.'

Hole

Pretty on the Inside

'Love is obsessed with people who are obsessed with her'

LOS ANGELES TIMES, 1992

Hole
Club Lingerie, Hollywood
(*Melody Maker*, 8 June 1991)

Courtney Love, singer with Hole, tells me I write like a lover, a *mean* lover.[1] Courtney Love would make a lousy lover. She'd fuck you once, make you fall in love and then leave you for dead. Still, any experience is better than none at all, I guess. As Courtney would say, fuck it! You want to go roll around in mud all day long,[2] you want to go masturbate non-stop or be a slut for four years? Fuck it! You can't rape the willing![3]

Hole. Yeah, right. Tonight in Hollywood, amid films of strippers and tales of anguish and exhilaration I witness the best . . . no, scratch that. Tonight I witness the *only* rock'n'roll band in the world. Something to do with equal amounts energy, luck, pain, passion, anger and the three major chords, I reckon. Courtney Love has been described (by me) as the 'illegitimate love child of Madonna and Lydia Lunch' and 'the drunk man's Madonna'. Both are accurate descriptions, if a little too glib for my liking. She consorts with various other Babes (most notably the ones from Toyland), has featured in various Alex Cox films, was a case history in the *NME*'s notorious sex issue of '86,[4,5] and her group's forthcoming debut album is produced by Kim Gordon (Sonic Youth) and Don Fleming (hiya, Don!). That's history time over.

Let's go back to this experience thing. Tonight, Hole cause me to lose sight of where I am and my feet to clump heavily back and forth the way they do only through fatigue or the most extreme noise conditions. And if I'm not in love this time, then I never fucking will be. Simply, this is awesome. Of course, bands being bands and dumb stupid creatures who would never hurt a fly unless it came up and peek-a-booed them on the nose, Hole reckon they've never sounded worse, roundly whipping the drummer for her sins and bad timing afterwards. Eric tries to throw his guitar at our brave photographer and that's that. Jesus! That was *bad*? Let's not throw the good at me too fast, huh?

Hole are . . . a fucking revelation.

So let's talk about the songs. *Songs*, right? 'Teenage Whore' is the most unsettling thing I've heard since Patti Smith uncovered 'Piss Factory' and then fucked off to become a middle-aged housewife, only it's way more personal. Like, you *feel* for her mother, when Courtney screams at us about how she got thrown out of the house for fucking around. 'Garbadge Man' (correct spelling) has the sexiest ending since Bongwater's Ann Magnusson whined '*I wa-a-ant one*' at the end of 'Nick Cave Dolls', and that's some sexy, I tell you.

'Good Sister/Bad Sister' is Beat Happening if they'd grown up feminist, over-sexed and *wired*.[6] 'Baby Doll' is lamest because it sounds like those middle-aged middle-class jerk-offs Sonic Youth.[7] Who cares? The sight of Eric and Jill rampaging possessed – and, believe me, you ain't seen no possession 'til you've seen Hole – across the strip-club stage more than compensates for that. And Eric plays Black Sabbath better than any white boy I've seen.

Oh, hell. Let's leave it here. Hole are sexy, happening, possessed and brutally honest. They make Brett Easton Ellis sound like a two-bit prankster. I came to LA thinking I knew everything there was to know about rock. I left a virtual beginner.

Hole are the only band in the world. It's the only way to feel.

Notes

(1) The 'lover' line is so transparent even I recognised it for what it was. Yet my rejoinder is astonishing, especially in light of everything that transpired. Many people took this, and the reference to Courtney wearing 'my' dressing gown in Hole's first interview proper, to mean that we were having sex. That was their interpretation. I've always loved to glamorise my own life. I even saw it as my duty, to give my readers something to believe in. One reason Courtney and I were attracted to one another was that we shared a common bond. We were both trying to invent and inhabit

characters that didn't necessarily have much relation to our real selves. We were both self-obsessed and suffered from monomania. Indeed, my best writing during this period came from what a fellow *MM* writer called 'sensationally deluded egomania, leavened with an element of self-deprecation'.

(2) The 'roll around in mud' line is a reference to the cover of the Slits first album, where the three female punks posed semi-naked and covered in mud in very un-erotic fashion. The album was a major influence on me, and I suspect Courtney may have claimed it as a reference for herself, too – possibly after meeting me.

(3) The 'slut for four years' line must have been hers. I've never made up shit like that. '*You can't rape the willing*' is a lyric from Hole's *Pretty On The Inside* 1991 debut.

(4) The *NME* sex issue. The editors had a brainstorm and commissioned a load of critics to write about sex, featuring rock music if they so desired. The result was brilliant and hilarious, and had indirect consequences such as *Melody Maker* being unable to print the word 'fuck' even a decade later. Questions were asked in Parliament about the irresponsible influence of youth media. One article was written by an earlier incarnation of myself, ranting about how celibacy – or, better still, virginity – was the most radical way rock music could go. I felt everything else was a cliché, particularly anything that celebrated those tired old passions of sex and drugs and alcohol. The article had two surprising results. First, another *NME* writer seduced me. Secondly, the cuties appeared, a bunch of Pastels and Orange Juice-inspired musicians who liked to dress down (as in schoolyard) and pretend they didn't know what sex was. How weird it was, then, the initial matching of Courtney and me.

(5) The first few meetings with Courtney where I was raging drunk and infatuated, I probably believed everything she told me. I'd never had anybody lie so outrageously to my face before. Courtney's memory was selective at best, so she'd get mad when I repeated some of her lies. Hence the famous 'knocking out a tooth' incident at Reading Festival '91 that didn't actually happen. Yes, she hit me playfully, in front of witnesses, but there was no damage. The story that later circulated erroneously – reported in disparate places including Andrew Mueller's excellent book, *Rock And Hard Places* – was fed by her and me, gluttons for publicity both. It was ironic, considering the physical barneys Courtney has had since.

(6) The Beat Happening line is so dumb. 'Feminist, over-sexed and wired . . .?' That's Beat Happening, exactly. I probably meant

something along the lines of 'Beat Happening, only not so scarily minimal'.

(7) Of course I like Sonic Youth. I wrote that line for emphasis.

Pretty On The Inside. Isn't that a great phrase? It's like when you're a little girl and all your friends have told you you're ugly, and you're crying and sobbing and stuff, so you go to your mum and ask her if you're beautiful, and she replies, 'Yes dear, you're pretty on the inside.'

Or maybe it's more Freudian than that. Maybe it's a reference to the vagina, the beauty that lies hidden beneath the surface, in all its folds and creases and secretions, the way it blossoms and fades and hardens like buds in spring. Or maybe it refers to the way everyone judges everyone else on their looks and their dress and how the ugliest people can be the best looking, and the most beautiful people can be the most repugnant.

Or maybe it's about pain, as the rest of life is, and how, no matter how much pain and torment you put your body through, you always have that inner core of bone inside you, that indelible something that keeps you sane and keeps you together. It's a great phrase, anyway. It's also the title of Hole's debut album.

(Opening lines of Hole feature, *Melody Maker*, 24 August 1991)

I remember the hotel.

Stepping down from the canopy into the cool, dark lobby, a haven from the oppressive heat. Laidback, hushed. The fairy lights twinkling among the tree borders like it was Christmas time already; the soothing, pastel colours; the ground level apartments; the concierge who didn't sneer at us as we walked in.

This was the hotel where Prince was rumoured to have indulged ladies with baths full of rose petals. This was the hotel where we lounged for days by the swimming pool, sipping beer and multi-coloured cocktails, basked in the LA haze and called record companies and industry people up on our mobile phones, eager to extend our stay. Desperately, we lounged by the pool and waited for folk to call us back. Every now and then, we'd call up London, just to smirk. 'How's the weather over there? It's raining? No, not really? What a shame.'

This then was the hotel where I first met Hole. I can still see them now, walking across the tiles at the far side of the pool to where we were idling in our English swimming trunks, the smog-filled sunlight catching Courtney's unkempt hair. In sharp contrast to the browned legs and light-coloured clothing of our fellow guests, they looked shockingly over-dressed and anaemic. Courtney's tights were ripped, drummer Caroline Rue boasted a chin stud long before they became fashionable, and bassist Jill Emery was a tiny dark-haired Gothic abrasion. The shy guitarist, Eric Erlandson, meanwhile, was almost the most startling of all – lanky like Thurston Moore, with his long scraggly hair and pale skin, it looked like he hadn't seen daylight for several years. The hotel management couldn't have dreamt up a bigger collection of hometown freaks in their darkest nightmares.

Courtney seemed very taken with our Englishness, laughing at our accents every opportunity she got. Or maybe it was the trunks. Eric refused to shake my hand because, he explained, then we would be friends. And it's not right, being friends with a journalist.

Nothing seemed more natural than Hole's presence there in that playground of the privileged. Nothing could've seemed more out of place. At the Sunset Marquis, even the cigarette machine is hidden away in the basement.

Later, we talked.

'There are two types of people,' Courtney told me. 'Those who are masochists and sadists, and those who are perfectly square, who have no desire to inflict pain or get pain, and that's the majority of people. You and me, Everett, we're in the minority. But then we're a little bit more sensitive than a lot of stupid people who are happy to be in a nice relationship and live a nice life and not desire anything else. They don't desire truth and they don't desire hate. They don't desire evil or decadence or purity . . .

'That's fine,' she continued. 'I envy these people, those Russian farmers who live to be one hundred and twenty on yoghurt with their simple lives. They don't have any stress. But it's so *fun*,' she said, drawing out the word like a plea for help, 'to be like we are and to me, the most fun part of it all is when you show bone. I'm so full of shit that when I'm honest enough to show some bone, it's almost like a Christ thing. It feels pure when I do it, even if it's a deep emotional lie.'

Courtney always was in tune with her dark side.

'Men are intimidated by me, but I'm past caring about it,' she said. 'They're intimidated because I wasn't raised coquettishly and don't know how to be real demure. I don't know the tricks in that realm, and I haven't taken the time to learn them because I feel I have other stuff to do. I have relationships with people who are brave enough to deal with me and I don't want to deal with people who aren't.'

'I've always been hated by the pen-pushers, the people who answer telephones,' she said. 'The people who love me are the people behind those telephones, people with power: Julian Cope, Elvis Costello, Alex Cox and . . . Everett True.'

That one cracked me up, I can tell you.

We talked long, ceaselessly, with energy and a burning passion. About everything, anything – anything that Courtney thought I wanted to hear. About her flirtations with ancient British rock stars and being bullied at school, the media's expectations of women, vaginal accoutrements, love, desire and hatred. We talked about showing bone and Jill's dad, a professional gambler. About Caroline's weird, studded friends and white-trash Wonderbread-and-gravy upbringing, and Eric's mother fixation.

Before we started, Courtney showered and carelessly changed into my white flannel hotel dressing gown. Her feet were uncovered, bare thighs prominently displaying their whiter-than-whiteness, laughing at Jill while the bassist grew more and more paranoid. Courtney sent all the other members away out of the room, so we were alone together, intimate.

For thirty minutes, I avoided asking the lady a direct question. I knew it would annoy her. Once she started to speak, my life didn't stand still for years, until late one summer when it ground to a juddering halt and has only barely moved on since.

But I'm getting ahead of myself.

```
Hi ET
   OK, my memory is shite too, but I do remember our
first interview with you and how evil you were and how
you were just trying to get into Courtney's knickers.
I remember getting Chinese food with you in Seattle
during those sad surreal days after Kurt's death. I
remember filming you push him out on stage in a wheel-
chair at Reading. I remember climbing fences with you
to go see Elastica in the tent at Reading. I remember
you getting up onstage with us in St Louis and singing
some songs. I remember shooting smack with you in
CBGB's. I'm joking, of course. Sorry. I remember the
VOX interview and photo session at Olympic studios.
   Eric
```

I have read so many part-truths and lies about Courtney and her group Hole that it becomes difficult to sort out fact from fiction even in my own memories. Did Courtney first meet Kurt in

Portland in 1989/1990, as was reported in Poppy Z Brite's *Courtney Love: The Real Story*? Not according to Eric, who was dating her back then. Did Courtney have any influence on her friend, Babes In Toyland singer Kat Bjelland's famed 'kinderwhore' look or music – a look and music Courtney later took for her own? Not according to Kat's Minneapolis boyfriend of the time, Chris Letcher. How long was Courtney married to her first husband, the cross-dressing Falling James of the Leaving Trains? Surely longer than to consummate the relationship the one time she told me about. There's so much I could write that I won't. Loyalty is important where I come from (Olympia).

There's a lyric on 'Asking For It' from *Live Through This* that is drawn directly from the second interview I did with Courtney in my Cricklewood flat in '91. '*Every time that I sell myself to you,*' she sings, '*I feel a little bit cheaper than I need to/I will tear the petals off of you/Rose red, I will make you tell the truth.*' The way she phrases the lyric is a reference to my somewhat penetrating interview technique. Likewise, 'Softer Softest', with its opening lines '*I tell you everything/I hope you won't tell on me*', is a reference to a relationship that went far beyond standard press/artist.

Sure, our relationship was ... what? Friends and peers tell me now how Courtney took advantage of me, how she used my position for her own ends and then dumped me, how she's manipulative and insanely ambitious and a bad, bad person. Others might say she's matured in recent years, grown into a fine actress and strong defender of certain rights, sometimes female. They usually agree on the relationship part, however. Sure. I'm prepared to believe all that. Except that Courtney never 'dumped' me. We drifted apart as our lives drifted apart, as often happens with friends. There was a Barney Hoskyns novel, *The Lonely Planet Boy*, that came out in 1995, based around the fictionalised relationship of a naïve male, middle-class English rock critic and a corrupting female rock star/diva, where she leads him into a sordid lifestyle of drugs and emasculating sex. The parallels seemed uncanny. That's what attracted all of us to her initially, right? The forbidden fruit is always the sweetest.

Courtney was insanely great fun to be with, had a most endearing way of turning to me for help and succour with her little-girl-lost eyes when she was at her most fucked-up, and could be relied upon to create a situation where none had previously existed. Is that bad? She made me feel special, like I was the most special person in the world when I was with her. Fuck all you dull nine-to-fives who can't perform that simple trick.

On our first meeting, I found myself rubbing whisky away from her groin. That was about as close as we ever got, and as close as we wanted to get. Whenever we'd first meet, I'd make her cry by being mean when drunk, which I always was – referring to her weight, or lack of voice or talent. I didn't want to be that way. She made me like that and, yeah, I loved it.

Oh, and listening back to some of the bootlegs of Hole shows from '91, '92 and '95 ... who's to say I didn't encourage her to misbehave, too?

Here's the secret of why I loved Hole initially: the music. Those first two singles I received, unsolicited in the post – 'Retard Girl' and 'Dicknail' – seemed like an entry to a darker, more turbulent world. Eric's guitars were laden with a claustrophobic intensity; the lyrics were spiteful and nasty and full of passion. The reason I fell for 'Retard Girl' was that all of its meanness and blackness and squirming reminded me of Lydia Lunch, Sonic Youth and my other secret eighties passions. I liked the fact nothing was cleaned up, that this was far removed from gregarious pop. The drums and bass were heavy, relentless. The guitar seemed to chuckle with maliciousness. 'Dicknail', meanwhile, was pure Babes In Toyland, and I wasn't going to resist that. Listen to the voice. Isn't the promise of trouble seductive in itself?

Even now, I'll hear Courtney lisping and howling her way through the Carole King song 'He Hit Me (It Felt Like A Kiss)' from the 1995 *MTV Unplugged* recordings, and my heart aches. I can't help it. She needs protecting. Still. She needs looking after – back then, but especially now, tormented in her easy life, however much her latest personal managers and trainers and manicurists deny it. I could be talking context here, knowing how some women really do feel the way that King wrote it. I don't think so, though.

Help never comes from those paid to smile. How sad is that, when you start dating your A&R man? Even now, if only Courtney wised up and started listening to Vic Godard rolling his vowels through 'Stool Pigeon' and OV Wright testifying on 'I'd Rather Be Blind, Crippled And Crazy', Al Wilson and Mavis Staples, Magazine mocking fashion on 'Boredom', there could still be hope.

Where would she get these records? From me, of course.

You've seen those rock movies with 'groupies' in, like Cameron Crowe's *Almost Famous*. They aren't fiction. These stories actually happened, albeit without the cosy, neat endings. It's strange. Ask me what I hate about rock music, and I'll tell you straight out. Axl Rose and those ridiculous things Steve Tyler ties round his head. Heroin and disrespect towards women. Crap situations where the people are there only for the party, the drugs – not the music. Johnny Thunders and the Velvets. The guitar used as a penis extension. Yet I lived through all of that, and I loved most of it.

I remember the flat.

I lived there after all. It wasn't much, considering the price. Just a couple of sterile rooms, a kitchen that connected with the living room by means of a hatch, a bathroom up back. A stairwell that was cluttered with three thousand tapes. Sometimes, I would wake there in the morning, smashed cassette boxes lying round my trashed body, the smell of defeat heavy in my nostrils. Posters adorned the walls – Beatrice Dalle, Betty Boo, the odd Edward Lear. Friends would come over just so they could watch the cappuccino machine in action and play Battling Tops. I hired a TV set when the rumours surrounding the forthcoming Gulf War became too much for me and ran out of the Phoenix cinema in East Finchley when I imagined the smell of gas. Cricklewood is good for getting into fights with cab drivers when they think you're too drunk to notice, good for cadging lifts from bands on their way out of London, good for entertaining – not that I usually did.

I remember the bedroom. How could I not? Two single beds pushed together in the centre in imitation of a swinging 'bachelor pad', wall-to-wall records, curtains the indeterminate colour of London afternoons. The window overlooked an unattainable pruned garden, three flights down. The rented TV took pride of place against the bathroom wall. A Debbie Harry poster stared down from the door. I don't think I ever managed to get off with a girl the whole time I rented that flat.

This then was the room where Courtney gave her first-ever, serious music press photo shoot: a piece of black cloth hastily gaffer-taped to the wall. First, though, she tore down the photo of her band above my stove. It showed her with her old nose. The photographer stood on the bed to escape the encroaching vinyl; Courtney pancake-white and over made-up, her lipstick the colour of blood, her hair the colour of dreams. Her eyes are what I mostly remember: fierce, wide and unblinking.

She knew what she wanted all right.

'There are two things you should know about me,' Courtney states. 'Two little stories about my life I'll tell you.'

OK. Carry on.

'Yeah, but you guys [points at Eric] have to leave. Leave! Just leave, though. Go on, get out!'

Eric, who's been sitting inoffensively in the corner listening to this ranting, departs for the bedroom.

'First one is, I went up for a play once. It was for *Snow White*, a really big production down in Portland. I studied the part of Snow White forever and had it down memorised. And they gave me, without even auditioning me, the part of the Evil Witch. And that was when I was eight.'

You're more like Rose Red, I interject, but she's away.

'The second one was after I came back from New Zealand and I had to go to this tough school. I didn't know anything about guys then, but I knew that you were supposed to desire them and they were better than horses or the Sweet or Bay City Rollers.

'I'd been at that school for a week and I was popular because I had this accent and I was into this Bowie thing. There was this guy and his name was Gary Graff and he was really nice to me and sweet and cool and funny, and followed me around, and everything. So we went out to the place where everyone smoked and he kissed me and gave me this hickey on my neck.

'So then these two incredibly popular girls asked me where I got my hickey and I was really proud and I said, "Oh, this guy Gary Graff," and they started laughing and cracking up. The deal was that Gary Graff was the biggest geek in the school and everyone made fun of him. I didn't want that to happen to me, so I ignored him. I did that to him.'

Her voice has dropped down to a plea again.

'So the point is, for the rest of my life I've been haunted by this Gary Graff thing, and in my relationships I just seek out Gary Graff. The revenge of Gary! Fuck punk rock jock boys, I don't care!

'All the Gary Graffs grow up to be incredibly powerful fuckers or they're forever stuck, trying to fit in. People should just accept their Gary Graffness and go on from there. Those who don't are bigger losers than normal people. Don't be bitter and mean because you don't fit in, it's a gift! Look at you, you've got your individuality, you don't have the herd instinct, you can read Nietzsche and understand it. Only dumb people are happy.'

For Gary Graffs everywhere: I give you Hole.

(*Melody Maker*, 24 August 1991)

On my first trip to LA, I visited Disneyland. There's something fascinating in the sight of Americans revelling in their own excess. I was there for eighteen hours and had to invent a plane crash to get to 'the happiest place on earth'. I returned at least twice afterwards, once with Hole and once with Melvins. Taking a band as screwed up as Hole to Disneyland seemed a brilliant juxtaposition.

'I remember this whole weird thing where she insisted on sitting next to you on all the rides, even though she was going out with me at the time,' Eric says. 'I was convinced that she'd fucked you, too – during that first interview when she changed into your dressing gown. She told me to keep quiet about our relationship to you. We kept it quiet for a year, and then we had a huge fight during which Courtney threw a trashcan through my car window. So it was hard to keep it a secret after that.

'She moved in with me the day we fell in love, on St Patrick's Day, 1990,' he continues. 'It was while we were recording "Retard Girl". She phoned up her husband James and said she wasn't coming home. When we met you, that was the beginning of the end. As soon as it became serious like that, with her sitting down and talking to journalists, there was a whole new set of rules. I remember that, during the first interview, you kept asking me odd, disjointed questions, like "How do you feel about aeroplane flights?" and I wanted to kill you. I was really taken aback by the way she was using her womanhood on you to get what she wanted.'

Eric was working at Capitol Records at the time. (It was from there he posted the first two Hole singles to me, Courtney having been tipped off by Kat Bjelland that I was a good contact.) The future lovers met after Eric answered an ad in an LA paper in June 1989 that was looking for a guitarist into 'Big Black, Stooges, ABBA and Fleetwood Mac'. Courtney called him back two weeks later at two a.m.

'I was completely in awe of how fucked up she was,' the guitarist recalls, 'and almost irresistibly embarrassed by the way she was acting. She used to pick on me for having one foot in her apartment and one in the hallway, because my car was always double parked when I'd visit her. I was totally into hanging out with her but not fully committed, thinking of my escape the whole time. I used to think that was a great metaphor for our relationship – yours, too. Except, of course, both of us eventually put both feet irretrievably in her apartment.'

I don't want to sound too cynical here. Everything that involved Courtney was a raucous good time certainly up to the end of '91, and many times after. That held true even when she phoned me up to boast about punching enemies out. I shouted at her then, unless I was in a position where I couldn't, like sitting next to the news editor in *Melody Maker*. After all, I was a target for violence myself, with my photo in *MM* almost every week.

The memories blur into one, endless night, me drunk and her whatever. We meet outside the Dominion Theatre in London; she sends her personal manager out into the crowd at the Phoenix Festival to find me; curled up in bed on drugs; arguing and screaming at the tops of our voices. Hanging out in LA, shopping in unrelenting sunshine, hours wasted in a dusty vintage dress shop. The initial round of UK press interviews with Hole, where Courtney slagged me off for the benefit of every last fanzine writer.

The first time Hole played England, they headlined at the Camden Underworld where the belligerent crowd, tanked up on hype and alcohol, molested Courtney. She leapt off stage after Eric had jumped in still playing his guitar, and had her dress ripped from her body. Tiny Delia kicked at the ankles of louts twice her size; Courtney screamed my real name from on stage like it was my fault; friends wandered around afterwards in tears of anger. Post-show, the two of us hid beneath the dressing room table as her friend Bill (the one with the monstrous moustache) fended off the curious. Courtney gave me a ring from her finger as a bond. I wore it faithfully for months afterwards until it broke. It was fake metal.

Why did I hang out with Courtney? What, are you going to resist gossip-dripping phone calls five days a week, lasting three hours, usually at four a.m. and sometimes with songs attached? (Once, the singer left a message where she was boasting to Kurt how I had made her a star and introduced the couple. So I put it on my answer machine. The first person to leave a message afterwards was, of course, Courtney. There was a stunned silence, and then she continued talking.) Are you going to resist the temptation to create mischief and upset and scandal at every turn? You're a duller person than I thought, then. When I drank, I drank without fear of the consequences because I had low self-worth. I partied like it was my last evening because it could well have been.

At the annual Reading Festivals, I could sometimes be badly behaved. So come 1991 – or was it 1993, it's hard to separate the years – I thought I'd take it easy. On the London train down to Brighton the night before, I bumped into Bobby Gillespie from Primal Scream. I had a bottle of whisky in my bag. One thing led to another, and we ended up playing old soul records and drinking red wine back at my place till five a.m. Ah well, I thought, I can get some sleep now.

Fifteen minutes later, the phone rang. It was Courtney in London somewhere, wasted. She wanted to come over. Instead, we chatted on the phone for two-and-a-half hours, and then it was time to leave for the festival.

In 1992, Hole played LA's Whisky-A-Go-Go with Superchunk in support. Courtney walked up to the 'Chunk's singer Mac and announced that 'you should pay attention because this man is going to make you a star'. It was the last time I saw Hole play with Caroline and Jill in the band. Courtney sang a drug-ravaged version of the Velvets' 'Pale Blue Eyes' dedicated to her new lover Kurt Cobain, while outside a storm-lashed sky changed colour every few minutes.

Brighton Zap Club, 1991; I feel frightened but irresistibly drawn towards the emotion directed straight at me from the stage. She's in her usual confrontational stance: feet on speakers, dress riding over the audience. London, the same tour, and Courtney ad libs between songs with Morrissey references that I'd instructed her to say. Backstage, she hurls a solid glass ashtray at Eric's head. It misses him by inches. This was one of many concerts where security tried to restrain us.

I hung out with Courtney because she was fun to be with. I hadn't even known what she looked like when I fell in love with her music.

From: Jerry Thackray
Date: Sunday, October 29, 2000 11:48 pm
Subject: hey, help!
Hey C. Tell me a couple of stories involving me and you because my fucking memory is crap and I have just over two weeks to finish this book on rock and write 40,000 words. Love, J

From: Courtney Love
Date: Tuesday, November 14, 2000 11.25 pm
Subject: Re: hey, help!
I don't remember anything. I'm the rock star, you're the writer but I'll try to help you. Focus man.

From: Jerry Thackray
Date: Wednesday, November 15, 2000 11:25 am
Subject: Re: Re: hey, help!
Oh ha, ha. I was the fucking rock star and YOU were the writer, don't you remember? How can I focus?

You want to know about the personalities behind the music, right?

So listen to the music. *Pretty On The Inside* is a fine reflection of Courtney's state of mind, the way *Live Through This* couldn't ever hope to be because it was too concerned with attaining the approval of its class. Or maybe the debut album was as false and misleading in its own right as the two that followed. I think not, though. Despite its obvious debt to Sonic Youth and Mudhoney, *Pretty On The Inside* has an unsettling passion that can't be masked. Hole's debut album is unfocused, but that's why it's so fascinating. Any record that attempts to extract a linear narrative from Courtney's thoughts is a lie. The lady isn't like that. She does herself and her art a disservice by pretending she is.

'Jeez, as much as I would love to hate Love,' recounts *Pretty* producer Don Fleming, 'I really thought highly of her and Eric. At the time she was such a fan of Kim's that she would do anything that we told her to, no real prima donna shit at all. I think we bashed out the record in about seven days including the mix. When it was time for Courtney to do her vocals, she was a total gung-ho pro. I remember her putting so much energy into the vocal performance that she was literally ripping her clothes off as she sang. Of course the drive and determination to be bigger than Madonna was already there, and I was quite sure that she would make her mark.'

Courtney's fascination with the beauty process is obvious on *Pretty On The Inside*. I misinterpreted her stance, thought that she cared as little as me for society's facades. How wrong I was. When Courtney sang *'there is no power like my pretty power'*, she was being literal. All she ever wanted was to turn pretty on the *outside*.

Want to know what Courtney was like back then? Listen to the music. It's catharsis. What she screams and simpers and sobs, she feels. That's why it was such great art, and that's how those of us who believed she had the potential to effect genuine change felt she betrayed us. We thought there was something behind the fierce ambition, didn't realise that Courtney was only interested in changing her own life, not anyone else's. Still, it's her art, not ours. I guess. The fact remains, though, that when Courtney let Caroline and Jill go at the end of 1992 and set about trying to recreate herself in her husband's image, she let us down. How dull. Hadn't we already heard a thousand times a thousand male bands making that music?

Hole
My Body The Hand Grenade
(City Slang)
. . . Back in the day when she cared FEROCIOUSLY what us little UK weeklies said about anyone, she would have read this.

But, alas, the last time she read a weekly, or even got close to one, was flirting with Alex James in the bathroom at the Video Music Awards at some fabulously debauched penthouse party, when she had the foggy realisation that the demarcation point forbidding Grungers and Britpoppers from fraternising was hopelessly outdated. And besides, in her 10,000-dollar free gown, the last thing she was, was a dirty old grunger.

Hole, I remember them well.

I remember the photographer telling the rest of the band to 'act like shadows' on their first photo session . . . Eric's the only one left. She used to always joke about Eric someday writing his memoirs and calling them *Poor Eric: The Story Of My Life.* I remember her promising me that when she made it to the top she'd give me a cut, and she wasn't going any place but . . .

I haven't seen a pence.

Now the battles have been mostly won and I suppose there are just a few skirmishes left before the war is over and she emerges number one. She sits at the new tables and eyes Madonna to the right and Demi to the left and notices she's the only one who's eating any cake, cos really she still kinda doesn't CARE, at least that's what she tells herself.

She's protected, no one can call her a mess – she's forced them to call her beautiful, she's not gonna let us have it ever so easy ever again, so naked, wide open and vulnerable. And why should she? What did she get when she gave that to us? Burnt at the bloody stake is what, a regular Joan de Arc. This record is not for her new demographic of the mainstream, this is a piece of cake thrown our way, to recall how fierce and hard and fucking insane it used to be and how a split open walking wound cannot fight forever. There are children and movies, there is Hollywood, there is Hole now, finishing up what she promises to be the perfect pop record, because she's not leaving till she's had that, the perfect pop record, and of COURSE you KNOW this is not it. This is a record of what it was, a recap of what it was, of what scared the shit out of us, drove us insane, made us hate her, love her, want to marry, bury, Scary her. And she's traded up on us, gone her own fucking way, and here is what we had.

Diva is a word only applied to women. It's a gorgeous word. It means divine, she who brings the divine, the divine dark and blood and pain of night too, like Persephone returning to her frozen hell. All Divas are not Venuses, few are. They show us their wounds so raw we turn our heads in disgust and revulsion, to see ourselves reflected so clearly is too much. We want the pop, the moment of escape. We don't want the trouble of our souls.

I cannot wait for the next Hole record, I fully expect it to save and redefine Rock as it sits boring and bad again, and we will have to be endlessly grateful that the diva we tried to bury has deigned to come back and inspire us.

This record shows us the value of what was Opera.

I did not write this, Courtney did.

(The above is a review of a compilation of Hole rarities, taken from the November 1997 issue of VOX. *The final line is true. Courtney responded to my plea for help – to write the review in my style, because I didn't want to – with the words above.)*

The Royal Couple

'This is the hardest job I've ever had,' the reluctant star begins. 'I can't believe it . . .'

He pauses.

'I like it, though!' he exclaims. 'I'm thoroughly enjoying myself. It's just a lot more demanding than I expected.'

He pauses again.

'You know, she can fart as loud as I can . . .'

'Oh, Kurt!' his wife interrupts, offended.

'And burp as loud as I can,' he finishes unabashed, smiling his mischievous little smile.

'Keep it down,' his wife scolds him. 'It's not feminine.'

But she's a baby. Babies are allowed to fart.

'Oh, OK,' the protective mother says, mollified, looking proudly at the wide-eyed child by her side.

Does having a baby make you see life in a different way?

'Definitely,' replies Courtney. 'Yeah . . .' She stops, distracted by the look in her husband's eyes. He's rolling them.

'Stop it! Why do you do this?' she shouts.

'Do what?' he asks, innocently, as Frances Bean reaches out for his hand.

'Switch off when the tape recorder switches on.'

'I've pretty much exhausted the baby opinions,' Kurt Cobain – America's most successful 'punk rock' star – says, defensively. 'I just don't have anything important to say. I mean, duh, it's fun, it's great, it's the best thing in life.'

Silence falls over the bedroom. We go back to watching the latest *Ren & Stimpy* cartoon, the new cult favourite of young

America. Frances Bean Cobain's nanny appears, ready to take the little one – a bouncing, almost nauseatingly healthy, blue-eyed child (Kurt's eyes, Courtney's nose) – downstairs for her nap.

Silence. Courtney takes a sip of lukewarm strawberry tea. I take a gulp of vodka. Kurt belches. We all have appearances to keep up.

(*Melody Maker*, 19 December 1992)

Think back to when Kurt started dating Courtney.

He was also seeing a sickly sweet Boston singer called Mary Lou Lord. Courtney was going out with her guitarist Eric Erlandson and seeing Billy Corgan on the side. She liked her male friends. I was a close friend and she was both insanely protective and jealous towards me.

My standard answer to the question 'what is the most rock'n'roll thing you've done?' is this: a pair of twins once came on to me because I was Everett True. I ended up with the blonde one. Years later I bumped into her brunette sister, who started chastising me for choosing her sibling because of her hair colour. So I ended up in bed with her. Anyway. Each time such an opportunity arose when I was with Courtney, she told the predator to fuck straight off. If you were Courtney's friend she had to be the most important *female* in your life.

I met Mary Lou during Nirvana's British tour in the latter half of 1991. She was faux-Olympian: not from the city, but taking on many of the city's superficial musical trappings. She had that irritating tweeness that latter-day K bands like the Softies misinterpreted the label as standing for, simply because Calvin wasn't conventionally male. Kurt hadn't invited Mary Lou along; she'd followed the band over, thinking the relationship was more serious than it was. Perhaps it could have been (Kurt told me he was in love) but Courtney was already getting interested.

'Kurt had a straight choice,' recounts Eric, who was still living with Courtney when she started calling the Nirvana singer up. 'He chose. He wanted to bite that apple. He chose the darker, more interesting one, but that doesn't make it right. Courtney's position was probably that Kurt had no choice, because she had decided she wanted him – but he did. I think Kurt wanted to live out his junkie couple fantasy with her, like Sid and Nancy. That was his way out of the fame that had suddenly come crashing in on top of him. What craziness. It was Christmas Eve, 1991, and they were living in a tiny room in someone else's apartment.'

Kurt's choice encapsulated the decision awaiting many of his peers. Mary Lou, with her jangling guitar and cutesy pixie personality, represented his adopted hometown of Olympia and, through it, hardcore. Courtney Love, with her myriad contradictions and attempted manipulation of the mainstream, represented punk rock. Hardcore and punk are similar musical styles but have different world views. The first aims to set up a counter-culture, an alternative to society. The second seeks to change society from within.

Kurt had to choose between hardcore and punk.

He chose the punk.

Kurt and Courtney's new apartment is prime LA near the top of a hill overlooking West Hollywood, surrounded by palm trees and winding pathways lined with foliage and security fences. You need an elevator with a private key to reach it. [This interview took place before the Royal Couple moved back to Seattle at the start of '93.]

Inside, one room is set aside for Kurt's paintings: strange, disturbing collages and images. He painted headless babies when his wife was pregnant. Now he paints angels and dolls.

There's a large, old-fashioned kitchen with a mirror running along the length of its back wall, sundry guest rooms up top. Upstairs, Courtney's walk-in wardrobe is crammed with antique 'baby doll' dresses and shoes. The closet is larger than some flats I've lived in.

Pizza crusts and half-full doughnut containers litter the spacious main room. There's a telescope, guitars, old rock books, clipped photos. Baby things are scattered everywhere with pride of place given over to a tasteful pink crib, bedecked in ribbons. A stereo in one corner blasts out Mavis Staples. The place has an air of being only half lived-in, as do many LA residences.

As I arrive, the couple are lying on the double bed in the master bedroom with Frances Bean ('Frances! Say hello to your Uncle Everett!' – Courtney). She: wearing a nightie; he: in pyjama bottoms and the ubiquitous scruffy cardigan and T-shirt. On the TV screen, three huggy male rock musicians wearing dresses surreally smash instruments, regardless of the backing track. It's the new Nirvana video for 'In Bloom'.

Courtney's sifting through a coloured box-load of Nirvana letters sent to Kurt by *just one girl*. There are 30 or 40 of them, painstakingly hand-coloured, hand-lettered and with audiotape accompaniment.

'Look, Kurt!' Courtney picks on one particularly lurid speci-men. 'She's spelled out your name over these envelopes . . . oh, here's a picture of her . . . (pause) . . . oh, she's got a muscular wasting disease . . . we have to write back! We've got to! She's an outsider, just like me!'

Kurt grunts affirmation. We pore over her scribblings with renewed interest, grateful that we've never been thus afflicted. Someone puts her name down on the Christmas card list.

Kurt decides he wants to tell us about his high school days, but then dries up.

'That's because you're a stoned retard,' Courtney teases him, in reference to the way he would often spend his school hours.

'Go on!' Courtney urges her husband. 'I always talk! I'm sick of it.'

Another pause. Frances gurgles slightly, a happy thought striking the Bean. There's no sign of the *Diet Grrrl* graffiti her father had drawn on her stomach for the photo session earlier.

Kurt sighs.

Kurt and Courtney have only given two joint interviews before this, both to American publications. They wanted to speak to *Melody Maker* to clear up certain matters, mostly arising from a profile of Courtney that appeared in the September issue of *Vanity Fair*, an upmarket fashion magazine.

Clearly, we'll have to tread carefully.

(*Melody Maker*, 19 December 1992)

Everything that happened between mid-1991 and mid-1994 is a blur.

Writing this book has been an exorcism. Sure, I had fun times but my religious upbringing – I was chief choirboy and a Venture Scout – means I suffer from self-hatred when I least expect it. It's not nice, looking back.

So a pregnant Courtney and Kurt got married in Hawaii at the start of '92, with the minimum of fuss. Kurt had been looking for a stable family unit for so long, it probably seemed a dream come true. Especially after old girlfriend, Bikini Kill's Tobi Vail, had rejected him in the wake of Nirvana's success. The rest of the year was given over to courting fame, drugs, hedonism, depression and preparing for the baby. Nirvana sold records and Courtney shop-ped. It didn't seem a fair swap, not least to those of us, increasingly in the minority, who felt that Courtney had a genuine talent beyond that of being able to attract rock star boyfriends.

Controversy followed controversy. There was the afore-mentioned *Vanity Fair* article where Courtney was pictured smoking while pregnant, and admitted to taking drugs. As loudly as

Courtney complained that the article's author Lynn Hirschberg had made stuff up about her and Kurt's drug use, Lynn was guilty only of writing the story as it was presented to her. Courtney would phone me after speaking to the journalist and recount what she'd told her. There was no telling her she was being naïve. Courtney remains convinced she knows best how to influence the media – and she's usually right. I guess.

The interaction between myself and Courtney over the *Vanity Fair* article got reported in Melissa Rossi's entertainingly trashy *Courtney Love: Queen Of Noise*: 'Before the interview sessions with reporter Lynn Hirschberg, who was known for well-crafted fluff pieces, Courtney ran into *Melody Maker's* Everett True; as always, he fawned over her. She asked him how she should act for the interview, and he told her she should be herself. The next time Courtney saw Everett, she said, "You gave me bad advice." '

Kurt Cobain announced 'Courtney Love is the best fuck in the world' live on British youth TV programme *The Word* in a dull parody of a bloated rock star, living out his Sid Vicious fantasy. Both Kurt and Courtney threatened a few enemies, revelling in and abusing their new power. A lengthy fax was sent to the authors of a proposed Nirvana book by Kurtney's management, detailing among many other points that (a) Courtney and myself had never gone on record as stating we'd had sexual congress, and (b) Nirvana did not think I was a 'wanker'.

One incident arose after Courtney phoned my house, and Beat Happening singer Calvin Johnson – the man who'd been such an influence on her husband – answered. I have no idea what he said to her but, when I finally spoke to Courtney, she told me she would hit Calvin next time she saw him. She did. There was already bad blood between Courtney and Olympia: before Courtney got famous, talented Olympian writer and singer, Lois Maffeo, had formed a band called Courtney Love after discovering one of her diaries in their joint Portland apartment building.

Courtney's band got put on hold while she pursued Kurt, but she hadn't been happy with Caroline or Jill for a while. I have no idea why but, knowing Courtney's infatuation with surface beauty, I suspect that the 'beauty process' had something to do with it. Both the bassists who followed – Kristen and Melissa – were clearly chosen for their talent *and* their looks. Forget Courtney's proclamations she'd be happy to have a fourteen-stone female musician join her band 'if she was a fourteen-stone goddess'. Both Caroline and Jill were goddesses, not even approaching fourteen stone, and it didn't help *them*.

Washington-born drummer Patty Schemel was the first to join towards the end of '92. I vaguely knew her from her Seattle band Kill Sybil: red-haired and fun to be around. She was a good drummer too. The story goes she was once considered for Nirvana.

It took a while longer to find a bassist. Minneapolis musician Kristen Pfaff, who eventually joined in 1993, was already in a band, the unrelenting Janitor Joe. Kristen was dark and intelligent, and a champion of underground music. Winona Ryder, as she was in *Night On Earth*, would have been perfect to play her. Minneapolis boasted two bands that were a major influence on Nirvana's sound – Hüsker Dü and the Replacements. ('Come As You Are' is essentially Hüsker Dü's exuberant guitar sound set to Replacements' singer Paul Westerberg's bleary lyrical outlook.) The city was also home to Babes In Toyland and Janitor Joe's label Amphetamine Reptile – a label that respected Kurt, but not his wife.

Indeed, many from the Minneapolis hardcore scene held Courtney up as the Devil, and were aghast when Kristen left her hometown for Seattle.

Courtney mumbles something from where she's sitting, behind the bed by the ghetto blaster. Sorry?

'You were wrong,' she says. 'I should have been sullen and demure.'

What?

'When I asked you that question a couple of years ago,' she explains. 'In a bar in LA.'

You can't hide your personality . . . well, most people can't. Maybe you can.

'I wouldn't have minded,' she whimpers. 'I used to be sullen and demure.'

Courtney is referring to the time she first met me, last year, when she asked me how I thought she should behave in her relations with the press.

'I used to be really loud and obnoxious,' Kurt interrupts. 'And then I stopped hanging out with people.'

Why?

The singer shifts from where he's lying, sprawled out on the mattress. Courtney moves to switch the TV off.

'Because I was tired of pretending that I was someone else just to get along with people, just for the sake of having friendships,' he replies. 'I was tired of wearing flannel shirts and chewing tobacco, and so I became a monk in my room for years. And I forgot what it was like to socialise.'

But didn't you drink?

'Yeah, I drank,' he agrees. 'And I was obnoxious when I drank too much. Then there was a period during the last two years of high school when I didn't have any friends, and I didn't drink or do any drugs at all, and I sat in my room and played guitar.'

Then, when you formed Nirvana, you started drinking and hanging out with people, and you were back to where you were a few years before . . .

'Not really,' responds Kurt, stretching. 'I still have the same best friends I had a few years ago. The scale of social activity that I have is so fucking minimal – nothing, my entire life – so the little bit of socialising I did at parties when I was loud wasn't much more than when I started socialising again in Seattle.

'I started hanging around with people like Mudhoney,' he continues. 'Mainly there were just other people in bands. I wasn't really part of a thriving Seattle social scene. Both Chris and I thought of ourselves as outsiders. We wrote that song "School" about the crazy Seattle scene, how it reminded us of high school.

'It hasn't got any different, I just . . .' The singer pauses, choosing his words carefully. 'I guess living in LA makes me more reclusive,' he says. 'I don't like LA at all. I can't find anything to do here. It's pointless going out and trying to make friends, because I don't have these tattoos and I don't like death rock.'

'Axl wants to be your friend,' Courtney reminds him, sitting back down again. 'Axl thinks that if I wasn't around, you and him could be backstage at arena rock shows, fucking self-hating girls.'

'Well, that was always my goal,' replies Kurt, sarcastically. 'To come down to Hollywood and ride motorcycles with Axl on the Strip . . . and then you came along and ruined it all.'

'That's what Axl says,' Courtney explains. 'Did you hear about that show where he got on stage and started saying something like, "Nirvana's too good to play with us. Kurt would rather be home with his ugly bitch . . ."?'

Well, that's true, isn't it? (Not the 'ugly' part.) Kurt would rather be home with you, bathing Frances Bean, wandering around in your nightie, than out bonding with Axl and the boys. Why should he act any differently? It's weird that famous people want to hang out with other famous people, just because they're all famous.

Do you like it here in Hollywood, Courtney, or are you simply fed up with running?

'I just always ended up back here,' she muses. 'Jennifer [Finch, bassist L7] lives here, and she's always been a pretty good friend.

I'd call her and say, "This town didn't work out!" and she'd go, "Oh, come back to LA!" It's so big it can just absorb you. People here are so . . .' She pauses, struggling to find the right word.

'We thought it might be easy to live here because people are trained to deal with fame,' she says. 'The thing is, however, it's not really like that. They don't stare, but they know who you are, and the second you leave the store, they're on the phone to their friends . . .'

She pauses again.

'It's not even that,' she corrects herself. 'I wouldn't have got in nearly as much trouble if I hadn't chosen to live here. I just thought that it would be interesting to go into the mainstream and fuck things up, because people always say they're going to, but no one ever does – and I didn't have any choice, really. It's weird here: nurses calling Cowboy Capers [a Hollywood delivery firm] for their Valium subscriptions. It's scary, because everybody wants fame.'

'Fame is more of a reality here,' her husband agrees.

'See, here's where it started too,' she adds. 'Before I became the poisoner of my husband, before I occupied the position I'm now in. But until we started going out, I never realised that's how the people in LA really are.'

(*Melody Maker*, 19 December 1992)

In March 1993, Courtney edited the *Melody Maker* letters page. The look on our editor Allan Jones's face when I showed him her unexpurgated 1,000-word viewpoint was a joy to behold. Disbelief at her complete lack of grammar was followed by bemusement at the idea we should be giving over space to her ridiculous ideas, and that was followed by anger.

'Everett, we are not printing this crap and that's final,' he shouted at me. Allan is an unrequited old school music journalist. He comes from the era of Nick Kent, Charles Shaar Murray and Lester Bangs. By and large, though, he was remarkably tolerant of our little foibles at *Melody Maker*. He loved the rock stuff I was championing from America, but wasn't so convinced by my infatuation with Grrrl-style feminism. Courtney editing a section of his beloved *MM* was pretty much the final straw.

(It's a bloody good job he wasn't around the following year when Courtney came in to review the singles the same week Kurt tried to kill himself in Rome. She projectile vomited into bins while nanny Cali DeWitt changed Frances Bean's nappy on our art editor's desk. The baby pissed on the page layouts.)

Jonesy eventually relented. Courtney's letters page and editorial appeared in *MM*, with several explanatory interjections from myself. She used the opportunity to talk about two of her favourite topics of 1993, the Riot Grrrls and feminism – she had recently fallen in love with Susan Faludi's powerful feminist screed *Backlash*.

'When Riot Grrrl began, I was very supportive of it,' she wrote. 'It seemed as though things were getting better . . . I gave a Bikini Kill fanzine to Everett, Kim and Thurston and *Spin*, and I would have done anything to promote it, to help it.'

That wasn't strictly true. I obtained my fanzine from Calvin, and almost certainly passed it along to Courtney, but whatever. It is true that Courtney initially aligned herself with my flatmates and Kurt's old girlfriend. Hearing about the all-girl concerts that Huggy Bear had been organising in England during 1992, she demanded that Hole should be allowed to play one.

By all accounts, it wasn't that well attended. Courtney, never one to bask in the glow of political correctness, called a female critic 'fat' from on stage. She soon tired of her new allies, especially when it became apparent they weren't prepared to court fame the way she'd been trained to. Also, her attempts to ingratiate herself within the suspicious and closed world of Olympia, to seek approval from her husband's former peers, failed miserably.

This change of heart was reflected in her hastily written *MM* column.

'I feel plunged back into the Dark Ages,' she complained. 'Riot Grrrl celebrates the anarchy but also the clumsiness and incompetence of *femme* musicians. That's like giving women high level corporate jobs even if they can't do the job correctly. I am NOT assimilationist. I am a populist. I believe that everyone, not just people that know Fugazi personally, has a right to revolution but I'm not going to be dumb about it. I'm going to understand the mechanics of the Empire that I am going to fuck with. I am going to insinuate myself with the best of them.'

Courtney's mistake here is rudimentary. She assumes there is only one way to write songs and judge 'competence' (her word) and storm the Empire. There are few parallels to be drawn between women making exploratory music and women holding down high-powered jobs . . . Maybe the fact Courtney thinks music equates with business might explain her subsequent musical direction.

'I've worked too hard and put up with too much to be dragged down by the incompetence of a few spoilt elitists,' she continued.

'Most of us aren't rich and spoilt, drinking gourmet coffee with soymilk and dreaming up daily manifestos for the few. Most of us feel ugly and are lonely, and want to be pretty (or handsome). Maybe some of us want to be pretty because it was, and always will be, powerful. Maybe some of us want to feel good about ourselves, and negotiate the world and have children and even give the Patriarchal Empire a run for its money.'

Enough. What Courtney is talking about in the above paragraph is peer approval, not beauty. The 'pretty' she is referring to can never exist because it is a false value placed upon the individual by an inconsistent society. The only 'pretty' that truly exists is on the inside. So 'pretty always will be powerful'? Surely then, the way forward is to re-educate, not reinforce stereotypes. What about wanting to be informed, intelligent, funny, wise, smart, sassy, crafty . . . a goddess in other words, Courtney?

Or is buying yourself a new nose really that important?

Do you feel poisoned by Courtney, Kurt?

'By Courtney, or by Courtney's stigma?' he asks. 'Poisoned by . . . the whole fucked-up misconception of our relationship. Everyone seems to think we couldn't possibly love each other, because we're thought of as cartoon characters, because we're public domain. So the feelings that we have for one another are thought of as superficial.'

'It's not everybody who thinks that, though,' Courtney adds. 'It's a couple of has-been, pontificating, male rock stars and mostly women who work in the American music industry. I think that's because, in the early eighties, if you were a woman and you wanted to play music, there was a real slim chance you would succeed. So a lot of women who wanted to empower themselves within rock without being self-loathing joined the music industry – and these are some of the most vicious women I know.

'I've heard industry women talking about how horrible L7 are, I've heard industry women talking about how unattractive PJ Harvey is, which is ridiculous . . . I just think these powerful women have this real competitive, jealous nature that manifests itself like this. And when I married Kurt, they went into overload.

'It's insane, this real complex issue . . . It's an attempt to create something out of nothing – the whole superstar thing. They at least try to take away my intellect and my ethics and create . . .'

She pauses again, jumbled. Her thoughts are pouring out too fast now for coherent speech.

You must find it annoying, Kurt, that people perceive you as this stupid hen-pecked husband.

'Yeah, there have been quite a few articles like that,' he growls. 'I don't know how to explain what happens to me when I do an interview, because I usually shut myself off. I just don't like to get intimate. I don't want anyone to know what I feel and what I think, and if they can't get some kind of idea of what sort of person I am through my music, then that's too bad.'

Jackie, Frances Bean's nanny, shouts from downstairs that Kurt is wanted on the phone. Kurt tells her to tell whomever it is to call back later. I take another gulp of vodka and continue. (*Melody Maker*, 19 December 1992)

Courtney never thanked me on the sleeve to *Live Through This*.

She was upset because I'd told her what I thought of the album after it was recorded in September 1993. She'd asked me my opinion, and so I told her the truth. I thought she was asking me as a friend. This was crucial. I'm a critic. I usually pass when asked for my opinion because it hurts.

I thought the production sucked. The songs were too refined, and you couldn't hear enough of Eric's guitars. I felt the structures were dull, traditional – a far cry from the passion of the debut album. The tracks I liked more were the minimal ones: the wicked and hilarious putdown of the Riot Grrrls from Kurt's former hometown, 'Olympia'; also 'Doll Parts', retained in a similar form to when Courtney played it to me acoustically down the phone; 'Jennifer's Body', too, has an evil resonance that reaches to me down through the years, especially when Courtney screams the lines '*I'm your brother, I'm your friend/I'm purity, hit me again/With a bullet, number one/Kill the family, save the son.*'

Sure, I liked the lyrics. But I also thought the single 'Miss World' (the first moment where I realised the extent of Courtney's vanity) was weak, thin.

I've never liked rock bands that don't rock.

Courtney didn't appreciate my candour. We rowed, not for the first time. Eric tentatively backed me up – he appreciated the comments about the guitars – but Courtney had become convinced the only way forward for her was to create an all-female rock band that came from the underground and sold as many records as her husband's. I disagreed violently. Friends sometimes ask me what I think of the rumours that Kurt co-wrote some of the songs on *Live Through This*. If he did, he did a bloody awful job.

Maybe I was disappointed that Hole had stopped being Babes In Toyland.

Maybe I didn't like all the references to myself on songs such as 'Asking For It'. That seems unlikely though. I'm as vain as the next critic, as narcissistic as the next person who leaps up on stage.

Maybe I was being too harsh, expected too much.

Hole were an incredible live band, fronted by a singer whose only equals in onstage charisma and passion were Calvin Johnson and Birthday Party-era Nick Cave. (I rated Courtney above Kurt as a front person.) I'd been disappointed by Birthday Party and bloody Nirvana albums too. Perhaps it was only compared to Hole's performances that *Live Through This* was a disappointment.

'One thing that's pleased me,' Courtney says, drawing on a cigarette, 'that I've been really surprised by and learnt a lot from, is the psychic protection I've got from so many girls and women . . .'

She pauses. I'm not sure what she's trying to say.

'I mean, it's really fucking obvious unless you're stupid,' she goes on. 'Like I walk around and say, "Oh, he should have married a model but he married me," with a straight face.'

This is more familiar territory. This is the line Courtney takes when she wants to wind up people who think Kurt's marriage to her was ill advised. Her argument is something like, who should he have married then? A model? The point being . . . *Kurt's not like that.*

'There were sixty sarcastic things I told *Vanity Fair* that they quoted straight because they're so stupid,' she says. 'Their whole attitude was like, "Let's be condescending to these wacky punk rock kids and make allusions to how, in their world, success is bad. Aren't they cute?" '

But Kurt, you never said that success was bad, did you?

'What kind of success?' he sighs. 'Success in general? Financial success? Popularity in a rock band? Most people think success is being extremely popular on a commercial level, selling a lot of records and making a whole bunch of money. Being in the public eye.

'I think of myself as a success because I still haven't compromised my music,' he continues, 'but that's just speaking on an artistic level. Obviously, all the other parts that belong with success are driving me insane – God! I want to kill myself half the time.'

People still don't get it. Nirvana catch a lot of flak from people because (a) Kurt Cobain whines a lot, and (b) Nirvana slag off corporate rock bands even though they're one themselves.

'Oh, take it back from him, the ungrateful little brat,' mocks Courtney.

'What I really can't stand about being successful is when people confront me and say, "Oh, you should just mellow out and enjoy it," ' explains her husband, interrupting her. 'I don't know how many times I have to fucking say this. *I never wanted it in the first place.*

'But I guess I do enjoy the money,' he relents. 'It's at least a sense of security. I know that my child's going to grow up and be able to eat. That's a really nice feeling, but you know . . .'

Frances will only be treated nice to her face. People will kiss her butt and stab her in the back at the same time.

'Yeah, but she'll know about it because she'll come from us and be cynical by kindergarten,' Courtney answers, looking fondly at the empty crib. 'She's already cynical.'

'I don't mean to whine so much,' continues Kurt. 'There are just so many things that I'm not capable of explaining in detail.'

'I am!' Courtney interjects.

'But people have no idea what is going on,' her husband complains. 'The sickening politics that are involved with being a successful, commercial rock band are real aggravating. No one has any idea.'

(*Melody Maker*, 26 December 1992)

So Courtney retreated to her bed with Kurt while they lived out his *Sid & Nancy* fantasy and their lives degenerated. Around them, band members fought, managers wheedled and insisted on bringing in more and more riches, and the outside world looked on in ever-increasing fascination. Whose story am I telling here?

Sure, I met Kurt's buddy Dylan Carlson a few times. He seemed a nice chap. Shy, awkward, talented – like most of us.

Sure, I met the nannies, even that scared fragile one in the Nick Broomfield film who should never have been given the burden of looking after the Bean. Sure I hung out with Hole, but the band hardly existed, barring a few concerts and recording sessions. It wasn't until the European tour in July 1993 to promote the City Slang single 'My Beautiful Son' that Kristen Pfaff agreed to join as a full-time member. Kristen was incredible on stage, as powerful and full-on challenging as Michelle Leon had been in Babes In Toyland. Eric fell in love with his new band-member and the couple started dating.

The single had been recorded the previous fall while Hole still lacked a bassist.

'We were waiting for Kurt to show up to stand in on bass because time was running out and I needed to start mixing the three songs we were doing,' producer Jack Endino recalls. 'Finally I said, "I'll just do it, lemme have the bass," and Courtney said, "Sure, why not?" There were only three notes in "Beautiful Son" after all, plus three other notes in the bridge. Kurt finally showed up around midnight when I was already well into mixing. He wasn't the least bit put out about it. Courtney played bass on one of the other songs herself, either "Dakota" or "Old Age", whichever one is not totally acoustic.

'Funny about "Old Age",' the grunge master continues. 'Kurt kept mum about it at the time which, with what I know now – he demo'd the song at the *Nevermind* sessions, before he knew Courtney – suggests he gave her the song intentionally and let her write the words. For him, it was a throwaway tune. But that's twenty-twenty hindsight, I suppose. Kurt wasn't credited on the single, but then neither was I nor anybody else, so Courtney may have been tarred a bit unfairly over this one. I did see him asking her to help him with lyrics one time.'

I have few memories of Hole's 1993 Phoenix Festival appearance, beyond taking Courtney, Eric and my teenage girlfriend out into the crowd to the funfair, where we split up in teams (Courtney and me, Eric and my partner) to go on the Big Wheel. The stall owner, recognising Courtney at the last minute, speeded up the ride far beyond its usual velocity. Courtney was terrified. Still, as she admitted when she phoned me the following week to inform me that her plane had nearly crashed on take-off because of a faulty engine, it put her in good training for the free-fall descent.

After the ride, Courtney took me to one side. 'You bastard,' she cried. 'Don't take this the wrong way, but I always thought you'd go out with a right dog. But your girlfriend is beautiful!'

Yeah, right on, Sister.

'It doesn't matter though,' Courtney shouts at her husband. 'You have your success but I've been victimised by it and, at the same time, I still haven't proved myself. Last year Kat came up to Chicago and we went to this bar and they started playing *Nevermind* – this was just as it was starting to get big. So we sat there and drank and drank, and got mad. Because we realised no girl could have done that. I want to write a really good record and I haven't done it yet.'

This is where I disagree with you, Courtney. *Nevermind* was a great record, but so was 'Teenage Whore'. *Nevermind* was made by a bunch of blokes. Why should it have been made by a bunch of girls?

'No girl could have come from the underground and done that,' she argues. 'It's just the fact that somebody did it. It's happened.'

But Hole were an astonishing band, particularly live. I can't think of many other artists who've come across on stage as powerfully and totally magnetic as you. I mean it.

'Yeah, but Everett, not many people remember that,' whispers Courtney, touched.

You're judging yourself on your husband's terms, and that's ridiculous. You don't write songs like Kurt writes songs. Why should you? You're completely different people. If the commercial market refuses to accept your music then it's a failing of the business, not your music. Your marriage and your pregnancy mean that your career has been on hold. You haven't written many new songs, you haven't had a record out and you haven't played live. This means that people who only know about you through Kurt have nothing to judge you on except your very public 'bad girl' image. The bottom line is, you have to get back out there and perform if you want to regain people's respect for your music. No amount of hedging will alter that.

'The fact I judge myself on Kurt's terms is part of me subscribing to the whole male rock ethos, too,' Courtney explains. 'Kim Gordon, like every woman I respected, told me that this marriage was going to be a disaster for me. They told me that I'm more important than Kurt because I have this lyric thing going and I'm more culturally significant, and they all predicted exactly what was going to happen.

'I disagreed,' she recalls bitterly. 'Everyone knows I have a band, everybody knows about my band, I can do this – my marriage is not going to be more important than my band.'

She pauses, then explodes.

'But not only has my marriage become more important than my fucking band, but our relationship has been violated,' she cries. 'If we weren't doing this interview together, no male rock journalist would dare ask Kurt if he loved his wife. "Do you love your wife? Do you guys fuck? Who's on top?" . . . I'm not saying you would, Everett.'

She's shaking with emotion now.

'Men are men!' she exclaims. 'They do the work of men! They do men's things! If they have bad taste in women . . . whatever! All of a sudden, Axl and Julian Cope and Madonna decide I'm bad taste in women and it's the curse of my life and tough shit. What can I say?

'I never experienced sexism before,' she says, agitated. 'I really didn't experience it in any major way in connection with my band until this year, and now I have. The attitude is that Kurt's more important than me because he sells more records. Well, fuck you! Suck my dick!'

There's a brief silence. Courtney's just taking a breather before going in for the kill.

'You wouldn't look good in leather,' Courtney says to Kurt, looking fondly at him. 'Kurt and others all riding around in a limousine, fucking women that are idiotic and self-hating that want to fuck them to get some attention for themselves, instead of grabbing their guitars and going "Fuck you, I could do this better with integrity and more ethics and with revolution and . . . fuck you!" I created this rock thing in the first place for my own amusement and I'm going to take it back.

'I always have lofty ideals about it and yet I deserve it.' She's resorting to sarcasm now she's so worked up. 'I deserve to get raped by a crowd if I stage-dive in a dress and I deserve to get raped if I go to a bar and I'm wearing a bikini. I deserve to get raped because I did all these things I said before, nipping a hot young rock star in the bud, having a baby, having been a stripper, having used drugs . . .

'And then to be perceived as a child abuser!' She exclaims anguished, off on another exclamatory track. 'We are two of the last people on earth that would ever hurt a child or a harmless person. *Ever*. I've never picked on harmless people. I've always picked on people that I felt were corrupt or more corrupt than me.'

Silence.

'All right,' she adds, gently. 'I'm done now.'

From far off comes the sound of a baby crying.

(*Melody Maker*, 19 December 1992)

Live Through This

'Everyone, over here NOW!' Courtney exclaims. 'Turn the fucking house lights up NOW! Do it. Just do it! Everyone, look at this man.'

The band stops playing. The house lights go up. Courtney walks over to the photo pit at the front of the 600-capacity Mississippi Nights nightclub. A strangely familiar face is using her guitarist's video camera to film her band and she wants to make sure she's got his identity correct. It can't be right. He's not even in America . . . is he?

She can't believe her eyes.

'This is Everett True, the man who discovered us, my husband's band, Pavement, Babes In Toyland, Sonic Youth, Madder Rose,' she babbles. 'Turn those lights on him. He's a very famous English writer and one of my closest friends. Be nice to him or he'll ruin you. Everyone, look at him now.'

The crowd crane their necks looking for the source of the excitement. Out the corner of one eye, I can see *MM* photographer Stephen Sweet grinning.

I pull Courtney over to the side of the stage.

'Listen,' I whisper urgently, 'would you like me to get up on stage and sing a few songs with you?' Courtney had been asking me to do this for years but I'd always refused, told her I'd do it when she least expected it.

So it was that Stephen took a series of photos of us on stage together – singing 'Teenage Whore' or 'Do Nuts' or God knows what, we were all trashed and the tapes have long been lost to posterity – with Courtney playing guitar on her knees in front of me, pretending to give me fellatio, in tribute to those famed David Bowie/Mick Ronson stage shows in the seventies. No, you can't see the shots. I'm a happily engaged man.

The crowd roared and my head ached. The previous night, my Chicago hotel room had been broken into and my passport stolen as I lay there unconscious, vomiting; no sleep and a twelve-hour drive followed before we joined our friends in Madder Rose and Hole in St Louis. I'd had to drink a bottle of whisky just to stay upright.

Courtney is even more wasted than me. I sing a few numbers and lurch over to Billy from Madder Rose, who thumps me on the back in congratulation. After the show, Courtney gives me $500 from her purse when she hears what's happened and asks me if that's enough, before stumbling off to her hotel. Later, I lead a parade of grumbling rock stars down to the river's edge in East St Louis to go gambling. No one wants to come along, but no one's going to argue.

For some reason, we don't make it. Foiled, we return to Eric's hotel apartment for a party and I promptly fall asleep on his bed, oblivious even to the tour manager drawing on my face.

The following day, freaked out beyond endurance by the alcohol and drugs and lack of passport, I refuse the pleas of Eric and the lovely and talented Melissa Auf der Maur, Hole's new bass-player, to come on tour with them. They entreat me, tell me that Courtney only becomes halfway manageable when I'm around. I refuse.

I no longer had any idea what was going on.

```
Hi ET
   St Louis. I just remember partying all night long in
my hotel room with you and Veruca Salt. I think you
slept for a bit on my couch or floor. You had just lost
your passport – in Chicago? You got up on stage that
night and sang – 'Retard Girl', 'Teenage Whore'? I
can't remember, and the tape doesn't have it. Drunken
fun.
   Eric.
```

The back cover of *Melody Maker* dated 16 April 1994 carried an advert for the new Hole album *Live Through This*. This was the record that was supposed to crash Courtney through into the mainstream. Her music had been honed and polished to glistening perfection, all interviews completed months earlier. The advance reviews had been positive, exclamatory. Everyone wanted to be in on the Mrs Kurt Cobain story. Finally, Courtney was going to be regarded as a serious artist in her own right.

It didn't happen. The same issue of *MM* had a front cover that carried a picture of her husband bordered in black underneath the words 'Nirvana Star's Shotgun Suicide'. Courtney had been fed up with Kurt's increasing inability to handle both his fame and his drugs; Kurt was disillusioned with Courtney, especially at the way she kept in contact with people he despised. (Like all lovers, Courtney knew which buttons to press to make her partner mad. Her public flirtation with Evan Dando was one of those sore spots. I don't think she actually had an affair with the Lemonheads singer, though.) Courtney would accuse Kurt of standing in her way as an artist, withdrawing his support when she most needed him; Kurt felt the same way, in reverse. Shortly after his Rome suicide attempt, he announced his intention to withdraw Nirvana from their proposed Lollapalooza headline slot, turning his back on a rumoured nine million dollars.

Some time earlier, Kurt wrote a will but never signed it.

Live Through This came out in the UK three days after Kurt killed himself. It still seems odd that someone at Hole (and Nirvana)'s record company Geffen didn't seek to delay the release, but it was probably unavoidable. Of course, the proposed tour starting on 3 May was cancelled and Geffen put all promotion for *Live Through This* on indefinite hold. Only a few weeks before, Courtney was set for superstardom: MTV, Tower Records and the US music press were agreed on that. Not any more. Hole's career was effectively over the moment Kurt pulled the trigger.

It seemed unreal: calls from Courtney where she suggested we enter into a joint suicide pact ourselves, and where she'd tell me about the ghosts running through her house. When she burned the first suicide note, from Rome, a gust of wind came down the chimney and threatened to set the house ablaze. I saw the greenhouse over the garage where Kurt killed himself, the candles lit in memory, the turned-away faces of former friends and patronising smiles of those paid to care. It seemed unreal after Kurt died, but it got worse.

On 16 June Kristen Pfaff's body was discovered in her bath. With bitter irony, it was the same day she had planned to leave Seattle to return to Minneapolis to rejoin her old band Janitor Joe.

Former beau Eric had stopped by the previous evening to say goodbye. He left after Kristen had gone to take a bath, where, unknown to anyone, she injected herself with heroin.

'I knocked on her bathroom door and thought I heard her snoring so I wasn't too concerned,' he told me. 'I thought she was asleep on the floor because she used to do stuff like that. Then I got a phone call from her boyfriend, Paul, the next morning saying she was dead.'

We didn't like to call each other in those sad final months of 1994. Every time Courtney or I picked up the phone, one or both of us would end up in tears. By our very presences, we linked one another to a previous life and friends who had so brutally been taken from us. We had to stop speaking to one another. There was no way we could help one another, our lives were too disparate. Our relationship had turned unhealthy.

I knew immediately. When Kurt died, I wasn't losing just one friend.

In the crazy months following Kurt's death, Courtney confided in everyone. She'd convinced herself that she had a job to do, that she was a singer in a rock'n'roll band, and it was important. Being so obsessed with fame, she probably appreciated the impact of Kurt's suicide more than many. Also, *you have to move on.* Life doesn't stop, whether you want it to or not. So Courtney got back on stage during 1994, ostensibly to help promote her album – though no one was paying any attention to *that* – but more obviously to try and find herself.

I would stand at the side of numerous stages, weeping for my friend who – always entertaining, always fascinating – was falling to pieces in front of my eyes. Some called her behaviour cathartic. To me, it was almost purgatorial. I had lived through too much to be in a position to appreciate such pure, unconscious performances of rock.

I could not divorce myself.

Sure, it was rock'n'roll when Courtney crawled on stage at Reading Festival a few months after Kurt's death to kiss a startled Lou Barlow, or when she gatecrashed Lollapalooza to rant at thousands of sheeplike masses. Sure, it's rock'n'roll to kick, punch and scratch your way across the years. In all probability, by any definition you care to throw my way, Hole were the Greatest Rock Band Ever during 1994 and 1995. How couldn't they be? Eric had suffered too, remember – as had Patty and everyone else around. I would never deny the lady her happiness, but damn it was a shame when someone finally convinced her she should get down from the stage and move into films, there was no way she was ever going to be as big as Nirvana.

It was sad, and strange, and painful though.

There's a concert at Amsterdam's Paradiso Club, where I'm interviewing Hole's support band Scarce. Courtney is sprawled out on her hotel bed when I show up, not caring how many people she reveals her intimacy to, as long as they're famous. Courtney demands I go for a walk with her. I tell her it means I'll miss Scarce and that she'll be late on stage. She says she'll go into town without me. I don't want the responsibility of a lone Courtney on my hands, so I agree to go with her. We eat a meal at a canalside café and nothing is discussed. By the time we show up at the concert – the tour manager is like, 'Thank God it was you with her, Everett'; my date for the evening is livid – the crowd are boiling over with rage at the star's tardiness. I watch from the side as fans heckle Courtney to live up to her bad girl reputation. Courtney loses it and clambers up the amplifiers onto the side of the balcony as Eric and I chase unseen foes across landings.

In Hamburg, Eric and myself play a two-song set before Hole take the stage, the guitarist providing noise from his drum machine. Courtney curtly tells us afterwards never to do that again.

It's Reading Festival 1994. Melissa has joined Hole two weeks earlier, recommended by Billy Corgan. A whole crowd of us are standing stage right, watching Henry Rollins pump iron. The cheeky Jesus Lizard drummer Mac promises he'll rush on stage and bring him down with a rugby tackle, like a couple of us managed with Evan Dando, if we can raise a hundred quid. Sadly, we fail to find the cash.

Impressions come thick and fast. Six-inch gold stilettos in the mud; gold dresses and a painfully inept performance; Patty's laughter when Courtney attempts to shock me by stripping naked in my presence; the constant arguments with security men who resolutely refuse to recognise the most famous person on site. (Of course, neither of us carried passes. We'd given them to needy friends long before.) During Hole's set, a section of the crowd chant my name when they spot me crouched down at the back of the stage, Courtney leading them on.

Watching Hole was so sad. It was obvious Melissa wasn't too familiar with the songs – and, yes, I missed Kristen. Also, Courtney was only fooling herself if she thought she was in any kind of state to perform. She changed the words in 'Miss World' from '*I am the girl you know/Can't look you in the eye*' to '*I am the girl you know/The one who should have died*', and stood with her arms raised in a crucifixion pose. The crowd response was both muted and sympathetic. Most people couldn't believe she was even up there.

Afterwards, the wasted singer decides there's nothing more she wants than to hang out with her English friend, Everett True, who's also trashed and in no condition to take charge of anyone, least of all Courtney Love. Her wise personal manager Janet Billig knows when to quit, however, and passes responsibility for the lady over to me. Eric is away somewhere else, being cute with his new girlfriend Drew Barrymore. (The guitarist met the actress after she threw up over his shoes outside LA's Jabberjaw venue at the end of 1993. He phoned me the same night to brag. I didn't believe him. Shortly afterwards, Drew got married to an English bar owner she'd only known for a few days . . . and then divorced him, and started seeing Eric. He'd been telling the truth. With sad irony, Eric and Drew's first date took place the same night Kristen died.)

So Courtney and I go out into the crowd . . .

I try to divert her from running on stage during Sebadoh's set by introducing her to Wedding Present singer David Gedge. She slaps his face because of an imagined enmity, and then, while I'm apologising, Courtney hugs confused Sebadoh singer Lou Barlow anyway. Lou ends up in hospital after breaking his guitar over his own head. Later, there are any number of fights, drinks and tantrums.

I really had no control over my circumstances.

To me, this was an exemplary way of behaving – to turn your anguish into art and music, to be a car crash victim who doesn't hide the scars.

Courtney Love was my definition of a diva as far back as 1991, but it wasn't until Kurt killed himself that everyone else caught up.

Tragedy, beauty, ambition, a sense of entitlement and purity: these are the five elements that go to make up any real diva – *not* a record contract with Disneyland or MTV.

Courtney had all of these elements.

Before Kurt, her wounds were mostly self-inflicted, but after Kurt she had it made. I remember being so impressed with her histrionic behaviour at their house in the days immediately following the suicide, and thinking that here was a diva-esque performance to rival the most legendary. So that's the tragedy: that Courtney was married to one of the most famous and talented musicians in the world, and still wasn't satisfied.

Beauty. That's an interesting one. Courtney is obsessed with being beautiful on society's terms, not her own. The title of her first album is ironic. Courtney never believed it mattered if you were beautiful inside. When we first met, she had an irresistible *anti-beauty*, both inside and out.

Hence, the ridiculous third album *Celebrity Skin* and all those photos of her attending film premieres with her breasts on full show, childishly proud that someone else could find her attractive. Sure, I understand why she does that. It's the only defence she has left. She pretends she doesn't care and so immerses herself in a world of superficiality where everyone pretends not to notice. Maybe I'm envious of that. It doesn't mean I can't criticise, though.

Courtney used to harp on about how no one noticed her 'until I got a nose job and then Everett wrote about me', but if only she had realised what a lie that observation was based upon. Sure Courtney has beauty. It never used to be the conventional kind. It was far more interesting than that. It came from the force of her personality and her evil charm and her energy and the fact she never ever bothered switching that sorting switch in her brain to ON, she just let it all tumble out. She would exhaust so many with her energy, her incessant questioning. Many of my colleagues at *Melody Maker* during 1991 and 1992 lived in terror of Courtney ever obtaining their home phone number.

Ambition is the one quality everyone agrees that Courtney has, in spades.

Everett: What do you suppose people hold you as a role model for? *Ambition?*

Courtney: I have ambition, but it's not Madonna ambition, it's the ambition of 'I have something to say, I'm a minority, I come from shit and all forces are aligned against me from what I was born into to what I had to get out of.' Did I achieve a significant

amount of the American dream? Yeah! That is a good thing. I have achieved that in my celebrity, which is a hobby and could go at any minute. Yes, I've done some retarded stuff in my work. Fuck you! I'm not going to low-ball, my stock is too important to me.'
(The *Stranger*, 25 February 1999)

Most critics say this is the only quantifiable one of Courtney's talents, her all-driving monomania. We used to have a game wherein we'd compare the number of songs written about us, but I guess she trumped me on that one. Sure, that's nothing to be proud of.

Does Courtney have a sense of entitlement? I'd say. The world fucking owes *her* a living. That's the mantra she's lived her entire adult life by.

Courtney has purity, though. Make no mistake. She's pure in her ambition. She's come out the other side. Those Hole live shows were some of the purest exorcisms I've ever witnessed.

What motivates you?
'I'm trying to embrace the main. I was talking with Melissa the other night, and all of a sudden the stupid fucking conflict starts: "Are Girls Against Boys watching us?" Our stupid bad training is kicking in. Lately, I've been splitting a lot of things up with Melissa, in terms of fronting, because Eric doesn't front, so it's a fifty-fifty deal, and she's a great rock star. Eric used to complain that "Courtney's furious that I'm not a fucking girl", and . . . oh my God, he's right! I feel like a failure that I never got to be the girl Beatles and I became a huge celebrity, whereas the intention was to be the Paul. I didn't want to be the John, but I couldn't find anyone to match me. Sometimes my posture is like Madonna, but it's relative to the punk rock I grew up in. Yes, I'm ambitious! But I'm not rapaciously ambitious. So I'm held to a higher standard than Jewel by a million miles, and life isn't fair and it sucks.'
Why haven't you written a book of bad poetry yet?
'That's not a stupid question. I could probably get a good advance, and I could do my lyrics and great collage stuff and our old flyers, and then some good prose pieces and poetry. People want it from their pop stars nowadays. I could give *King Ink* [Nick Cave] to the mainstream. It's like Michael Stipe said last night – everyone says they're going to subvert the system from the inside and then everyone gets mad because no one ever does it.

But they do! Michael does! I totally do! We have stock, but we also want to be populist. I watched Kurt Cobain sell ten million records and it made me kind of crazy. But there's nothing wrong with being a huge artist that sells two million records.'

You seem much more conscious onstage nowadays, probably because you were going through an exorcism last time I saw you.

'Yeah, I was trying to deal with that. I do not want to be a hack. I remember in the suicide note, he [Kurt] wrote "I don't feel it anymore. That is why I want to die", which I felt was silly, but the few moments it slipped away from me . . . oh my God! I am more conscious now. I'm not in a delusional haze, I'm not on a load of drugs and I'm not getting rid of the Kurt thing and the craziness and the insane fury in front of people. Some of it will always be there, but trans-gender and trans-genre shouldn't be our shtick anyway. Is being conscious onstage a bad thing?'

Not necessarily.

'Frankly, I didn't feel like a freak show when I was working it out [in 1994]. I was pure and coming from my source, and if my source at the time was wounded and raw, then, OK, that was what you got. Even now, I will not stand there and come from a fake place. If I feel it's happening, and I have a little bit, then it makes me want to quit. I don't need the money. I sell records, I make movies and I've made good investments. I don't know what my problem is.'

(*Melody Maker*, 26 January 1999)

Of course I returned to Seattle on several occasions after Kurt and Kristen's deaths.

In the early days, Courtney paid for me to fly over to her Seattle home. We'd stand around in the kitchen: the singer, her gay friends and me. Courtney is a self-proclaimed 'fag hag'. She claimed it didn't matter I wasn't homosexual because I had no sexual presence. (Why? Because I wouldn't sleep with her?) We'd go down Capitol Hill, whoever was looking after Frances Bean at the time and I, and drink cappuccino milkshakes, thick and delirious with sugar and caffeine.

Sometimes, Eric would be staying in town with Drew. We'd drive past their apartment and Courtney would hurl abuse at the window, want to go upstairs and rush the couple, angry that her old lover should be dating someone more famous than herself. One time, Courtney sat on my shoulders and Drew sat on Eric's, and we did battle down a deserted Rendezvous in Belltown.

Courtney took photos and gave me the film afterwards, instructing me to sell copies to the British tabloids 'because they'll be worth thousands'. I didn't.

Celebrity Skin

In April 1997, I got a phone call at home around seven a.m.

Oddly, I was up. I can't remember why, maybe it was my new job as editor of *VOX*, the former '*NME*' monthly' that I'd been charged with turning mainstream. Anyway. I didn't pick up the phone since I figured it would be a fax sent from Bikini Kill drummer Tobi Vail to my flatmate Jon, ex-Huggy Bear. The pair were dating at the time, and had a habit of communicating at odd hours of the day. It wasn't a fax. Instead, when the machine kicked in, a slightly slurred voice started singing down the line.

How nice, I thought. Tobi is singing Jon a couple of her new songs.

So I sat down next to the phone with my mug of tea, and listened, not wanting to pick up the receiver and disturb the flow. The half-formulated songs sounded intriguing, like US Riot Grrrl crossed with Cheap Trick soft rock – New Wave, American style. I felt nostalgic as I listened, thinking back to the times from '91 through to '93 when Courtney would leave me similar messages. The caller spoke a few words after the second song, but so rapidly I couldn't understand her.

Later I woke Jon up and told him that Tobi had left a message for him. We listened to it together.

'That's not Tobi,' he exclaimed.

'So who is it?' I demanded, adding, 'It's certainly not anyone I know.' We needed to hear the tape several more times before we could divine the truth.

'This is a really good song that you'll actually really love,' the voice commented before the second number, 'because if you don't, you're fucking stupid.'

Oh my God! It was Courtney! Stung by some comments I'd made in a review of a PJ Harvey album in *Melody Maker* about how she didn't listen to music anymore, the Hole singer had called me up to sing demos of 'Awful' and 'Reasons To Be Beautiful' from her new album, with Eric playing guitar in the background. '*Swing low sweet cherry,*' she crooned from across the Atlantic, sounding like she'd been taking elocution lessons. '*It's your life, it's your party, it's so awful.*'

It was such rich irony to mistake her for Tobi, especially on a song that attacked Riot Grrrls.

COURTNEY LOVE: Nick Broomfield was using me as this false archetype based on the fact I went out with Kurt. You know that, you introduced us. But before I met Kurt, I was already destined for trouble and for hugeness – for my *own* trouble, not as a satellite of this fucking golden boy. So here's Nick, he's made a documentary on Margaret Thatcher, dominatrixes, Heidi Fleiss . . . so a Fleet Street boy who wants to get the shit beaten out of him by a matriarch puts me into that set as the ultimate. It's lurid. Get the fuck over it! Even the tabloid press in America is over it.

EVERETT TRUE: I saw that documentary he made, *Kurt And Courtney*. I was laughing most of the time. There were a couple of parts I would've preferred not to see, especially the interview with the scared nanny and where Kurt's old friend Dylan was talking. You know who the star was? It was your old Portland boyfriend, Rozz.

CL: Absolutely. That part where he's quoting me on how to become famous – Number One: Make Friends With Michael Stipe – has to be true. Well, duh. Who else was there to become friends with? Wouldn't you?

ET: No.

CL: In one version of 'Teen Spirit', Kurt sang the line *'Who will be the king and queen of the outcast teens?'* Glamour aside, there could be no more perfect couple at the time. We were so right for each other because we were the most antisocial people in our entire area. It was great . . . and it was horrible because of all the drugs and the pain and the fear. So I come back to Seattle to play a concert and I get this feeling in my chest, and I realise that the reality of our life was so much scarier than I realised back then because of the numbing effects of the drugs. Kurt was a sweet, sweet guy. People think I look upon that relationship as dysfunctional, and I am a bit disdainful in public because it's not my job to hold that goddamn flame, but I will honour and adore that person because I loved him.

(The *Stranger*, 25 February 1999)

Understand this. There is a symbiotic relationship between artist and journalist. In the unenlightened public's eye, it's OK for musicians to use the media. That's expected. That's playing the game the way it's supposed to be played. The other way around is just some loser writer trying to latch onto the coat-tails of stardom, of glamour, of rock'n'roll excess. I've said it before and I'll say it again but *simply because you get up on stage doesn't make you any more interesting than the next person.* It's what you do with the exposure that counts.

'I'm coming from the purest place possible, and it's not an exorcism,' Courtney told me after Hole co-headlined Seattle's Key Arena with Marilyn Manson in December 1998. 'It's intent. I'm delivering something. You know what? People change. Bob Dylan went fucking electric. His Albert Hall concert CD is so brilliant. You can hear the shout of "Judas" really loud. The betrayal is palpable. Tonight, we segued "Pretty On The Inside" from our debut album into our most pop song "Heaven Tonight". They're the same, in some ways. One's based in this fury and anger and hate and real self-loathing and one's based in this incredible fucking moment of feeling I was loved. For me to be able to express that is breaking down such a wall of my own training. It's like Kurt firing Jason [Everman] from Nirvana and having the balls to say, "Hey, I don't want to be Soundgarden, I want to be myself." It's almost impossible to write about love if you're intelligent. I woke up in Las Vegas the other morning and started wondering whether Shania Twain had done six miles on the Treadmaster of hate.'

Nothing changes. Courtney and I were first attracted to one another because we were at a similar stage in our careers. Rock music had something we needed. Acceptance. It gave us a sense of belonging and a chance to stop being outsiders. For a while, our lives ran parallel. We were the loudest voices at the party. We'd blast out random opinions, not caring where they fell. All that mattered was being heard. If you weren't heard, you didn't exist.

So who won and who lost? Isn't it obvious? Courtney got her fame and fortune, her Versace fashion shoots, private schooling for her kid, tea with Madonna. Her name is known the Western world over. Her skill as an actress in films such as *The People Vs. Larry Flynt* and opposite Jim Carrey in *Man On The Moon* has been praised numerous times, even if she is only reprising her real-life role. She flies all over the world, and stays in the plushest hotels. She's got her own website at www.hole.com, complete with a willing audience for her densely argued, haphazardly punctuated ravings about whatever caught her eye in the last twenty-four hours, or some old imagined enmity.

Or, if it's not her, it's someone able to imitate her style brilliantly. *'in the depths of my soul – God – what would i ever be able to have be about trenbt?'* someone calling themselves 'Courtney' posted on the hole.com message board on 12 March 2001 under the title 'What Could Be About Trent?'

umm . . . isnt it a litttle pretentious and tacky to have a black terry cloth robe with 'trent' embvroidered in gold lettters on it? i dont know just asking.

ive only ever really loved three men and trent isnt one of them – by – a long shit so dying is not about him

its about my true love dave.

no im not telling you guys who its about it would ruin it – its a secret.

actually thre truth is since i didnt write it – as with everything – i wouldnt know who its avbout someone just handed it to me in its present form cos i gave good head.

I have no idea what this is about, except that, after Trent Reznor from Nine Inch Nails decided he didn't want to have an affair with Courtney in the fall of 1994, she turned nasty and hasn't been able to resist an opportunity to attack him since. 'Dying' is a track from Hole's third album *Celebrity Skin*.

Courtney's opinions are relentless. In the months following Kurt's death, she took solace in her love of the Internet, relishing its immediacy. Seven years on, Courtney still enjoys using e-mail as a tool to gain attention. On 7 March 2001, someone using her name posted the following comments on the Hole website under the heading 'I Heart Anok' (Anok is a member of Hole's online community).

yer so frickin sassy.

this was leaking like crazy anyway you know and it hasnt been ann0ounced = what would you like me to do? i spent all last night doing twenties songs with daniel lanois - that was fun, i played around with hip hop people = the dmx ones whow ere hard and weird – that was fun. but i like rock - im sorry i didnt buy you know – two turntablesandamicrophone and start signifying for your amusement – lets see how it TURNS OUT anyway dudee? shall we my princess?

But what do you do when youve always really just wanted to play with your own gender and you never got around to it? like when you CRAVE to just go ina room and playw ith other women? when theres a teensy limited pool of females to play with who are up to your speed and have a similiar objective - rock as opposed to singer songwriter bleh. How many girls do you know canmake a great skynrd reference and play atari teenage riot songs too?

Anyone wanting a crash course in Courtney's reference points, please don't write to me. That's not my job any more . . . and, besides which, I haven't a clue what she's talking about.

After a two-year hiatus living abroad, I ended up back in English suburbia: no alcohol or drugs, none of my sought-after fame and comparatively little money. When I travel, I prefer to stay on friends' floors. When I go out, I try to return to my fiancée and my Brighton home as soon as possible.

Both Courtney and I have been damaged by our experiences during the early nineties. The damage manifests itself differently. I think Courtney suffers from paranoia: overhauling her managers and trainers every six months, suing her old record company for restraint of trade. She's almost completely estranged from her guitarist Eric, the man who has given her so much support over the years. She may come across as a more mature and complete person in interviews, but that's because she has that whole superficial LA style that masks a thousand worries. I suffer from paranoia, too. But I don't go around parading my fears in public. I'm English. I don't like to put across a false impression of the 'real' me in public, at least not right now.

Sure, I resent Courtney's good fortune. It's never easy being the one left behind. Except, who has won here? Is there only one way to judge success? Like a distant echo, I hear Kurt's words in my mind: 'Most people think success is being extremely popular on a commercial level, selling a lot of records and making a whole bunch of money. Being in the public eye.'

'Why am I alive right now?' Courtney muses. 'It's because I had a child. So, for me, even in my darkest hours, to leave, to pass on to the other side, would have been ruthless. Obviously I used to think about it. That was the first thing – "I will be an empty vessel devoid of life and love and spirit and spark, but I will be here physically in her presence and I will love this child." And you build from there. Other values started to come to me. Like "What can I contribute to society?" "What are my responsibilities?" Then you get this super-ego voice, this elder sister mentor person, Madonna on the phone, saying that you've got a responsibility with your lyrics and you start hearing a voice go: "You can't sing", which never happened to me before. So my challenge was to stare that voice down and tell it to shut the fuck up and leave me alone.'

Courtney is a disappointment. In her joint interview with Kurt, she talked about self-hating girls fucking rock stars to grab attention instead of grabbing their own guitars. Who exactly was she describing there?

'I'm getting to be sober, sober in thought and deed,' she says. 'I'm not all the time, but to a certain degree. I'm becoming a responsible member of society. When teenage children are telling you that they've done self-destructive acts because of you, you really have to sit down and think, "OK, what am I giving here? And how can I give what it is I have to give without being fake?"'

Hold on. Who is talking here? Courtney Love or Madonna?

I liked Courtney when she was on edge and emotional, unable to control her art, manipulative and nasty. That was fun. She's swapped that for society's approval. Is society really so *fun*, Courtney? Did these new peers of yours do anything of interest to reach their positions of power, or did they achieve it by stepping on all those Russian peasants with their simple lives and yoghurt that you once professed to despise? In 2000, Creation Records boss Alan McGee, the man who started me in the music business after he saw me dancing to his band and asked me to contribute to his fanzine, went on record as saying, 'Courtney is the most punk person I know.' He's at least five years too late. Only outsiders are punks. Give me that small solace, at least.

'You know,' she told me in 1998, 'you go from your starter kit when you're in pop, and you're a writer, and you're dark, you go from your Leonard Cohen/Baudelaire/Rimbaud starter kit and if you can end up inspired by Yeats and Rilke, then you're going in the right direction. What Rilke did – write tragic, epic, gorgeous love poems to the spirit of God – is so much tougher than to write sexy morphine/opium poems to the cats. The hate spark dies much quicker than the love spark, and the love spark is much harder to achieve. If you're going to keep your inspiration going, you've got to have some light. That's what I'm trying to do with *Celebrity Skin*. It's not that it isn't cynical in parts, but it's like, "Build a new one, man! Build a new one."'

This would be a great defence, if only *Celebrity Skin* wasn't so crap.

Courtney's forays into Hollywood don't hold me in thrall, nor do her apologists' homilies. She still says what she thinks I want her to say, only now it's tempered with a slightly patronising manner – the tone all famous types obtain when surrounded by enough yes people. Courtney's passions nowadays have no relevance to me, just to those desperate for validation. She even admits in public to liking Heart and Smashing Pumpkins. That's not maturity. That's relapsing into the most neurotic of adolescent experiences.

'You're going to lay into the album, aren't you?' Eric complains. 'That's not fair. I spent so much time on it. It could have turned out a lot worse, considering what I had to work with.'

Point taken, old chum. Point taken.

* * *

From *VOX*, June 1998.

So what's Courtney Love really like?

A lot healthier, fitter, more muscular and happier than *VOX* remembers from meeting her last. Annoying, inspiring, arrogant, funny, witty, gracious, paranoid, sometimes rambling, often incisive, a control freak . . . She's been burned badly by the media as a result of her own candour several times in the past and is determined not to let it happen again. Her strength of character has given her the ability to continue.

VOX remembers a conversation with Courtney, held about six months after the death of her husband where she repeatedly avowed her determination 'not to let the assholes get the satisfaction of seeing me kill myself'.

Do you feel ghosts run your life?

'Yeah,' she agrees. 'Well, I feel that it's run by myths. If I don't keep my head about me and I don't perform daily spiritual rituals – and I mean this in all sincerity and not in a doozy way – for instance, drugs are a ritual, as are self-destructive acts and acts of self-love . . . I perform my rituals, which is chanting [Courtney is a Buddhist] and I also do a lot of yoga and I juice and tonight I'm drinking a fuck of a lot of tequila . . .

'You know what's great about people knowing that you could punch them out because you've done it before?' she continues, momentarily diverted. 'You never have to because everyone's terrified that you might do it again. You have a security through people knowing that you've lived real hard.'

So how did you live through this, Courtney?

'My solution and my advice to all the British kids, all the scenesters who are going through their Seattle 1991 game right now, is to change your fucking social life!' the singer cries. 'Seriously. Have a child. Change your social life. The first thing I did was to deny my ridiculous dependency on substances. And you know what? When you're motivated it's not hard, it's fucking easy! Now, I just don't hang out. The second thing I did was to remove God from my life because I didn't buy it any more. The atrocities were too heavy and the sins committed against my karma were too large, so I got into Darwinism – that this is Survival Of The Fittest and there is no gender politic . . .'

Hold up. Is Courtney now saying she's not a feminist?

'I'm pretty depressive, but my depressions are more panic attacks,' Courtney continues regardless. 'I had this whole deconstruction period when I dealt with all my problems, where I went into an isolated society and chain-smoked for a month. When I left that place, I had real spiritual problems because I started seeing everything in Darwinian, nihilistic terms, which I'd never seen before, because at the core I've always had a real innocence and optimism . . . It was through Jungian ideas and Jungian archetypes that I started to realise that, even if Jung was a bit of a fascist and a sexist, the sentence isn't "God is dead" but "God is dead, comma, because man is alive." And then I started to see a divinity in things through archetype and symbolism and my own participation in a cultural myth . . .'

You say it's easy to sort out your dependencies when you're ready. But you're one of the few people I know who can use drugs, not let them use you.

'Yeah,' Courtney agrees, 'but I got ensnared into my own archetype, so at a certain point I became a slave. Who I hung out with very much influenced me because I'm such a girl about stuff a lot of the time. I thought Nick Cave and Johnny Thunders and Keith Richards were so fucking cool. Whatever. Change your lifestyle. It doesn't mean you have to get on a stump and start whingeing about other people's experiences. Part of growing up and being disaffected and being youthful and being tortured is having a drug experience. But I've never spoken out about this because that's what people like Steven Tyler [Aerosmith singer] do when they give public service announcements like, "Oh, don't do drugs, kids, even though I did them for forty years and had a fucking great time." That's fucking absurd.'

HOLE Celebrity Skin (Geffen)

Some facts.

(1) I don't like this record. I come from the tradition of the Slits and Young Marble Giants, not mid-American classic rock. How could I like this? It's too polished, too rounded-off. It sounds like Fleetwood Mac or Heart, and this fact is paraded as a virtue. What is it with you Americans? These people were WRONG! Hole have often suffered from severe schizophrenia during their turbulent career, from wanting to sound like Sonic Youth (*Pretty On The Inside*) to wanting to sound like Nirvana (*Live Through This*) to wanting to sound like a mid-seventies FM radio band (*Celebrity Skin*). Hopefully, one day soon they're going to realise they're best off sounding like themselves. Courtney's voice has been so double-tracked and ultra-trained on this record it's not even recognisable in places. Is this a plus? You tell me.

(2) I don't like it. I come from the underground and damn me if I'm not sidling back there rapidly. This record is corporate. It's been designed to shift units, and to please radio programmers. Some songs even sound like the Smashing Pumpkins. Now, you tell me, am I going to like that? A reputed two million dollars plus has been spent on making *Celebrity Skin*, and you can best believe that that's bought a whole lot more than an eight-track cartridge player. The Pumpkins are heinous: fake angst boiled down to a lowest common denominator. The drawn-out, druggy, Pumpkins-influenced 'Use Once & Destroy' is possibly the worst song Hole have ever recorded.

(3) I don't like it. I can't stand LA. Songs such as 'Malibu' and 'Boys On The Radio' are dying to be played cruising down the freeway to Santa Monica, hatchback down. You think I'm going to relate to that? I'm a bitter, twisted, stunted Brit. Why do you think I moved to Seattle? For the weather? Only one song here, the magnificently brooding 'Northern Star' – where distant drums roll like thunder, where the sound of the acoustic guitar is like rain lashing on the windowpane – recalls Seattle. Otherwise, it's all film stars *this* and film stars *that*.

(4) I don't like it. I always hated the Primitives. Courtney has stated that she wanted 'Heaven Tonight' (the love song she wrote for her daughter Frances Bean) to sound like the Primitives. No, no, no! They were closet goths who happened to once hear the Shop Assistants' genius buzzsaw, Ramones-influenced guitar sound. Go to the source. Go to the source! 'Hit So Hard', meanwhile, is a Crystals-style girl group song extolling the virtues of being beaten up by your celebrity boyfriend. Is this to be encouraged?

(5) I don't like it. Both the terrible 'Awful' and rampant 'Playing Yr Song' could be construed as cheap pot shots at Olympia. And you all know how I feel about Olympia.

(6) I don't like it. There isn't a single song that connects with me on any level, barring 'Northern Star'. The aforementioned LA driving songs are great radio-pop songs, albeit totally commercialised. This record says nothing to me about my life, nor is it intended to. How could I like it?

(From the *Stranger*, 25 February 1999)

Here's where the story ends.

I met Courtney and Eric when they were over in England at the start of 1998 when they were trying out Spice Girls producer Mike 'Spike' Stent at London's Olympic Studios. We hung out at the Met Bar, the three of us, incredibly drunk and lairy, Courtney exactly how I remembered her. Fun. The *VOX* interview smacked of grand farce. A few days after it had taken place – Courtney had called me to set it up, not the other way round – I got faxes from her management totalling 25 pages, seeking worldwide rights for both copy and photographs, and plenty of other restrictions besides.

I told them to fuck off.

Courtney and I still have a dysfunctional, co-dependent relationship. It's unlikely we'll ever lose that, assuming it survives her reading this book (which she will). We've been through too much together. I've deliberately distanced myself from her while writing *Live Through This*. All the e-mails I've sent have been along the lines of 'Virgin would like you to write the intro for my book. PS: fuck off.' I feel bad not calling her, but what can I do? She has her film star friends and her manicurists, while I have my writing. There isn't too much in common there.

The last time I spoke to the lady was in the final few months of 2000. She was in London, fraternising with my old pal, Alan McGee. So she did what came naturally, phoned up her English friend, Everett True, asked him to come up to town and hang out. I refused. I was about to embark on a writing project (this book) that I knew would drain me, and that I had no desire to be compromised on. We chatted for a while, and then I lost my temper with her because she'd been helping a Seattle journalist I have no respect for write a book on Nirvana.

That's it. We've exchanged e-mails since. These included a classic 'glad to see you've got a conscience, now that you can afford one' one-liner from me in response to an online article she'd written about the evils of the music industry. That amused her. She wrote back, detailing the latest news concerning her child.

The last time I met Courtney in person was in Seattle, start of 1999. There was little change in our rapport, although I wasn't allowed to be present when Hole held their band meeting. I no longer possessed *that* power. Hole had a new drummer, Samantha, who had replaced Patty for reasons that escape me now. Onstage at the Key Arena, Courtney seemed disinterested, more obviously an actress in command of her emotions than I'd seen before. I rejoiced for Courtney the person, but yearned for Courtney the artist.

There was no hanging out at a bar afterwards. Courtney feels she's too recognisable for those simple pleasures now, especially in Seattle. She only likes to co-exist with people on the same level as her: managers and celebrities. Aren't we all like that? Don't we all prefer to run in our own social circles, scared of outsiders? So the drinking honours were left to Eric and Melissa (who shortly afterwards left Hole to join Smashing Pumpkins). The three of us stood at the bar in the Cha-Cha Lounge, unrecognised by all except the most hip, and happy in our anonymity.

We still knew how to enjoy ourselves.

I have nothing else to say.

These people have nothing to do with me anymore. I live in a world of Garden Centres and badminton lessons and failed meringues. Courtney has become the face of credible Hollywood, disconnected, there to stare at on a TV screen: to admire, to aspire to, to stare blankly at while I sip my tea. My life may not have moved on, in rock terms – fuck, I'm still not famous! – but I'm more or less cheerfully domesticated. I'm engaged, I have a book deal and I don't have to take part in the nine-to-five grind. That's not too bad. I find myself increasingly unable to deal with the utter banality of people in clubs but, if I need entertainment, I have some great memories of a reckless, carefully spent youth. Oh, and don't underestimate me. My life as an insurrectionary and catalytic agent isn't over yet, not by a long chalk.

You know what? There isn't anything that bad about living a simple life, trying to treat others the way you'd like to be treated, having respect for people and not trampling all over them. Sure, I miss the past, but rock as a lifestyle always sat uneasily upon my shoulders. Too many assholes showing off too loudly, me included. Me, I disconnect from you.

Rock'n'roll may not have given me the best years of my life, but at least it paid for my house. And for that, I'm grateful.

Epilogue

My problem with *Celebrity Skin* is that I don't like any of the bands you aspire to be on it.

'But can you tell on the final product?'

I can, because you told me. It's classic cause and effect.

'I don't care if you don't like it,' Courtney pouts. 'I still like you . . . (Laughs) . . . That's mature of me.'

And I like you. You're asking the wrong person to comment, anyway: my favourite music this year . . .

'Is Julie Ruin?' the celebrity asks, referring to a previous phone conversation.

No. It's me playing Tom Waits songs badly on the piano to my girlfriend. That's the truth.

'OK,' she laughs, resigned to my intransigence.

I'm trying to find myself right now. You know me, I subject any kind of . . .

'. . . town to its reign of terror,' Courtney completes the sentence for me. 'That's why I don't think you should leave. Seattle deserves its reign of terror.'

(From *Hit It Or Quit It!* Fanzine, 1999)

When I was fourteen, fifteen, I learned to play piano using a Beatles songbook borrowed from the library. I'd never heard the Beatles beyond the occasional snippet on a shop radio, but something about the airbrushed illustrations in the front of the songbook attracted me to them. I'd never seen airbrushing before, and for a brief moment in time it seemed sexy, new, to me. So I taught myself to play via the Beatles: painfully, one note at a time, one finger at a time, no discernible sense of rhythm, singing along to such childlike, deceptively simple melodies as 'Nowhere Man' and 'Love Of The Loved'. The lyrics attracted me as well. They seemed so wise, so understanding, so directly related to my situation: boys having no luck with girls. Boys vowing revenge on girls because they had no luck with girls. Boys knowing how alone they are. Boys knowing what bastards girls are. Boys being sensitive and, hence, misunderstood by girls.

Yes . . . these were good lyrics.

I would sing those songs for hours on end, picking out the bass harmonies with one or two fingers on the keyboard. Not having any reference point against which to judge my own work, I would endlessly rework the songs, creating my own rhythms, cadences, harmonies, interpretations, meanings. It pleased me to do this. Later, when I made a handful of friends who listened to punk (in 1977, the pop charts were full of punk), we would create our own concept albums. Usually, they would have Daniel Johnston-esque sad themes – boy sees girl, girl doesn't want to know boy, boy kills himself – and the music would be less than rudimentary. Hammered out chords on the piano. Packs of cards rifled through close to the tape player's microphone. Recorders blown down for no apparent reason. Electric plugs banged against something. Words solemnly intoned, then forgotten.

I'm sure we would've used guitars if we could have afforded them.

This was our alternative to what was going on outside. Boys being successful with girls, friends being beaten up in pubs, sports . . . there were always people going on about how good at sports they were.

I was safe at home with my piano, safe within my own alternative world.

Soon, I grew to discover the outside world. Comics, music, the odd book or five hundred . . . I liked it. I particularly liked the punks, the way they seemed so curiously sexless and sexual simultaneously. They seemed unafraid to flaunt their feelings at outsiders. Me, too. Except no one wanted to listen to me. I liked the punks, though. Their music was angry, assertive, a source of annoyance to those on the outside. It made my feet want to move, my body want to shake. It filled my ears with a glorious resonance. Even more importantly, women were part of punk. They had feelings, too! And hard as it was to believe by someone as messed-up by the single sex, elitist English public school system as I was, it seemed that it wasn't just men who hurt.

Beyond wearing my school tie with an Essential Logic T-shirt and getting spat at by the straights in the streets of Chelmsford, I never joined the punk movement, though. Probably because I believed all those proclamations by people like Johnny Rotten and punk fanzine editor, *Sniffing Glue*'s Mark Perry, and sadly forgotten punk poet Patrik Fitzgerald that you should think for yourself, never follow leaders. Anyway, wasn't it obvious? As soon as the alternative to the mainstream is recognisable as an alternative to the mainstream, it's time to leave and move on. I never thought that punk could provide anything for me, aside from a temporary escape. I liked punk because it made me dance, and I found the rhythms of disco mostly too repetitive and unimaginative to dance to.

That was it for punk, though. Good dancing music.

Fast-forward 25 years, and I've seen too much and experienced too little. I've found myself dragged into a music industry that never had much to give me, except for spineless backstabbers, several thousand free drinks and regurgitated cigar smoke blowing in my face. I've found myself talking to people I never wanted to talk to, drinking with people who I don't believe should ever have been fucking allowed to live. Somewhere along the line, my very natural desire to dance – *I only ever wanted to dance!* – has been turned into a career and a life and a job and a house by the seaside and free trips to America and the irritation of being known only because of those I know. Is this an alternative? I don't think so.

I'll tell you where the only alternative, that I know, lies.

At the start of 1998, I had my precious piano returned to me from my mother's where it had been lying dormant for several years. Around then, I was almost physically unable to listen to music – any music, Nirvana, Beat Happening, Slits, Stax Records . . . even Dexys Midnight Runners. It was too irritating, too painful, too close to home. I was disillusioned with recorded music. I felt only charlatans and frauds created it. So I returned to my roots, picking out the same Beatles songs fastidiously, singing lustily and soulfully along. I played Tom Waits and Nina Simone and blues songs, and tired old sixties classics, with my stiffened fingers, barely able to hold down the melody. I was back in my alternative reality, safe in my alternative world. Except now a proper girlfriend who, wonder of wonders, professed to enjoy my singing, had replaced my old Chelmsford friends.

I bought a Nirvana songbook for piano recently. I haven't opened it yet but I know that, when I do, I'll find melodies to pick over and oblique words to suit many moods. I'm not saying that I think Kurt's lyrics are genius. I don't. I prefer words more direct than the ones he wrote. It doesn't matter, though. What's important in music is the expression you give a certain phrase, not the phrase itself.

I don't think Kurt ever did hit top F in 'Smells Like Teen Spirit' like my book claims, either, but hey! If I do end up singing his words then at least it'll be a way of paying tribute, separate to everyone else. And I think he would have liked that.

everett_true@hotmail.com

Discography

This list isn't anywhere near complete and it's not supposed to be. It's merely a guide to some records I think are very fine and which also have relevance to the book. Hence, there is no reference to Nirvana's *Unplugged* but both Pigeonhed and Liliput are here. All are CD albums, and hopefully available, unless otherwise indicated. The dates and labels usually refer to the most recent edition.

Chapter 1
NIRVANA: *Bleach* (Sub Pop, 1989), *Nevermind* (Geffen, 1991), *In Utero* (Geffen, 1993)

Chapter 2 (Riot Grunge)
ATARI TEENAGE RIOT: *Sixty Second Wipe Out* (Digital Hardcore, 1999) – Riot Grrrl meets electronica
THE AVENGERS: *Died For Your Sins* (Lookout!, 1999) – great retrospective of early eighties female-led LA punk band
BEAT HAPPENING: *Beat Happening* (K, 1985), *Jamboree* (K/Rough Trade, 1988), *Black Candy* (K/Rough Trade, 1989), *Dreamy* (K/Sub Pop, 1991), *You Turn Me On* (K/Sub Pop, 1992). Each CD is vital, but start with *Black Candy*, or save your money for the promised box set
BIKINI KILL: *Pussy Whipped* (Wiiija/kill rock stars, 1993), *The Singles* (kill rock stars, 1998), *Reject All American* (kill rock stars, 1996)
BIKINI KILL/HUGGY BEAR: *Yeah Yeah Yeah Yeah/Our Troubled Youth* (Catcall/kill rock stars, 1993)
BILLY CHILDISH/THEE HEADCOATS: *I Am The Billy Childish* (Sup Pop, 1992) – great collection of English garage king
BLOOD SAUSAGE: *Happy Little Bullshit Boy* (Wiiija, 1993) – ten-inch only
BRATMOBILE: *Pottymouth* (kill rock stars, 1993)
BUILT TO SPILL: *There's Nothing Wrong With Love* (Up, 1994), *Keep It Like A Secret* (Warner Bros, 1999) – the Grateful Dead of the International Pop Underground
CADALLACA: *Introducing Cadallaca* (K, 1998) – Sleater-Kinney meets sixties girl groups
THE CANNANES: *Witchetty Pole* (Feel Good All Over, 1993) – collection of early material from genius Australian counterpart to Olympia
CAUSTIC RESIN: *Body Love Hate Body* (CZ, 1993), *Fly Me To The Moon* (Up, 1995) – signifiers of that peculiar Boise acid party that produced Tad Doyle and Doug Martsch
COMET GAIN: *Casino Classics* (Wiiija, 1995), *Magnetic Poetry* (Wiiija, 1997) – garage-fed English Riot Boy
THE CRABS: *Sand And Sea* (K, 1999) – dreamy Beat Happening-influenced Portland group

DEAD MOON: *Strange Pray Tell* (Music Maniac, 1992) – Portland's answer to the Cramps: all records are equally fine

DUB NARCOTIC SOUND SYSTEM: *Boot Party* (K, 1996) – Calvin's dub project

JAD FAIR: *I Like It When You Smile* (Paperhouse, 1992) – features J Mascis and Don Fleming, contains 'Angel'

JAD and DAVID FAIR: *26 Monster Songs For Children* (kill rock stars, 1998) – original line-up of Half Japanese

JAD FAIR and DANIEL JOHNSTON: *It's Spooky* (Paperhouse, 1993)

THE FRUMPIES: *Frumpie One Piece* (kill rock stars, 1998) – Tobi Vail's garage band

GIRL TROUBLE: *Hit It Or Quit It* (Sub Pop, 1988) – classy Tacoma minimal garage rock

THE GO TEAM: any single (K, no albums available)

HALF JAPANESE: *Fire In The Sky* (Paperhouse, 1992), *Music To Strip By* (Paperhouse, 1993), *Charmed Life* (Paperhouse, 1993), *The Band That Would Be King* (Paperhouse, 1993). Last three are reissues, with oodles of extra tracks

HALO BENDERS: *God Don't Make No Junk* (Fire/K, 1995), *Don't Tell Me Now* (K, 1996), *The Rebels Not In* (K, 1998) – Calvin Johnson and Doug Martsch, and even better than that sounds

HEAVENLY: *Le Jardin De Heavenly* (Sarah, 1992) – where cutie became politicised

HEAVENS TO BETSY: *Calculated* (kill rock stars, 1994) – classic Riot Grrrl

HUGGY BEAR: *WeBitched* (Wiiija, 1992), *Taking The Rough With The Smooch* (Wiiija/kill rock stars, 1993)

DANIEL JOHNSTON: *1990* (Shimmy Disc, 1990), *Continued Story/Hi How Are You* (Homestead, 1991), *Artistic Vice* (Shimmy Disc, 1992), *Fun* (Atlantic, 1994), *Rejected Unknown* (Pickled Egg, 2000). These are only the start: now buy his tapes on the web

KICKING GIANT: *Halo* (Loose Leaf, 1993) – classic Olympia

LE TIGRE: *Le Tigre* (Wiiija, 1999) – Kathleen Hanna's latest band

LILIPUT/KLEENEX: *Liliput/Kleenex* (kill rock stars, 2001) – killer collection of Swiss seventies female punks

LOIS: *Butterfly Kiss* (K, 1992) – as delicate as the title suggests

LOIS MAFFEO and BRENDAN CANTY: *The Union Themes* (kill rock stars, 1999) – Lois and the drummer from Fugazi. Excellent

THE MAKE UP: *Live At Cold Rice* (Dischord, 1996), *Sound Verite* (K, 1996), *After Dark,* (Dischord, 1996), *I Want Some* (K, 1999) – James Brown comes to Washington DC

MARINE GIRLS: *Lazy Ways/Beach Party* (Cherry Red, 1988) – pure pop minimalism

MATRIMONY: *Kitty Finger* (Frock, 1989) – Australian influence on Bikini Kill

MECCA NORMAL: *Mecca Normal* (Smarten Up, 1986), *Calico Kills The Cat* (K, 1988), *Dovetail* (K 1992) – Canadian agit-pop guitar/voice duo who helped split open the rules on instrumentation

MODERN LOVERS: *Rock'N'Roll With . . .* (Beserkley, 1977), *Precise Modern Lovers Order* (Rounder, 1994), *The Modern Lovers* (Rev-Ola, 1994). At the International Pop Underground Festival in 1991 a huge photocopy of Patti Smith was on the women's restroom door, a huge photocopy of Jonathan Richman was on the men's restroom door – cool, tough, cold, poetic Patti and warm, sensitive, narrative Jonathan

NATION OF ULYSSES: *13 Point Program To Destroy America* (Dischord, 1992), *Plays Pretty For Baby* (Dischord, 1993) – two albums that invented Huggy Bear

ORANGE JUICE: *Orange Juice/You Can't Hide Your Love Forever* (Polydor, 1991), *Ostrich Graveyard* (Postcard, 1992) – two very different versions of the same classic 1981 Scots debut. Major influence on the Pastels

THE PASTELS: *Up For a Bit With The Pastels* (Glass, 1987), *Suck On The Pastels* (Creation, 1988), *Sittin' Pretty* (Chapter 22, 1989), *Truckload Of Trouble* (Paperhouse, 1994), *Mobile Safari* (Domino/Up, 1995), *Illumination* (Domino, 1997) – got them? Good. Now buy all the other stuff

THE PEE CHEES: *Do The Math* (kill rock stars, 1996), *Life* (kill rock stars, 1998) – California's stuttering answer to the Make Up

THE RAINCOATS: *The Raincoats* (Rough Trade, 1979), *Odyshape* (Rough Trade, 1981) – rightly venerated

JULIE RUIN: *Julie Ruin* (kill rock stars, 1998) – Kathleen Hanna's dub-fuelled solo project

SANDY DIRT: *Sandy Dirt* (K, 1996) – collaboration between Pastels and Some Velvet Sidewalk

THE SHAGGS: *The Shaggs* (Rounder, 1988) – contains everything you'd ever need by these most engaging of sisters

SHONEN KNIFE: *712* (Rockville, 1991) – cute Japanese pop

SHOP ASSISTANTS: *Will Anything Happen?* (Overground, 1997) – Ramones meets sixties girl group meets Mary Chain in the mid-eighties

SKINNED TEEN/RAOUUL: *Bazooka Smooth* (Wiiija/Lookout!, 1993) – youthful a cappella British Riot Grrrls

SLEATER-KINNEY: *Call The Doctor* (Chainsaw, 1995), *Dig Me Out* (kill rock stars, 1997), *All Hands On The Bad One* (kill rock stars/Matador, 2000) – the carriers of the flame

THE SLITS: *Cut* (1979), *Untitled (Bootleg Retrospective)* (1980), *Return Of The Giant Slits* (1981), *In The Beginning* (Jungle, 1997) – the original Riot Grrrls, without equal. *Cut* is still the place to start

SOME VELVET SIDEWALK: *Avalanche* (K, 1992), *Whirlpool* (K, 1993) – Olympia's own Nirvana

TEAM DRESCH: *Personal Best* (Chainsaw, 1993) – classic riot grunge

VIC GODARD AND THE SUBWAY SECT: *Twenty Odd Years – The Story Of . . .* (Motion, 1999) – two-CD collection of the most underrated punk band around. The Pastels and Orange Juice started here

TALULAH GOSH: *Backwash* (K, 1996) – great compilation of seminal English cutie band

TELEVISION PERSONALITIES: *And Don't The Kids Just Love It* (Rough Trade, 1981), *Mummy Your Not Watching Me* (Whaam!, 1982), *They Could Have Been Bigger Than The Beatles* (Whaam!, 1982), *The Painted Word* (Illuminated, 1985), *Privilege* (Fire, 1990) – all of these are vital. *The Painted Word* is one of the most chilling albums ever

UNWOUND: *New Plastic Ideas* (kill rock stars, 1994), *A Single History* (kill rock stars, 1999) – metal, Olympia-style

THE VASELINES: *The Way Of The Vaselines* (Sub Pop, 1994) – all you need to know

YOUNG MARBLE GIANTS: *Colossal Youth* (Rough Trade, 1979) – spooked minimal pop

Chapter 3 (Sub Pop Grunge)
STEPHEN JESSE BERNSTEIN: *Prison* (Sub Pop, 1992) – Seattle's own tormented Beat Poet, produced by Steve Fisk

CODEINE: *Frigid Stars* (Sub Pop, 1990)

COME: *Eleven:Eleven* (Placebo, 1992), *Don't Ask Don't Tell* (Beggars Banquet, 1994), *Gently Down The Stream* (Domino, 1998)

DWARVES: *Blood Guts And Pussy* (Sub Pop, 1990)

EARTH: *Earth 2 Special Low Frequency Version* (Sub Pop, 1993), *Phase 3 Thrones And Dominions* (Sub Pop, 1994) – as basic as music gets

FASTBACKS: *New Mansions In Sound* (Sub Pop, 1996)

GREEN RIVER: *Rehab Doll* (Sub Pop, 1988) – contains all you need

KYUSS: *Muchas Gracias* (east west, 2000) – the band that spawned Queens Of The Stone Age, and reinvented grunge as stoner rock

MARK LANEGAN: *The Winding Sheet* (Sub Pop, 1990), *I'll Take Care Of You* (Sub Pop, 1999)

LIVE SKULL: *Live Skull* (n/a, 1983), *Bringing Home The Bait* (Homestead, 1985) – Sonic Youth, UT and Live Skull; this was eighties foxcore

MODEST MOUSE: *The Lonesome Crowded West* (Up, 1997), *The Moon & Antarctica* (Matador, 2000) – Edge City wildness

MUDHONEY: *Superfuzz Big Muff* (Glitterhouse/Sub Pop, 1988), *Mudhoney* (Glitterhouse/Sub Pop, 1989), *Every Good Boy Deserves Fudge* (Sub Pop, 1991), *My Brother The Cow* (Reprise, 1995), *March To Fuzz* (Sub Pop, 2000) – the latter is a killer compilation

PIGEONHED: *The Full Sentence* (Sub Pop, 1997) – Steve Fisk takes on the dance world, and wins

QUEENS OF THE STONE AGE: *Queens Of The Stone Age* (Loose Groove, 1998), *Rated R* (Polydor, 2000) – metal, as she used to be wrote

REVEREND HORTON HEAT: *The Full Custom Sounds Of . . .* (Sub Pop, 1993) – the vicar of vice

SCREAMING TREES: *Even If And Especially When* (SST, 1987), *Invisible Lantern* (SST, 1988), *Dust* (Epic, 1996). First two are full-on psychedelic splendour, latter is classic warped Americana

SKIN YARD: *Hallowed Ground* (Toxic Shock, 1987) – producer Jack Endino's band

SOUNDGARDEN: *Superunknown* (A&M, 1994)

TAD: *Salt Lick* (Sub Pop, 1989), *8-Way Santa* (Sub Pop, 1991)

THE WALKABOUTS: *Rag & Bone plus Cataract* (Sub Pop, 1989)

Chapter 4 (Grunge Lite)

FOO FIGHTERS: *Foo Fighters* (Capitol, 1995) – it's not bad, you know

Chapter 5 (The Real Grunge)

BABES IN TOYLAND: *Spanking Machine* (Twin Tone, 1990), *To Mother* (Twin Tone, 1991), *Fontanelle* (Warner Brothers, 1992)

BIG BLACK: *Atomizer* (Touch & Go, 1992), *Songs About Fucking* (Touch & Go, 1992), *Hammer Party* (Touch & Go, 1992), *The Rich Man's Eight Track Tape* (Touch & Go, 1992) – CD reissues from Steve Albini's kick-ass eighties group

BLACK FLAG: *The First Four Years* (SST, 1988) – seminal US hardcore, before Rollins joined and ruined everything

BOSS HOG: *Drinkin', Letchin' & Lyin'* (Amphetamine Reptile, 1989)

BUTTHOLE SURFERS: *Brown Reason To Live* (Alternative Tentacles, 1983), *Live PCPPEP* (Alternative Tentacles, 1984), *Psychic . . . Powerless . . . Another Man's Sac* (Touch & Go, 1984) – very influential eighties art-fuck rock

COWS: *Cunning Stunts* (Amphetamine Reptile, 1992), *Old Gold 1988-1991* (Amphetamine Reptile, 1996) – warped psychosis

DICKLESS: *I'm A Man/Saddle Tramp* (Sub Pop, 1990) – seven-inch

FLIPPER: *Generic Album* (Sony/Columbia, 1999) – reissue of classic US punk album; major craziness

GOD BULLIES: *Mama Womb Womb* (Amphetamine Reptile, 1989) – AmRep's answer to the Buttholes

HALO OF FLIES: *Singles Going Nowhere* (Amphetamine Reptile, 1989) – Hazel-myer's mod hardcore band

JANITOR JOE: *Big Metal Birds* (Amphetamine Reptile, 1993) – Kristen Pfaff's main band

THE JESUS LIZARD: *Goat* (Touch & Go, 1991), *Liar* (Touch & Go, 1992)

KILLDOZER: *Intellectuals Are The Shoeshine Boys Of The Ruling Elite* (Bone Air, 1984), *Snakeboy* (Touch & Go, 1985), *For Ladies Only* (Touch & Go, 1989) – the latter is a bad ass set of cover versions

LAUGHING HYENAS: *Life Of Crime/You Can't Pray A Lie* (Touch & Go, 1990) – punk blues from the mid-West, produced by Butch Vig

L7: *Smell The Magic* (Sub Pop, 1990)

LUNACHICKS: *Babysitters On Acid* (Blast First, 1990)

LYDIA LUNCH: *Hysterie* (Widowspeak, 1989), *Widowspeak* (New Millennium, 1998). The woman who invented Courtney Love; these two compilations are great starting points

MEAT PUPPETS: *Meat Puppets* (Rykodisc, 1999), *Meat Puppets II* (Rykodisc, 1999), *Up On The Sun* (Rykodisc, 1999) – seminal skewed hardcore. If you're looking for a primer in male early eighties US punk, buy the debuts from Meat Puppets, Minutemen, Flipper and Minor Threat

MELVINS: *Ozma/Gluey Porch Treatments* (Boner, 1993), *Houdini* (Atlantic, 1993) – the finest albums of their genre

MINOR THREAT: *Complete Discography* (Dischord, 1990) – Ian MacKaye's pre-Fugazi hardcore band, and a zillion times more vital

MINUTEMEN: *Introducing The Minutemen* (SST, 1998) – more classic hardcore, great compilation

PUSSY GALORE: *Corpse Love: The First Year* (Caroline, 1992) – raw-boned rock'n'roll

SCRATCH ACID: *The Greatest Gift* (Touch & Go, 1991) – pioneering noise/deliverance from future Jesus Lizard men

THE SONICS: *Here Are The Sonics!!!* (Norton Northwest, 1999) – *the* sixties Northwest garage rock group

STP: *Hey Bastard!* (Circuit, 1990) – seven-inch only

TEEN ANGELS: *Daddy* (Sub Pop, 1996)

TODAY IS THE DAY: *Supernova* (Amphetamine Reptile, 1993)

UT: *In Gut's House* (Blast First, 1987), *Conviction* (Blast First, 1987) – fans of early Babes should check out this intense NYC female trio

Chapter 6 (Pop Grunge)

AFGHAN WHIGS: *Up In It* (Sub Pop, 1990), *Congregation* (Sub Pop, 1992), *Gentlemen* (Blast First/Elektra, 1993)

THE AMPS: *Pacer* (4AD, 1995) – as fine as the Breeders

BEASTIE BOYS: *Licensed To Ill* (Def Jam, 1996), *Paul's Boutique* (Capitol, 1989), *Ill Communication* (Capitol/Grand Royale, 1994)

BECK: *One Foot In The* Grave (K, 1994) – if you really must . . .

BLAKE BABIES: *Nicely, Nicely* (Chewbud, 1987), *Rosy Jack World* (Mammoth, 1992) – pop passion

THE BREEDERS: *Pod* (4AD, 1990), *Last Splash* (4AD, 1993) – the first is miles better produced

BUFFALO TOM: *Buffalo Tom* (SST, 1989), *Let Me Come Over* (Beggars Banquet, 1992), *Asides From . . .* (Beggars Banquet, 2000) – start with the compilation

ED'S REDEEMING QUALITIES: *More Bad Times* (Flying Fish, 1990) – reminiscent of the Cannanes

GIRLS AGAINST BOYS: *Venus Luxure No. 1 Baby* (Touch & Go, 1993)

GUIDED BY VOICES: *Vampire On Titus* (Scat, 1993), *Under The Bushes Under The Stars* (Matador, 1996), *Do The Collapse* (TVT, 1999) – actually all 50,312 albums are rather fine

HÜSKER DÜ: *Everything Falls Apart* (Reflex, 1992), *Metal Circus* (SST, 1983), *Zen Arcade* (SST, 1984) – this is where pop grunge was invented, and never bettered

THE LEMONHEADS: *It's A Shame About Ray* (Atlantic, 1992), *Come On Feel The Lemonheads* (Atlantic, 1993), *Car Button Cloth* (Atlantic, 1996)

LUSCIOUS JACKSON: *In Search Of Manny* (Big Cat, 1993) – slinky NYC female hip hop

MADDER ROSE: *Bring It Down* (Seed, 1993)

PIXIES: *Come On Pilgrim* (4AD, 1986), *Surfer Rosa* (4AD, 1988), *Doolittle* (4AD/Elektra, 1989)

THE REPLACEMENTS: *Let It Be* (BMG, 1991) – reissue for classic snotty post-punk album

RODAN: *Rusty* (Quarterstick, 1994)

SCARCE: *Deadsexy* (Paradox, 1995)

SLINT: *Spiderland* (Touch & Go, 1991) – the best album ever, according to Steve Albini, who produced it

SUPERCHUNK: *Tossing Seeds (Singles 89-91)* (Merge, 1992) – actually, you only need 'Slack Motherfucker'

TEENAGE FANCLUB: *A Catholic Education* (Paperhouse, 1990), *Bandwagonesque* (Creation/Geffen, 1991)

THROWING MUSES: *House Tornado/The Fat Skier* (4AD, 1988), *Hunkpapa* (4AD, 1989) – contemporaries of the Pixies, and just as unsettling

URGE OVERKILL: *Saturation* (Geffen, 1993)

THE WIPERS: *Is This Real?* (Sub Pop, 1993 reissue), *Youth Of America* (Restless, 1981), *Over The Edge* (Restless, 1982) – major influence on Nirvana: singer Greg Sage produced the first Beat Happening album

Chapter 7 (Art Grunge)

B.A.L.L.: *Bird/Period* (Shimmy Disc, 1989), *Trouble Doll* (Shimmy Disc, 1990)

BONGWATER: *Double Bummer* + (Shimmy Disc, 1990), *The Power Of Pussy* (Shimmy Disc, 1992) – the first is a cool box set, but the latter is the classic album

BOREDOMS: *Soul Discharge 99* (Shimmy Disc, 1990), *Pop Tatari* (Reprise, 1993), *Super Roots 7* (WEA Japan, 1998) – insane Japanese noise pop

DAS DAMEN: *Das Damen* (Ecstatic Peace, 1986), *Triskaidekophobe* (SST, 1988) – NYC contemporaries of Soundgarden

DINOSAUR JR: *Dinosaur* (Homestead, 1985), *You're Living All Over Me* (SST, 1987), *Bug* (Blast First/SST, 1988), *Where You Been?* (blanco y negro/Sire, 1993)

DOGBOWL: *Flan* (Shimmy Disc, 1992) – my main man

THE FLAMING LIPS: *In A Priest Driven Ambulance* (Restless, 1990), *Hit To Death In The Future Head* (Warner Bros, 1992), *Transmissions From the Satellite Heart* (Warner Bros, 1993), *Clouds Taste Metallic* (Warner Bros, 1995), *The Soft Bulletin* (Warner Bros, 1999). You probably don't need the one that requires four CD players to hear it, not yet . . .

THE FOLK IMPLOSION: *Take A Look Inside . . .* (Communion, 1994), *One Part Lullaby* (Domino, 1999) – go for the first, devastatingly human, release first

FREE KITTEN: *Nice Ass* (Wiiija/kill rock stars, 1994)

GALAXIE 500: *Today* (Rykodisc, 1997), *On Fire* (Rykodisc, 1997), *This Is Our Music* (Rykodisc, 1997) – buy these reissues, then buy the live album (or the box set)

GUMBALL: *Super Tasty* (Big Cat, 1993)

JON SPENCER BLUES EXPLOSION: *Extra Width* (Matador, 1993), *Orange* (Matador, 1994) – before the ex-Pussy Galore singer turned to parody

J MASCIS & THE FOG: *More Light* (City Slang, 2000)

MERCURY REV: *Yerself Is Steam* (Beggars Banquet, 1992), *Deserter's Songs* (V2, 1998)

PAVEMENT: *Slanted And Enchanted* (Big Cat/Matador, 1992), *Crooked Rain, Crooked Rain* (Big Cat/Matador, 1994)

ROYAL TRUX: *Twin Infinitives* (Drag City, 1989), *Royal Trux (#2)* (Drag City, 1992), *Cats And Dogs* (Drag City, 1994) – seriously deranged, Stones-influenced rock

SEBADOH: *Sebadoh III* (Homestead, 1991), *Bubble And Scrape* (Domino/Sub Pop, 1993), *Bakesale* (Domino/Sub Pop, 1994), *The Sebadoh* (Domino/Sub Pop, 1999)

SILVER JEWS: *Starlite Walker* (Domino/Drag City, 1994), *The Natural Bridge* (Domino/Drag City, 1996), *American Water* (Domino/Drag City, 1998) – a skewed American visionary, slightly ramshackle, but very beautiful. Malkmus contributes

SONIC YOUTH: *Confusion Is Sex* (Blast First/Neutral, 1983), *Bad Moon Rising* (Blast First/Homestead, 1985), *Evol* (Blast First/SST, 1986), *Sister* (Blast First/SST, 1987), *Daydream Nation* (Blast First/Torso, 1988), *Goo* (DGC, 1990), *Dirty* (DGC, 1992), *Experimental Jet Set, Trash And No Star* (DGC, 1994) – these are only a guide . . .

SPACEMEN 3: *Playing With Fire* (Taang, 1996) – eighties drone rock from England, big influence on Mudhoney and Queens Of The Stone Age

VELVET MONKEYS: *Rake* (Rough Trade, 1990) – the mythical soundtrack

Chapter 8 (Hole)

HOLE: *Pretty On The Inside* (City Slang/Caroline, 1991), *Live Through This* (Geffen, 1994), *My Body The Hand Grenade* (City Slang, 1997)

Index